THE EVOLUTION BOOK

THE EVOLUTION BOOK

SARA STEIN

Photography by Rona Beame

Illustrations by Sara Stein

WORKMAN PUBLISHING, NEW YORK

Library of Congress Cataloging-in-Publication Data
Stein, Sara Bonnett.   The evolution book.
Summary: Text, experiments, projects, investigations,
and plentiful pictures show the reader how to unlock
the secrets of the earth by investigating woodlands,
beaches, and mountains.
1. Natural history—Experiments—Juvenile literature.
2. Biology—Experiments—Juvenile literature.
3. Evolution—Experiments—Juvenile literature.
[1. Natural history. 2. Earth sciences. 3. Evolution]
I. Beame, Rona, ill. II. Title.
QH48.S7915 1986   508   84-40682   ISBN 0-89480-927-X

Book and cover design: Susan Aronson Stirling
Cover illustration: Ponder Goembel
Additional photography: Suzy Raywood, pages: Dedication, 24, 25, 32, 47, 56, 77
Photography sources: See page 391

Workman Publishing Company, Inc.
708 Broadway
New York, NY 10003

Manufactured in the United States of America
First Printing October 1986
10 9 8 7 6 5 4 3 2

To
Aram Gabriel
evolving

THANKS & THANKS

The "finished" manuscript of *The Evolution Book,* fresh from my computer, was the neatest thing you ever saw. I handed it in to my publisher with pride. Eight weeks later it was returned to me a mess. Every page was littered with penciled corrections and plastered with questions and criticisms on separate slips of paper called flags. For this mess I have to thank three people: Suzanne Rafer, Carol Mark, and Michael Bell.

Suzanne was my editor. Her notes to me in the margin were baffled, and brief. It doesn't take much space to say "I don't get this," which means "write it over again."

Carol was my copy editor, something like an English teacher, but more so. Her hand was everywhere, moving commas, correcting spelling, smoothing bumpy sentences, and, on flags, objecting: to my arithmetic, my logic, my facts. Carol had a nasty habit of catching me when I was dead wrong.

Michael was my vetter, an evolutionary biologist whose job it was to read the manuscript as an expert in the field. Oh, he was the worst of all! He doubted me at every turn, scolded me for speculations, harrassed me with contradicting evidence, wanted me to add some bison, subtract some chimpanzees, and stop putting my foot in my mouth. "NO!" he would begin, and a lecture would follow.

The *real* finished manuscript was the messiest thing you ever saw when, a whole summer and umpteen revisions later, I reached the last remark, my grade. "Good job!" scrawled Michael on the final page. By then, he was right. Now it is my turn to grade my tormenters.

Suzanne, Carol, Michael: You all get As.

Thank you, Suzanne. You were right about rewriting the beginning of life, the end of the dinosaurs, and all those boring or puzzling passages that would have bored or puzzled readers. Thank you, Carol. What a knack for accuracy! You saved me from being caught in public with my facts down. What if kids had found out that I added 5 and 13, and came up with 22? And Michael, thank you twice over, first for your thoughtful consideration of the manuscript, and second for your thoughtful consideration of me.

I intend to do something I have never done before: save the manuscript. Its messiness is a record of how a book is really written—with a lot of help from one's friends.

CONTENTS

• The Hand and the Foot of It • And More and More and More •
Clean as a Bone • Depend on Your Fungus • Waste Not, Want
Not • Faithfully, the Sloth • Traitorously, the Fig • Monstera • An
Eye for Color • Why Avocados Are Not Extinct

Haywire Hayfever • Ready or Not, Here I Come! • Wuchaks •
The Longest Meal • Double Digesters • Anybody Home? • Giant
Squirrels • Kissing Cousins • Albinism • Spreading Out and
Hunkering Down • Plain and Fancy • Nature's Noncompetition
Clause • Safe Traps • Funny as a Ferret • Stamp Feet • A Warning
About Handling Dead Animals

The Source • Spilling Mountains • Blowing Its Stack • No
Straight Lines • No Men Allowed • Shoo Fly! • Exhibition Games
• Ride a Ring of Horses • Why the Camel Has Its Hump •
Lambikens • The First Dog? • Ganging Up • Winning Chemistry
• The Sniff Test • Say It With Your Body

The Monkey Business • Noah's Ark • Eat Your Jicama, Dear • No,
Thank You • Reliving the Past? • Skull Bones • Easy Cutters • Easy
Containers

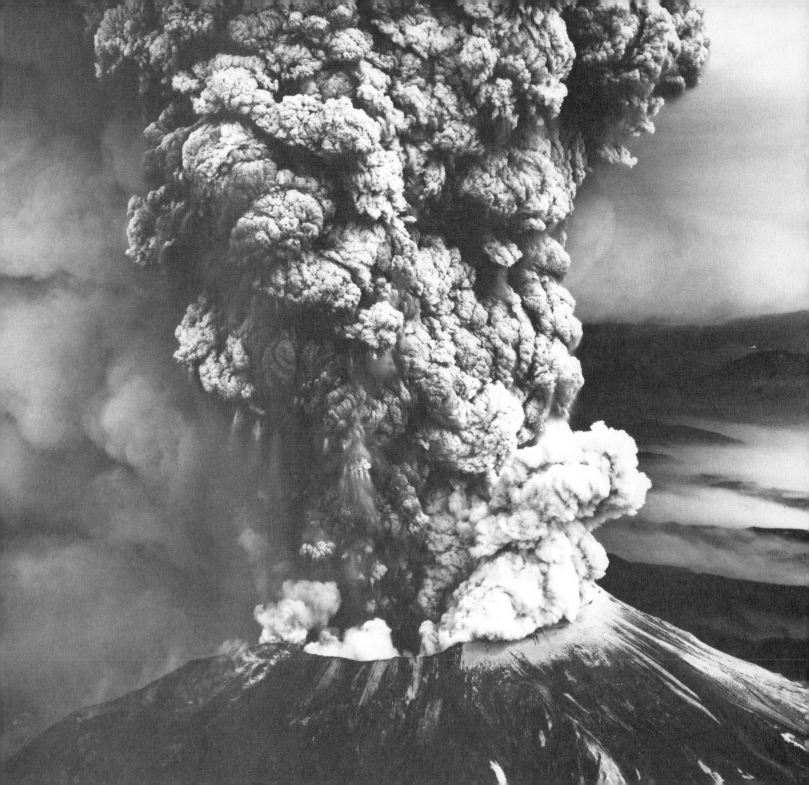

SETTING OUT

When I was 10 years old, I climbed Mount Saddle-back. It's one of the hundreds of bumpy hills of the same name all over our land that barely rise above the timberline. Still, it was a long walk uphill. At the summit, I turned to look down at the countryside laid out like a map below, and got the shock of my life: Clouds make shadows.

The darkness that comes over you when the sun "goes behind a cloud" is a shadow. Nobody had ever thought to tell me that. I had never thought to ask. A cloudy day is just a big shadow.

You can catch things looking different when you look at them in different ways. Lie on your back and look at the ceiling. Seen topsy-turvy, what a place to play! Look at your skin through a magnifying lens. That's a whole new world.

Nothing changes the world you live on so much as seeing it through the lens of time. Time is a brand new lens for us. A few generations ago, people couldn't imagine a time longer than a few thousand years. They thought the world, even the whole universe, was 6,000 years old. Now we know that the world, aged 4,600 million (close to five billion) years, is a youngster compared to the universe, which is at least three times that old.

We're on a mountaintop now, looking down at the map of everything that has happened before today. The world has changed. The landscape is more beautiful, more fascinating, than anyone had ever guessed.

SEASHELLS ON MOUNTAINTOPS

Having no idea how old things were made certain oddities, such as shell-shaped stones, hard to understand in our forebears' days. Maybe shell-stones were shaped that way by coincidence, as frost on a window-pane happens to be shaped like ferns. But, the fact that such shell-stones are found at the top of the Alps caused a brainstorm: Maybe they really were seashells, left there by a flood. When found, gigantic bones were even harder to explain. Perhaps they were dragons.

The discovery that time goes back really far began with simple observations. A farmer and amateur geologist named James Hutton, who was born in 1726, wondered why, if soil is always being washed off the land and out to sea in storms and streams, there is any soil left. New soil must be added as old soil is washed away. New soil could come only from above, from highlands where rock is eroded into stones, pebbles, sand, and mud. Highlands, too, would wear down in time. New rock must push up as old rock wears down, figured Hutton.

That's how shells climb mountains. Fossil shells were once where they belong, on the ocean bottom. New rock pushed up under old rock, lifting the shells sky-high. Checking out his idea by examining layers of rock, old and new, Hutton was flabbergasted by how long this business had been going on. He found, he said, "no vestige of a beginning, no prospect of an end."

SHELLSTONES AND DRAGON BONES

That didn't explain why there *were* shellstones and dragon bones. Again, someone became curious about simple things. In the early 1830s, the well-educated son of a successful English country doctor, Charles Darwin, noticed that finches living on different islands off the coast of South America had oddly different beaks, although they were very close relatives. One finch's beak was long and curved, another's was short and powerful. Of nine species, each had a beak that seemed perfectly designed for eating that species' particular food. Darwin figured that bodies must change to suit their environment.

Each individual is unlike any other individual. Those that are most suitable for their environment get along better, those that aren't don't fare very well. Those that fare better than others sometimes pass on to their offspring the characteristics that allowed them to fare well. Hence, generation after generation, characteristics that help individuals thrive can become common. The more suitable are in this way "selected" to continue and

to change further, the less suitable die out. Shellstones are shells. Dragon bones are dinosaurs. Both are fossils of forms of life that worked well for awhile, then died out or evolved into new forms. Evolution means that each form of life is related to the one that came before it. "There is," Darwin said, "grandeur in this view of life."

PEA GAMES

But there were mysteries, too. No one knew how a creature could change, or how that change could be passed along to other generations, until the beginning of this century, when the forgotten work of a monk who enjoyed gardening was rediscovered. Gregor Mendel had experimented with peas in the century before ours, dusting the pollen of one kind into the flower of another kind. The seeds produced were wrinkled or smooth, yellow or green, depending on which parent plants he had used to produce them.

Each plant, Mendel decided, must contain instructions that are passed to the next generation. Depending on how those instructions are mixed, the new plant might be very much like one parent, or quite different from both parents.

Although Mendel did not realize the full significance of his discovery, he was "evolving" new varieties

of peas by selecting only those plants whose instructions he wished to see in the next generation. That's how life changes.

PUTTING PIECES TOGETHER

Loose ends remained. Some fossils in Africa are identical with some fossils in South America, but the continents are an ocean apart. How could creatures have crossed the Atlantic? And since they couldn't have, how could identical creatures have evolved in such different places?

In the 1920s, Alfred Wegener looked at the shapes of continents as though they were pieces in a jigsaw puzzle. Africa and South America, he noticed, fit together nicely. The kind of rock the west coast of Africa is made of is the same kind of rock the east coast of South America is made of. Fossils found on one coast match fossils found on the other coast. They must once have been joined together. Since then they must have drifted apart.

No one believed Wegener. He himself had no idea how continents could drift. Everyone thought he was a crackpot to the day he died and after. But Wegener was right. So were Hutton, Darwin, and Mendel. New rock is being made right now, new life forms are evolving, your instructions are different from those of any individual on Earth, Earth's continents are drifting all over the globe, and the amount of time all these things take is mind-boggling.

THE TROUBLE WITH TIME

Wegener was a geophysicist and meteorologist, but Hutton, Darwin, and Mendel were just amateur scientists. The things that made them curious might make anyone wonder. What they noticed, you could notice. What they figured out is simply sensible. But none of it is imaginable without the imagination needed for understanding how long time is.

The trouble with our human minds is that we are smart enough to read the truth in rocks, fossils, and all the life around us, and yet we can't imagine the slowness with which things happen, or the immensity of time itself. Geologists call this "deep time."

Utah was an ocean beach 500 million years ago. Now North America is coming apart in the West, and Utah may become a beach again. The time that has passed between then and now amounts to only one-ninth the age of Earth. Ninety-five percent of our history so far was over by the time dinosaurs left their fossil bones behind. It took bacteria

1,500 million years to evolve into the types of cells that we are made of. All multicellular life, from algae to zebras, has evolved in the 1,500 million years since then. We humans are about 2 million years old—the final two-thousandths of the fossil record. Even Hutton admitted that his mind grew "giddy by looking so far into the abyss of time."

TAKE A WALK

This book is a journey through an amount of time too long for humans to easily comprehend. Begin at wetlands alive with the first cells and walk only a few yards up fish-filled streams; you will have traveled 3,550 million years. Walk farther uphill, following the path fish took as they lumbered ashore on stubby legs, and you will pass the time when all the continents of Earth crashed into one another, and myriad kinds of creatures became extinct. That was 230 million years ago, and there still weren't any dinosaurs.

Cows, Christmas trees, cockroaches, and you are descended from the remnants of life that survived that catastrophe. The story can be read in days. In an hour, you can walk from the warm, wet lowlands where life first clung to the cool, dry heights where life can live today. The effect will be like a movie in which the frames are unreeled before your eyes so fast that events fairly gallop. If you were to slow the reel down and look at the movie frame by frame, you would see as little difference from one frame to the next as you would see between the Rocky Mountains today and the Rocky Mountains tomorrow—even though they are eroding to stubs before your very eyes.

The descent of present life forms from previous ones, the movement of continents, and the inheritability of traits are facts. They are events that are happening now in measurable ways so that there is no doubt about their reality. As to how or why these things happen—by what forces they occur or what rules they obey—those are theories. A theory is an explanation. People are born theorizers. Ask a three-year old what makes the wind, and he may with no hesitation at all explain that leaves make wind when they move. Theories can be tested. A good theory accounts for the known facts, and predicts new ones that have not yet been observed. The three-year-old's wind theory is not a good one. It doesn't account for the fact that the wind blows in winter, when the trees are bare, and it predicts that there will be no wind in a desert, where there are no trees.

Theories proposed by scientists are subjected to just such tests. Suppose a biologist were to guess that snails with thick shells evolved because thick-shelled individuals could not be crunched and eaten by predators, whereas thin-shelled individuals were eaten up. That theory predicts that there will be a relationship between shell thickness and predation. The scientist can go out, as you can go out, to look at snails and their enemies. If, in fact, thin-shelled snails live in places where they have few enemies, and thick-shelled ones live in places where predators are a threat, the theory will have passed a test.

No matter how many tests a theory passes, it can never become a fact. Facts don't change, but someone might easily come up with a better theory to explain them. Perhaps thick shells evolved because thin-shelled individuals were crushed by the surf.

This book includes many theories. Some have passed so many tests over such a long time that they are very likely to be correct explanations of the facts, and few people argue about them any more. Others are newer, less tested, and therefore still argued about. A few are no more than good guesses supported by so few facts that they are not yet, and may never be, testable. That is the case, for example, with theories that explain how we got to be so smart that we can think up theories.

Not only *can* we think up theories; we must. We can't, even at three years old, see leaves move and feel wind blow without trying to put two and two together. We hunger to understand, to get it! But just try to tell the child meteorologist about Earth's spin, ocean currents, cold air, hot air—the ingredients of the grown-up meteorologists wind theory. You will only spoil his fun, for a theory is a thrill only when it puts together facts that have gone begging for an explanation, and little kids don't know all the facts meteorologists know.

I have divided the story into three sections, Dawn, Noon, and Dusk. Dawn, of course, is about the beginning of life. It is filled with jellyfish, seaweeds, and all the other life that began or still lives in the sea. That section covers 3,600 million years, and ends jarringly with the greatest extinction of life the world has ever known.

Noon is about a harsh, pioneering time when life moved ashore over bare rock, into glaring sun and drying winds. Although the time covered is shorter—340 million years—Noon feels like a summer day, when the hours stretch out almost forever and every sort of adventure seems possible, and even happens. Noon was the time of the dinosaurs, of flowers, butterflies, and birds.

The last section, Dusk, is harder to explain, because the title may make you think of dark pollution, nuclear warfare, or extinction. It is true that the last 65 million years has not been easy. The section starts with the catastrophe that extinguished the dinosaurs, and includes the Great Ice Age, and us. But I do not think night is falling on life's evolution on Earth. Simply, the book ends at the end of the story of life as we know it so far. Whatever light we have been able to shed falls back over the past. We cannot see into the future; it is as impenetrable to us as night. Still, I expect the sun to rise over Earth's tomorrow as warm and rosy as ever. I expect life to continue in the future as wriggling with energy, and as full of surprises, as it has always been.

In all the time that has passed, and with all the astonishing things that have happened, we are the first and only creature that can read the story. We are the only ones who can pick up an arrowhead and think about when it was a lump of quartz, and when that lump was sand scoured off the first rocks, and before that, when those first rocks were the original, small island that was to grow into North America.

No other creature can look at a cow and see that it is the whole world to its bacteria, or understand that we, the bacteria, and the cow are all chemical factories recycling energy trapped in plants, which are made of little but air and water.

You may not be able to go to all the places mentioned in this book. That doesn't matter. If you can't see a clam at the seashore, you can see a snail in the park. Wolves are rare, but dogs are common. Dinosaurs are extinct, but birds are descended from dinosaurs. Flowers bloom in pots; algae and insects grow everywhere. The entire journey of life from the sea 4,000 million years ago to Ice Age plains peopled with people is only as far as from the soggy foot of a hill to its dry summit. Each square inch of that hill takes on new meaning as you think about all the inches below, all the time they took to accumulate, and all the evolution that led to the weed, the bug, and the human observer that have an interest in it.

No square inch of the world will ever look the same to you again.

Sara Stein
September, 1986

DAWN

4000 MILLION YEARS AGO

The Craton · Clay Organisms · Bacterial Smells · The Oxygen Crises

Life began on Earth because Earth was in the right place in our solar system. Here, and only here, is water watery. And that's what life needs. Every living thing is juicy. Prick a finger, bite a peach: there's juice in everything. You yourself are 70 percent water. There's not a dry spot in the human body; water brings to every bit of every body everything it needs to live.

It's strange to think how easily the chance for life to start might have been missed. There's a difference of only 100° Celcius (180° Fahrenheit) between the freezing point of water, where it turns into solid ice, and the boiling point, where it turns into airy vapor. The temperature on Venus averages about 480°C (900°F), way above boiling, and the temperature on Mars hovers around −23°C (−10°F), way below freezing, even on a "balmy" summer day. On Mars, farther from the sun, water is a solid: ice. On Venus, closer to the sun, water is a vapor and exists only in clouds. Just a small change in the distance from the sun is the difference between life and no life.

Earth is a small planet. If it were big, like Jupiter, it couldn't be called Earth because it wouldn't be solid. You can't stand on Jupiter. There's no surface. It's 99 percent gas. Jupiter is so big that six Earth-

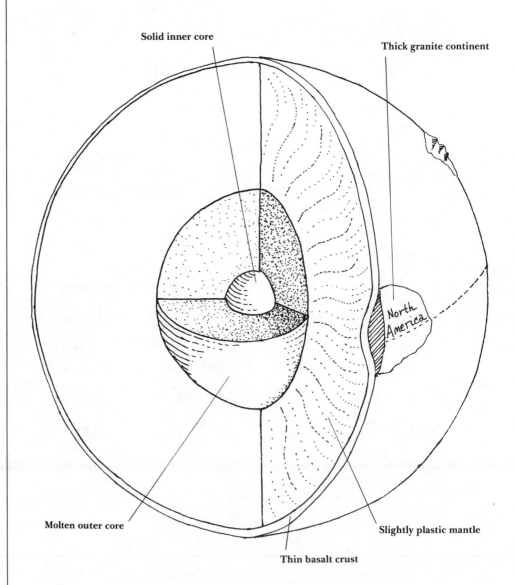

Solid inner core

Thick granite continent

North America

Molten outer core

Slightly plastic mantle

Thin basalt crust

The thickness of Earth's crust is very exaggerated here. The size, shape, and position of North America when it first formed is not known for sure. It was probably very small, and it may have been on the equator.

size planets could fit into its Great Red Spot, the eye of a humongous storm that has been raging there for centuries. Earth, which consisted mostly of hydrogen and helium when it was born, was so small that its gravitational force couldn't hold on to much of the gases. The substances you can see and feel—hard iron, yellow sulfur, glassy silicon, powdery calcium, smudgy carbon—are what are left over. You walk, breathe, and bathe in the "dregs."

But then again, our planet isn't *too* small. If it were as small as the moon, its gravity couldn't even hold on to a cloud. There would be no wind, because there would be no air. No air means nothing to trap the sun's heat, which melts ice, which makes oceans, seas, lakes, rivers, ponds, puddles, rain, and juicy life.

Our sun—our star—also happens to be the right size for life. Bigger stars have so much gravity that they pull into themselves the whole cloud of dusty gas that is their raw material and leave nothing to form planets. Little stars are too cool, and burn out too fast. Life needs a warm and steady sun.

Look up at the night sky. Among the stars there are billions like our own. Around them circle planets like the ones in our solar system. Some of those planets are in the right place. What has happened here may be happening right now on some small planet with earth, air, water, and sun. Or life may have begun there when it began here, and some organism, watching the stars fade in the morning sky, is looking in your direction and wondering.

It is dawn, 4,000 million years ago, and life is just beginning.

A BALL OF SOUP

There are worm burrows in rock 1,000 million years old, fossil threads of algae in rock perhaps 1,500 million years old, and round microfossils (they can be seen only through a microscope) in rock that formed fully 2,000 million years ago. The oldest fossils of all are more than 3,000 million years old and look very like the bacteria and algae living today. By the time they formed fossils, the ancestral bacteria and algae had already been evolving for 1,000 million years, ever since rain fell and rocks hardened. Life seems to have begun almost as soon as there was a place to live. All life still lives within an incredibly thin zone at the surface of our planet.

If you drew a circle and called it Earth, the pencil line would be too thick (in relationship to the rest of the circle) to represent Earth's crust. The crust is only about 30 kilometers (18½ miles) thick, of which only the top few meters support life. The temperature climbs the deeper you go. Below the crust for nearly 3,000 kilometers (1,860 miles) is the mantle of hot, oozy rock that slowly swirls and flows. The very center of the earth is the heaviest part of it, a core of iron and nickel. Our planet is a ball of simmering soup with a scum floating on its surface.

Earth's scum is composed partly of granite, the rock that continents are made of, and it floats. Put enough weight on granite and it sinks. The weight of water sank land under Hoover Dam eight inches into the mantle when the dam's reservoirs were filled. Heavy as granite feels, it is the lightest part of the soup, the fat that rose to the top of the broth during Earth's hot beginning 5,000 million years ago. The rest of the scum is denser rock called basalt, that now covers the

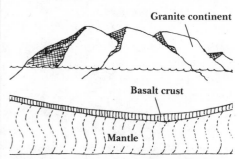

Granite continent

Basalt crust

Mantle

Continents float on the mantle; the thickest parts, the roots of mountain ranges, float deepest.

GRAY GRANITE

R ock is made of minerals, and often of many different kinds. The grayish background mineral in granite is feldspar, sparkling bits are mica, glistening black is hornblende, rusty red is iron ore, white is quartz. Some granite contains large crystals of garnet, a wine-colored jewel.

whole earth below the oceans and continents. Before 4,000 million years ago rafts of rocky crust hardened only temporarily and then melted again.

Oceans formed as soon as the atmosphere cooled enough for steam to settle out of it as the first rain. After the rains came, water may have covered the whole world, crust and all. We will never know for sure. The first rock that stayed cool enough to stay solid must have eroded away. No one has found a trace of rock quite old enough to be the original.

The oldest rock that still exists is nearly 4,000 million years old. These oldest rock formations are called the craton. Our craton is the original America, one that never saw the deer and the antelope play. Now most of the old rock is buried thousands of feet deep under newer rock. A bit is exposed at the lowest portion of the Grand Canyon, more than a mile below the rim, and a portion lies nearer the surface at Lake Superior and northward all the way to Greenland. Only in a very few places is the original surface still naked; you can touch the craton in parts of Canada.

BARE ROCK

Rock isn't something that simply *is;* it is something that has happened.

Even an amateur rock hound can see some of the past in outcroppings and in the exposed rock of highway cuts, and pick up rock history in a chip of marble. Geologists have learned to read in a rock's form, texture, color, and chemistry the whole story it has to tell.

North America appears to have been made of many granite rafts, not just one. As the rafts pushed into one another, they squeezed up mountains. Between 3,800 million and 1,000 million years ago no fewer than six huge mountain ranges, each as great as the Alps, were raised up and eroded away on the North American continent.

Rock is different at the seams between granite rafts. It is a denser, darker, solidified lava called basalt. While molten, the basalt oozed through weak spots in the crust, or broke to the surface through the holes of volcanoes. One of the craton rafts was cracked open from Lake Superior to northeast Kansas, and was flooded by the hot stuff under it. Lava filled in the hollows until the whole landscape was smooth.

HOW TO MAKE A ROCK

Rocks are named according to how they formed and the materials they are made of. Rock that arrives mol-

BLACK BRIMSTONE

Basalt is hardened lava. Sometimes this dark, very hard rock is streaked with the green mineral olivine, but often its mineral crystals are too small to see, even with a hand lens. These basalt pebbles have been smoothed by surf on the beach of an old volcanic island off the coast of Maine. They can be kept as shiny as they are when wet by rubbing them with a little Vaseline. Some people display colored beach pebbles in glass jars of mineral oil.

PAGES IN THE ROCK BOOK

There are many different kinds of layers you might see along a highway that has been cut through hills of sedimentary rock. Some, such as black coal, are easy to recognize; when you see coal, you are looking at the remains of an ancient swamp. A flood washes away finer sediments, leaving heavier pebbles to form a lumpy sort of rock. Sand dunes keep their wavy shape as they become rock, and the original cut of a stream is preserved as the stream bed fills with sediments. Deep ocean muds become rock nearly devoid of fossils, whereas the bottoms of shallow seas contain lots of fossil shells. Each season, the mud that drifts to the bottom of a slow river adds a layer, perhaps paper-thin, to the rock it becomes. Lava seeps upward, then flows over the land and hardens. Each of these layers was once the surface of the land or sea.

Layers are originally horizontal. Later, mountain building can fold them into humps, tilting the layers. Wind and water erode the tops of humps, leaving just the vertical portion.

Geologists examine layers of sedimentary rock to discover the history of the place where they formed. Some sediments are built up quickly. A hurricane might heap up mud or sand many centimeters deep. That layer, turned to rock, would represent only a day or so of time. Some sediments build up slowly, only one millimeter in a thousand years. A leap over a few feet of such sediment layers would carry you millions of years through time.

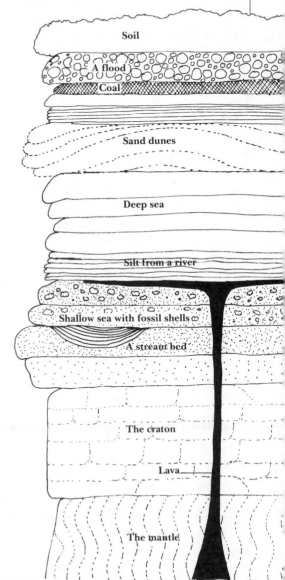

Soil

A flood

Coal

Sand dunes

Deep sea

Silt from a river

Shallow sea with fossil shells

A stream bed

The craton

Lava

The mantle

ten at the surface from deep down is called igneous (fiery) rock. Granite and basalt are igneous rocks; they have different names because they are made of somewhat different minerals.

All other kinds of rock are recycled from igneous rock. Minerals dissolved out of them form clay; grit eroded from their surface accumulates as sand and mud. As layers of these materials accumulate, they are pressed into rock under their own weight. Rocks made into layers by being pressed are called sedimentary rocks. The deeper the sediments are buried, the more they are squeezed. Squeezing causes a form of friction, and friction heats stuff up and bakes it hard. Scrunched sand becomes sandstone. Brownstone houses are made of sandstone of a particular color. Each grain of sand is still visible in it, and as the surface wears, you can sweep up little piles of sand. Sand is made mostly of silicon, a common element that is glassy. In fact, the glass windows in that brownstone house were made by melting and refreezing sand.

Rock made of fine clay that drifted to the bottom of a lake or spilled over in floods is called shale. Each spring's floodful of clay will be a layer in the shale it becomes. Shale splits easily into its original layers.

MICROMINERAL COLLECTION

The large mineral crystals displayed in museums and sold in stores are rare and hard to find. Tiny crystals are common, and are often more perfect in shape. With a hand lens, check rocks you find for the flat surfaces, called facets, that all crystals have. The outside of a rock is usually badly worn; unworn crystals are inside. To find them, put the rock on something hard, such as a stone terrace or concrete floor. Cover it with a piece of cloth so no chips fly. Hit it hard a few times with a hammer. Then pick through the pieces looking at each with a hand lens to find one that includes a pretty crystal. The rock chip might be no bigger than a pea, and the crystal only the size of a pinhead.

To display microminerals, cut a piece of cardboard to fit the bottom of a clear plastic box. Using white glue, glue the minerals to the cardboard in rows. Use a field guide to find out their names (*The Audubon Society Guide to North American Rocks and Minerals* has the best pictures).

A powerful hand lens will let you see the tiny mineral crystals in ordinary rocks. One that folds into a case, can be worn around the neck, and is no bigger than your thumb can be bought at stores that sell other optical equipment, such as telescopes and cameras. Eyeglass stores can also order a folding hand lens for you. Ask for a "10x" lens, which means it makes things look ten times bigger than they really are.

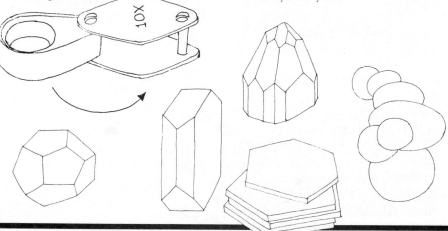

HOMETOWN GEOLOGY

To learn your local rock history, ask at nearby natural-history museums, nature centers, or parks. Some offer "geology walks" to the most interesting sites, or have booklets about the rock formations in your area. Town historical societies usually know the locations of old quarries where samples of granite, limestone, sandstone, slate, marble, or mica can be collected. Many parts of the country have fossil-rich rocks.

A fossil is an image of a creature, not the flesh itself. Some very rare ones are prints. A jellyfish buried very deep and very fast in velvety silt slowly evaporates, leaving behind a film of carbon that is like a drawing of the original. Most fossils are made of minerals that didn't belong to the original creature. Porous shell or bone is gradually invaded by harder minerals as the original material dissolves. Or, a hollow left when a shell dissolves fills up with minerals. These boys have found mollusk fossils in the limestone lobby of a New York City skyscraper.

Mollusk shell

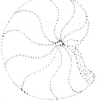

Hollow left when shell dissolves.

Mineral fossil formed in the hollow.

PRESTO CHANGO

Half-baked sedimentary rock that heats up more, becomes rubbery or even melts, and rehardens is called metamorphic rock. It has changed (metamorphosed) into something else. When shale is pressed and baked more, it becomes slate, hard as a blackboard and smooth as a pool table. Slate is the best blackboard material and the best surface for a pool table, and it is very likely to be the hearth in your home. The shale it was made of may have felt gritty but the grit has been transformed into crystals so tiny that slate feels velvet smooth. In the hardest slates, mica crystals may be large enough to see.

All these kinds of rock—granites, basalts, sandstones, shales, and slates—were being formed as life began, and are still forming now. But other kinds weren't in production 4,000 million years ago. Organisms that harden their bodies with lime evolved only 1,000 million years ago. The shelly remains of these organisms form chalk, limestone, and marble.

Lime is calcium carbonate, the same white powder that is spread on lawns to help them grow. As calcium-using organisms die in sea or lake, they drift to the bottom and leave layers of white lime. Over tens of millions of years, that lime may pile upward into deposits thousands of feet thick.

Lime is chemically identical to shell, chalk, limestone, and marble. The differences of texture and hardness among them are a result of differences in the heats and pressures under which they formed.

White Florida beaches are largely the raw material itself, mere skeletons of lime. Powdery lime mashes under pressure into chalk, the silkiest of limestones. No limey stone is as old as the oldest granite, but the chalk you use in school could be hundreds of millions of years old.

Coarser lime wastes scrunch up, heat up, and harden into limestone. Along the coast of Florida there is a very coarse limestone so stuffed full of shells you would think it had washed up yesterday, except that it is not very easy to pry apart. It is real sedimentary rock about a million years old; human beings walked the earth as it was being made. Many of the most elegant city buildings are made of limestone. You can sometimes see the shapes of shells if you look closely, especially in lobbies where the limestone has been polished.

Cook limestone at enormous pressure and temperature and you get marble, a metamorphic rock. Wherever lime deposits have become embroiled in the cooking and crunching of mountain building,

ROCK HARDNESS KIT

Rock collectors use the numbers 1 through 10 to describe how hard a rock is. The softest chalk has a hardness of 1; a diamond is a 10. Quartz has a hardness of 7, and limestone a hardness of only 3 or 4. These numbers are used in field guides to help identify rock specimens.

A scratch test is used to see how hard a rock is. You can put together your own scratch-test kit, beginning with your fingernail, which can scratch rocks that are softer than about 2½. A rock that can be scratched by a copper penny is no harder than 3½, one that can be scratched by a knife blade or a piece of window glass has a hardness of up to 6. A rock as hard as 7 can be scratched by a hardened steel file, and one as hard as 9 can be scratched with the kind of sandpaper called emery cloth.

there will be marble. Marble is all over New England. The shells are gone, melted away. But minerals, melted and mixed with the once-white limestone, have marbled it with color.

Rock hardness alone tells you

something of a stone's history. Lime that is still chalky enough to write with hasn't been pressure-cooked very much. If it is limestone, it has. Marble is the well-done stuff, fired to a turn inside the kiln of a mountain range.

ROCK PRINTS

As mud, sand, and lime turn into stone, traces of life buried in them turn into stone, too, and are preserved as fossils. Worm holes, snail tracks, dead weeds, and empty shells become a record of life that has literally left an impression.

Where layers of rock have been undisturbed, fossils can be read like a book, but backward. The soft surface of mud bears the marks of your feet, printed there only this morning. As you peel back the underlying rock layer by layer, you come closer to the beginning of life's story.

Not every layer of North America's history lies beneath its present land. Some layers were fractured in mountain building or were crumbled and washed off the surface long ago. Wind erosion scrubs away great thicknesses of rock.

The edges of the continent were built too recently to show traces of the earliest life. North America was just a big island when life began. Only in the middle of the continent are all the layers in place, like a giant wedding cake. Under the Midwest's flat-as-a-pancake fields lie flat-as-a-pancake sandstones, limestones, shales, and slates, and under them lies the flat-as-a-pancake granite of the craton, its mountain stubs buried at its roots. The craton is our heartland, and our most ancient history. Fossils started when it was spanking new, more than 3,000 million years ago.

A STEW OVER THE CRATON

The world as it was when life began would have killed you. The atmosphere was poisonous: a concoction of ammonia and hydrogen sulfide (what you smell when you sniff a bottle of household ammonia or let an egg get rotten) and deadly methane gas, which has no smell but which you can see as the flame of a gas stove. There was plenty of water, molecules made of two hydrogen atoms and one oxygen atom, and written H_2O. But there was no free oxygen. Without free oxygen, the ozone layer of the atmosphere, which now protects you from the full strength of the sun's light, couldn't exist. Your skin would have burned much worse than any sunburn you have ever seen. Flesh deep in your body would have been destroyed. You couldn't have survived the heat anyway, or the radioactivity. Radioactive elements hadn't had a chance to decay much, so the continent was one big "hot spot," and volcanoes spewed boiling lava everywhere.

Uplands were rain-scrubbed rock, very clean and fresh. But low places were sticky with clay, and with a reddish brown sludge made of organic molecules. Any molecule with carbon in it is called organic, whether or not it is made by an organism. Some organic molecules have fruity, meaty, or cheesy smells. One of the simplest, most common organic molecules is sugar. So the ancient sludge might have been smelly and sweet (see Molecule Making).

In fact, you might have been able to digest it. You are what you eat, and what you eat is organic molecules: carbohydrates, for instance, which include starches as well as sugars; and proteins, which are assembled from smaller organic molecules called amino acids. In your experience, foods to feed your life are made by other lives—carrots, or cows. But the stuff in long ago puddles was food before there was a life to make it or to eat it.

The basic ingredients for organic molecules—atoms—were in the poisonous air: carbon mostly, and nitrogen, hydrogen, and sulfur. Other necessary elements became available as rain dissolved them from the crust and deposited them

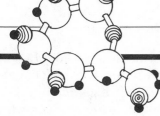

MOLECULE MAKING

Life's chemistry—organic chemistry—is built on carbon atoms. Carbon is unusual because it has four "sticky" places to which other atoms can attach. When you're gluing two pieces of something together, the attachment between them is called a bond. The word "bond" is also used for the joining of atoms. Organic molecules are made by bonding other kinds of atoms to carbon's four bonding sites. The other atoms also have a typical number of "sticky" places. Hydrogen has a single bonding spot where it can "glue" itself to

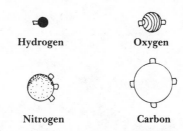

Hydrogen   **Oxygen**

Nitrogen   **Carbon**

spots. Oxygen has two. Nitrogen, which is in all proteins, has three. A carbon atom can share a single bond with a neighbor, or two bonds (called a double bond), or three (called a triple bond), so long as all four bonds are used to make the finished mole-

cule. The arithmetic of organic chemistry is easy.

Use polka-dot stickers in different colors and sizes to invent all sorts of molecules that actually exist: chains built from strings of carbon, branched forms, or carbon rings bristling with other atoms or groups of atoms. You can find other examples not illustrated here in high school chemistry textbooks, or you can make up your own. Made-up molecules are quite likely to exist, providing your arithmetic is correct.

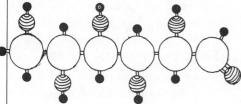

A glucose molecule. It has 6 carbon atoms, 12 hydrogen atoms, and 6 oxygen atoms.

Its chemical formula is an abbreviation, $C_6H_{12}O_6$, and sometimes it is shown as a diagram, in which the lines stand for the number of bonds between atoms, like this:

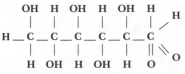

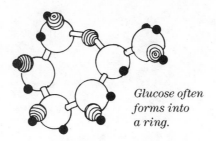

Glucose often forms into a ring.

Two glucose rings bump into one another.

A molecule of water, H_2O, escapes.

The two glucose molecules now stick together as the double sugar maltose. The maltose molecule will come apart again if H_2O is added. In other words, the sugar will dissolve.

WHERE LIFE BEGAN?

Life may have begun in the "pan" of a mud flat like this one, where evaporation concentrated the chemicals brought in with each tide until the broth was rich enough for complicated molecules to form. You can see how chemicals become concentrated by doing your own evaporation experiment.

Make a quart of hot salty water using as much salt as will dissolve in it. Pour some into a shallow pan, and let it evaporate in the hot sun. That should take only a few hours. Do it again. After a dozen "floods" and "droughts," there will be a crust of salt in the pan, and each new flood will be saltier than the one before.

in the form of clay. And, of course, there was water. It took energy to push elements together into molecules, and that energy came from bolts of lightning and from sunlight.

But not even the simplest form of life is made up of only simple organic molecules that fell together. If you were to order all the molecules that you are made up of from a chemical supply house, the bill would come to $10 million. That's not because you're made up of precious stuff like gold and platinum, but because you're made up of molecules that are tremendously difficult to manufacture. So is a bacterium and, no doubt, so were the first living creatures.

There also is a chicken-and-egg sort of problem. To be alive, an organism must be organized into a community of molecules that can do two things: metabolize, or rearrange molecules from outside itself into molecules of itself; and replicate, or make copies of itself. Metabolism is handled by protein enzymes, which rearrange the molecules that you eat into the molecules that you are. Proteins can't replicate themselves. Replication is handled by DNA, which can copy itself and also carry information for assembling the proteins from which you are made. But here is the catch: DNA doesn't work without

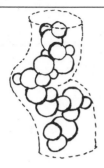

Proteins are built in such complicated ways that they are very hard to draw. (1) Shows atoms in a protein chain. The protein molecule is actually very much longer; to avoid drawing thousands of atoms, the molecule might be illustrated as a tube.

But the chain of atoms coils, like a spring; coiling is also hard to draw, so often it is ignored by placing an imaginary second tube around the first, coiled one (2).

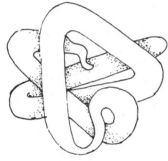

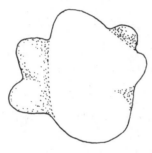

However, even the coil in its pretend tube is bent into a very complicated shape like (3).

To avoid spending hours drawing such difficult shapes, proteins are often drawn as though they were inside a bag like (4).

protein enzymes that "unzip" its double strand for copying. So the first life had to have both types of molecules, for neither can do its work without the other.

DNA and the proteins it depends on are high-tech chemicals, not the sort of organic stuff that forms in puddles, where the meeting and making of molecules is as haphazard as the formation of words in a bowl of alphabet soup.

Some scientists reason that there must have been a chemical supply house capable of assembling difficult organic molecules, of introducing them to one another at close quarters, and of favoring those that are now life's basic tool kit before they, in turn, could assemble one another. Some think the supply house was clay. One such clay is kaolinite, an ingredient in kaopectate, which is a medication used to relieve diarrhea. What a thought! But it's not crazy.

The scientist who champions this possible origin of life, A. G. Cairns-Smith, compares the process to how a stone arch is built. At first sight, it seems impossible to build an arch. The sides will not stay up until the keystone is in place, yet the keystone can't be placed unless the sides of the arch support it. But once you realize that a heap of sand (or a pile of stones, or a wood scaffold) is used to support the arch until the keystone can be dropped into place, the feat seems easy. The supporting sand is then removed, and the arch stands on its own.

Clay is a good supporting structure for the building of difficult organic molecules. It is formed of minute crystals, often of complicated shapes, that form a scaffolding within which smaller molecules are held in position for assembly into larger ones. Clay grows in layers as more minerals crystallize against its surface. Certain organic molecules may help it grow by making it less soluble in water, or by attracting more minerals. Clay also evolves. Irregularities that develop

PROTEINS IN ACTION

P rotein enzymes assemble molecules, and disassemble them; other proteins move molecules from place to place in clever ways.

Assembling a Molecule

1. Two molecules bump together, but they are not in the right position to bond together.

2. An enzyme manipulates them into the right position for bonding with one another.

3. Once bonded, they stay together even after the enzyme leaves.

Moving a Molecule Through a Cell Wall

4. A protein opens in the cell wall like a cup to receive a molecule from outside the cell.

5. The protein springs into another shape to dump the molecule inside the cell.

Disassembling a Molecule

6. An enzyme is "cocked" by a regulator molecule.

7. The molecule to be disassembled settles into place.

8. That releases the regulator, and the enzyme springs open, pulling the large molecule apart.

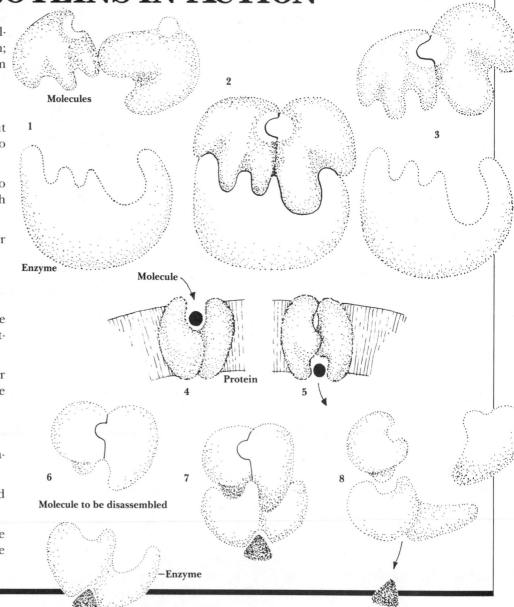

Molecules

1

2

3

Enzyme

Molecule

Protein

4

5

Molecule to be disassembled

6

7

8

—Enzyme

Regulator molecule

in its crystal structure are "inherited" in each new layer that forms thereafter. Organic molecules produced by clay evolve with it, for as the structure changes, so do the possible shapes into which they can be assembled. Cairns-Smith calls such communities of clay and organic molecules organisms. They do, after all, grow, replicate, and evolve. If that is so, there is truth in what religion tells us: Life came from clay. Or were clay organisms already alive?

BLOBS ALIVE

Organic molecules within a clay community would also have aided one another's evolution. DNA that included instructions for its own untwisters and unzipperers would naturally have increased the population of both its proteins and itself. All they would need to leave the shelter of their parent clay would be a body. That, apparently, is not a problem. Very ordinary organic molecules, low-tech puddle types, form bodies and behave in lifelike ways even in a laboratory flask. The organic molecules clump together into droplets. The droplets are invaded by sugars and proteins, which accumulate inside them. The protein enzymes rebuild sugar into starch. The starch migrates to the surface of the droplet, forming a thick jacket. There is even a waste

THE SMALLEST FACTORY

The DNA molecule is two very long twisted strands of nucleotides held together by links like the rungs of a ladder. Although DNA contains all the instructions for making proteins, it cannot make them itself. That job is done by single strands of nucleotides called RNA— messenger RNA that carries a set of instructions out into the cell, and transfer RNA that carries amino acids to the place where they will be assembled. After enzymes "unzip" a portion of DNA, its instructions are copied into a molecule of messenger RNA.

1. Portion of a DNA molecule before it is "unzipped."

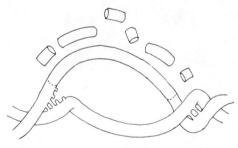

2. An unzipped portion being used as a pattern for assembling a length of messenger RNA.

3. The finished RNA messenger molecule leaves the nucleus carrying instructions for making a protein.

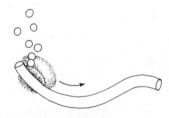

4. Out in the cell, a structure called a ribosome moves along the RNA assembling amino acids, brought to the site by transfer RNA, in the right order.

5. The finished protein chain will then detach from the ribosome.

RAISING BACTERIA

S team rises from this manure heap because of the bacteria living there. The heat is the energy they release during glycolysis. If a bacterium is warm enough, wet enough, and has plenty to eat, it can double itself every 20 minutes, becoming 50,000 bacteria in six hours. If none died, they would weigh 2 million kilograms (over 900,000 pounds) after only 24 hours.

Raise your own bacteria by building a compost heap for them to eat. Pile up grass clippings, weeds, and leaves. Dampen the pile with a hose every few days. After a week, plunge your hand deep into the pile to feel the heat bacteria produce as they digest the food you provide.

Turn the pile over every week. By the end of the summer, bacteria will have digested it completely. It will be soil.

product, which is expelled from the starchy blob into the surrounding water (you could call it primitive pee). The blobs grow. When they reach a certain size, they break apart into several "daughters."

Imagine giving such blobs DNA that could copy itself, its unzipperers, and its sugar-digesters. Those blobs would be self-perpetuating as long as there was enough sugar for them to eat. We would have to call them alive.

Lifelike behavior of organic molecules is ordinary chemistry. It may be not only a common outcome, but an inevitable one. This much we know: Somewhere over the craton 4,000 million years ago, some blobs became alive.

SMELLING IS BELIEVING

The blobs had a very simple diet and didn't use any oxygen at all. Even now, the most primitive organisms eat glucose (a simple sugar), cut it in two, and use the energy that had held it together for their own life processes. The broken sugar is cut up even smaller into molecules of lactic acid (the sourness of sour milk), alcohol (as in wine and beer), and carbon dioxide (the gas in rising dough). This short disassembly line is called glycolysis ("glucose cutting") and that way of getting energy is called fermentation. If you don't believe it, then feel it, taste it, smell it. First, savor the sweetness of wheat, milk, and grapes before any organism has eaten their sugar. Then feel the spongy airiness of bread, taste the acid tang of yogurt, smell the alcohol fumes of wine. They have all been glycolized.

The oldest microfossils found in rock are of bacteria. Bacteria are so tiny that tens of thousands fit into the space of a single skin cell, and even a skin cell can't be seen without a microscope. Bacteria aren't much to look at anyway: plain

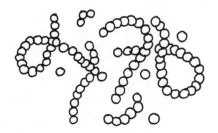

spheres, rods, spirals. It's their chemistry that's important, and you can smell that anywhere these smallest of all cells take their meals, including public toilets and your own armpits.

The world wouldn't smell the same without bacteria. Sweat and urine come out of your body with only the mildest of odors, and without bacteria. The raunchy odors they develop in time are not your waste products, but those of the bacteria eating them. Feces are smelly from the start, because they are loaded with billions of bacteria that thrive in your bowel on food you yourself can't digest. When you're gassy, you've fed them well. Hard-to-digest beans are the "musical fruit" because so much of a bean supper is leftovers for bacteria. Their waste product is methane gas. The methane gas that burns in your stove was made as bacteria decayed swamp plants.

If bacteria weren't eating every-

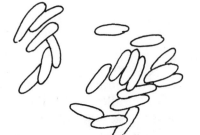

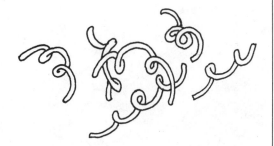

THE BACTERIUM'S COMPASS

L arge, heavy organisms like us know where down is because that's where gravity pulls us. The lighter (less dense) an object is, the less it is pulled by gravity. Bacteria are so small that they may be unable to sense the force of gravity at all, but they still know which way is down. Those that swim with twirling flagella head downward using a compass made of tiny grains of the iron ore called magnetite that they collect inside them. Bacteria in the Northern Hemisphere turn north. Because the Earth's magnetic field slants inward like the pattern of iron filings sprinkled around a bar magnet, that path takes them down. Bacteria in the Southern Hemisphere head south to head downward.

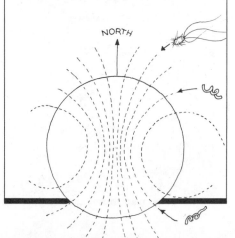

NORTH

thing from swamps to beans, nothing would fall apart. Leaves would dry out, but they wouldn't decay into soil. Sniff the good earth; that's the smell of bacteria. Without bacteria, fish would die, but they wouldn't rot. Breathe the salt air; that's laced with the whiff of bacteria, too. Meat uninhabited by bacteria would never spoil. Hold your nose near the garbage pail, where bacteria are doing their importantly smelly work.

Most organic molecules don't easily fall apart by themselves. Bacteria dismantle them when an organism dies, and they are then recycled by new life. Without bacteria, life would long ago have run out of materials.

NOT SO HOT, AFTER ALL

Bacteria get all their energy for recycling life's materials from glycolysis. But glycolysis doesn't give a cell very much energy to use. For every glucose molecule a bacterium eats, it gets only two usable units of energy. The rest is wasted as heat. You can see the wasted heat by turning a manure heap on a cool morning: The heat will rise as steam. Manure used to be heaped against barn walls to give heat all winter. You can feel heat in rotting compost, too, where bacteria are fermenting in their ancient way.

If a cell could find a way to extract more energy from its environment, it could live an easier life and manufacture more copies of itself. The evolution of cells in the clay scum over our basement rock involved increasingly efficient ways to grab energy.

The greatest breakthrough was photosynthesis, a way to get energy without eating. It was invented by cyanobacteria. Cyanobacteria are among the organisms that tinge puddles green. They trap an outside source of energy—light from the sun—in a pigment, green chlorophyll. The extra energy frees cyanobacteria from

GO AHEAD AND GLYCOLYZE

The original form of metabolism, glycolysis, was never lost. When you exercise so hard that not enough oxygen can get to your muscle cells, they do without. Going back to the old way, enzymes in the muscle cells cut glucose to supply the cells with energy. If your legs get tired during a hard run it is because your glycolyzing muscle cells are filling up with their ancient waste product, lactic acid. When you are absolutely exhausted after a race, the supply of glucose in your muscle cells is probably exhausted too.

the need to find sugar molecules in their environment. Instead of eating, they use the extra energy to make their own sugar from water (H_2O) and carbon dioxide (CO_2). When the sugar is completed, there is a leftover molecule of oxygen (O_2).

That should have been the end of that chemical experiment: Oxygen meant instant death to the early bacteria. Unless oxygen is tied up with other substances—with hydrogen as water, with iron as rust—it is an explosive gas that can simply fry bacteria to a crisp. Until the cyanobacteria did their experiment, there was no free oxygen in the air, and no way for the poison to get inside a cell to burn it up. But cyanobacteria evolved an ability to tie oxygen up with other molecules inside them. They were able not only to tolerate the poison, but to use it. They learned to breathe.

Instead of disassembling the two pieces of glucose leftover from glycolysis and excreting them as wastes, cyanobacteria combine the pieces with their oxygen molecules and continue processing them. When the processing is complete, they have removed from the original sugar molecule not the two units of energy retrieved through glycolysis but 38. Breathing grabs 19 times more energy than does fermenting.

THE OXYGEN CRISIS

Cyanobacteria changed the world. The oxygen they released accumulated in the atmosphere and is the oxygen you breathe today. Many of the fermenting bacteria that had peppered our oldest rock with microfossils were poisoned by oxygen and became extinct. Others survived by staying in murky depths where there was no oxygen; they inhabit those places still—the Dead Sea, for instance, and geysers in Yellowstone Park.

There are bacteria that can stand only very small amounts of oxygen and that use it for only a few reactions. Bacteria that infect hangnails and cuts can't tolerate much oxygen. That's why bandages are porous, to let oxygen get through to poison them.

As oxygen built up in the atmosphere, new species of bacteria arose that could survive larger doses and use it for longer and longer procedures for manufacturing all sorts of complicated molecules that could not have come together by themselves.

By about 1,500 million years ago, oxygen had accumulated to about half the amount present in our atmosphere today. Ozone had begun to form a protective layer above the earth. The new air created an opportunity for a new kind of cell, the eucaryotic cell that we and all the plants and animals of earth are made from. It uses oxygen, and plenty of it. But the most remarkable thing about it is the organization within its cell.

The chemical factory that is a bacterium is a sloppy sort of place. There is a short loop of DNA that carries instructions for all the worker enzymes that run its assembly lines, but that Boss DNA has no office separate from the rest of the cell interior, nor are any of the jobs carried out in separate laboratories.

The new eucaryotic (the name means "true nucleus") cells of 1,500 million years ago organized the factory. DNA was wrapped inside a membrane: the nucleus, the Boss's office. A network of pathways stretched from the nucleus to every area in the cell. Along the pathways, RNA—molecules similar to DNA that act as its translators and messengers—hustled amino acids into proteins destined to be the workers for various jobs. Chemical production lines were separated into their own rooms, called organelles.

The difference between bacteria and eucaryotes is something like the difference between a warehouse in which parts are strewed everywhere on the chance that what is needed is within reach, and an in-

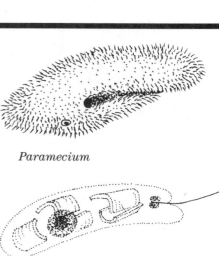

Paramecium

Euglena

Ameba

BRING 'EM BACK ALIVE

Eucaryotic cells are much larger than bacteria. They can be seen through a microscope in water collected from a pond. Inexpensive microscopes sold in toy departments do not have good enough lenses for seeing cells. Use a school microscope if you can.

Collect eucaryotes by sucking up water close to the leaves and stems of pond weeds with a basting bulb (a rubber ear syringe, available from pharmacies, is better because its smaller tip can be held closer to the underwater surfaces where eucaryotes are most numerous). Carry them home in a jar. Use an eyedropper to put one drop of water on a microscope slide. Cover the drop with a cover glass. Examine it under the 100 power (100x) lens, moving the slide slowly to scan the drop. Some common critters you might see moving about are euglena, amebas, and parameciums.

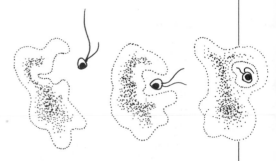

Ameba engulfing its food.

dustrial plant in which each production line enjoys its special location stocked with needed parts.

A STRANGE STORY

There is nothing simple about even the simplest eucaryotes, the single-celled creatures called protozoans. A paramecium, for instance, is covered all over its slipper-shaped body with fine, short hairs called cilia that move in waves like a millipede's legs to flow food into a groove at its rear end that acts as a mouth. The end of the groove's "throat" forms a temporary sort of bubble stomach that engulfs food. Following a particular path through the network inside the creature, the bubble moves forward toward the paramecium's front end. As it moves, it is joined by small packages of digestive enzymes supplied by another organelle. The bubble stomach distributes digested food as it goes. As the food is being distributed, the bubble loops back toward the paramecium's rear end, where it disgorges the leftover waste products through an anal pore, and disappears, to be replaced by new bubble stomachs that form as they are needed.

Protozoans are very active; they have had to be. With everybody eating whatever the water held, ready-made organic molecules, those that came together all on their own

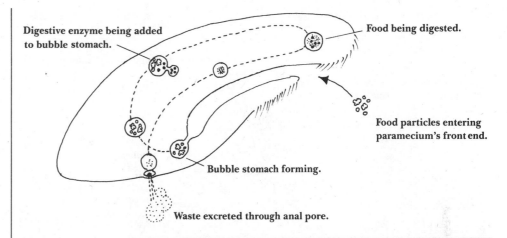

Digestive enzyme being added to bubble stomach.

Food being digested.

Food particles entering paramecium's front end.

Bubble stomach forming.

Waste excreted through anal pore.

rather than as part of an organism became scarce. Protozoans developed three ways to get around. Those with cilia (for example, parameciums) wave themselves through water. An ameba moves by partially liquifying a portion of its body so that it flows, then resolidifying it to pull the rest of the body along. Euglena and many others whip themselves forward with flagella, which are long hairs that wave like a rope.

But locomotion didn't solve the food shortage. There simply wasn't enough to go around. Eucaryotes began engulfing one another.

And so a strange thing happened. Perhaps a protozoan, perhaps its ancestor, swallowed a cyanobacterium and found it undigestible. The photosynthesizing cyanobacterium lived on, reproducing itself inside the host cell and

distributing copies of itself to its host's daughters, and evolving to the point where it no longer looked like a cyanobacteria. The descendants of these tiny invaders are called chloroplasts; it's their chlorophyll that colors plantlike protozoans and every green plant today.

Other large eucaryotes swallowed small bacteria that had another special talent. They made a "storage-battery" molecule that kept lots of energy on tap. They, too, proved indigestible; their descendants live on as the mitochondria that energize protozoans, plants, and animals today.

Chloroplasts and mitochondria have their own DNA, and it is looped like that of bacteria. The eucaryote cells they inhabit have very long unlooped strands of DNA. Mitochondria don't even speak exactly the same language as

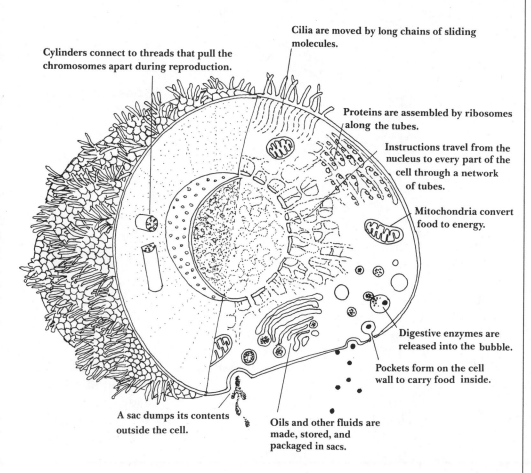

Cylinders connect to threads that pull the chromosomes apart during reproduction.

Cilia are moved by long chains of sliding molecules.

Proteins are assembled by ribosomes along the tubes.

Instructions travel from the nucleus to every part of the cell through a network of tubes.

Mitochondria convert food to energy.

Digestive enzymes are released into the bubble.

Pockets form on the cell wall to carry food inside.

A sac dumps its contents outside the cell.

Oils and other fluids are made, stored, and packaged in sacs.

Not all eucaryotic cells have all this equipment, but some have even more. Plant cells have, in addition to most of this machinery, chloroplasts that use the energy from light to manufacture food and rooms for storing starch granules and oil droplets.

their hosts. For example, a sentence in mitochondrial DNA may contain the same sequence of letters as a sentence in nuclear DNA but may spell the instructions for a different protein.

Some instructions that mitochondrial DNA carries have been duplicated unchanged for at least 1,500 million years and are being duplicated this very second in your own invaded body. So have bits of your nuclear DNA, such as bacterial instructions for glycolysis.

If every bit of DNA remained unchanged, however, the world would still be inhabited by nothing but bacteria—and every one alike. More likely, the experiment of life would have failed entirely.

SCRAMBLED MESSAGES

Luckily, DNA is not the strongest of molecules. It breaks when jarred by energy or disrupted by chemicals. Sometimes, bits change places, thereby changing the order of letters and the amino acid word those letters spell. Sometimes larger fragments exchange places when the chain has been broken, or a whole section comes loose and is lost altogether. An exchange of words or a loss of words changes the sentence and the protein that is assembled from it. Fragments can migrate from one place to another, and insert themselves in a new position,

CHROMOSOMES IN ACTION

3 *The supercoiled chromosome looks like a thick X or K.*

8 *The daughters divide. This time the doubled chromosomes come apart, so that each daughter gets a single chromosome.*

1

A single chromosome is a very long strand. This one is copying itself in preparation for reproduction. Its duplicate, not shown here, is copying itself at the same time. Both are doing so inside the nucleus of a cell.

4   **5**

The pair of chromosomes, each attached to its own copy, move next to one another inside the cell nucleus. Their "arms" cross.

The crossed portions trade places during a process called crossover. Now the original chromosome and copy are no longer identical to one another.

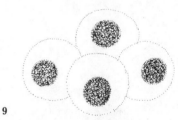

9

They are now sex cells. Their chromosomes relax. They look like grains within the nucleus.

6

The cell in which all this has been happening divides.

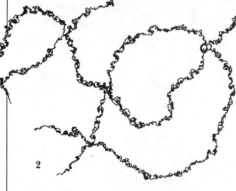

2

The chromosome is now doubled. The two identical copies remain attached to one another. The strands are coiling tighter now, and so appear thicker, shorter, and darker.

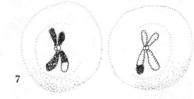

7

Each daughter gets one of the doubled chromosomes.

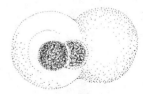

10

Two sex cells from different parents, each prepared the same way, come together. The new individual again has a pair of chromosomes, but it is different from the pair either parent had.

A LIFETIME'S KNOWLEDGE

Each girl is born already carrying the approximately 450 eggs that can become her children. Each boy will produce many billions of sperm during his adulthood. No two eggs and no two sperm are alike. No wonder everybody looks different!

The amount of information in a single human chromosome is equal to about 500 million words. That would fill 2 million pages, or about 4,000 volumes of 300 pages each. We have 46 chromosomes, or a library of 184,000 volumes. That's more books than are housed in most large libraries. Is that the amount of information necessary to specify how to make and run a human? It is much more than enough. Apparently a great deal of our DNA is repetitive, or is downright nonsense. Like a good scholar in a large library, enzymes discard useless stuff and copy into messenger RNA only the valuable information.

where their message interrupts another message and therefore is read differently.

Alien DNA can also sneak in, often carried by viruses. Viruses may have evolved from bacteria that had lost most of their innards; they are merely a package of genetic material (DNA or RNA) wrapped in a jacket. They "come to life" only by tricking the assembly lines inside living cells to produce viruses instead of their usual products. This they do by invading a cell, and shucking their jacket; the host then reads the bare genes' virus-making instructions and makes viruses. During the confusion that follows, viral genes may be left behind in the host cell, or the virus may pick up a fragment of its host's DNA, which is then spread to other cells in other bodies. You, for instance, make a mouse protein, the long ago gift of a virus.

Each of these changes to DNA changes the chemical assembly line—perhaps making too little difference to matter, perhaps preventing a necessary chemical from forming, perhaps creating a new and better one. When an organism reproduces by duplicating itself perfectly, these accidents, called mutations, are the only way it can change, even over a million generations. If the environment were always the same, a creature would be better off sticking to its own DNA and not gambling with whatever changes may have happened to another's DNA. But environments seldom stay the same. Sugar gets scarce, oxygen poisons the air, and those who lack the chemistry to deal with such crises become extinct. An organism that has changed in a way that allows it to cope with a crisis will be more likely to survive.

Even bacteria have to cope with changing environments. Usually they just split in two without benefit of a partner, and each daughter cell's chemical instructions are identical to those of the mother cell. But occasionally they exchange DNA with one another in a crude form of sex. Two bacteria that differ genetically form a bridge that connects them. One bacterium copies a small portion of its DNA, which travels through the bridge to the other. The receiver of this new DNA incorporates the fragment into its own loop and destroys the old section that has been replaced. The new section is rarely identical to the old one, so the receiver's instructions are changed, and the receiver becomes a somewhat different individual than it was before. When it splits, both daughter cells inherit the change.

Still, the rate of change among bacteria has been something less than impressive. Between 3,000 million years ago and the oxygen revolution 1,500 million years later, bacteria hardly changed. In fact, in the 1,500 million years that have passed since, they have remained the same old itty-bitty spheres, rods, and spirals. Meanwhile, eucaryotic cells have evolved into redwood trees and elephants. They have done this by allowing the complete invasion of one another's DNA. They invented sex.

THE SEXUAL REVOLUTION

Information exchange among the eucaryotes became generous to the point of selflessness. They have an enormous amount of information to offer one another. A bacterium has only a little loop of genetic material. But eucaryotic DNA is arranged in strands called chromosomes that are so long that even under the strongest microscope they appear to be a tangled mass of granules. What's more, a eucaryote's nucleus holds two copies of its library of information, and some copies may differ slightly in detail. Both libraries are used in everyday workings. Before exchanging information with another individual, a cell duplicates the two libraries, mixes them, and divvies up all the knowledge among four offspring. Each offspring has one complete library, but the information in it is unique to that individual.

Two such cells, prepared by different parents, then unite into one, pooling their information completely. With this combination and recombination system called sex, no two individuals carry identical instructions. Evolutionary change can't happen unless individuals are different from one another. Sex makes the difference. With it, every individual is a brand new experiment in life.

During the time of the first sexual experiments, North America was still the size of its original craton, lacking what are now our Western, Southwestern, Southern, Atlantic, and New England states. One mountain range after another had been scoured down by wind and rain and stood shoulder deep in their own rubble. Sand that had brushed off the continent rimmed the shore and spread for miles out to sea. Strolling along the beach, you would have sunk in thick brown mats of one-celled life and slipped in slimes of microorganisms. You would have recognized an old nuisance, the green fuzz that clouds fish tanks and makes the insides of flower vases slippery: the first green algae.

You may not think much of a simple strand of alga even if you examine it closely under a hand lens. Each filament is just cells strung end to end; there are no body parts. The whole plant is only one cell thick. Yet algae may have been among the first organisms to have invented the way to ensure that DNA keeps pace with changing times.

The repercussion of this sexual revolution was an information explosion that within another 500 million years had left the sea awash with weeds, afloat with jellyfish, and squirming with worms.

1000 MILLION YEARS AGO

Sexual Seaweeds · Jelly Animals · An Explosion of Shells

By 1,000 million years ago, even the most recent of the six great mountain ranges that had risen in North America as life was getting established were eroding away. Volcanoes were subsiding. Valleys were filling with sediment. The whole continent was becoming smooth and flat. Oceans washed inland over this low land, forming shallow seas. Beaches, coves, spits, and islands glistened white in the sun. The continent, its bare rock groomed by wind and rain, was much cleaner than the land today.

Cells had moved into bulky communities. They had weight; they had shape. In a way, communities of cells were nothing new. Back then, as now, bacteria tended to congregate with their own kind, if only because what suited one suited the others. Some bacteria strung along together like strands of beads; some algae assembled together in round mats.

What was new was the degree of organization. In a simple strand of alga, every cell can photosynthesize and reproduce. In simple algae that still have the protozoan's flagella, every cell has its own to wave. If the plant is disassembled, each cell can survive on its own.

Somewhere around 1,000 million years ago, communal cells began to differ from one another. Some

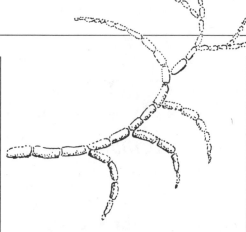

In a simple strand of alga, every cell is like every other cell, and what one can do, all can do.

could move; others couldn't. Some could digest or photosynthesize; some relied on others to do that work for them. Only certain cells were capable of the preparations necessary for sexual reproduction. Those that could do one thing lived here in the community, others lived elsewhere. Things began to take shape.

The simplest shapes were disks, spheres, and leaf shapes. More complicated shapes evolved from the simple ones. Take a hollow sphere, punch it in like you would a rubber ball, and it becomes the shape of a jellyfish. Turn the jellyfish shape so that its opening is at the top, squeeze it into a vase, and it is the shape of a primitive sponge. Or roll the basic jellyfish shape into a French pancake and you have the tube shape of a worm.

These new shapes allowed more cells to live together and benefit from one another's abilities, and also to move in new ways, and to explore new places to live. Multicellular life escaped from the shallows and moved sedately away from the shore.

BOYS AND GIRLS COME OUT TO PLAY

As complicated as the larger algae look, waving feathery fronds as the tide rocks them, strewn in tangles along the beach, or washed in as great rubbery strips many yards long, they have no roots, no stems, no leaves. Most of the hairy looking seaweeds are branching filaments of cells laid end to end, one cell thick. Sea lettuce, a brilliant green, leaflike alga that looks good enough to eat, is only two cells thick. Almost all the cells of an alga are identical, even though they can arrange themselves to form a thickened midrib, a flattened frond, or a branching filament. What each cell does depends on where it finds itself.

On many kinds of seaweed, only the cells that hold the fronds fast to a surface are specialized for their job. Other than the cells of these holdfasts, any cell can do any other job, including reproducing new plants. Even with so simple a plan, however, the kelps, those rubbery brown algae with the snaky midrib and holdfasts that grip like claws, may grow to a hundred feet and live a dozen years.

A favorite alga is rockweed, the branching stuff that has air bladders just made for popping (the alga uses them as floats to keep its fronds upright and spread out in the water). Often you'll come upon a rockweed that seems to hold out more promise than the others, for the tips of its fronds are swollen into super-big bumpy bladders that should, when squeezed, give a super pop. But squeeze away; they will deflate with only a faint hiss of air. They are sex organs, not air bladders, and the bumps are pores that lead to batches of male or female reproductive cells.

Back when algae had just begun to try out new shapes, sex didn't require the sexes. Any two cells could unite and pool their information, and each did it exactly the same way as the other. Protozoans still have sex without sexes. The real difference between a male reproductive cell and a female reproductive cell is size. The eggs are large enough to hold enough food to feed daughter cells until they can feed themselves. The sperm are specialized for movement; their work is to get to the egg, which is too big to do anything but stay put and wait.

This specialization isn't practical when a single cell is also the whole organism, for the organism must swim to eat and eat to swim, and it had best do both equally well. Only as cells came to live in groups in which each member could depend on others to do some of the work was there the luxury to be something special.

COME TO THE BALL

Various green algae, ranging from just a few cells to very many cells, show step by step how eggs, sperm, and multicellular life all evolved together. The most primitive in the group *Gonium* is a shallow saucer of four to 32 cells that communicate with one another well enough to beat their flagella in unison, which keeps the whole crew moving in the same direction. Each of the cells can live alone, any of the cells can reproduce, and all of them are alike.

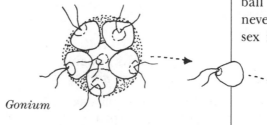

Gonium

A slightly more advanced relative, *Pandorina*, has about the same number of cells, but they form a sphere. One end of the sphere is its front, the other its rear, and the community swims with its front end forward. Remove a cell from the group and it will die. This alga always produces two kinds of cells that unite sexually, larger ones and smaller ones. Both still have flagella, and both swim away from the colony to meet one another.

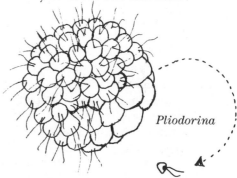

Pliodorina

In *Pliodorina,* an alga with up to 128 cells, the large reproductive cells remain embedded in the colony, where they are easier for small swimmers to find. *Volvox* (see page 51), with at least 500 cells, is a real ball of a colony. Cells to the front never do any of the reproducing; sex is left to the cells in the rear.

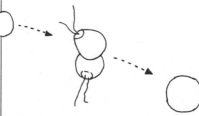

The big cells—they can be called eggs now—have lost their flagella entirely. The most advanced *Volvox*

SEAVEGETABLES

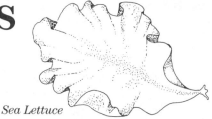

Sea Lettuce

W hat are sea*weeds* to us are sea*vegetables* in other parts of the world. Seavegetables are about as nutritious in protein and carbohydrate as oats are. Some have more vitamin C than lemons, more vitamin A than eggs, as much iron as whole-wheat bread, and as many B vitamins as many fruits and vegetables. These are a few beginner's recipes made from very common and easy-to-recognize marine algae that you can gather fresh from the sea. There are two cautions: Don't gather in polluted areas, such as where the shore has been closed to swimmers or clammers, and if you are an inexperienced cook, ask for help with the recipe for kelp chips, as the frying fat tends to spatter.

Most seaweeds are dried before they are cooked. Rinse them well under running water, chop or cut them up, and spread the pieces on a terry cloth towel in the hot sun for a day to dry them crisp.

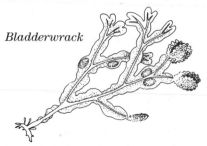

Bladderwrack

Bladderwrack Tea
(*Fucus vesiculosis*,
also called rockweed)

Use the tender, young tips of branches only. Rinse, chop fine, and sun dry. For each cup of tea, put 1 teaspoon of dried bladderwrack and 1 cup of boiling water into a teapot and let it stand for a few minutes. Strain through a tea strainer. The tea leaves a sweet flavor in the mouth.

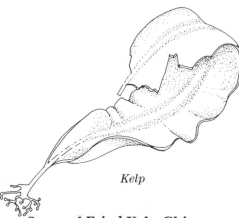

Kelp

Sugared Fried Kelp Chips
(various species of
Laminaria)

Rinse, cut in small squares, and sun dry. In a frying pan, heat ¼ inch of vegetable oil over medium heat until a haze begins to form. Fry the kelp chips a few at a time until crisp. Drain on paper towels. Eat sprinkled with sugar.

Steamed Sea Lettuce
(various species of *Ulva*)

Sea lettuce is eaten fresh, not dried. Rinse young fronds in cold water. Melt a pat of butter in a frying pan over a very low flame. Add a handful of sea lettuce, cover the pan, and cook for about 10 minutes, or until tender. Sea lettuce is good sprinkled with lemon juice.

Irish Moss Pudding
(*Chondrus crispa*)

Irish moss is the "carageenan" that is used to thicken packaged pudding and ice cream.

Rinse and sun dry the seaweed, then crumble it. Soak ¾ cup dried, crumbled Irish moss in tap water for 30 minutes. Put the soaked moss in a square of cheese-cloth and tie the corners together with a piece of string. Put the bag in a deep saucepan with 1 quart of milk. Simmer it over low heat for ½ hour, stirring frequently and pressing the bag with a spoon to extract all the thickening in the algae. Throw away the bag and algae. Sweeten the thickened milk to taste with sugar or honey. Pour into custard

cups and chill for several hours until it is like pudding.

Eat Irish moss pudding plain or with crushed fruit. You can also make fruit puddings by adding 2 cups of thawed frozen peach chunks or strawberry pieces to the thickened milk and blending in a blender before chilling.

Irish Moss

may contain up to 50,000 cells, but only a few of those are egg cells. Each egg cell is so large and has stored so much food that, once fertilized by a swimming sperm cell, it can produce an entire new colony.

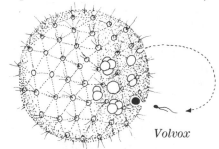

Volvox

Large seaweeds—yellow, brown, purple, red, and green—make both eggs and sperm. But these thick, branched, and leafy forms of algae took some hundreds of millions of years to evolve. The algae of 1,000 million years ago were mostly very small.

THANK THE PLANKTON

The smallest algae are the most important form of life there has ever been, then or now, for they are the basic food on which all marine life depends. Altogether, one-celled algae make up most of the floating life called plankton. Plankton is the pasture grazed by animals from the tiniest shrimp to the largest animal in the world, the 160,000 kg (176 ton) blue whale. If you doubt the ability of an organism as small as those that form plankton to nour-

ish a creature as large as a whale, consider this: The total bulk of all free-floating microscopic algae is 95 percent of all the plant life in the sea.

Plankton is at the very bottom of the food chain. A food chain is like a list of who eats what (or whom). Small floaters such as infant shrimp eat algal plankton; shrimp in turn are eaten by others who in turn are eaten, all the way up to the top of the food chain—tuna fish or us. The dead debris from algal plankton drifts to the sea bottom and is eaten by marine worms and mollusks. Leftovers go to bacteria that, digest and recycle their substance into the water. In one way or another, plankton feeds every animal in the sea and many on land. Plankton also releases oxygen as an end product of photosynthesis. Without plankton, life would suffocate.

THE SMALLEST SKELETONS

Some tiny algae swim like sperm, waving their flagella behind them. You would have to use a microscope to see one, and it wouldn't be impressive. But other one-celled algae called diatoms encase themselves in skeletons. They are simply gorgeous.

Diatoms take up the glassy mineral silica from seawater to build their microscopic bodies into prisms, boxes, disks, and stars more

HOW TO MAKE A PLANKTON NET

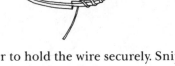

The teeming life of plankton pastures can be gathered in a net and examined under a school microscope. The net, attached to a pole, is dragged along the surface of the water from the back of a boat. The plankton accumulate in a jar tied to the open bottom of a net so fine that it can strain out blood cells. You may need help in drilling the hole in the pole, and with sewing the net.

You need:
Roll of 12-gauge galvanized wire
Grease pencil
Hacksaw
Tape measure
Roll of 20-gauge galvanized wire
Masking tape
Wire snips
Scissors
1 yard 200-mesh silk-screen cloth
  (available at art stores)
Sewing machine or no. 8 needle and
  sewing thread
Strip of muslin or other strong
  cloth, 6 inches wide by 30 inches
  long
Pencil
Iron
Straight pins
Eyelet kit (available in sewing stores
  or departments)
Nylon mason's line
Drill and $3/32$-inch bit

Wood dahlia pole, 5 feet long
  (available at garden stores)
1⅝-inch large-eye eyehook
Small glass jar with lid

1. Make a double loop of 12-gauge wire that is 27 inches in circumference. To do this, pick up two loops of the wire from the roll. Mark the second loop with the grease pencil where it meets the free end of the wire. Cut the wire halfway through at that point with the hacksaw. Then bend it to break off the double loop from the roll. The two ends of the double loop should meet exactly, and the circle they form should measure 27 inches in circumference. You can check this measurement with a tape measure. This will be your net's rim.

2. Strengthen the rim by wrapping it with the thin wire. To hold the loops together as you wind, wrap them first with a few strips of masking tape. Remove each piece of tape as you get to it. The thin wire winds should be about ¼ to ½ inch apart, except at the beginning and end where you can do a few winds very close to-

gether to hold the wire securely. Snip off the end of the wire with the wire snips.

3. Measure, mark, and cut out two pieces of silk-screen cloth according to the pattern. Sew them together along the sides ½ inch in from the edge. Use a sewing machine if possible, silk-screen cloth is hard to stitch through by hand. If a sewing machine isn't available, use a needle and thread and a running stitch.

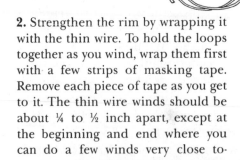

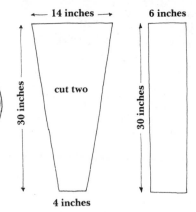

4. Turn the long edges of the muslin strip in ½ inch and use the iron to press the folds down. Pin one edge of the muslin strip to the wrong side of the net and about ½ inch down from

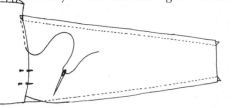

the top. Sew the strip to the net. The strip will be too long. Don't trim the excess yet. Turn the net right side out.

5. Slide the wire rim over the muslin strip to about 1-inch up from where the muslin meets the net. Fold the muslin strip over the wire rim, and pin it in place. Now you will be able to tell how much excess length to trim off. Trim to ½ inch longer than where the muslin is attached to the silk-screen cloth. Turn under the extra ½ inch. Now stitch the muslin strip in place by hand.

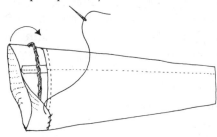

6. With a pencil, mark the muslin where the three eyelets will go. They should be about 9 inches apart. Fol-

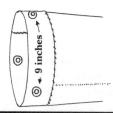

low the instructions that come with the eyelet kit to attach them in the muslin just below the rim.

7. Measure, cut, and tie a 2-foot piece of nylon mason's line through each eyelet.

TIE THE NET TO THE POLE:

8. Drill a short hole down the center of one end of the wooden pole, and screw the eyehook into it. Pull all three net strings through the eyehook. Holding onto the strings, let the net hang below the pole and fiddle with the ends of the string

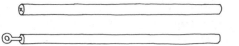

until the net hangs straight. Tie the three strings around the eye hook as shown.

9. When you're ready to use the plankton net, pull the open bottom of the net part way over the glass jar and tie it in place with nylon mason's line. Keep the lid so that when you have dragged the net for a while, you can carry the plankton-rich water home without spilling it.

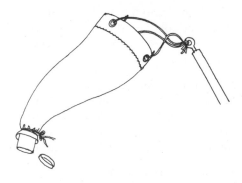

Note: If 200-mesh silk-screen cloth isn't available locally it can be mail-ordered from Arthur Brown & Bros. Inc., 2 West 46th Street, New York, NY 10036. Write first to ask the price.

ALGAE COLLECTION

This is a way to dry and mount seaweed in its natural, spread-out shape.

You need:
Freshly collected seaweeds
Pocket knife
Bucket
Bathtub
Several sheets of watercolor paper, large enough to fit the algae you want to mount
Waxed paper
Newspaper
Plant press (page 197) or several heavy books

1. Collect young, undamaged plants. Use a pocket knife to scrape hold-fasts free from the rocks or shells they cling to. Keep the seaweeds in a bucket of seawater until you're ready to mount them.

2. Float the plants you've collected one at a time in several inches of water in the bathtub. Use your fingers or anything pointed to tease fronds apart until they look natural.

3. Under the alga slip a piece of watercolor paper large enough to hold it. Gently lift the paper, with the alga on it, from the bath. Put that sheet aside. Use separate sheets of watercolor paper to remove each remaining specimen from the tub.

4. Place a piece of waxed paper over each specimen. Dry the sheets stacked between thick layers of newspaper in a plant press or under heavy books.

5. Change the newspapers every few days and continue to press the seaweeds until they are dry. Peel off the waxed paper. No other mounting is needed for your seaweed collection. A dried algae will stay stuck to the watercolor paper without glue or tape.

intricate than jewels. There are more diatoms in both fresh water and salt water than any other kind of plankton. A gallon of seawater may contain two million of their glittery bodies. When diatoms die, they sink to the bottom and form deep layers of fine abrasive mud that has been used in polishes, detergents, and toothpaste.

Some algae that use calcium live on shallow ocean bottoms and look very much like corals (real corals are animals, not plants). These coralline algae are seen as flat pink patches that spread over the surfaces of rocks and living shells. Older colonies form layer upon layer and become bumpy and stony to the touch. Other coralline algae sprout short, stiff branches, that are pink and white. Both the flat and the branched kinds are common in northern waters and are easy to spot as you poke around rocky tidal pools at low tide. In warm waters they grow so well that they help to build reefs high enough to become land. They helped to build Florida, which you wouldn't have found 1,000 million years ago, because it hadn't yet been built.

The spread of algae of all sizes created a new world to live in, but one that by our terrestrial standards was topsy-turvy. Pastures of green plankton floated high above forests of large seaweeds anchored to the bottom. Between pasture and forest fell a continual rain of edible debris. Into this new world came the first multicellular animals.

SPONGING

Judging by their simplicity, sponges might have been the very first animal visible to the naked eye. Pick up a sponge corpse and you'll notice that some holes are small, others are large. The small holes are canals through which water flows inward in the live animal. The big holes are sluices through which water flows outward. The sponge used as a bath sponge is a more complicated version of the simpler body plan many sponges enjoy, in which all the small canals lead into a central cavity, and the only large hole is at the top.

You can cut a live sponge into as many pieces as you like without finding out any more than this about its insides. That's because it doesn't have insides. There are no organs at all: no heart, no blood vessels, no stomach, no intestine, and not a single nerve.

A sponge gets along quite well with only four kinds of cells. Along its exterior is a single layer of "skin" cells that feel rather like the outside of raw beef liver. A second kind of cell is shaped like a tube; it lets water into the animal. A third kind of cell is equipped with fla-

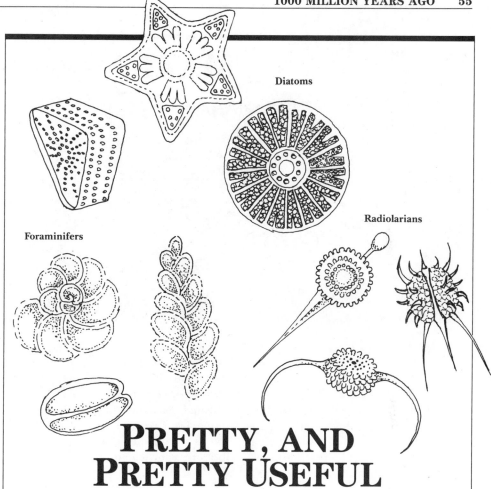

Diatoms

Radiolarians

Foraminifers

PRETTY, AND PRETTY USEFUL

Size does not limit how beautiful a life form is, or how useful. These beauties are all just one cell big. The shell- and leaf-shaped foraminifers build their shells of calcium. Most chalk is made of their remains. Glassy radiolarians, whose spiky shells are made of silica, live in deeper water. Accumulations of their corpses become the ocean-born rock called chert. Flint, from which early man made his best blades and struck his first sparks, is a form of chert. Diatoms are so numerous that they build layers of an abrasive substance called diatomaceous earth as their corpses accumulate. Diatomaceous earth is used in many kinds of polishes, including toothpaste.

SMALL WORLDS

The strip of land between high tide and low tide is called the littoral. It is home to many creatures that can live neither deeper in the sea nor higher on land; they spend their whole lives in the small world where tides ebb and flow. Some of the creatures run their lives by the tides. Bar-nacles may seem dead to the world when the tide is lowest, but as the sea rises again into the pools they inhabit, they open up and move the rich water through their bodies with feathery tentacles. Creatures that live in tidal pools would die quickly in a bucket because they would suffocate for lack of the twice-daily dose of oxygen the whirling, rushing, splashing, tide brings to them.

Other animals can live only in what is called the continental shelf, on or under the ground that stretches be-neath the sea from the low-tide line to the true edge of the continent, where the land plunges to the bottom of the sea.

Even the water is divided into zones. Most ocean life inhabits the photic zone, where sunlight pene-trates enough for photosynthesis. Fish may swim below the photic zone but the deeper you go, the darker it becomes, and the scarcer the rain of nourishing corpses, and the greater the pressure of the water above on the body. Only very specialized creatures can live in the crushing pressure and permanent night of the deep ocean zone known as the abyss.

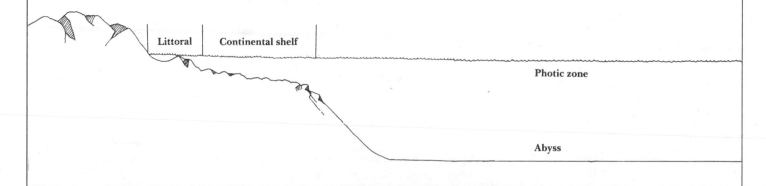

Littoral   Continental shelf

Photic zone

Abyss

gella that whip water along toward the exit hole. The fourth kind acts like an ameba and wanders among the others, engulfing and digesting particles of food for them that float its way. Sometimes the flagellated cells capture food and pass it to their neighbors for digestion.

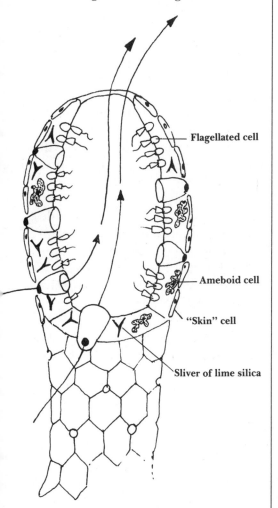

Flagellated cell

Ameboid cell

"Skin" cell

Sliver of lime silica

SPONGING

A live sponge won't hurt you, nor can you hurt it. Even if you use a pocket knife and slice a sponge off the surface that it clings to, it feels no pain, for it has no nerves.

Live sponges don't look like those you see in the bathroom. The natural bathroom sponge is the dried skeleton of a sponge, not its juicy flesh. The type of sponge we use in the bathroom lives deep in warm water like that in the Gulf of Mexico. It is a fleshy blob laced together with an elastic stuff that stays squeezably soft after drying. But most sponge skeletons are stiff, not spongy. They are usually a network of either sticks of crumbly lime or slivers of glassy silica. If you dry such sponges, they are likely to cut your skin or fall to bits when you squeeze them.

Many sponges come in flower colors of rose, marigold, or violet. Avoid any green sponge you might find. It may be the crumb-of-bread sponge that has a terribly bad smell.

All of these cells can move on their own. Disassemble a sponge entirely by squeezing it through fine silk, and its individual cells move into a clump, putter about for a bit, and before long rearrange themselves into a sponge.

RIGHT-SIDE-UPS AND UPSIDE-DOWNS

Early animals specialized in digestion. A sponge is a digestive skin; a jellyfish is a stomach with the weird ability to turn inside out. A sea

MOON BABIES

The moon jellyfish is common all along the American coast from New England to Florida, around to Mexico, and up again along the western edge of the continent. You can recognize it by the outline of a clover on its upper surface. The pretty pattern is sex cells. Some jellyfish specialize in making sperm and are therefore male; others make eggs, and are female. The clover pattern of sex cells is milky white when the animal is young, pinkish in an older female, and more yellow in an older male. Moon jellyfish won't do anything horrible to you, but

some people get an itchy rash from touching the tentacles that hang down from the central stomach.

Moon jellyfish spend their earliest months like anemones—inside out and attached. Wade out to search for them at the end of a pier at low tide toward the end of summer. Look into the water along the wood pilings for slender, clinging, anemone-shaped creatures no more than a quarter of an inch long. These are the polyps— the sexually reproduced babies—of moon jellyfish. The polyps will cling to the piles all winter, through cold and storm. In early spring, their long bodies will begin to constrict in places. They are budding, nonsexually, into a generation of offspring. Each constriction will pinch off a bit of the polyp from the top down, and each pinched-off bud will swim away as a tiny jellyfish.

anemone is a right-side-up jellyfish, and a jellyfish is an upside-down sea anemone, unless it's the other way around. There's no way to be sure, because so many of the coelenterates (the name means "intestine") spend part of their life tentacles-up like a sea anemone, and part of their life tentacles-down like a jellyfish. In either position, these creatures shoot tiny poison darts from their tentacles to paralyze prey. Sea anemone poisons are not strong enough to hurt you, but the sting of a jellyfish can be painful and even dangerous.

Sometimes a strong wind will wash moon jellyfish close to shore, and sometimes the surf will strew them helplessly across the beach by the thousands. Before the next tide can carry them away, they have evaporated, leaving only round stains behind them. There isn't much to jellyfish. The top of their umbrella shape is a thin, transparent layer. The bottom of their umbrella shape is a thin transparent layer. In between they are stuffed with trans-

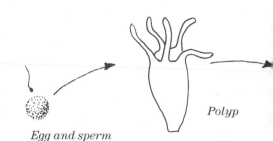

Egg and sperm   *Polyp*

parent jelly. You can see right through a jellyfish, and you are looking mostly through water.

Still, a jellyfish is a more complicated animal than a sponge. Embedded in its surface are cells that work together to contract and relax. These cells were the first muscles. The signal to contract is spread by a net of electrical and chemical transmitter cells. These were the first nerves. In the old style of moving, in which a cell communicated chemically with only its immediate neighbors, and in which only cilia or flagella were used, a creature as large as a jellyfish wouldn't have gotten far. Ever since the jellyfish evolved a way to coordinate muscular movement over a large area, animals have really gone places.

A FLABBY ELEVATOR

Slip a live jellyfish from the surface of the sea into a jar of seawater. The jellyfish contracts its umbrella, forcing water from beneath it, and rockets toward the surface. When the jellyfish relaxes, the springy jelly inside restores it to its open shape and it slowly sinks.

This is the only movement a jellyfish can make, up and down like a flabby elevator. Invisible to us, however, is the awful drama that takes place as the jellyfish sinks. As the umbrella descends through plankton, it entangles a multitude of microscopic browsing animals among its long, central tentacles, shoots deadly darts into their bodies, envelops them in its overhanging stomach, and digests them. The larger jellyfish can paralyze whole fish trapped in their tentacles. Some jellyfish grow to over seven feet across and have drifting tentacles 120 feet long. They can kill humans.

Jellyfish in the ancient seas left

about as good an imprint of themselves as they do today—almost none. The piddling puddles of stranded jellyfish are barely recorded in the rock of ages, although jellyfish were certainly there.

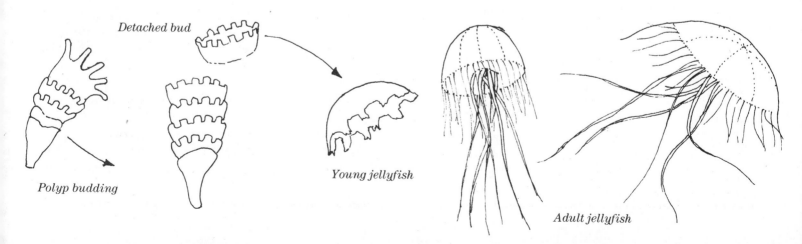

Detached bud

Polyp budding

Young jellyfish

Adult jellyfish

BIG-TIME BUILDERS

Corals are upside-down jellyfish: Their fringe of tentacles wave upward. These flipped creatures live in large communities and take calcium from the water, building from it crusty tubes to live in. From hundreds of thousands of stony rooms, coral animals wave their tiny tentacles, armed with poisoned barbs, toward whatever dinner floats their way.

Corals are fussy about where they live. Apparently the ancient seas were just right: clean, bright, and about the temperature of a plastic kiddy pool on a summer day. Clear across North America, they built coral reefs that eventually became limestone. Corals are just as fussy nowadays, but our harsher world offers them less choice of where to live. You can observe coral communities only off the coast of Florida and the Gulf Coast, where their standards of cleanliness, light, and warmth are met.

Each coral animal waving its arms above its home looks like an individual, but the polyps, as the individuals are called, are connected by tubes to the stomach cavities of all the other polyps, so although each may capture food on its own, digestion is a community affair. The top layer of the communal animal ages and is eventually overgrown and killed by new polyps. Coral reefs therefore build upon themselves inch by inch, foot by foot, to depths of more than a thousand feet. The sub-basement of Chicago is a vast coral reef. So, though the jellyfish didn't leave much of an imprint, its relative, the coral, did.

The thickness of these reefs is

THE ALIENS

The very earliest well-preserved fossils of whole animals are a group of large, handsome critters called the Ediacaran fauna that lived about 700 million years ago. Some were shaped like plumes, with a stalk for attachment to the sea bottom, and seemed to be the ancestors of corals. Others were more like jellyfish, and some, a full meter (3.3 feet) long, were considered early worms. Scientists hoped to find in these Ediacaran ancestors the story of how hollowness evolved. The only trouble was, the "worms" had no mouth. None of the others did either, and every type was just as flat as could be.

It is possible that they were related to nothing on this Earth now: They were not hollow. In fact, their body plan was alien to every life form we know. The Ediacarans apparently conducted all their multicellular business at their outside surface, which was plumed or deeply quilted like an air cushion to increase its area.

It isn't even certain that they were multicellular. Unlike their contemporaries, who left such disappointing fossil traces of their soft bodies, the Ediacaran fossils are precisely sculptured. They must have been covered with a cuticle. Given a large surface area, little thickness, and a tough coating, there is no reason why a single-celled animal can't be, like a single nerve cell in an elephant's leg, about 6 meters (20 feet) long.

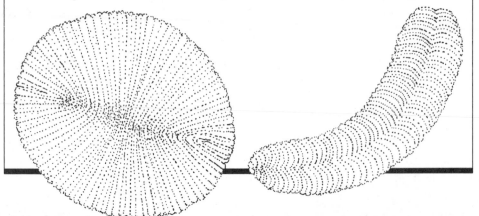

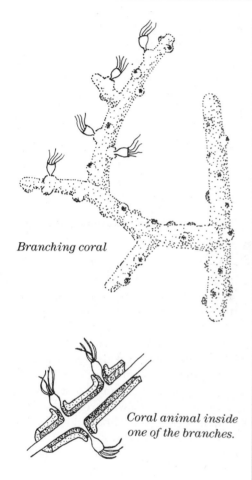

Branching coral

Coral animal inside one of the branches.

hard to understand, because corals won't grow more than 45 meters (150 feet) below the surface of the sea, and they can't have risen into the dry air above the surface. The explanation seems to be that thick reefs like the one that underlies Chicago weight the crust, sinking it down into Earth's plastic mantle as they grow upward. The whole mass sinks about as quickly as its new layers rise—over millions of years, of course.

If you can't get to coral-growing waters, you might instead get to see a close relative of coral, the equally upside-down (or right-side-up) sea anemone. A sea anemone is much larger than a coral polyp—maybe an inch or more across—and it lives in cold water as well as warm water. You will find sea anemones on both coasts in the lowest tidal pools and in deeper water, waving one or several rows of chubby pink, red, or yellow tentacles.

Unlike the moon jellyfish, which can multiply in the polyp stage by budding off medusas and multiply in the medusa stage by sexually producing polyps, corals and sea anemones never produce a jellyfish stage, and many jellyfish never produce a polyp stage. But the fact that some jellyfish are found in both the right-side-in and inside-out polyp and medusa stages reveals that creatures as unlike one another as hard coral and squishy jellyfish are true cousins.

THE IMPORTANCE OF BEING HOLLOW

No matter how large an organism becomes, each of its cells must be surrounded by a sea. Life's chemicals are more concentrated inside a cell's jacket—the cell membrane—than outside it, yet outside the cell membrane are the raw materials of life that the cell needs to replace and repair itself. All of these raw materials are either dissolved in water or transported by flowing water. They can't get into the cell without it. Without water, waste products can't be gotten rid of either. Even in a terrestrial animal like you, the lymph fluid that bathes your cells (and fills a blister) is very like seawater, and so is plasma, the liquid that remains when solids are removed from blood. Both taste as salty as the sea.

Looking at the spectacular shapes of marine organisms, one would think these life forms were free to be wildly inventive, but their basic shapes are really very limited by the need to keep the sea handy. Algae remain thin; they are nothing but surface, with no inside at all. Sponges and jellyfish are surfaces folded into shapes that allow water to be waved through their interior. The larger an organism becomes, the more surface it must have, lest cells lost in its depths starve or suffocate for want of food and oxygen. Even a marine worm has only rolled its surface into a tube through which the sea flows. No multicellular life forms are solid. They all have hollow places through which water flows.

Some marine worms are as long

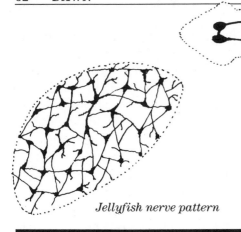

Flatworm nerve pattern

Jellyfish nerve pattern

A jellyfish's nerve cells connect with one another like the strands of a net. A worm's nerve cells connect with one another like avenues with streets in between. One advantage for worms is obvious: A message traveling from here to there in a jellyfish wanders all over the place. A message traveling through a worm goes straight from head to tail.

as your arm and as thick as your wrist. They could grow so big because hollowness can be shaped as easily as the container around it. A tube can branch and pouch to extend the hollow out through thicknesses of cells. These branches and pouches evolved into the interior spaces of lungs, guts, kidneys, blood vessels that all increase the surfaces at which cells conduct their ex-

A TASTE OF WORMS

Worms are a confusing lot: There are segmented worms (many marine worms as well as their terrestrial counterparts, the earthworms) and roundworms, flatworms, tapeworms, and several others. That's not to mention the "worms" called maggots and caterpillars, which are not worms at all, but the larvae of insects.

Roundworms, also called nematodes, have no segments; they are smooth from end to end. Most are so small that they aren't visible to the naked eye, yet nematodes live everywhere in such numbers that if all the other substances of the earth were to evaporate, the whole shape of our planet would still be outlined in a haze of worms. Some larger ones are parasites that inhabit puppies and other animals.

Tapeworms are all parasites. Their "host" does all their digestive work for them; a tapeworm's body is mostly reproductive equipment. What appears to be segments is really an egg production line. The rear compartments are completed egg cases.

Many flatworms are parasites, too, but an appealing quarter-incher called a planarian makes an amusing small pet. Planarians live on the undersides of rocks and debris in fast-flowing streams, where they can easily be collected. Keep them in a shallow glass dish in their own stream water, frequently changed. They will eat bits of raw meat, though not at the head end where you see two eye spots. The mouth is smack in the middle of the belly.

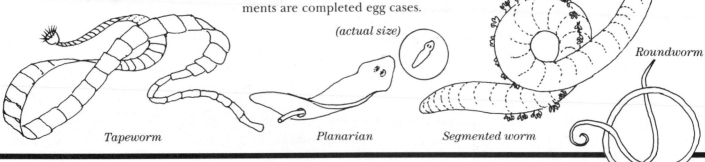

Tapeworm

(actual size)

Planarian

Segmented worm

Roundworm

changes with the outside world and with one another. These surfaces bared to an inside sea can be increased again with more folds, loops, and crinkles, while the outside can stay smooth.

HIGH-CLASS WORMS

The "lowly worm" certainly hasn't been given the credit it deserves. Compared with a sponge, which is no more than a perforated skin, or with a jellyfish, which might be called a floating stomach, a worm is definitely high-class. First, it has a head. A head is an amazing invention. Marine worms have eyes on their heads, antennae, and little biting jaws so tough that they survived as the first worm fossils, to be followed about 600 million years ago by whole fossilized worm bodies. Inside a worm's head is a genuine brain.

Having a head with sense organs and a brain gives an animal a firm sense of where it is going. A sponge has no front or back, top or bottom. It is wise to stay put. A jellyfish has a top and bottom, and knows how to rise up and fall down. But a worm, with back up, belly down, tail to the rear, and head to the front, knows where it is going.

A worm's body is modular, like a building of identical stacked units. Each unit is a segment of its body, flapped or bristled outside with a

WORM HUNT

Nightcrawlers used for fishbait are earthworms. They are captured at night by flashlight when they come out of the ground. You can catch marine worms in the daytime. Hunt marine worms that burrow in sand with a shovel, bucket, and large, coarse sieve. Quickly dig a deep shovelful of sand from where you see signs of a burrow. Dump the sand into the sieve. Then pour buckets of water through the sieve to wash the sand away through the holes. If you have dug fast and deep enough, you should have your worm.

pair of appendages, powered by a middle layer of muscle, and equipped inside with its own portion of central tubing: gut, vein, and artery.

Such a body plan helps a worm get organized—literally, it has organs. Unlike sponges and jellyfish, who defy dissection, since one part is just like any other, the tube systems of worms are things that you can easily see. You can open a marine worm (or an earthworm) and see a genuine intestine. For the first time in the animal world, in these early worms and their relatives, food went in one end and out the other.

No animal has ever improved upon the worm's basic plan. The tube body is the basis for the spatial system by which advanced animals organize themselves into vast communities of cells. From our hollow gut to our segmented backbone and our paired arms and legs, we are organized like a fancy worm.

AS PRETTY AS A WORM

Marine worms are much fancier than their earthworm relatives. There are green ones, iridescent ones, ones with flame red bristles and plumes of sunny yellow. And big worms. The leafy paddle worm, common along both coasts, is lined with pale jade or olive paddles and grows to 46 cm (1½ feet) long. It hides among stones and algal holdfasts below the low tide line and hunts freely in the water for smaller animals that it bites and chews and swallows.

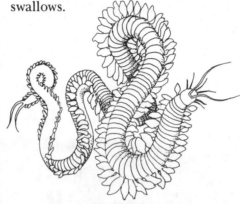
Leafy paddle worm

Other worms stay put in burrows and feed on whatever sinks to their level. A coiled pile of fine sand on a tidal flat marks one end of a U-shaped burrow built by a lugworm. The other end is a shallow dimple in the sand a few inches away. The lugworm lives in the bottom of the U, moving forward up one arm of the tube to wave a feathery plume in search of food, and backing up the other arm of the tube to cast away coils of undigested debris.

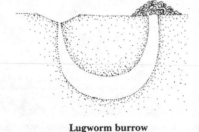
Lugworm burrow

The parchment worm, a pale, many-paddled creature 25 cm (10 inches) long and 2½ cm (1 inch) thick, builds a stout-walled burrow that rises above the sand in two chimneys. The walls are made of a parchmentlike material for which the worm is named. You can see these chimneys sticking up above the tidal flats along the Atlantic and Pacific coasts, except along northern shores. The chimneys are very narrow, and you won't notice any worm. It never leaves its burrow, because it can't; the chimneys are too small. So the worm paddles a steady stream of water through its burrow, bringing its dinner along in the flow. Besides supplying itself with sturdy walls and running water, the parchment worm can brighten its home by lighting up like a firefly. The light is so strong that it shines out the chimney tops at night.

Tube worms, like corals and algae, use calcium to build their homes. Each tube is as sinuous as a worm, and often they are heaped upon one another in a twisted tangle. Beachcombers find lumps of these tangles on rocks and shells that wash ashore, or on hard surfaces—including boat bottoms—below the low tide mark.

The ability to accumulate calcium from seawater and secrete it into protective or supportive struc-

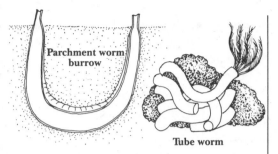

Parchment worm burrow

Tube worm

tures was invented by algae and again and again by animals unrelated to one another. By 600 million years ago, the talent had become quite advanced. Mollusks had evolved, and they were making the first seashells.

A VERY OLD FEAST

Some hundreds of millions of years after the first worm made its burrow, mollusks began to strew their shells all over the place, from the sea floor that is now the 8,848-meter (about 28,300 foot) summit of Mt. Everest to sediments now buried deep beneath the corn fields of Iowa. The sea over the craton would have been a shell collector's paradise. There were long spiralled snail shells, and round plump ones. There were bivalves you might have mistaken for clams and oysters; perhaps you could have eaten them. There were chitons and limpets on the rocks, among the algae, just as there are today in tidal pools all over the world. Some have hardly changed.

THE OLDEST SEA MONSTER

An ancient relative of the little squids sold in fish markets today was the world's first genuine monster. Unlike our cephalopods, whose remaining bit of shell is buried in their head, this giant poked its tentacles from a pointed shell more than 3½ meters (12 feet) long. That's the width of the average living room. Squids and octopuses have eyes remarkably like our own; this monster probably could have seen you as well as you could have seen it.

SHELL SHAPES

The shape a shell becomes depends on the way it grows. Growth happens only at the edge of the mantle (see page 68), where new rings of lime are secreted. Seashells have flaring shapes because the mantle itself grows, so each new addition to the shell is wider than the one before. If the mantle secretes evenly all the way around, the shell becomes a cone. But the edge of the mantle needn't secrete evenly all the way around. Thinking about the humps, hollows, twists, and turns that result from uneven growth is good exercise for the imagination.

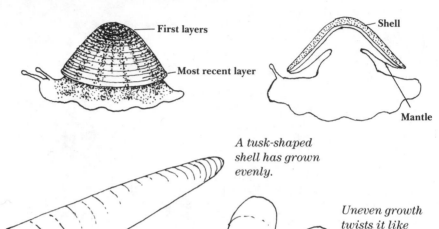

First layers

Most recent layer

Shell

Mantle

A tusk-shaped shell has grown evenly.

Uneven growth twists it like corkscrew.

Top and bottom shell have grown about at the same rate.

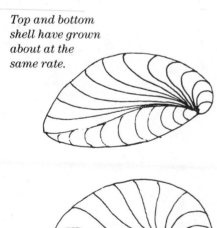

An even greater difference in growth rate coils a tusk into a snail.

Faster growth of the top shell twists it into a spiral.

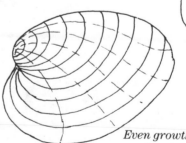

Even growth produces a smooth edge.

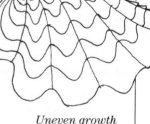

Uneven growth produces a scalloped edge.

All of these lime-shelled creatures, even the present-day squid whose shell is only a scrap beneath its skin, are mollusks. They have rather complicated little bodies. A whelk, like other snails, has a head with eyes on the ends of two stalks. Land snails also have a pair of feelers that can pop out and pull in like the fingers of a rubber glove. The flat pad a snail creeps about with is called a foot. Its stomach is on top of its foot instead of slung underneath, as it is on other animals. Beyond the stomach, the rest of the body is cleverly coiled to fit its shell exactly.

It would not work at all for a snail to get rid of wastes at its rear end, since that end is curled up into the dead end of the shell. Snails get around this problem by having a looped intestine. The mouth, where food comes in, and the anus, where wastes go out, are right beside one another in the head. For convenience, a snail's penis is in its head, too, where it can be poked out for mating. A few snails have managed to make one feeler serve as a penis, and one outrageous snail can protrude its penis from its mouth.

Small as it is, a snail can be a monstrous predator of other underwater life. Inside its innocent round mouth is a drill: a long tongue called a radula barbed like a

BEACHCOMBING

Shells washed up on a beach are often damaged. The more perfect ones found in tidal pools or clinging to seaweed are still occupied. Kill the mollusks by boiling them in a pot of water for a few minutes. Cool them under running water. Pick snail flesh out with a toothpick. There may be a cap called an operculum over the opening. Stuff the empty shell with a bit of cotton, then glue the operculum back in place. Bivalves such as clams will open when they are boiled. Opened bivalves will eventually break apart at the hinge. After clean-ing the flesh out with a table knife, hold the shells shut with string or freezer tape. They will be dry enough in a few days to stay shut when the string or tape is removed.

Cleaned and dried shells can be kept in glass bottles with a wad of cotton on top to keep them from getting broken, or in bottles filled with mineral oil to preserve their bright color. You can also display shells by gluing them to a piece of cardboard with white glue. Or, to keep the collection from becoming dusty, glue the shells to the inside of a large, shallow gift box that has a lid.

SHELL HUNT

Common species of mollusks that vary from one individual to another, such as Atlantic dogwinkles, make interesting collections. Smooth dogwinkles have inherited a combination of genes that is different from that of the ornamented, raspy ones. Dogwinkles of different colors—ice-white, chocolate-brown, butter-yellow, tangerine—have been eating different kinds of food. A winkle that's striped has been switching diets, eating one sort of food while one band was forming, another while the next one grew.

Populations of thick-shelled mollusks have been heavily preyed upon: the fragile, thin-shelled ones have been eaten; the tough ones have survived.

rasp with razor sharp teeth. A snail known as an oyster drill climbs aboard an oyster and drills a hole right through its stony shell into the tasty body inside. It rasps off bits of flesh from the living animal and pulls them through its mouth down into its gullet.

CLAP, CLAP

Oysters, clams, and mussels have lost their heads. With their gentle way of life, they are able to get along with nothing more than a mouth and an anus stretched out into siphons for sucking in nutritious bottom water and squirting out the leftovers. A clam pulls its feeding siphon in at low tide, leaving a hole in the sand through which, as the tide comes in, it pokes its siphon up to eat.

Inside the shell itself, a nubbin of muscle reaches from top to bottom to clap it shut. When the muscle is relaxed, the shell's elastic hinge automatically opens it. A thin tissue clinging to both halves of the shell is the clam's mantle, a sort of cape that spreads out over its topside stomach and drapes down about its foot.

The shell of a mollusk, whether it is twisted and turned like a conch or is as plain as a clam, is formed by secretions from the mantle. Picture the mantle depositing layers of shell along its outer edge. The

MOLLUSK STEW

Whelks, clams, mussels, and limpets are all easy to find and good to eat. Before gathering mollusks for a meal, though, be sure you know what they are, and that the water they live in is not contaminated. Use a field guide to shells, such as Audubon's, to check identification. Check with the Coast Guard about water pollution. Sometimes no mollusk gathering is allowed because the mollusks are temporarily poisonous from an alga that thrives in hot weather, and sometimes areas are closed to protect species that have been gathered too much. Mollusk gathering is done at low tide.

Mussels come in bunches stuck by strong threads the animals spin out to hold them onto rocks or wharves. Tear them away and toss them into a bucket. Pick up whelks and winkles at low tide. Limpets cling flatly and tightly to rock surfaces. Pry them off with a pocket knife.

Clams dig down into the sand or mud of tidal flats. You must dig for them with a clam fork or with a gardener's hand fork. Look for holes that squirt at you. Rake out the sand there to a depth of at least 15 centimeters (6 inches), plucking out clams as you uncover them.

Rinse snails and limpets under running water to get rid of the sand; scrape the "beards" and clinging seaweed off mussels with a small knife as you rinse them. Let clams "spit" their insides free of sand by submerging them for an hour or so under seawater, then rinse them, too. Cook them right away or, if you must wait a few hours, keep them in the refrigerator so they stay alive. Bacteria quickly multiply in dead mollusks, and can make you sick.

Put edible mollusks in a pot with a little water—2 inches for a large kettle of clams, only a half-inch for a small pot of whelks. Put the lid on, and heat over medium heat to boiling. Little fellows like whelks, winkles, and limpets are done at this point. Clams and mussels are done when their shells open. Remove snail types from their shells with toothpicks, and clam types with a fork. Eat them all with melted butter.

smaller mantle of a baby clam secretes the first ridges you see at the hinge. On a snail, the first ridges are in the center of the spiral. As the mantle grows, it lays down a new layer of shell along its edge, so each band of shell is broader than the next.

Because a clam stays buried in mud all its life, it really doesn't need eyes. The scallop is another story. It, too, lives at the bottom of the sea, but not sedately. When disturbed, a scallop claps its shell and rockets away like a dancing pair of false teeth, peering at its enemy with two rows of bright blue eyes strung along its mantle.

The world that the first seeing animals looked upon slowly turned to stone. Shells and limey corpses piled layer after layer over the sea bottom, covering the craton with its first frosting of limestone. Their world is still there. After the ages of mountain building, there came a time of peace in the heartland which has been unbroken to this day. The whole Midwest has been unmoved for more than 500 million years. Layered over the oldest sea floor lies the fossil record of marine life the likes of which the world has not seen since.

500 MILLION YEARS AGO

The Drowned Continent · Strange Fish · Legs, Pincers, Claws, and Feelers

After the craton had been scrubbed flat by scouring wind and rain, there was not much of it left to stick up out of the sea. And there was a lot of sea then. There was no ice anywhere to trap the water into icebergs or glaciers. The ocean bottoms seem to have been "fluffed up" higher, so that their basins could not hold as much. The sea rose and spread over the craton, covering at one point nearly two-thirds of the North American continent. The only dry areas were the high shoulder of the craton in Canada, which stretched from there like a narrow peninsula as far south as Arizona, and a scattering of islands.

You could have waded waist-deep from Pennsylvania to Nebraska. You would have crossed the equator. The continent was far south of its present position, and also turned somewhat around so that the equator ran up from Texas through Oklahoma, Nebraska, and the Dakotas. (By now this floating continent has drifted nearly to the North Pole in its journey over the globe.) The water was as warm as a bath and was swarming with life.

Your ankles would have become tangled in algae as complicated as seaweeds are today. That algae was the latest fashion 500 million years ago, the height of evolution in the world of plants, the very best that plants could do. You might have snorkled among waving fronds where Cincinnati now stands, spying on a community of marine animals so abundant that you could not have taken a step without treading on one.

Maybe you wouldn't have needed a face mask. The sandy bottom washed off the absolutely clean craton that gleamed white below crystal water as transparent as a swimming pool.

Life simply exploded. Relatives of today's sea stars and sea urchins waved their tentacles atop 21-meter (70-foot) stalks. Worms donned armor, grew legs, eyes, feelers, and pinching claws—they were the first crustaceans. You could have gone fishing: the highest form of multicellular life, the vertebrates, already swam the spreading seas.

STAR-SPRINKLED LILY MEADOWS

Wading across Ohio, sloshing through Wisconsin, paddling along toward Utah 500 million years ago, you could have stopped to admire vast beds of sea lilies bowing their flowery heads atop waving stalks. They were crinoids (and they were animals), and they still grow today in meadows on warm seafloors. Most of our waters are too cold now for crinoids, but in the ancient bath

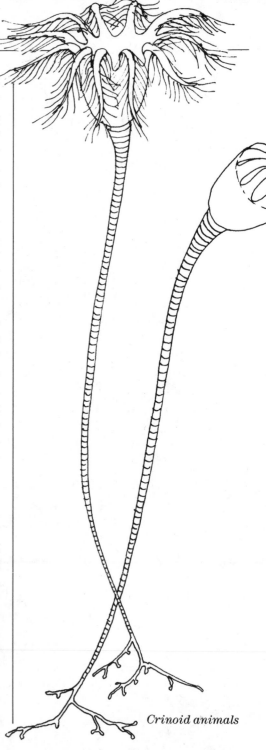

Crinoid animals

of the Midwest they grew so thickly that they left great slabs of limestone made up almost entirely of their graceful fossils.

Living on a limy stalk has its advantages. Given rich plankton hunting grounds, a sea lily can stay put and not worry that it will drift to poorer waters. On the other hand, its hunting grounds are only as broad as its tether will allow, and even the amazing 21-meter stalk of the longest sea lily was still a leash. What if there were more to eat just a ripple to the left, a step to the right? Well, then one would need feet.

A couple of crinoid cousins took just such a course 500 million years ago. Sea stars and sea urchins learned to creep slowly on rows of sucker-tipped tentacles called tube feet. These feet poke out through the animals' spiny skin. (The animals' scientific name is *Echinodermata*, which means "spiny-skin.") The skin is made up completely of interlocking, limy plates each bearing a spine. The spines fall off sea urchins when they die and dry up. Then the plates themselves are easy to make out.

The animals' system of moving gave them the advantages of both staying put and moving off. A sea urchin can hold so tightly to the rocky shore that even the crashing surf of an ocean storm can't dis-

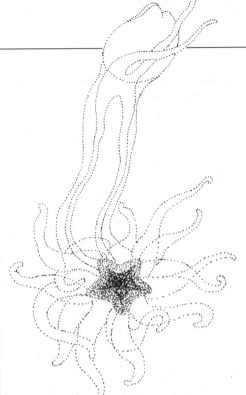

A sea star develops from a larva that swims vigorously.

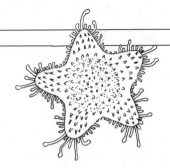

The species shown here drops to the ocean bottom as soon as the sea star forming at one end grows tube feet. It then detaches from the rest of its larval body, and takes up its creeping way of life.

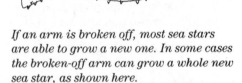

If an arm is broken off, most sea stars are able to grow a new one. In some cases the broken-off arm can grow a whole new sea star, as shown here.

lodge it from its lair. It can also move out over its prey to chew it up with the most complicated and efficient crunching mechanism in the world. Sea urchins eat almost anything, alive or dead.

Although sea stars, too, cling to the bottom as tides wash in and out, they get about somewhat better than sea urchins, because their tube feet line the undersides of their five bendable arms. A sea star, however, has nothing at all to bite with. Its mouth is just a soft hole in the middle of its belly. However, it has no need to bite; its powerful arms and suction feet pry open clams, mussels, and oysters, which it digests whole.

Though sea stars have explored a mobile way of life at greater speed than urchins, they are stuck with a limited navigation system. Among the thousand or so tube feet at the end of each arm there is one that is particularly sensitive to touch. Using these touch organs, a sea star more or less feels its way along. As it moves, the tip of the reaching arm is tilted up. The gesture lifts to the light a tiny red eye (look closely—there is one on each arm

VIEWBOX

A viewbox is a wooden frame with a Plexiglas bottom that floats on the water. Use it as a window to see underwater worlds clearly while wading, or while lying on a dock. When viewing the underwater scene from a rowboat, take care not to tip the boat: Bring the boat to a halt; float the viewbox behind the boat, not to either side; hold it close to the boat with the rope, and let only one person at a time look into it.

The viewbox takes some carpentry skills. You may want to get help from an adult, or use this as a school shop project.

You need:
Plexiglas, 14 inches by 14 inches
Pencil
1-inch by 6-inch pine, 6 feet long
Handsaw
Carpenter's glue
Hammer
6-penny box nails
1-inch brads
Quarter-round trim, 6 feet long
Shellac
Paintbrush
Alcohol for cleaning the paintbrush
Silicone caulking
Two 1⅜-inch large-eye eyehooks
Clothesline

1. Using the piece of Plexiglas as a ruler, make a pencil line on the shelving to mark the length of the first side of the box. Cut that piece with a handsaw. Mark and cut the second piece the same way.

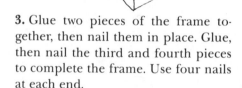

2. Set these two sides on their edges with the Plexiglas lying snugly between. That will give you the measurement for the other two sides of the box. Mark and cut both of them. Put the Plexiglas aside.

3. Glue two pieces of the frame together, then nail them in place. Glue, then nail the third and fourth pieces to complete the frame. Use four nails at each end.

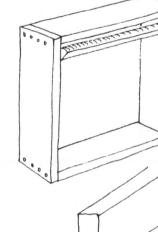

4. Use the quarter-round trim to make the inside ledge that the Plexiglas will rest on. Mark, saw, and glue each piece into place before marking the next piece. Nail the trim in place with the small nails, and let the glued joints dry overnight.

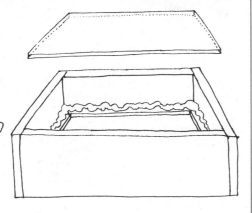

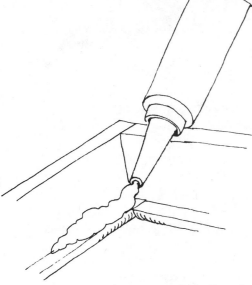

5. Brush on two coats of shellac to waterproof the wood. The second coat can be done as soon as the first is dry, usually after a few hours. When the second coat is dry, squeeze caulking generously along the top of the bottom ledge.

6. Ease the Plexiglas into place. Caulk around the upper edge of the Plexiglas and up the inside corners of the box. Turn the box over to caulk the bottom seams.

7. Screw an eyehook into each of two adjacent corners of the box, as shown in the illustration of the finished viewbox. Tie a 2-foot piece of clothesline in between. The rope can be used as a handle to hang the box up when not in use, or to tie a line to when the box is used from a dock or behind a boat.

tip). But sea stars can barely see. They can't tell a rock from a mussel, a weed from an arm. In fact, a sea star's five red eyes can tell the difference only between dark and light—helpful for finding the way to a hiding place and finding the way out again, but not good for much else. What looks like an eye on the top of a sea star is actually a sieve through which the animal takes in just enough water to keep it properly plump.

WATER PICKLES

The least likely member of this tribe of spiny skins is the sea cucumber. Unlike pretty sea lilies, sea stars, and sea urchins, the sea cucumber looks worse than a pickle. One kind has been described as a large black pudding. Another looks like an emaciated piece of cactus. Our ordinary North Atlantic species is murky, wrinkled, and flabby. It is hard to tell which end is which, but the animal itself is not confused.

You won't find a sea cucumber easily. Not that they are rare—they are very common in all the seas of Earth. But these water pickles don't hug the tidal pools like sea stars, or hang in bunches from a pier like mussels. They bury themselves in mud or creep along the bottom beyond where beachcombers might come upon them. The best way to

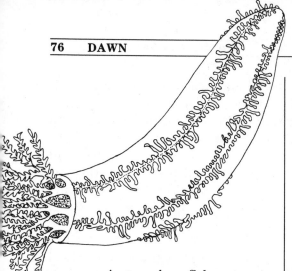

see one is to ask a fisherman or lobster hauler to save for you whatever odd things stumble into his net or trap.

Sea cucumbers are built in the same circular design as their relatives, but they are stretched out and lie on their side, as though one had taken an urchin and rolled it up to look like a sausage. The five rows of tube feet running down its body correspond to the five arms of a sea star. A sea cucumber has a mouth at one end and an anus at the other. In between is a genuine coiled intestine. The limy plates, which in sea stars and sea urchins cover the body completely, are in the sea cucumbers mere slivers scattered about within the body wall. The animals feel soggy, rubbery, or leathery to the touch.

Unlikely as it seems, soft sea cucumbers and their prickly kin share a common ancestor with bony animals like us. The ancestor—or rather its fossil—has not been

PICKLED URCHINS

Almost any small marine animal can be preserved in alcohol. Inexpensive rubbing alcohol becomes cloudy; only expensive grain alcohol stays clear. Choose small specimens and small bottles. Don't be greedy: There is no reason to preserve a dozen animals when a single specimen will do. One each of the small creatures found in a tidal pool would show the typical life forms there without wasting a lot of little lives.

You need:
1-cup measuring pitcher
1 quart of grain alcohol (available at liquor stores or drugstores)
1 of any or all of the following: urchin, shrimp, sponge, snail, mussel, or crab
1 small bottle for each specimen

(half-pint preserving jars would work)

1. To preserve an urchin in a half-pint jar, fill the measuring pitcher with ⅓ cup of alcohol and ⅔ cup of water. Drop the urchin into the jar, and pour the alcohol solution over it. Let it soak three hours.
2. Pour off the first solution and replace it with ½ cup of alcohol and ½ cup of water. Soak the urchin in this stronger solution for another three hours. Alcohol dehydrates the animal, or removes water from its flesh (sadly, its color will also be removed).
3. Pour out that solution, and cover the urchin with the final pickling juice: ¾ cup of alcohol, ¼ cup of water. Screw the lid on tightly. Any small creature can be kept in this last alcohol solution almost indefinitely.

found, and probably never will be. It would be recognizable only by certain similarities in its larval stage to echinoderm larvae and to vertebrate embryos that are too brief and delicate to make it into the stony record of extinction. But sometime before 500 million years ago, one branch of its descendants had stiffened their bodies with a notochord, a flexible rod embedded within the back. By 500 million years ago, they had strengthened the rod with bones, vertebrae strung along it like beads on a string.

By that time the sea had risen to cover almost the entire continent. You could have sailed clear across America, beaching your boat on an island somewhere in northeastern Canada. There hasn't been that much water over Earth since. Fish, the first vertebrates, were already swimming the ocean gray.

THE OCEAN GRAY

Perhaps you are imagining the sea over the craton colored turquoise like the Caribbean, or as blue as the blue Pacific. Blue is the color of sky and water, because both absorb the other colors of sunlight and reflect back to our eyes nothing but blue. But blue water is sterile water. The blue water that is 90 percent of our seas and oceans is as empty of life as a desert.

DRIED SEA STARS

S ea stars can be gathered from their rocky haunts at low tide. The only equipment you need to collect them is a bucket or, to see the animal walking on its tube feet, a jar filled with seawater. The creature will pull its tube feet up into its body when you disturb it, but settled down in the jar for a few minutes, it will poke them out again and move slowly about. The sea star is soaked in alcohol to dehydrate it before the drying is finished in sand. There is no way to preserve the lovely lavender and apricot colors of live sea stars. Museum display specimens are painted with acrylic paints after they're dry. Choose only one specimen to dry; let the others go.

You need:
1 sea star
Quart jar
1 quart of rubbing alcohol
Small corrugated carton, with its lid
Enough dry beach sand to fill the
**   box ⅔ full**

1. Put the sea star in the jar, cover it with alcohol, and let it soak for three hours. Pour off that alcohol, and repeat the soaking with fresh alcohol. Again, pour off the alcohol and give it a third soaking in fresh alcohol, this time for several days.

2. Fill about one-third of the carton with the dry sand. Take the specimen out of the alcohol and place it on the sand, leaving plenty of space on all sides. Fill the box about two-thirds full with more sand, and close the lid. Store it in a hot, dry place for a month.

3. Carefully pour out the sand and remove the sea star from the drying box. A thoroughly dry sea star is light and hard.

The remaining 10 percent is grayed, browned, greened, or reddened by plankton and the thronging life plankton supports. The North Atlantic, for instance, is gray with life.

Plankton, on which all marine life depends, needs nutrition as well as light. Its fertilizer is mainly nitrates and phosphates recycled into the surface water from the decaying bodies of dead organisms that have sunk to the bottom. But how does the bottom get up to the top? Think of any body of water as a bowl of soup. Unless the soup is stirred, whatever has sunk to the bottom stays there. Ocean water near the mouth of a river is stirred by the flow of water pouring into it, and is doubly blessed with mineral-rich silt that the river has carried from the continent's interior. But other portions of the bowl can be stirred only by something that, like a great spoon, will skim surface water off to one side, letting rich bottom water well up to replace it.

That spoon is the wind. World wind maps in a good atlas will show you that winds to the east of the continent blow steadily and strongly northward in a great sweep along the coast, driving the ocean in their path. The ocean current founders as it hits the shallow offshore bottom, breaking up into a powerful confusion of whirling water that stirs the rich bottom water up. It's not hard to guess the places where strong currents meet rugged obstacles. They are where we catch the most fish—off New England and Newfoundland, for example.

On the other side of the continent, especially to the south, an atlas shows weaker and more faltering winds that often blow away

from rather than along the shore. The ocean currents therefore can stray out to sea too far and deep to be thrown into a tumult. You can go fishing in the blue waters off San Diego, but you cannot hope to haul the huge catches netted in the North Atlantic. Most sterile of all are places like the Gulf Stream—warm, calm, blue, and lifeless.

Because the sea over the craton left a solid carpet of fossil marine life behind, you can bet your buttons it wasn't blue.

High Roads, Low Roads, and Everywhere In Between

Early fish were blunt-skulled, armor-backed, flattened creatures who bellied along fertile bottoms in the gummy mouths of rivers, sucking up soft foods with jawless mouths. Some fish, such as the lampreys found in the Great Lakes, suck the juices from other fish, that still have no jaws. But almost all other species nibble, nip, bite, and tear with the toothsome hinged traps called jaws. There are over 19,000 species of fish, more than all the other vertebrates put together. The secret of their success is simple: They can swim anywhere.

Marine life lives in layers. Plankton and floaters that eat plankton live in the top layer, where there is the most light for photosynthesis.

At the bottom, animals live off one another and off dead plankton drifting down from above. In a sea so shallow that you can wade through it, these layers aren't apparent, because light shines through right down to your toes, and life throngs everywhere. But—as you can imagine if you picture North America as a mound—while the sea spread inland during this time of fluffing ocean basins, the sea also deepened at the underwater continental edges. The middle layer in deeper portions could not have been too lively. If an animal enjoyed any vertical travel at all, it amounted to one floating trip up after hatching to browse or prey on baby food, and one sinking trip back as an adult to browse or prey on bottom dwellers.

As the sea deepened, more space was added between the "ceiling" and the "floor," but no elevators. So fish moved in. They had evolved their powerful motion in mud; the same motion moved them out of the mud, into deep water. Even now the middle of the sea is occupied by fish who can swim, and don't need elevators.

Even the tiniest fish can swim more powerfully by far than a wriggling worm or a clapping scallop. Because they can swim where they please, they can eat where they please. Medium-size eels in coastal

waters swim to the bottom to eat crustaceans, to the top to feast on insect larvae, or anywhere between to chase the young of other fish.

Stuffy Water

Cut open the belly of a fish you've caught and you'll see an efficient arrangement of all the major organs found in any vertebrate: intestine, stomach, liver, heart, and yes, lung. At some time in their lives most people are taught that fish, who live in water, breathe through gills, and land animals, who live in air, breathe with lungs. The fact is that primitive fish breathed with both, and so do a few fish that live in stuffy water today.

Stuffy water comes about when water lies stagnant, without wind or waves to whip air into it, or when there are so many oxygen-using bacteria that they use up all there is. Carp can be seen gulping good fresh air right at the surface of a stuffy pond. The earliest fish that evolved in shallow, stagnant places gulped water when it held enough oxygen, passing it through a sieve of gill rakers to separate out food or dirt, and forcing it out over the gill surface where oxygen was absorbed through moist tissue directly into the bloodstream. When water was stale, they swallowed air from the surface into their lungs.

The lungs of most fish were later

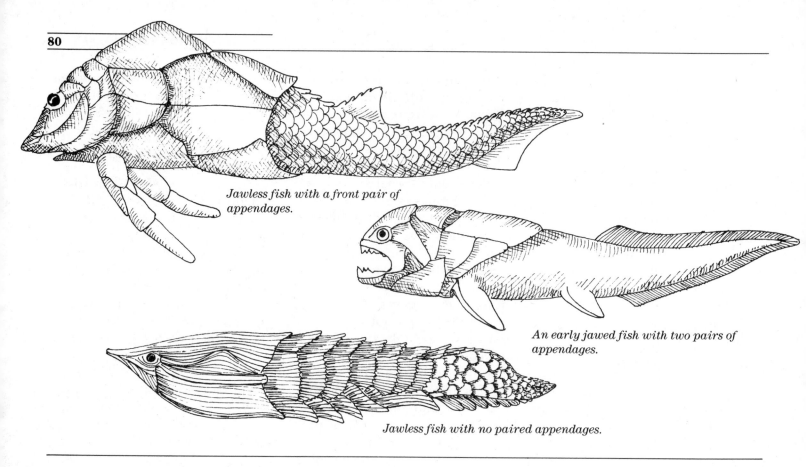

Jawless fish with a front pair of appendages.

An early jawed fish with two pairs of appendages.

Jawless fish with no paired appendages.

converted to swim bladders. By inflating or deflating the swim bladder, a fish can compensate for changing water pressure at various depths. The fish deflates its bladder to descend, inflates it to rise, and at any level can remain in the same spot without either rising or sinking.

A CUT TO THE BONE

Fish were the first animals to have an inside skeleton. You may have been told that the purpose of a bony internal skeleton is to support the body; without it, an animal would collapse into a squishy lump. This is not true of the first inner skeletons that evolved.

A fish is of almost exactly the same density as water; it lives weightless, like an astronaut, and has no need of a skeleton to prevent its collapse. Therefore, fish bones are often light and delicate, nothing like the steel structure of a building to which bones are often compared. The joints between a building's beams and girders are rigid, designed more to prevent movement than to allow a building to swivel, bend, or fold. Skeletons are jointed both for rigidity and for motion. In a fish skeleton, the skull is made of many bones joined rigidly for skull strength, while the fin bones are jointed in such a way that they swivel or fold flat. Backbone joints bend sideways in either direction, but only so much. They don't bend up and down at all. The way a fish's backbones fit against one another controls its range of motion and protects its body from dangerous overbending.

The long spiny ribs sticking out from each vertebra run between muscles. They serve as attachment surfaces against which muscles pull as they contract. A fish swims by contracting first one side of the body as far as it will easily bend, and then the other, so that the whole body moves like a series of waves.

A fish's body is made for the wave motion of swimming, but the engineering that speeds an eel on its way did not come quickly or all at once. Early fish, weighted with bony plates and finned with a single long flap on each side, had little speed and few controls. At most, their flaps might have offered some lift and saved the beast from tipping. As bony armor gave way to light scales—a change as wonderful as that from clanking breastplates to fine chain mail—fins began to come in useful pairs.

Fish now use their fins for hovering motions that keep the animal in one place, or for paddling motions that delicately maneuver it into position for nibbling, turning, lifting, diving, or stopping. Some fish that remained on the bottom or adapted to very shallow water developed lobed fins—bony fans set on rugged stumps for grappling forward through sticky mud. Free swimmers developed the folding fin—a web of skin supported by

THE LONG HAUL

The common eel that can be trapped by the dozens in the mouths of east coast rivers and along the Atlantic coast arrived there after a year's journey from the Sargasso Sea, northeast of the Caribbean Islands. They were mere larvae, thin and transparent, while traveling, and were only elvers (baby eels) a few centimeters long when the trip was over.

The Sargasso Sea is really not a sea at all; it is more like a floating island made of rafts of the seaweed *Sargassum* that have broken away from their offshore holdfasts and drifted with the ocean current to an area where rich nourishment wells up from the bottom. This floating island is home to a multitude of animals, some found nowhere else. As adults, eels travel back to the Sargasso Sea and lay their eggs among masses of the floating seaweed alive with a delicatessen of small browsers that are easy prey for the tiny babies when they hatch.

horny rays. Many fish today can raise the spiny rays of their back fin to fan it out for stability when moving slowly, and can lower it for speed. Pairs of rayed side fins and belly fins also fold back for speed.

Most fish are slippery. The mucous covering that makes an eel as slippery as an eel smooths its streamlined body, which cuts through water like greased lightning.

BABY JAWS

Ocean-going fish have a problem: where to keep their eggs. A fish that just dumps them in the deep blue sea loses almost all of them. Floating fish eggs are caviar to plankton predators; sinking ones risk hatching in starvation land at the very depths of the ocean basin. Most open-ocean fish have solved this problem by laying millions of eggs. After all, only one survivor per herring keeps the herring population steady. Others have gotten around the problem by avoiding it. They continue even now to lay their eggs in the shallows they swam so long ago. Coastal marshes, protected inlets, and river estuaries are the hatcheries for such otherwise far-out fish as salmon.

But not for sharks. They found many ways to have babies in the deep, and you may well have stumbled upon one of their inventions while beachcombing. Those odd, black, four-horned objects called mermaids' purses are the tough, un-

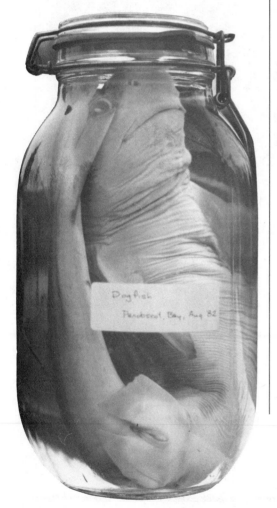

The amount of alcohol needed to preserve a creature as big as this dogfish shark would cost a great deal. This one was bottled in formaldehyde.

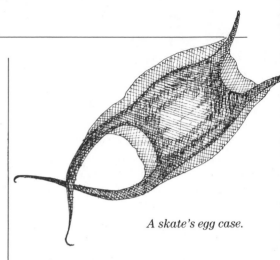

A skate's egg case.

appetizing floating nurseries of skates—shark relatives. That particular egg case is small as shark nurseries go. The whale shark makes an egg case larger than a basketball.

There is no lack of food in the nursery. Inside an egg case is a generous supply of fertilized eggs. The embryos—the unhatched fish—that grow the fastest eat the eggs around them. Buoyant, inedible, well-stocked nurseries provide a deluxe cruise ship that the shark embryos enjoy until they are large enough to break out and fend for themselves.

It's not easy to raise a shark embryo to even mini-Jaws size. Many species can't get their own food until they are at least a third the size of Big Mama, or bigger than they could possibly grow inside an egg case. The solution is to forget the nursery and carry embryos within the belly, where there is more room for food storage. Such sharks are born live, like mammals. One kind of shark carries inside her an egg the size of a softball as food for the single embryo she will finally give birth to.

Other sharks have gone further. Hammerheads use an early version of the placenta—a yolk sac which provides additional food after the embryo has used up the substance of its own egg. Like a mammal's placenta, the hammerhead's yolk sac transports the embryo's waste products into its mother's bloodstream for disposal, and carries nutrients and oxygen from her blood to the embryo.

Then again, there are sharks who simply make small eggs in large quantities and assume the embryos will manage somehow. They do—by eating one another. The tiger sand shark, an eight-footer that lives off our South Atlantic coast, produces pea-size eggs in batches of 15 or 20. Within the mother's belly, the developing embryos gulp down their brothers and sisters until only one is left. The winning cannibal then continues to grow by eating new batches of eggs as they arrive. Within a year, Baby Jaws is ready to be born—a full 120 cm (40 inches) from snout to tail.

A WANDERING EYE

Newly hatched fish don't usually look like the adults they will become; they are larvae who still have

GILL BONES TO JAWBONES

Jaws were not invented until after the first hundred million years of fish history. The cartilage or bone support that forms the lower jaws in sharks and mackerels were originally gill supports or gill arches. Put both your hands up behind your ears and pretend you feel the curve of arched gill supports back there. Now slide both hands down toward your mouth—that's the travel route of the pair of gill arches that moved forward in a V to form the upper and lower jaws. At first the jawbones were just embedded in muscle to which they were attached by tendons, giving the fish a weak sort of mouth. Later, the jaw became hinged to the skull on both sides, giving the shark its powerful crunch.

Infant fish

Right eye migrating over the top of the head, to the left side.

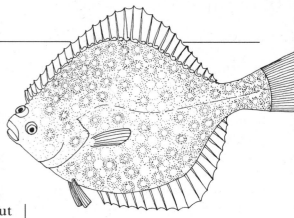

Adult flatfish lying on its right side with both eyes facing upward.

a good deal of shaping up ahead of them.

Larvae show relatedness much better than adult forms do. It is as though cells assuming the shape of an organism do first what they have done longest, and only then go on to more elaborate constructions. You wouldn't be able to tell the difference between a fish larva and yourself as a young fetus (as we call our own larval stage) during the first weeks of life.

One of the ways a larva assumes its unique form is by cell migration. Among fish, the most amazing cell migration takes place in the larvae of flatfish. Flatfish (including the ones called flounder, halibut, plaice, sole, and turbot) start out life as normal fish swimming upright and with eyes where they belong. As the larva grows, however, its body shape and fin position begin to change. Gradually, one eye migrates around the head until both lie on the same side. The flatfish then quits swimming like a normal fish, sinks, and takes up a sideways sort of life in the bottom ooze.

Flatfish have thus made a round trip from their primitive beginnings as mud-dwelling bottom scavengers, up to the high life of the free swimmer, and back down to the bottom again. That evolutionary round trip is repeated in every flounder generation.

LITTLE FISH GO TO SCHOOL

Almost all little fish are the steady diet of larger predators. We ourselves eat sprats, smelts, herrings, sardines, whitings, and anchovies. To protect themselves from predation, these little fish swim in schools.

At first thought, it seems stupid to swim in schools. After all, if a tuna is after you, why call attention to yourself by joining a large and

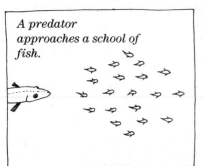

A predator approaches a school of fish.

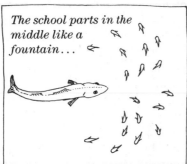

The school parts in the middle like a fountain . . .

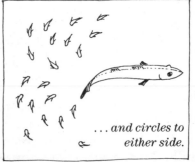

. . . and circles to either side.

The school is now behind the predator.

very visible group? And why, when so many fish are congregated together, aren't they easily gobbled by the dozen? But try to catch a minnow in the shallows by the shore and you'll see how difficult it is.

The sheer number of fish is confusing. Even if you can single out your intended victim, the darting around of dozens of other fish while you are trying to concentrate on one is completely distracting. A predator actually has more success zeroing in on one fish among six than on one among twenty. More likely, the whole group escapes by performing a high-speed water ballet.

Fish schools have three such maneuvers for escaping predators. To avoid your hand, for example, they would simply turn in another direction; your hand is so slow in the water that this is usually their easiest escape. A faster predator that

KNOW A FISH BY ITS SHAPE

You can tell at a glance some things about how a fish lives. A dogfish is shaped broad and flat; its mouth opens underneath. Dogfish live mostly along the seafloor and feed on crustaceans and other bottom-dwelling creatures. A mackerel is perfectly streamlined, and its mouth is smack in the middle of its face. Mackerels spend their lives chasing prey at high speed straight through the sea. A herring is narrower than a dogfish and wider than a mackerel, and its mouth opens upward. Herring feed on plankton near the surface, and are not speed swimmers.

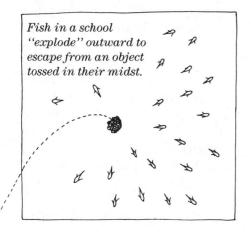

Fish in a school "explode" outward to escape from an object tossed in their midst.

darts quickly toward the minnow of its choice is baffled by a different strategy. The minnow school parts in the middle, spills like a fountain to either side, and rejoins to the rear of the enemy, who is left facing empty space with its dinner behind it. Plunk a rock into the midst of a school and you can see what happens when the attack is a complete surprise. The entire school explodes outward like a bursting bomb, leaving the attacker with no particular direction to follow.

FOOL THE SCHOOL

Humans have no trouble at all catching small fry like these minnows by hauling long nets through their schools. When herring come into shallow coves to spawn in the spring along the New England coast, fishermen simply wait until the huge schools are in the cove, then spread nets straight across the water to catch them as they swim back toward the open ocean. The catch is canned; you call it sardines.

Tunas use the same strategy by swimming in an arc, herding their prey closer and closer together, then closing up like a bag to trap their dinner.

ALL TOGETHER, NOW

Minnows and other fish are able to move as one by using their senses and doing some rudimentary arithmetic. Their nostrils—pits in their snouts—allow them to identify members of their own species through the particular shapes of the scent molecules they give off. Recognizing the smell and the look of their fellows lets fish of a kind get together in the first place.

To move in unison, fish use their eyes and a type of hearing. Along a fish's side is a line (you can see it on any fish) within which are ciliated cells in a fluid-filled canal (you have similar cells lining your fluid-filled inner ear). There are also canals beneath the surface of a fish's head. The system is sensitive to vibrations bouncing off objects in the water, though whether a fish senses vibrations as noise or as touch is anybody's guess. Using that vibration sense, a fish can tell the size, distance, direction, and speed of a fish or of any object nearby.

Using vision and vibration, the fish applies three rules that coordinate its movement within the school. The first rule is that a distance closer than about a third of the fish's body length is too close for comfort. The second rule is that any distance greater than a full body length is too far for comfort. The two rules work in opposing ways. The sight of another fish is attractive, so neighbors tend to swim closer together; vibrations are repelling, so neighbors tend to move farther apart.

The third rule tells a fish to swim roughly parallel to those fish that swim on either side.

To adjust course, the fish takes

into account the movements of all the individuals in the group, weighs that reckoning somewhat in favor of what its nearest neighbors are up to, and comes up with a course that represents the group's activity as a whole. Each fish in the school is therefore a follower, and the whole group is the leader.

AS WARM AS A FISH

Touch any ordinary fish and it will be as cold as the water surrounding it—unless it's a warm-blooded fish. Most tunas and a few sharks keep their bodies warmer than the seas in which they swim. The job of being warm-blooded in water is much harder than it is on land. The reason has to do with breathing. Fish get their oxygen from water that contains only a little more than 2 percent of the amount of oxygen from an equal volume of air. To get enough to breathe, they must circulate through their gills far more water than the amount of air we must circulate through our lungs. Worse, water absorbs about 3,000 times more heat than air absorbs. The heat lost from breathing water rather than air can be 100,000 times what would be lost if fish could get out of the sea.

Yet most species of tuna manage to keep the core of their body 10°C (18°F) warmer than the surrounding water temperature. They do it

WHITE MEAT, DARK MEAT

Expensive tuna fish is white; the cheaper cans contain dark tuna meat. The cheap, dark sort is the most valuable meat to the tuna itself. It's the muscle served by the blood-rich, heat-exchange system, the one that is the warmest part of the tuna's body, and the one that powers its long, hard swims.

The color of a muscle, whether it is chicken meat or tuna, shows the kind of activity that muscle is capable of doing. Dark muscle can work almost continuously because it contains a dark, iron-rich, oxygen-storing protein, a sort of bank from which oxygen can be drawn when blood cannot supply it fast enough. Light muscle lacks that extra store of oxygen. It works sporadically—fast and furious until it outstrips the oxygen supply, then wearily or not at all while it recovers. A chicken's dark meat powers its legs, which can walk all day without a rest. Its light meat powers its wings, which can flap fast, but can't flap long. You might suspect that a strong swimmer like the streamlined mackerel is dark fleshed, while a sedentary fish like a flounder is light fleshed. True. Eat them and see.

by a heat exchange system. Blood cooled by its trip through the gills travels into a network of tiny arteries within the large swimming muscles. These arteries lie smack alongside small veins flowing with blood warmed by the working muscles. By the time the freshly oxygenated blood reaches its destination within the muscle, it has picked up enough heat from nearby warm veins to be warmer than the surrounding sea. The stale blood flowing back toward the gills has lost almost all of its heat. This is the same thing that happens in a home where hot and cold water lines have been installed too close to one another. The cold water reaches the faucet lukewarm, and so does the hot water.

The difference between a warm fish and a cold fish is power. A fish that is 10°C warmer than another fish can contract and relax its muscles three times faster than the colder fish can. Therefore, the warm fish is three times more powerful than the cold one. That extra power is put into high-speed swimming. Some tuna streak at 64 kilometers (40 miles) per hour.

That kind of speed was way beyond the sturdy but clumsy fish that

ONE OF BILLIONS

The commonest fossil trilobite has large round eyes like a dragonfly's and a plated body that could curl into a ball when the animal was frightened. Usually, a trilobite fossil's legs are missing, but there is a ridge where each leg would have been. You can imagine a trilobite walking the rippled white sand of Wyoming long ago. Too bad they're not alive now. Trilobites never got close to the present. Some evolved from little things to great beasts 77 centimeters (30 inches) long with golf-ball eyes, and some diminished to eyeless miniatures no longer than about 1 centimeter (about ⅓ inch). They vanished altogether when the shallow seas dried up, more than 250 million years ago. But you can still hold the fossil browser in the palm of your hand, a shape so old nestled on your fresh-made skin.

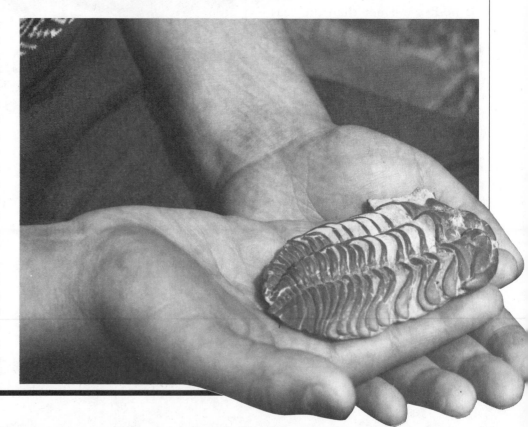

first explored the middle realm of deepening seas. Strangely enough, the worms of the day were probably faster. Though some were worms no longer.

HERDS OF TRILOBITES

Marine worms who had not been busy perfecting a wormish way of life or evolving into mollusks had been busy experimenting with something much more exciting: how to get about on legs, how to crawl, how to scuttle—and how to do it as safely armored against fish as fish were armored against all comers. The whole experiment took a very long time. But in the seas 500 million years ago, an early scuttler was already running about on stubby legs. There were hundreds of them, thousands, millions, and they moved in herds like so many hard-shelled sheep eating their way along the bottom of the sea. They were called trilobites. Trilobites were a dead end in evolution. They became extinct, and they left no descendants. But with a certain stretch of the imagination you can see in a trilobite fossil the basic plan for the remarkable features mere worms were working out: eyes made up of many lenses, mounted on a body divided into three parts, perched on jointed legs, all molded from an altogether novel sort of armor. All creepy-crawlies that

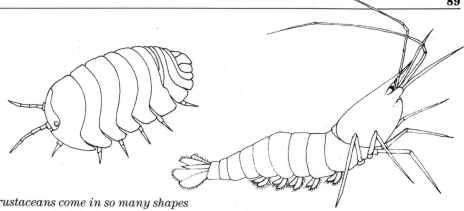

Crustaceans come in so many shapes that many don't look like relatives at all. The wood louse, a terrestrial crustacean that lives in damp places such as under rotting logs, is 6 millimeters (¼ inch) long, with stumpy legs and the ability to curl into a ball like a trilobite.

A shrimp has a more typical crustacean shape. This is what one looks like before its front end is lopped off for the fish market. Some shrimp are as small as a wood louse, others are as long as your hand.

share this basic plan are *Arthropoda*, a major division (phylum) of life forms that includes crustaceans such as crabs, shrimp, and lobsters, arachnids such as spiders, ticks, daddy-longlegs, insects such as roaches, moths, and honeybees, and other groups less common or like trilobites, extinct. Arthropods are the most numerous—some say the most successful—of all animals. Altogether, they make up 80 percent of all the animal species in the world.

THE MOBILE SHELL

The arthropod shell that worms invented outclassed the snail's immovable shell, or even the scallop's clapping shell. A crustacean's ele-

SHELL GAMES

A clam shell breaks; a crab shell bends. The material that makes a crab shell flexible is chitin. But crabs don't wear a cloak of chitin alone: They harden it with lime.

You can get an idea of this double-layered material by soaking a crab's carapace in vinegar. After a few days, the acidic vinegar will have dissolved the lime, leaving only a floppy layer of chitin. A cookout on the beach provides an opportunity to see how much of the carapace is made of lime. Burn a crab's shell. The chitin is consumed in the flame. All that will be left is a small pile of white lime.

THE CRAB'S SECRET

Turn a crab belly up. At the rear edge is a segmented section of shell that at first looks like it is simply part of the belly shell. Actually, it is the crab's tail, miniaturized and folded neatly under like a flap. Lifting the flap will tell you whether the crab is a girl or a boy. If you see a pointed penis, the crab is a male.

gant exoskeleton was certainly superior to the weighty outsides of the earliest fish. The light exoskeleton armored the entire animal, yet allowed it to move flexibly and speedily. The material was made of fingernail-like chitin, sometimes fortified with lime. A modern shrimp shell is made entirely of chitin, bendable and transparent. Crabs and lobsters strengthen chitin with calcium. To grow, a crustacean (and other arthropods, too) sheds its shell and grows a new one. Chitin is secreted all over its body before it sheds its old shell; then calcium may be secreted into the body to harden it. Soft shell crabs are crabs that have shed but have not yet hardened their shells.

Because the shell is secreted over a crustacean's entire surface instead of along the mantle edge like the shell of a mollusk, the armor conforms to the body plan beneath it. The body plan of a worm is in segments. The shells of a shrimp and lobster are also in segments, with pleats in between that act as joints. Legs are jointed, too. The shell of a lobster's leg is stiffened with calcium, but the pleat in the joint is not.

Legs, of course, must have muscles to move them. Another great advantage of this form-fitting shell is that muscles can be attached to it anywhere; the shell provides the surface to pull against. With the invention of joints and a muscle-attachment surface that completely clothed the body, a crustacean could walk the seafloor using a powerful push from one part of itself to advance the rest of it forward. The motion is so powerful that crustaceans do not need the many legs that worm ancestors and trilobite relatives had. Some legs disappeared; others evolved skills no worm has ever had. A worm can't pick up its dinner and put it in its mouth. A crab can.

JUST BEING CRABBY

Crabs take the raw materials of nature and make clever things of them. The materials they use now are ones that were at hand when crabs first evolved. One sort of crab bedecks itself with an anemone. When the anemone captures a meal, the crab shares the scraps. Another crab wears a coat of sponge. It plucks up a fragment of a living sponge and attaches it to its back; the growing sponge will eventually cover the crab's back. Crabs are a favorite meal for many animals besides humans, but almost no one dines on sponge or anemone. A cloak of sponge or a cap of anemone not only disguises the crab, but makes it unappetizing.

Hermit crabs dispense with their own armor entirely and use a harder mollusk shell instead. They enter an empty shell backward and jam the opening shut by folding a large claw within it. At rest in a tidal pool, a hermit crab looks like a discarded whelk shell lying on the bottom—until the "whelk" scuttles away on little crab feet.

Behavior leaves no fossils; behavior is the invisible side of evolution, the ghost driver of change. For a crab to evolve a body that fits a snail's shell, the crab must be in the habit of seeking shelter, and it must prefer shells for shelter. Then, any minute, accidental change in body shape that made a crab fit better into a shell shelter would help that individual live long enough to reproduce, and pass its better-fitting body on to its descendants. And vice versa: the better the fit, the more helpful the shell-seeking behavior; the best-fitting crabs that were the most attracted to shell shelters survived the best of all. Gradually shell shelters replaced the crab's shell entirely, and hermit crabs had evolved. In evolution, all changes—in body and in behavior—affect one another all the time. And those changes are affected by the realities of surviving in a particular environment. Why would a hermit crab seek shelter unless its little crab body and its sweet crab flavor gave it no better choice?

Crabs have been pushed into their protective ways of living by harsh reality. They may lay 25,000 eggs at a time, but hardly any will live to be adults. Crustacean eggs hatch into larvae so tiny and transparent they are barely visible to the naked eye. They don't look at all like crabs or lobsters, although you might say they are roughly shrimp-like. Unlike the bottom crawler that a crab will become, these crab youngsters swim high to browse the upper plankton pastures. The catch is, they thus become plankton, too. Very few will eat and not be eaten.

Those that escape gradually become shorter, leggier, and more crablike. Abruptly, they lose the ability to swim and sink to the bottom of the sea to crawl crabwise into adulthood.

THE LIVES OF LOBSTERS

The problem of being good food for others haunts even a large crustacean like the lobster. Not only must a lobster survive the perils of living in plankton, but when it finally reaches its crusty adult form, a human, cod, seal, or larger lobster will catch it if it can.

Too large by far to hide under a shell or an anemone, lobsters seek shelter in dens. The den is likely to be inside a natural crevice or under an overhanging ledge of rock, but a lobster will dig a burrow if it must.

CRAYFISH TRAP

Crayfish, close cousins of lobsters, live in fresh, briskly moving streams and rivers all over the country. They hide under rocks and debris near the banks and come out to scavenge for food at night. Catch crayfish with a trap similar to a lobster trap, baited with a chicken neck. The wire mesh from which it is made is not easy to work with. You might want to get adult help, especially for the cutting and bending. Watch out for sharp edges!

You need:
Yardstick
Grease pencil
¼-inch mesh hardware cloth, 36 inches wide by 36 inches long
Metal shears
Wire snips
Roll of 24-gauge wire
4 binder clips (available at stationers)
Heavy string

Make the body of the trap:

1. Using the yardstick and grease pencil, and following the pattern, measure and mark the hardware cloth to the size of the trap's body. Cut the cloth with the shears. Carefully snip off the sharp ends of wire at the raw edges.

2. Following the pattern, measure and mark the hardware cloth where it will

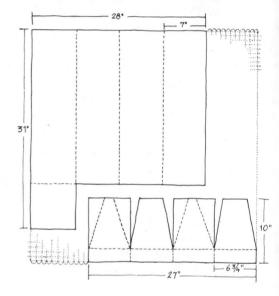

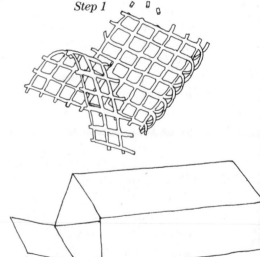

Step 1

Step

be folded to form a box (broken lines on the illustration). Crease the cloth into the shape of the box along the lines.

3. Use the wire snips to cut a 4-foot piece of 24-gauge wire. Thread the wire through the long edges of the box to join them together. Cut another piece of wire, and wire the end of the box in place.

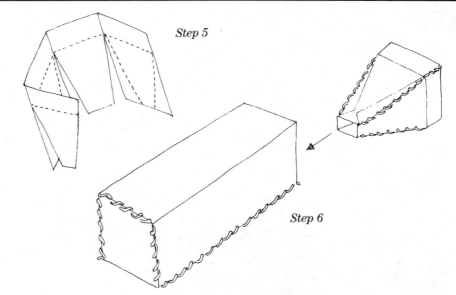

Step 5

Step 6

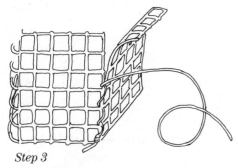

Step 3

Make the funnel:

4. The funnel through which the crayfish will enter the trap can be cut from the remaining hardware cloth. First, following the pattern, use the yardstick and the grease pencil to measure and mark the lines to be cut. Cut along those lines and trim off the sharp ends of the wire.

5. Mark the crease pattern (broken lines on the illustration), and fold the hardware cloth into a funnel shape. The large opening of the funnel should fit inside the body of the trap. The small opening should measure 4 inches wide and 1 ½ inches high.

6. Snip four 2-foot pieces of 24-gauge wire. Thread the funnel together. Push it into the open end of the trap, small opening first. Hold it in the trap with the binder clips. Attach a long string to the funnel end of the trap.

7. Bait the trap with a chicken neck or wing. Set the trap in the water, about a foot from shore, with the funnel end facing the bank. Tie the string to a stake, tree, or rock so you can find the trap again. Leave the trap in the stream overnight. Crayfish walk easily down the wide funnel ramp into the trap, but can't find the high, narrow exit.

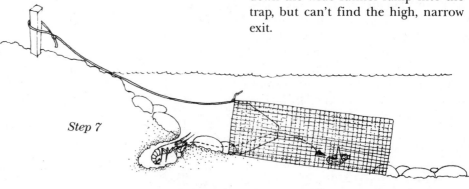

Step 7

THE RELICT

Along the Atlantic coast lives one of the world's most ancient creatures, the horseshoe crab. It is not a crab at all, but a relict from a group whose members have almost all been extinct for many millions of years. Fossil relatives include eurypterids—scorpionlike animals that may have been the reason why fish developed armor, for they shared the same river estuaries with fish, and some eurypterids grew to be 2⅔ meters (9 feet) long. Although a full-grown, 31-centimeter (1-foot) long horseshoe crab is scary looking, it's not dangerous unless you step on its upraised spike of a tail.

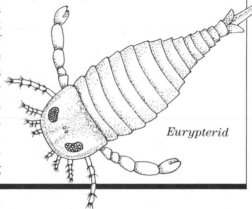

Eurypterid

Playing safe, lobsters stay inside their dens all day, coming out at night to hunt.

The lobster has no nose, but hunts by smell. If you look at a lobster closely you'll see that it is quite a hairy beast. The hairs act as more sensitive smellers than any noses known. The arrival of a single scent molecule on a single sensory hair is registered in the lobster's nervous system. Once nearby food has registered its scent profile in the lobster's front leg hairs, the legs start walking straight to the source.

Lobsters use both claws for eating. The larger claw crushes such shelly prey as clams and mussels. The smaller, nimbler one pinches up moving prey—a little crab, perhaps—and may pass it to the crusher if necessary, or pop it whole into the mouth.

The night's hunting over, the lobster heads for home and always finds it, even through the gloom of night and the confusion of a hundred other lobster homes along the way.

ONLY LADIES NEED APPLY

Lobsters don't share their homes with one another, but they do live in communities that may number several hundred dens. For some reason, they spend part of each night wandering around the neighbor-

These lobsters are only a few years old and weigh about two pounds. A lobster that escapes the hazards of being delicious may live longer than a horse and grow as big as a dog. Some live to be 40 years old, and the largest ever found had grown to a monstrous 123 centimeters (4 feet).

hood visiting one another. Maybe they like one another, or maybe it's important to know who is who and where they live for finding the way home, or for moving to better real estate when the opportunity arises.

The exception to the rule of "no visitors allowed" is when a female comes to a male's den. The purpose of her visit is always the same—she is ready to mate—and she announces her purpose with a squirt of scent molecules that say so. The male allows her to enter.

The female soon sheds. Mating can take place only during the first 30 minutes after shedding, but haste must not give way to carelessness. The female, having just stepped out of her split-down-the-back covering, is of the tender consistency of raw lobster, and just as floppy. Her suitor wears armor; his hands are claws. Still, he is able to place the female beneath him tenderly, and transfer his sperm carefully. He then protects her in his den for the week or so it takes for her new shell to harden. If she tries to leave, he firmly bars the door with his large crusher claw.

Crustaceans never left the shallow sea, but the shore that was the boundary of their wet world was only the beginning of the whole dry world beyond. As fish were swimming out to sea, arthropods were evolving variations that were to move shoreward as spiders, scorpions, millipedes, centipedes, and insects.

After nearly 3,500 million years of evolution, plants and their browsers were ready to move up out of the water onto dry land.

400 MILLION YEARS AGO

Rising Land · Greening Shores · An Invasion of Insects and Spiders

Earth has peaceful times and violent times. Seaweeds and trilobites evolved in a peaceful time. Their relatives, mosses and bugs, evolved in a violent time.

The funny thing is, if you had been around then, you would have been no more aware that anything was going on than you are now. Right now, in the Atlantic Ocean, magma is flowing up from below, creating new crust that is spreading the ocean floor apart and is pushing North America away from Europe. Africa is breaking in two. The Alps are growing. You are aware of the violence only when the crust suddenly slips, causing the ground to shake in an earthquake, or when lava erupts suddenly through a volcano. Usually the earth moves in such slow motion no creature notices. Speeded up, geology is raw drama.

Most of North America was still under water about 400 million years ago, when the ocean floor to the east bulged, then cracked. Plumes of steam and magma surged through the crack. This newborn crust shouldered the older crust aside. The ocean floor was on the move. North America stood in its way.

The oceanic crust was thinner and more supple than the continental crust. As it pushed against the continent's unbudging edge, the oceanic crust squeezed down at an angle beneath the continent. There, it melted from the pressure, spurted up as lava, and lifted overlying crust into island bulges.

Those islands rode the oceanic crust on a collision course with the continent. Too bulky themselves to cram beneath the North American continent, the islands crunched up against its edge. The edge buckled, folded, broke, and slipped inland, raising mountains as grand as the Alps and as high.

The shock of this mighty undercut was felt clear across the craton. Over the next 20 million years, as the ocean plate continued to plow under and heat up the land, the basement lifted, the shallow seas fell away, and, like some unimaginable leviathan, nearly the whole continent slowly surfaced.

The morning of Earth's history is over. The sun is climbing now toward noon. It is 400 million years ago, and America is greening.

ON THE MOVE

Earth's hot innards have driven its crusty skin restlessly across its surface for all the time in its rock-written history. The energy from that circulating heat is enormous. It has broken all the land at the surface into pieces, and driven them from one side of the Earth to the other; from the equator to the poles.

Each piece is called a plate. Some carry a thick continent on their back; others are jigsaw pieces of thin ocean floor. Some plates are huge, some quite small, and they can fuse together along their seams or break apart anywhere. At various times in the past there have been both fewer and more than the 20 plates there are today, and this number will change in the future. Right now the North American plate is breaking in two through the Great Basin in the far west. We have already named the unborn fragment: the California Plate.

A continent is merely a thick portion of a plate; its shape says nothing about the shape of the plate itself. When the ocean plate began to spread apart and undermine the land 400 million years ago, it wasn't a part of our continent. Now, our plate extends eastward all the way to the middle of the Atlantic Ocean, where, along its edge, upwelling lava is pushing America and Europe farther and farther apart.

Violence is greatest at the rifts where a plate is breaking apart, and at the seams where it is colliding with and fusing to another plate. Mount St. Helens lies along our western rift. The crust is thin there, and melted rock is bulging underneath it, and once in a while erupt-

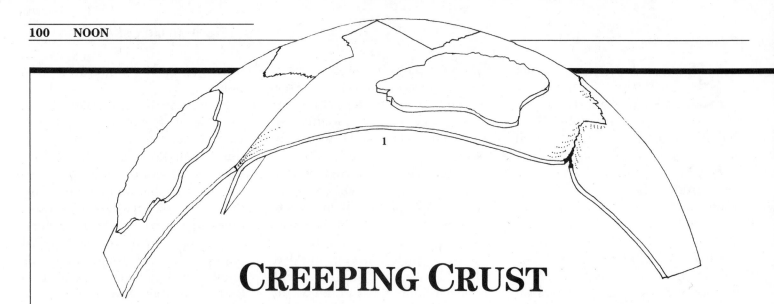

CREEPING CRUST

1. Earth is entirely covered with plates of crust. New crust rises through ridgelike seams, such as the ocean ridge shown here. At the opposite end, the plate descends back into the mantle through a trench. Here, two plates carry continents, but plates at the horizon are completely under water.

2. A plate can rift through even a thick continent. As the two pieces move apart, the land bulges, swollen by heat. In the center of the rift, slabs of land sink as their bottoms melt. Heat melts the mantle near the rift, and the molten lava seeps to the surface through cracks, where it forms pools that then harden into new rock. The lava can also burst up over the land through volcanoes. The cone of a volcano grows as the lava coming up through its center hole flows outward and hardens into rock.

3. As an oceanic plate underthrusts a continent, rock melted by friction can erupt as lava through volcanoes. Rock begins to melt at a particular depth, where it is already quite hot. Here, ocean crust is descending at such a steep angle that it reaches that depth offshore, under the continental shelf. Volcanoes arise as volcanic islands, like those of Japan.

When ocean crust plunges under a

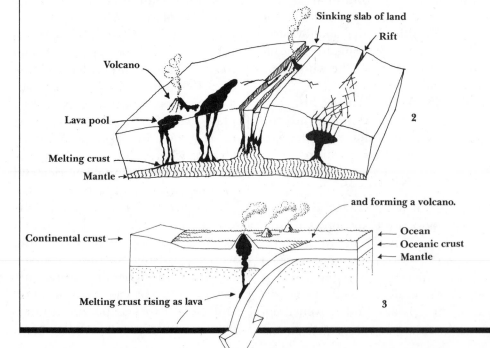

Sinking slab of land

Rift

Volcano

Lava pool

Melting crust

Mantle

2

Continental crust

and forming a volcano.

Ocean

Oceanic crust

Mantle

Melting crust rising as lava

3

continent at a shallower angle, it doesn't reach melting depth until it is below the land. In that case, volcanoes such as those in the American northwest grow inland rather than out to sea.

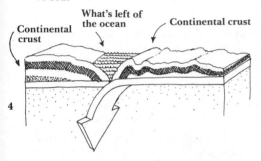

4. When the oncoming plate includes a body of land, there will be a collision like what happened between Asia and India. The ocean between them narrows, and the land, unable to squeeze into the trench, crumples.

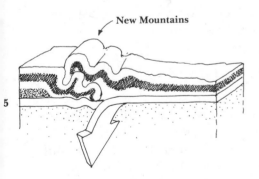

5. As the plate continues to move, land piles on land, and the continental edge is raised up into mountains like the Himalayas.

ing through to the surface. In Europe, the Alps are being raised where the piece of crust called Italy is colliding with Europe, pushing it skyward.

When ocean crust plows underneath a continent, tremendous heat is generated. Both the invading crust and the mantle below it melt. Molten lava, in turn, melts rock above, and the liquid bubbles up to the surface. It may simply flow out, or it may explode out, popping the plug of rock above it like a cork.

Wherever a column of molten lava breaks through to the surface, it solidifies into new rock. Each ooze or eruption builds another layer of rock. A crater is formed; a volcano is born. Columns of magma may rise inland, forming volcanoes like Mount St. Helens. They may rise out at sea, forming volcanic islands like Japan, or like the arc of islands that grew off the eastern shore of North America until their summit rose above the water 400 million years ago. That island arc still rode its ocean plate, no longer thin, like oceanic crust, but a great chunk that couldn't slip beneath the continent. Japan is even now riding a collision course toward the Asian mainland, but people go about their business there as calmly as trilobites conducted themselves while the whole continent was being raised and its edge was being scrunched into mountains.

BACKGROUND COLORS

The rising surface of North America was a mosaic of white, tan, gray, and black. Some of it was bare rock—black basalt belched up from deep in the crust, and the old, original gray granite. Much of the surface was sand, its color depending on where it had come from.

Florida sand is now white with fragments of shell and coral. There were vast stretches of those relics of shallow sea life even back then, and also salt stretching to the horizon where the seas had dried. Gray California sand is colored by black basalt that had flowed up in oozes, exploded up in eruptions during a more recent collision. Weathering ground the basalt to grit, and rain washed the grit down the volcano's flanks to the shore, where it mixed with paler sands and turned the beaches gray. In the east where the volcanic islands were forming, there would have been sand grayed that way with basalt, and sand like Connecticut has now, multicolored with flecks of brown feldspar and with quartz, clear and colorless, or tinted amber, peach, and pink. Quartz and feldspar are abundant in granite, and granite is what the craton is mostly made of.

A GRAIN OF SAND

Sand seen from a distance looks all the same. Close up, grains are very different from one another. Look for patches of very fine black-speckled or reddish sand. Swirl a magnet in the black-speckled sand. The dark grains are magnetite, a magnetic iron ore that will cling to the magnet or, less strongly, to anything made of iron. Red grains of sand are garnets that appear in shades from pink to ruby when viewed through a hand lens. A hand lens might also reveal grains of quartz as clear as glass, and flat crystals of sparkling mica. Some sand grains are rough edged, like broken gravel; others are rounded, like water-smoothed pebbles. Rough-edged sand is new, eroded from rock maybe 10,000 years ago. The rougher a grain of sand, the newer it is. Rounded grains of sand have had their rough edges worn off by rubbing against one another. The rounder a grain is, the older it is.

Blowing winds and falling rain scoured off the high spots of the continent and dumped the debris in the low spots. Rivers carried burdens of this eroded grit and silt thousands of miles as they carved channels and gorges through the bare rock.

What was dumped then is there now. So much of the continent has been dumped into the Gulf of Mexico by the Mississippi River that, standing on the beach there, you are perched atop 5 miles of disassembled highland. A grain of sand might be a bit of the Rocky Mountains to the west or a piece of the Smokies to the east. At the very bottom of the Gulf there may be crumbs of the great mountain ranges that grew when life was starting out. And somewhere in the middle layers are grains of 400-million-year-old America that, just then, was turning green.

THE COLOR GREEN

The green slime that you now see rimming puddles and coating rocks represents the first filaments of life to reach out to land. In that dull-colored world of 400 million years ago, algae pioneered ashore, brightening the few feet where splash of tide or spray of waterfall could keep them wet, rimming streams and ponds as though someone had out-

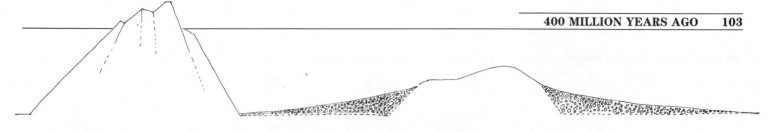

As a mountain pushes up from below, it is worn down from above. Old mountains are nearly buried in their own rubble.

lined them with a great green crayon.

To algae, life beyond a film of wet was out of the question. Bare and sprawling under the sun, they would soon have dried out even a few feet from the water. Though in time the green slime spread throughout the world, it never escaped its watered-down way of living. Green algae creeps along damp foundations, spreads along the trickle of a leaking pipe, climbs moist tree trunks, colors waterlogged shingles, and stains the shores of even smallish puddles. But algae slimes even a thousand miles from the sea live flat out in a film of water.

MOSSING OVERLAND

The first plants to work toward a way to live in drier places were the mosses which, when they are very young, look a lot like the filaments of green algae from which they are probably descended. Lay an alga on its side, let some of its filaments grow down into the ground and others grow up into the light, and you have the basic body plan of a moss plant. In fact, that is the basic body plan of all land plants: The bottom digs down into the damp, and the top protects the damp spot from drying by shading it.

The parts of a moss that reach into the ground are branches, not

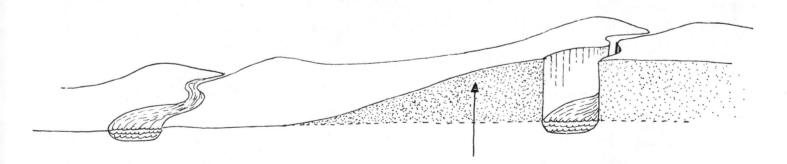

A river that cuts a gorge doesn't cut any deeper than it was originally. The land under it rises; the river stays at the same level. The lower Mississippi, for instance, meanders along through countryside that rises gradually uphill from sea level. Even during a flood, when enormous quantities of soil are washed off the surface of the land out into the Gulf of Mexico, the bed of the river remains at the same average level: It cannot cut deeper than the surface of the sea, for that is the bottom of the slope down which it flows. If, however, the coastal plain were to rise, the waters of the Mississippi, still flowing slightly downhill to sea level, would cut a gorge through the rising land.

GREEN COMPASS

Because algae can live only in a film of water, you will find it growing mostly on the north sides of rocks, trees, and walls, where the sun never shines and the damp seldom dries. You can use algae as a rough compass pointing toward the north.

roots, although they do a root's job of absorbing water and minerals. The branches that grow upright do the special job of manufacturing food. The leaflike parts that give the plant its mossy look are only one cell thick except in the very middle, and, lacking veins, pores, and layers of different kinds of cells, are much too simple to be called leaves.

Mosses must stay almost as moist as algae, and almost as low to the ground, if they are to grow. But they can get through brief dry spells by a kind of living death in which all growth stops. A place that is emerald with moss in spring may turn brown and crunch under your feet during August, only to become green again with the fall rains.

What is called "moss" should really be called "mosses." One moss is

MOSS MILK

Grow moss by planting moss spores. Look for a low-growing, carpeting type of moss covered with the short stalks to which the spore cases are attached. Use scissors to harvest a cupful of ripe spore cases. Put them in a blender, add a cup of milk, and blend thoroughly to break open the cases and release the spores. Add more milk to make a quart of moss milk. Pour this mixture into damp crevices between bricks or stones (moss will grow even in crevices filled with sand or grit instead of soil). The milk provides nourishment for the spores, but you must keep the planted places moist. The first sign of life will be a green fuzz. It will soon grow into a mossy carpet. Water the carpet during dry spells and feed it twice a summer with a liquid houseplant fertilizer. The moss will spread by itself.

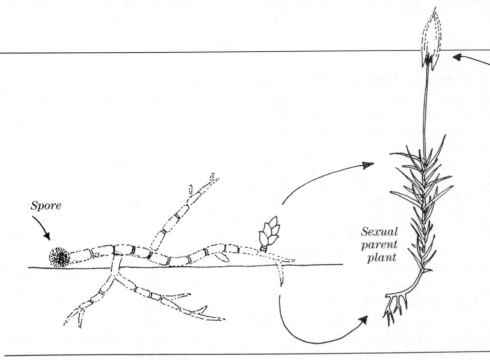

Parasitic spore plant

Spore

Sexual parent plant

A moss spore grows into a tiny plant that resembles a simple alga. Side branches that grow into the ground provide water and minerals. A bud along the main branch grows into the fuzzy moss plant that produces sperm and egg. After fertilization, an egg develops into the parasitic plant that sits atop its parent. It is the parasitic plant that produces the spores that will begin another generation of mosses.

one tuft; mosses are a group of tufts crowded against one another. Each tuft, a separate plant, is a sex organ. While you settle down on a patch of these sex organs for a rest, they are very likely sending sperm swimming about in the damp beneath you in search of eggs, which they are also making. Fertilization occurs right out there in the open, with no more protection than the film of water that gives the patch its pleasantly cool feel.

The fertilized egg has no way of moving off anywhere. It grows right on the parent moss plant. In fact, it grows into it. Each slender brown stalk, topped with a small capsule, is a separate plant grown from a fertilized moss egg, and it grows into the tuft of the green moss par-

ent from which it, like a parasite, gets most of its nourishment.

The parasitic moss plant is asexual, producing spores instead of sperm and eggs inside the capsule at its tip. The capsule opens after a time, and hundreds of very tiny, ripe spores, caught by the wind, travel overland great distances.

If it weren't for spores, mosses could not spread, nor could they survive long periods of harsh weather. The spore is encased in an amazingly tough and watertight wall that allows it to survive harsh conditions even for years. When there is at last enough moisture and warmth for growth, the spore develops into that familiar alga-like strand which, when adult, is a green and sexy moss plant.

From Fuzz to Forest

At the time when only green algae and flat mosses were exploring life on land, picture the landscape as

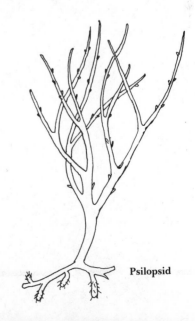

Psilopsid

VEIN PATTERNS

Leaf veins do two jobs: They carry sap, and they stiffen the leaf so that it can hold itself out flat to the sun. All sorts of vein patterns have evolved to suit the shapes of all sorts of leaves. They are usually easiest to see on the bottom side of a leaf. Interesting patterns you'd like to save can be preserved as rubbings. Lay a soft, thin paper such as a fine letter paper over the underside of the leaf and gently rub the paper with a thick, soft-leaded pencil.

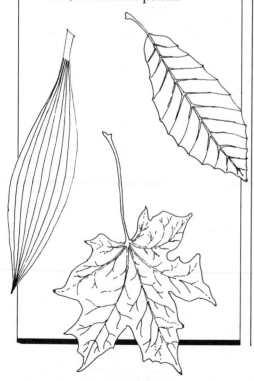

dimples and wrinkles of green fuzz wherever water collected. On flats where water dried up or on slopes where it drained away, no plant could live. In order to push any farther onto the moonscape of that time, plants would have to keep a reservoir of water inside rather than depend on a wet skin, and would have to use that water when it was available as insurance against the times when it was not.

Mosses never accomplished these improvements, and that makes a certain point about evolution. The life form that is most advanced in its own day isn't necessarily the forebear of tomorrow's winners. It was the humble green algae that once again, as it evolved into the 395-million-year-old group of plants called psilopsids, reached tentatively outward from the damp. If you could find a living psilopsid today—there is some argument about whether or not it is extinct— you would be looking at a meager thing only inches high, bare of leaves, and merely stuck, not rooted, in the soil. However, inside its branches would be the all-important reservoir of water and the tubes through which the water could reach the cells of its thickened stems. Psilopsids were the first vascular, or veined, plants.

Ten million years after the first psilopsids arrived, still another adventurous green alga pulled another first: real roots and real leaves on a really lovely plant called a club moss (which is not a relative of a moss at all). Club mosses survived, and you can find one called ground pine (or princess pine) in moist woodlands today. Ground pine, as pretty as its ancient relatives, is sometimes cut and wired into ropes and wreaths for Christmas decorations, although in some states where it is becoming rare it is protected by law and can't be cut for any purpose.

Club mosses were followed some millions of years later by horsetails, other veined, rooted, stemmed, and leaved plants that survive today. Our common horsetail is sometimes called "scouring rush," because its stem is stiffened with silica, which gives it a rough surface useful, in the days before Brillo, for scouring pots. It is also called "joint grass," because its stem is divided into segments that are neatly jointed; they can be pulled apart, then stuck together again.

Club mosses and horsetails have *merely* survived; they are not at all the grand things they once were. They were once as tall as trees are now, with trunks so hefty you could not have wrapped your arms around them.

Get down, cheek to earth, and gaze upward through a grove of

LOOKING DOWN

Look at plants from above instead of from the side to see how they are designed to trap light. The leaves of many ferns and palms fan out from the center of the plant. On other plants, each leaf may grow from the stem at a different angle so that from above they, too, form a circle in which no leaf shades another. A fir or spruce tree, cone-shaped from the side, looks like layers of circles from above. Each circle is smaller than the one below it, so all of the branches are laid out in the light. Elm branches spread their leaves to the light by arching outward like a fountain, and even the mighty oaks arrange their branches in a spiral around the trunk—that way, no branch leaves another in the dark.

The club mosses and horsetails of today are miniature versions of plants that once grew into towering forests.

Horsetail   **Club moss**

ground pine or horsetails. From this ant's-eye view you can get some idea of what it might have been like to see the world's first forests.

The word forest is no exaggeration. Horsetails and club mosses grew thickly together and spread over vast areas. Horsetail roots reached many yards into the soil.

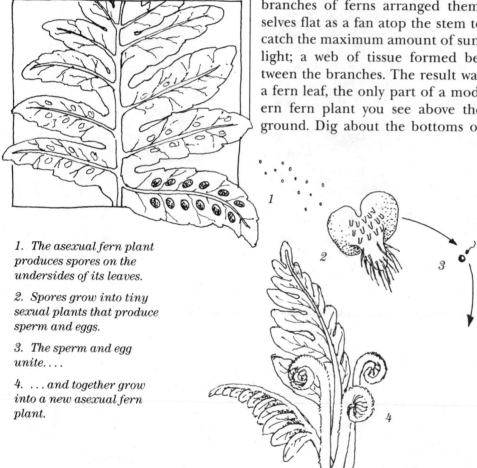

1. The asexual fern plant produces spores on the undersides of its leaves.

2. Spores grow into tiny sexual plants that produce sperm and eggs.

3. The sperm and egg unite....

4. ...and together grow into a new asexual fern plant.

The scant shade you can see under today's pitiful remnants was nevertheless the first shade barren shores had known.

LEAFING OUT

Plants marching inland and upland changed as they went. Psilopsids, some think, evolved into ferns, the first plants with leaves. The branches of ferns arranged themselves flat as a fan atop the stem to catch the maximum amount of sunlight; a web of tissue formed between the branches. The result was a fern leaf, the only part of a modern fern plant you see above the ground. Dig about the bottoms of spreading (rather than clumping) ferns, and you can easily see the stem lying on or just below the soil surface. The stems of some ancient ferns didn't sprawl like that; they grew up out of the ground treelike, and tree-size. Like the few tropical tree ferns still alive now, they stood like feather dusters on trunks as tall as palm trees spreading out their broad leaves to grab more sunlight than any other plant around.

The fern plants everyone is familiar with are as asexual as the parasitic phase of a moss plant and, like them, produce spores. The spores are contained in the brown dots you can find on the undersides of fern leaves, and it is they that, after a wind-blown journey to a favorable moist spot, grow into the sexual plants. These bitty, heart-shaped sexual fern plants are all around you in the forest, but they are dots of green no bigger than a fingernail, and so they are seldom noticed. The sexual plant, like the mosses' sexual tuft, produces eggs as well as flagellated sperm that swim to the eggs through a film of water. But fern sperm have a less hazardous swim than moss sperm. The sexual plant lies flat on damp soil; fertilization of the eggs takes place on the underside, where, swimming all the way, the sperm can reach their target before drying out.

MUSHROOM MYSTERY

Mushrooms are funguses, and funguses are strange. They don't belong to the plant or the animal kingdoms; they are so different from other forms of life that they are a kingdom of their own. Some funguses, such as baker's yeast and brewer's yeast, are one celled. Most grow as long strands of many cells laid end to end. A mushroom cap is a bunch of those strands packed tightly together. Underground, the strands spread through the soil. Dig anywhere in the woods, or lift the bark from rotting logs. You'll see thready white or yellow strands of fungus reaching in every direction.

The strands, called hyphae, digest. They release enzymes that disassemble organic materials outside the fungus, and then they absorb what they have digested, along with water and minerals. Mold funguses digest every kind of human food—and shoes, shower curtains, books, pipe insulation, paint, wax, and even diesel fuel.

Nothing grows like a fungus. A single individual can grow a kilometer (.6 mile) of new strands every 24 hours. Mold can fuzz basement walls in a day. Crops of mushrooms can spring up overnight. The mushroom cap you pluck and the tiny dots atop mold fuzz are the funguses' fruiting bodies, short-lived structures that make spores for a few days, and then disintegrate. Put a mushroom cap on a piece of paper for a couple of hours. When you lift it you will see a dusty pattern of the millions of spores it has dropped. Each one can grow into a new fungus.

The oldest fossils that might be fungus spores are from way back when algae first began, 900 million years ago. No one knows what they evolved from. Fungus cells are coated with chitin, as are shrimp shells and beetle wings, not with the cellulose that stiffens seaweed and celery. They do not have the cilia or flagella that most one-celled creatures and all multicellular ones have. In some funguses, there are no separations between cells. Their jellylike inside flows freely, like the inside of an ameba. There can be many nuclei within the jelly, and strangest of all, completely different sets of genes within those nuclei, as though the fungus were strangers come to live together.

Even this smart method of protecting the sexual generation is quite limited. The farther up you climb from streambed or bog, the rarer ferns become until, where soil is quite dry, there are apt to be no ferns at all.

THE INVASION OF THE CRAWLERS

The giant club moss, horsetail, and tree fern forests that flourished by about 380 million years ago were stuck in wet lowlands. The forests were more like the Everglades of Florida than a woodland you could stroll through. Flatlands all through Pennsylvania, Ohio, and westward were swamp, pond, puddle, and muck. You would have squished and slogged your way along—swatting at bugs.

With all the creepy crawlies that inhabited the ancient waters, it shouldn't be surprising that some of these followed the green algae onto land. The scum was, after all, the same meadow browsers ate in the water, and it was there for anyone inventive enough to reach it. Once browsers had emerged, predators were sure to follow them.

These first land-dwelling animals were all arthropods: scorpions and their kin, the spiders; centipedes, millipedes, and insects. All were better equipped for life ashore than plants were.

Whereas pioneer algae could not stand up to gravity and held no water, arthropods had been hollow water containers for ages, and their chitin shell (called a cuticle in insects) supported their bodies at the same time that it kept them from drying out. If the going got dry, arthropods could crawl back into the bath; their larvae, less well-covered than the parents, probably stayed in the water until adulthood. The problem of a safe swim path for sperm had been solved long before these creatures ventured onto land: Like lobsters, males passed their sperm directly into females.

One thing, however, each pioneer arthropod had to discover on its own: how to breathe in the air. Most terrestrial arthropods have evolved an intricate system of tubes called tracheae, which take in air through valved holes in the cuticle and deliver oxygen to every cell in the body. (Some have a different system, or even two systems; many spiders breathe with external organs called book lungs, others have both book lungs and tracheae.)

The various groups of arthropods did not inherit their breathing system from one another. By the time spiders, centipedes, millipedes, and insects had climbed out

THE SNEEZING TRUTH

Many people think they are allergic to feathers, and so they sleep on "nonallergenic" pillows stuffed with synthetic foam or fibers. These are not squeezably soft, and maybe their users would really prefer a feather pillow if only it didn't make them stuffy and sneezy. In fact, they are more likely allergic to a microscopic mite that eats skin scales. Skin scales are shed in great quantity every day, mostly in the bedroom, where people dress, undress, towel, brush, toss and turn, and otherwise scruff off their outer layer. The mites live in any bedroom dust, but prefer pillows and mattresses, where skin scales accumulate.

One can be desensitized to a mite allergy, or one can clean bedding and pillows with a hand vacuum daily. Then maybe one can again sleep softly as well as sneezelessly.

of the water, they were already very different from one another, and each group had invented breathing tubes on its own. Given a similar challenge, each of these creatures met it in the same way indepen-

WEB HUNT

The messy sort of spiderweb called a cobweb is easy to find indoors high up in corners and along the ceiling, where it often becomes tattered with age and covered with dust. The occupant does not actually live in its web, but prefers to hide in a nearby crack. The spider is small, spindly, and pale.

Spiders that spin neat, funnel-shape webs are more rugged looking. The web may be in the corner of a window frame (probably outside rather than inside), tucked into a rock wall, within a bush, or nestled low in tall grasses. The spider lives deep in the central part of the funnel, usually out of sight. Often it can be tricked into an appearance by tickling the outer edge of the web with a stalk of grass to mimic the vibrations of an alighting insect. If that trick doesn't work, dropping a fly-size live insect into the web certainly will.

The most beautiful webs are the round ones called orb webs. Look for them early in the morning in meadow or woodland before their owners eat them up. Their whereabouts is advertised in sparkling dew. Orb weavers are elegant, large-bodied, long-legged spiders. They are often prettily marked. A few stay in touch with the radiating threads of their web by remaining motionless at the very center. Others feel for the vibrations of trapped prey along a master thread leading off to one side, where they wait in hiding. Try the tickle trick or a small, live insect. The route the spider uses to investigate is made of non-sticky threads. All the other threads are strung with globs of glue visible through a hand lens.

The web of an orb weaver.

dently of the others. A spider today may breathe the same way as a fly, although the two are as distantly related to one another as each is to a trilobite.

HUNTERS SINCE BUGS BEGAN

Long before any of the arthropods had ventured ashore, spiders hunted down insects. That's what they stalked in the water; that's what they devoured among ancient moss and ferns; that's what they eat all over the world today. There are no spiders who are not hunters, and the largest pounce on mice.

Spiders are among the very few creatures on earth who bring down prey larger than themselves. To do this requires either cooperative hunting parties, like those of wolves and men, or ingenious weapons, like those of men—and spiders. All spiders use poison fangs. Whether a spider you find is no bigger than the head of a pin or as large as your big toe, it kills its prey by injecting the prey with a paralyzing poison through its hollow fangs.

Some spiders pounce upon their prey from ambush, others stalk their game, but most spiders snare the insect before killing it. The creating of the silk used to build snares is a whole industry. It can be manufactured as glue-beaded strands for trapping prey, or plain strands for the spider itself to walk upon. Some spiders eat damaged webbing to recycle its proteins. The recycled raw materials are respun into new traps, additional rope to tie up a victim, lining for a burrow, air balloons for breathing under water or rising into the sky, wrapping for eggs, safety harnesses with which to drop out of danger, or kite string on which to ride the breeze to a new location.

All this can easily be watched. Infant spiders off to set up housekeeping and males on the prowl for a mate unfurl their "kite string" in front of your eyes. A female who has built her web in a window frame can be watched by lamplight as she lays and wraps her eggs at night. A fresh web stretched between grass blades one night will be eaten up by midday and rebuilt by nightfall. To watch the action of the hunt itself, you need patience. There are so many insects in the world that few spiders bother to run about after them. Their hunting is a waiting game.

JERRY-RIGGED WORMS

There are more species of insects than there are of all other creatures put together. And there is more odd paraphernalia among these species than science fiction could

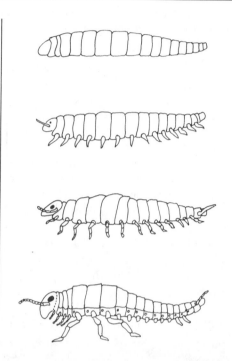

What were originally legs in a worm have evolved into antennae, mouthparts, and reproductive equipment in insects. In an insect, the first six segments have fused into a head. The next three segments still bear legs; they have fused into the chest, or thorax. Rear segments have lost their worm legs, except those at the hind end, which are specially shaped for transferring sperm, laying eggs, or stinging. Occasionally a mutation occurs that reveals insects' wormy past: An insect will hatch with a pair of legs on its head where antennae ought to be.

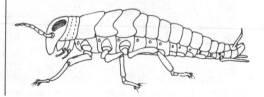

concoct. Insects have appendages that allow them to walk, leap, fly, bite, grab, bore, suck, sip, spin, squirt, inject, and lay eggs. This extraordinary variety of parts, evolved from the ancient worm of their very distant past, has enabled insects to take up ways of life that absolutely boggle the mind.

The ancestors of the insects (and of other arthropods) probably resembled the marine worms of today. Their bodies were composed of many identical segments. In the insects, the segments gradually changed and fused into three distinct body parts, each of which does a particular job. At the front is the head, which has a mouth and keeps in touch with the world through major sense organs. In the middle is the thorax, or chest, which specializes in locomotion. To the rear is the abdomen, which contains digestive and reproductive organs. The marine worms had spread-out nerves; nerves in the insects are bunched together into three centers, each serving its own body part.

The ancestral worms had a pair of legs on each body segment. Slowly, of course, insects developed joints in their legs and rigged them into every sort of appendage a mad inventor could dream up. At the front, they were reshaped into biting and sucking parts as various as the curlable sipping straw of the

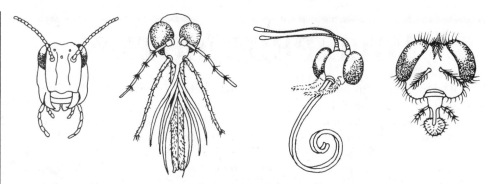

This rogue's gallery of insects shows how different mouths can be. From left to right: The grasshopper has sawtooth jaws from chewing, the mosquito pierces for its supper, the butterfly straightens its curled straw to sip its food, and the vulgar fly simply sponges.

CREEPY CRAWLIES

In the Catskill Mountains, where thousands now vacation in summer resorts, were found the oldest known fossils of land-living Americans. They are: a daddy longlegs sort of spiderlike creature; some inch-long centipedes complete with all their legs; a single mite; and one tiny fragment that might have been a silverfish. They all lived when princess pine first grew, 380 million years ago.

If that fragment is actually a fossil of a silverfish, then the silverfish is the oldest true insect known. You can still find descendants of this wingless little fellow living between cracks in basements and bathrooms, even in the Catskills.

Silverfish enlarged

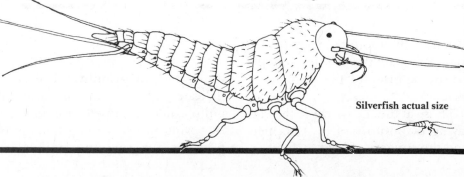

Silverfish actual size

MILLIPEDE MOTION

The word "millipede" means "thousand legs." This common arthropod does not live up to its name; still, with two pairs of legs per segment, it has a lot of legs to move. How does it keep from stumbling? Lift rocks in damp woodland to find a millipede. It will curl into a spiral at first, and may take a few minutes to uncurl and creep away. Watch the legs. They move in a wave that starts at the front and proceeds toward the rear. The wave of movement is controlled by a nerve signal sent down the body from the brain. As the signal reaches each segment, the legs there step. By the time the first signal has traveled only a fraction of an inch, the next signal from the brain is starting another wave rearward, another step forward. There is no other kind of message to a leg; either it is stepping, or it is still. Millipedes don't stumble because they can't send mixed messages.

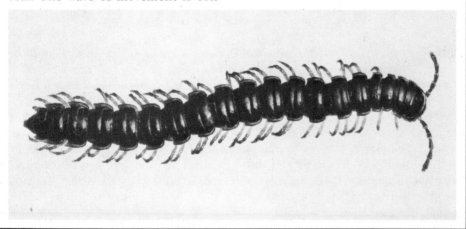

bumblebees, are tipped with suction cups in houseflies, and are bent into fearsomely toothy claws in the preying mantis.

That's an example of how ingenious evolution is. New body parts are made by revamping old ones, so that whether what sticks out from an insect walks, bites, or lays an egg, it is only a newfangled leg. Occasionally, mutations undo these transformations and then, like a spell lifted, the appendage is revealed as what it was: The insect grows legs where its mouth parts ought to be, or it grows legs on

butterfly, the toothy pincers (called mandibles) of the beetle, and the poison squirter of the soldier termite.

Those at the rear became the egg-laying ovipositors of grasshoppers and the stingers of bees.

Even the three limb pairs in the thorax that are used for walking didn't remain primitive. They are delicate and very long in the mosquito, come equipped with an elastic spring in the leaping flea, have pouches for carrying pollen in every segment of its abdomen, where there have been none since bugs began.

TAKING WING

It was already amid an abundance of wonderful appendages that the first land animals crawled out of the swamp. Walking along bottom-lands, over moss-covered ground between the trunks of tree ferns, you would have stomped on herds of silverfish—mere bathtub dwell-ers now—and crunched scorpions underfoot. Millipedes would have curled in their damp haunts under fallen horsetails, and spiders high-stepped delicately among fronds of princess pine. A cockroach might have scuttled by. The equator then ran from San Diego through New England. Most of the land was a muggy, marshy place—perfect for dragonflies, you might say, and so it was.

By 320 million years ago, insects were aloft. Insect wings grew from the locomotion-specialized thorax. They seem to have sprouted from mere flaps on the thorax, but how or why remains a mystery. Mayflies had them, and danced above the water then as they do now. One dragonfly wore them with a ven-geance: its wings were 30 inches from tip to tip. Most insects that didn't evolve wings became extinct. Today, only a very few of the most primitive insects—including the wingless silverfish—are unable to take to the air.

WATER BABIES

Primitive insects such as dam-selflies, dragonflies, and may-flies lay their eggs in water, as the first insects did. Their babies, called na-iads, spend their youth in the water and breath with gills, which sprout from their rear or along their sides, as the ancestors of insects must have done. As they grow, they shed their stiff skin, just like other arthropods do. With the final molt, they emerge from the water full-grown, winged, breathing air, and ready to reproduce.

But they have not grown very large. There have been giant trilobites, eu-rypterids, crabs, and lobsters. Why no giant insects?

The problem is their air-breathing system. Each cell of a terrestrial ar-thropod's body has to be supplied with oxygen directly from an air-transporting tube. Thick tissues, in which cells are heaped atop one an-other, can't be reached. The biggest insect there has ever been was a drag-onfly whose wings spanned 76 centi-meters (30 inches). Its thin body might have been a solution. The larg-est terrestrial arthropod now is skimpy scorpion-size; any thicker and it would suffocate. Those giant hor-nets in scary movies are not possible.

THE LORE OF THE LURE

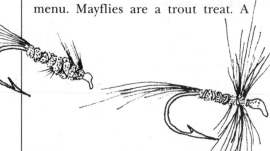

A trout "fly" is more than a gaudy fake. Trout learn what foods are good to eat at various times of the year, and won't snap at strange or out-of-season foods. Fishermen match their flies to that day's—sometimes that hour's—natural menu. Mayflies are a trout treat. A fisherman may tempt a trout with a breakfast of fake mayfly naiad, a "wet" fly made to sink into the stream. As the day warms, naiads molt and begin to leave the water as small-winged young adults. The fisherman switches to a "dry" fly with perky tufts of wing that skims the stream surface where trout are madly snapping up the real thing. By the following day, mayflies have undergone a final molt, mated, and are falling back exhausted into the stream where they will lay their eggs and die. Fishermen now tie a droopy, "spent" mayfly to lure the hungry trout.

In Ancient Company

In this book, "primitive" doesn't mean crude, simple, stupid, backward, or any of the other insulting meanings for which the word is commonly used. Primitive simply refers to an organism's position in time. The more primitive an insect, the earlier its origins and the more similar it is to the first insects.

Termites are primitive insects that evolved along with cockroaches from a common ancestor. The most primitive of the 2,000 species of surviving termites will eat anything organic, including rubber, leather, hair, ivory, and plastic (plastic is organic; it's made from petroleum, which was originally plants). None of these products was available until a hundred million years after termites began to chew. They spent the time consuming woody debris, and that is still the main course.

A termite, however, is not able to digest its own food. Digesting is done by protozoans and bacteria that spend their lives inside the termite's gut. A termite that lives in the Southwest harbors no less than 500 species of microorganisms—about a billion individuals per termite. Some of the species are unknown in the outside world; they exist only in the termite's gut, and can't survive beyond it.

This can only mean that some one-celled critters, at least, have been there an awfully long time. Perhaps they were just passing through the gut and stayed for dinner; perhaps they were parasites who knew better than to harm their host. By now, these microorganisms have gone much further than simply inhabiting a new niche. They have created a world.

It's a Small World

The species of microorganisms living in the termite all contribute to a balanced economy. Some secrete the enzymes that digest wood, providing nourishment for themselves, for their host termite, and for their fellow protozoans. Others literally provide atmosphere by expelling needed gases into their world, or by ridding their world of toxic wastes. One provides transportation for another: The main cellulose digester, a large zeppelin of a protozoan, is propelled along by several thousand tiny bacteria that arrange themselves in spiralled rows over its surface, all twirling their flagellae in unison. That's just a glimpse of what goes on inside the primitive termite.

Termites hark back to the good old days before insects had fancy stages of life. A "baby" butterfly is a caterpillar, but baby termites hatch from the egg looking pretty much like adult termites, except they are smaller and have buds where their wings will grow. As these nymphs grow, they shed their skins many times. Their wings develop fully after the last molt.

To grow, an infant termite must eat. To eat, it must have its company of little microorganisms inside. The termite is not born with them: they must be swallowed when offered from the rear end of another termite. Some of the protozoans and bacteria that now live in termites have been handed down anus to mouth in every termite generation for a couple of hundred million years. In fact, the most primitive termite can exchange protozoans with the most primitive cockroach by the same method, and the ancestors of those protozoan species may well have been passed down the same way from one of the very first insect species to walk the earth.

Join the Club

Because termites die of starvation if they are deprived of their inner life, they must live communally, and exchange microorganisms at least at every molt. This need to live in "eating clubs" apparently led to the incredible social lives of termites today.

A social life can only happen when individuals perform services that are needed by others and that will be returned either in kind, such as when individuals mutually exchange a digestive zoo, or in some other currency, as the zoo itself exchanges food for fresh air or waste disposal. If a creature can do everything by itself, it has no need to be social and never is. The earliest termites were only in the first stage of social evolution. As in a school of fish, all members of the group were similar, and all offered to others the same service each got in return.

Unlike fish, however, termite-to-termite communication is necessarily intimate. Today it includes mouth-to-mouth exchange and licking of one another's bodies as well as anal feeding. With each mouthful of one another's body products come the very chemicals that make a termite tick. Those chemicals evolved into the code of conduct on which modern termite society is based.

NO-NO'S

Using only this chemical code, termites develop into castes, or types, that are very different in appearance, in behavior, and in the services they offer. The code is a negative one: A dose of a chemical says what *not* to be and do. At the lowest dosage, an individual develops into a winged adult. It hasn't been told

JUNGLE BEASTS

Cockroaches live for the most part where they evolved, amidst the damp and edible litter of the jungle floor. Those species that have moved in with us live amidst edible litter in warm, moist cellars, steamy bathrooms, and humid kitchens. Cockroaches haven't had to change to move in with us. We give them little jungles to enjoy.

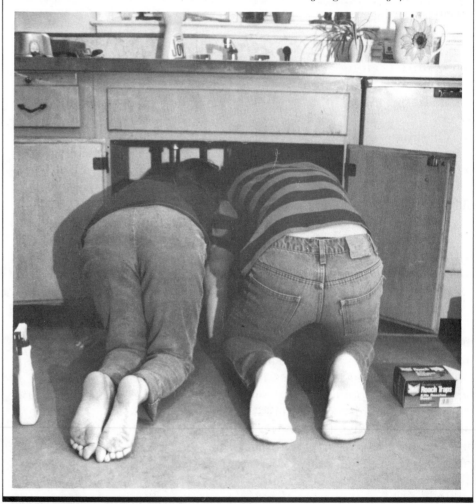

not to, so it does. Winged males and females of this reproductive caste fly off and choose a mate. The couple land, snap their wings off, and copulate. The two then dig into the ground to build a small egg gallery and raise the first generation of workers.

The sons and daughters of that mating will be a new community. When the eggs hatch, the nymphs turn to the parents for their various body products. Among them is a chemical that says "no" to growing up. The nymphs will grow to a good size but remain wingless and childless. They are the second caste, the workers. As their mother and father continue to reproduce, all offspring receive their dose of no-no message—until there are so many nymphs that some don't get a large enough dose. Those underdosed nymphs are not told not to grow so they will grow up and become winged and sexually mature. They will start new colonies.

The sterile sons and daughters of the first brood are all workers. They perform a host of services, including feeding and grooming their mother, caring for her eggs, expanding the nest into new passageways and galleries, controlling its temperature by opening and closing ventilation shafts, obtaining food, feeding youngsters, and exchanging their own body chemi-

ODD BODIES

Termites have come a long way from their cockroach ancestor. Workers and soldiers have no wings. The queen's wings are used only once, when she flies from the nest to mate. Then they fall off, and only the broken stubs remain. Her huge abdomen is filled with eggs.

Two kinds of soldiers are shown here. The one with the giant pinching jaws slashes and crushes intruders. Some are blockheaded, too; they use their enlarged head to butt entrance holes shut. The soldier with the bulbshape head squirts a chemi-cal concoction at intruders; another kind of soldier has a nozzle like a paintbrush with which it daubs chemicals onto an enemy's surface, or into wounds. The chemical may be a horrid-tasting or evil-smelling stuff, or it may be an irritant, blood thinner, glue, solvent, or downright poison.

Strangely, soldiers' weapon-heads make them the most helpless members of termite society. They have no eating mouthparts, and must be fed by workers.

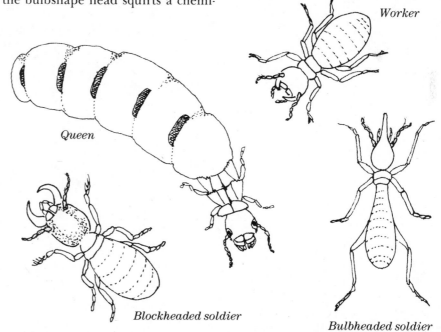

Worker

Queen

Blockheaded soldier

Bulbheaded soldier

cals. Before long, however, some of the nymphs in later broods will develop into a third caste, the soldiers.

Again, it is the scarcity of an inhibiting chemical produced by the mother that allows soldiers to develop. As her colony reaches a certain size, and there is less of the substance to go around, the nymph that gets the least of it will continue its development into a soldier. More soldiers develop as the colony continues to grow bigger. Soldiers themselves produce the inhibiting substance, so that as they fall in battle and their chemical contribution is lost, nymphs that would otherwise have remained workers become soldiers. In this no-saying way the proportion of each of the three termite castes is kept always the same.

Living this way, a colony of termites can survive with its original mother for more than half a century. How's that for primitive?

Primitive but advancing fast, creeping at first but flying soon, insects quickly pulled ahead of all other arthropods. They became, as they are still, the most numerous, varied, beautiful, awful, valuable, destructive—and amazing—animals there have ever been.

At the time of the swaying fern forests, however, many of the insects that now swarm, buzz, and flutter had not evolved. There were no pollen bearing plants, nor any flies or bees to eat pollen. There were no flowers, no nectar, and no butterflies to sip it. And other insects were missing, too.

Dung-eating beetles were absent. Who would have provided the dung? Carrion-eating beetles weren't around yet either: no corpses. Nor were there biting flies or blood-sucking mosquitos. There wasn't anyone to bite. There were no animals bigger than an insect in the first forests. The fiercest predator was simply a spider.

300 MILLION YEARS AGO

The Collision of Pangea · Coal Forests · Watertight Trees · Furry Reptiles

Mountains aren't forever. By 300 million years ago, rain and wind had worn down the alpine ranges in the East. The landscape was soft curves: rounded hills that had been mountains, rolling dunes that had been rock, and meandering rivers flowing gently by.

Standing then on the bare uplands of New York, you would not have seen the seascape of today—you would have seen Europe. The old ocean plate, still moling along, had carried the whole continent to our shore. That continent had met this continent in a collision that shook both to their roots.

They had approached like the blades of scissors, meeting first to the north, then closing against one another southward until they were smack against one another, with no more ocean between. Along the wound gigantic mountains rose again. They are the various ranges of the Appalachian system, oldest in the north, youngest in the south. Great chunks of rock were broken loose and shoved miles inland. North America warped into bulges and basins throughout its width; great chunks of it were lifted and tilted from east to west. Europe and North America became a supercontinent called Laurasia.

There was more to come. Up from the south another supercontinent—Gondwanaland—was plowing northward. Pieces of Gondwanaland are today South America, Africa, Australia, and Antarctica. Siberia, perhaps already glommed onto the northwest coast of North America, sutured with Europe along its free side, pushing up the Ural Mountains, while various microcontinents sailed into it, completing most of what is now Asia.

By 225 million years ago, every major land mass was the logjam of continents called Pangea, which means "all lands." All around Pangea spread a single ocean called Panthalassa, which means "all seas." Had you been around, you could have walked from Antarctica to Siberia, and from California to China. Land was everywhere—and now there were footprints on it.

FOOTPRINTS IN THE MUD OF TIME

For a hundred million years after the first collision of continents, the sea periodically rose and fell. There were dry times when the entire West was a dune desert like the drifting sand fields of Mars, and wet times when the West was a low-lying marshland criss-crossed with freshwater streams. When the sea was at its highest, the only large land areas were the new mountain ranges; the rest of Pangea was a dotting of islands. When the sea was at its lowest, most of Pangea was high and dry.

For the teeming life that had evolved during the previous eras of the greatest shallow seas the world has ever known, these were hard times. There were wholesale extinctions of creatures unable to live in fresh water or in stagnant water, or who were stranded as ponds dried to puddles, and puddles to mud.

Lurching along in just such puddly places were lobefin fishes. First their finprints, then their footprints, left in the mud of Pangea.

A FISHY LESSON

The lobefins' rise from mucky bottom to muddy shore is an example of what's called pre-adaptation. These fish evolved into amphibians—animals that spend part of their lives in water, part on land—not because they were able to change drastically, but because they hardly had to change at all.

They lived in stagnant water, and they kept their primitive lungs. Instead of mere dimples for nostrils, a lobefin had nostrils that penetrated clear through into their mouth, and were used for breathing. That was an invention, but not for land life. Nostrils simply allowed these fish to breath close-mouthed in murky bottoms, where a mouthful of water meant a mouth full of mud.

Lagoon

Ocean

Reef

Continent

OLD SALT

Sprinkle salt on your food and taste the sea over Pangea. Your table salt is probably the actual salt that was in that water. Salt accumulates behind great barrier reefs built by coral animals. A barrier reef forms a dam between the sea and the shore. The basin of water behind a barrier reef, called a lagoon, is like a gigantic tidal pool. Waves from the open sea slosh salty water over the reef into the lagoon. There the water is trapped. As water evaporates, salt becomes more concentrated, and the lagoon becomes much brinier than the sea. When the sea level fell over Pangea, the brine dried up in lagoons near what is now Chicago. The huge quantity of salt left behind is now Morton's salt, a genuine antique.

They got themselves through gluey ooze on stoutly boned and muscled fins. It was already their habit to heave themselves upon the weedy shore when ponds shrank during dry spells. They already knew how to nibble their way through thickets of horsetails, pond to pond.

An organism can't move into a new environment and then evolve to suit it, for its life would be snuffed out in days, whereas evolution takes thousands of years. What has suited it to its accustomed lifestyle must in advance suit it for a life-style that is not detectably different, but is becoming so. An organism undergoing evolution remains entirely unaware of it; it is only living its life.

Every life, however, is continued by many offspring that carry its genes into the next generation, or is continued by only a few, or is not continued at all. The sheer arithmetic of what works and what doesn't work constitutes evolution.

The stuff of evolution is inherited variation, and the force that drives it is selection.

Variation simply means the differences among individuals; the more ways in which they differ from one another, the more variation—the more raw material—there is to select from.

Selection is the circumstances under which one individual has a

ALPHABET SOUP

Get an idea of how selection works by playing Mother Nature with dried alphabet noodles. Throw all the letters into a paper bag. They represent all the characteristics in a population of fish. You play the part of nature.

Pick four letters at a time out of the bag. Throw back into the bag any O, G, F, or R that you find. Those letters stand for characteristics that help these fish survive. Cast any other letters aside; they stand for characteristics that aren't useful or are harmful. Little by little, you will get rid of bad traits and concentrate good ones in the bag. Sooner or later, a draw of four letters will happen to spell FROG. You didn't plan it that way; neither did nature plan for fish to evolve into amphibians.

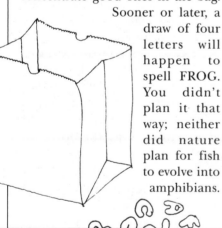

better chance of spreading its genes through descending generations than another individual. Natural selection works only on individuals. The spread of a helpful characteristic to other members of the species living at the same time isn't necessary for that characteristic to evolve and doesn't happen. Individuals that don't have the new characteristic simply leave fewer descendants than individuals that do have the new characteristic. Unfortunately, we cannot go back in time to keep breeding records of which individual lobefin fishes had the most children, grandchildren, and great grandchildren. We can only suppose a sensible story, in which individual lobefins who had stronger limbs than others were selected by the circumstance of a drying climate. We imagine they could go farther between ponds, and get more to eat, live longer, and have more babies. Each baby, a unique individual, would also have been subjected to natural selection. Evolution begins anew with each individual that is born.

The lobefins had in each fin a single long bone surrounded by a number of shorter bones. Any mutation or regrouping of genes that lengthened that central bone or spread the smaller bones apart was an improvement: that individual's fins had a broader "walking" surface and a firmer structure. In each generation there were more and more individuals with this characteristic because those fins-becoming-feet gave a reproductive advantage to their possessor. As long as there were droughts, this evolutionary track continued, until finprints were footprints, and fish were amphibians. Although lobefin fish do exist today, there are not many of them, but any pond is ker-plunk with frogs.

THE MYSTERY OF THE MISSING LINKS

If evolution happens only by the accumulation of thousands of tiny changes, so that the transformation from one kind of creature to another takes as long as millions of years, one should be able to find all the steps preserved in the fossil record. That sometimes happens. But more often the fossils of a creature's ancestors continue unchanged for eons; then suddenly the "new" creature's fossil appears. Where are the missing links, the fossil creatures that are somewhat different from the ancestor, but not yet quite like the descendant?

They may be there still waiting to be found, or they may be genuinely missing. Gaps in the fossil record happen when organisms live in areas where their bodies rot before

YOUR EVOLUTIONARY ADDRESS

O ver a million species of living animals, 325,000 species of plants, and even greater numbers of organisms that are neither plant nor animal are known. To "place" so many species, each has been given an evolutionary "address." The human evolutionary address (here written casually rather than scientifically) is:

Animal Kingdom
 Chordate Phylum
  Vertebrate Subphylum
  Mammal Class
   Primate Order
    Hominid Family
     Homo Genus
      sapiens Species
      Homo sapiens Species

The address lets you know how related you are to another organism whom you know only by address. If both you and a stranger are in the animal kingdom, you are more related to one another than either of you is to a carrot, even if the stranger is a clam. If you share the same phylum, you are closer still—both of you have a stiffened spine, even if one of you is a fish (if you share the vertebrate subphylum, as you and fish do, the stiffening is a backbone formed of vertebrae). Class gets pretty chummy; in your class, every species produces milk. Order is more intimate still—

the primate order includes mammals with thumbs, from marmoses and monkeys to gorillas and us. Unhappily, when you look for members of your own hominid family, you will find none: They are all extinct. The

same is true of your genus, *Homo*. Those who once shared your genus were human, but all except us are known only as fossils. Our closest relatives of all are in the species *Homo sapiens,* ourselves.

"The evolutionary 'address' of domestic cats and man are identical from kingdom to class, but differ from there on. The genus name is used as the first name of the species, so that a pet cat is Felis catus *while its wild ancestor is* Felis sylvestris, *or just the initial is used, as in* F. catus *or* H. (for Homo) sapiens.*"

they can be fossilized (that is most areas on Earth), or where the rock in which their fossils are embedded later erodes to dust (that is most of all areas where fossils once formed). If the number of fossils today are even one-billionth of the organisms that have lived, every stone would contain an imprint of vanished life.

Of course, the slower evolution occurs, the better is the chance of catching it in the stop-action of a fossil. Think of a movie. If the movie is very long, but hasn't much of a plot, you might be able to understand the story from a very few still photographs chosen from the thousands of frames in the reel. If the story moves fast, you would need many more still photographs to understand the plot. Evolution is usually so slow that one picture—one fossil—every few million years is enough to get the meaning of its plot. But occasionally evolution moves so fast—in thousands, not millions, of years—that "in between" fossils are very rare, or even nonexistent. Then the action seems to be as jumpy as a James Bond

movie, and new species appear as abruptly as the twists and turns of a spy thriller.

Rapid evolution is possible when a small group is promptly and completely cut off from the larger population. In a large population, where anyone can breed with anyone, rare genes are swamped by the more common ones. As long as circumstances remain the same, a quirky bit of DNA offers no advantage to an individual already getting along just fine. For that reason a species can go on and on in the same dull way for millions of years. The lobefin fish of today are not very different from those of their ancestors who stayed together in places where droughts were not severe.

But if a few individuals get trapped away from their fellows, and the place where they are trapped makes demands on them, quirks may come in handy. Rare genes and brand new ones spread

down through the generations. New species arise from strange individuals too fast to leave telltale fossils behind them.

FISH AFOOT

The first amphibians looked like nothing more than fish on feet. Those feet, sticking out sideways just as fins had before them, could barely lift the animals off the ground. Amphibians belly-dragged along the muddy shore. Their teeth were like fish teeth, evenly sized points all along the jaw that were no good for chewing. They pulled weeds and bolted down each mouthful whole, or snapped up insects and bolted them down whole. The slippery mucus that helps fish slip through the water also protected the first amphibians from drying. Even modern amphibians, though they are far less fishlike than their ancestors, still carry their fishy past within them.

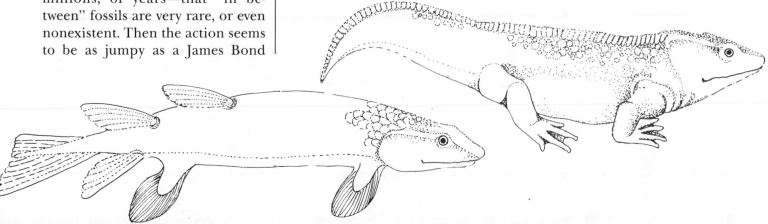

JELLY EGGS

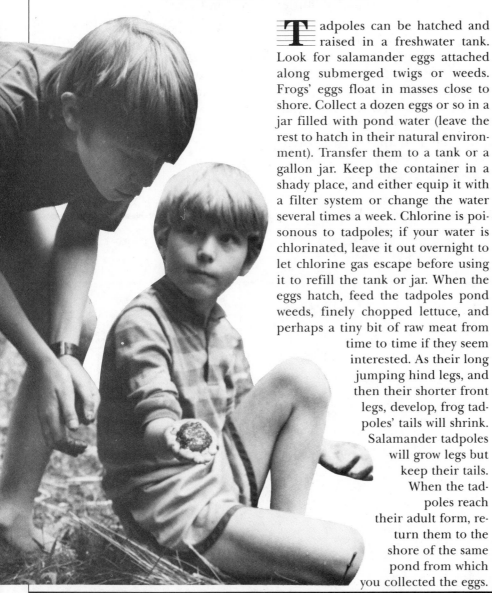

Tadpoles can be hatched and raised in a freshwater tank. Look for salamander eggs attached along submerged twigs or weeds. Frogs' eggs float in masses close to shore. Collect a dozen eggs or so in a jar filled with pond water (leave the rest to hatch in their natural environment). Transfer them to a tank or a gallon jar. Keep the container in a shady place, and either equip it with a filter system or change the water several times a week. Chlorine is poisonous to tadpoles; if your water is chlorinated, leave it out overnight to let chlorine gas escape before using it to refill the tank or jar. When the eggs hatch, feed the tadpoles pond weeds, finely chopped lettuce, and perhaps a tiny bit of raw meat from time to time if they seem interested. As their long jumping hind legs, and then their shorter front legs, develop, frog tadpoles' tails will shrink. Salamander tadpoles will grow legs but keep their tails. When the tadpoles reach their adult form, return them to the shore of the same pond from which you collected the eggs.

Salamanders can get up speed only by a fishlike movement of the body very similar to the way their fish-fathers swam in water. Only the frantic dash of a hungry salamander lifts that belly off the ground.

Like fish, frogs and salamanders must keep their eggs wet. Even the toad that can live beneath your doorstep travels each spring to lay its eggs in water, most likely the same pond in which it was born. It will return to the same pond year after year. If you leave amphibian eggs exposed to air, they dry up like jellyfish do on the beach.

The tadpole inside each egg is nourished by yolk, and the amount of yolk determines at what stage in its development the tadpole will hatch. Some amphibians provide so much yolk that their young grow out of being tadpoles altogether, and hatch looking just like adults, only smaller. Those with less yolk hatch at earlier stages of development. Watching a tadpole develop inside its transparent egg is like observing an embryo develop before its birth.

STOP ACTION

All tadpoles have fishy tails. If they are salamander tadpoles, they keep their tails, although the fishlike fins usually disappear by adulthood. If they are frog tadpoles, their tail is absorbed and its useful materials are recycled into new body parts.

This reshaping of the body, called metamorphosis, isn't very different from the changes in body plan that other embryos, even mammals, undergo in the course of development. In amphibians, legs grow from limb buds—hind legs first, then front legs. External gills used for breathing in water are resorbed, and the gill opening closes. Lungs develop from pouches, and the blood circulation is reorganized to make lung breathing possible.

We have gill slits (but not working gills) during an early part of our development, our limbs grow from limb buds, and we resorb our little tails.

The difference is that the embryonic stage of amphibians can continue unchanged for a long time, even their lifetime. Some tadpoles remain embryos for a year or more, living an aquatic life as vegetarians until changes in the environment trigger them to continue growing into terrestrial carnivores.

The instructions for how to grow up are there all the time, but the chemical trigger is released only by the right combination of temperature and length of day. Inside the animal, different chemicals, called hormones, control different sets of instructions. Mud puppies (a type of salamander) never produce enough of the hormones that instruct legs to grow large or gills to disappear. But they do produce enough of the hormone that tells reproductive organs to mature.

HI, SIS!

Experiments have shown that some species of tadpoles can recognize kin. In these experiments, each tadpole was hatched in isolation in its own private tank. When a tadpole was several weeks old, it was moved into the middle compartment of a three-section tank. Beyond the wire screen at one end of the tank lived unrelated tadpoles; beyond the screen at the other end lived a batch of brothers and sisters. The tadpole spent most of its time swimming as close to members of its family as the screen allowed, apparently not only recognizing them, but preferring their company.

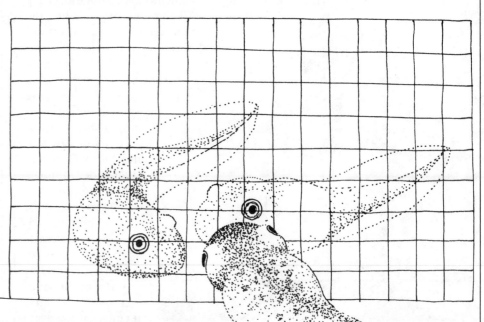

Mud puppies spend their whole lives as water babies, yet they have babies of their own.

A WEAK CHEST

Amphibians breathe by a swallowing motion that appears as a beating of their throat muscles. Try the motion yourself: not much air moves in and out. Squeeze a frog gently in the middle, and you'll notice that it has no ribs at all. In fact, since amphibians don't have a muscular diaphragm to separate their innards into two portions, they can't be said to have a chest. Without ribs to form a chest cavity, and without a diaphragm to control the size of it, they must gulp to draw in air. All amphibians supplement the meager ration of oxygen absorbed through their lungs by absorbing air through their skin. But what about the fact that cells are unable to get oxygen unless they are bathed in seawater? Feel an amphibian's skin; it is always moist.

That moisture, sometimes watery and sometimes gooey, is produced in glands that evolved from mucous glands in fish. Toads feel dry to the touch; their moist skin surface is inside the warty looking glands for which they are famous. A puppy, innocent enough to bother a toad, discovers that it produces a nasty irritant, too. Some frogs produce nauseating substances, and some

GESUNDHEIT!

Runny noses flush out invading viruses. Coughs and sneezes blast them away. Fever heats the body too hot for bacteria. Pus is the corpses of cells that died while engulfing and digesting invaders. But the system for detecting and destroying strangers is not foolproof, and luckily so. Millions of harmless aliens come in with every breath we breathe and every bite we eat. It is a waste to wage war on pollen, for instance; the symptoms of such mistaken battles against pollen, cat hair, or strawberries are evidence of a disorder called allergy. And what if eggs rejected sperm? Every ovum that was ever fertilized by a sperm must certainly have turned a blind eye to that foreign invader.

tree frogs in the tropics make lethal poisons that paralyze and kill. Even very ordinary amphibians exude distinctive smells. The common toad smells like vanilla, and others smell like onion or garlic.

BROTHERLY LOVE

The gross smells we can detect are nothing compared with what amphibians discern. Tadpoles can tell in a sniff whether other tadpoles are relatives. The ability to recognize kin by smell is related to the ability to distinguish self from nonself. Both talents go all the way back to bacteria.

Every individual of every life form is uniquely marked with its own chemical "profile." That unique chemical marker is on the surface of each cell in an individual's body. When an individual is invaded by another whose chemical profile is different, the invader is recognized as nonself. Even a single cell bumped up against another single cell can judge its neighbor's similarity to itself. Bacteria that go about in informal strands or clusters choose to do so with those most similar to themselves. When a bacteria exchanges DNA with another, it does so with an individual unlike itself. The judging of similarity is done at the cell surface, profile to profile, so to speak.

Tadpoles do much the same thing when they sniff out who is family and who isn't. The same bit of DNA that codes for an individual's inside chemical profile also codes for an individual's outside smell. The more genes that two individuals share, the more likely they are to share portions of chemical profile as well, and to smell somewhat the same. Smell molecules are long-distance versions of cell markers—they communicate the profile through air or water to the curious nose, a chemical sensor.

The chemical receptors inside the nose are not really part of the nose at all. They are the ends of brain cells. The brain (in fact, the whole nervous system) develops in the embryo from cells that will mostly become skin. Brain cells and their sniffing ends can be thought of as the *outside* of the organism, safely pocketed inward and still doing what bacteria do: judging who's who at the surface, profile to profile. Most mammals do as well as tadpoles in recognizing kin. Mice concentrate their self-smell in urine. Baby humans recognize the unique smell of their mother's milk.

SAY IT WITH CHEMICALS

Chemical sense exists in cells, whether or not they are in the nose. Cells of various sorts respond not only to a who's who of cellular profiles bumping up against them from the outside world, but also to the many internally circulating chemicals that are the fundamental communication system in every sort of life. These internal chemicals—hormones that circulate in the bloodstream, and neurotransmitters found mostly among nerve cells—are recognized by and fitted to receptors on the surface of a great variety of cells. The filling of receptors signals the cell to do something, or to stop doing it. That action may in turn trigger other changes, including the release of still other chemical messages that may lead the organism to lay an egg, shed a skin, make sugar, or feel depressed.

It used to be thought that this internal communication via hormones and neurotransmitters was so sophisticated that only vertebrates could do it. Now, insulin—which lets us know when we're short on sugar—and many other hormones and neurotransmitters have been found to be manufactured by organisms as humble as bacteria, funguses, and protozoans. These organisms have the same kind of receptors for them, too. Apparently, long before insulin circulated cell to cell in anybody's blood, it circulated from bacterium to bacterium in seawater. It served then the same purpose it and all these chemicals serve now: long-distance communication.

Chemicals that carry messages from one organism to another are called pheromones. Pheromones are those chemicals that termites use to guide one another's development, and those that many female animals use to advertise to males when eggs are ready to be fertilized. When an internal messenger chemical like the hormone insulin is sent between one organism and another, it also is a pheromone. In either case, the cell receiving the message is tuned to life's basic language, whether we call it hormone or pheromone. The only difference, after all, is that one-celled individuals converse with one another in insulin, while a multicellular one talks insulin only to itself.

IN THE BLACK AND IN THE RED

From the time when amphibians first waddled, and for millions of years after, the wetlands where they lived were undergoing an evolution of their own. They were changing into coal. Puttering through strip mines today, you can find carbon imprints of tree fern leaves, and of the wings of dragonflies that flitted among them. Some traces are so perfect that fossil hunters have found holes in leaves chewed by insects hundreds of millions of years ago.

Although these places that are now coal were once forests, you

WOOD TO CARBON

The coal that could be made from a whole bale of peat pressed for millions of years beneath a swamp would be a lump small enough to hold in your hand. Under the heat of pressure most of the peat would vaporize, leaving only carbon behind. A similar thing happens as you sit around a campfire. The burning wood vaporizes; everything except the carbon goes up in smoke. What's left is charcoal: carbon not yet pressed as hard as coal.

would have needed a boat to get around in them. Rampant vegetation grew from muck flooded with water so stagnant that not even decaying bacteria could live in it. When a tree fern died and toppled, it became waterlogged and sank rapidly without rotting. As more and more layers of dead material accumulated, the deeper layers were pressed into peat, the same stuff harvested in bogs today and used for improving soil texture. Over millions of years, the peat was compressed further under thousands of tons of dead forest. Pressure heated some of the trapped organic stuff to vapor, and it escaped. What was left was rich in carbon, black as coal.

The mass burial of many millions of years worth of dead wood had an extraordinary effect on the face of the earth. Pangea's rampant green jungles released a great deal of oxygen into the air. Ordinarily, a lot of that oxygen would combine with carbon to form carbon dioxide, CO_2. But since so much carbon was buried out of circulation, oxygen combined instead with iron in rocks and soil, and rusted the continent.

Over all the lands that were once united in Pangea lie thick layers of iron-rich and rusty sedimentary rock called red beds. Red sandstones, red shales, red layers in the

SAVING OLD-TIMERS

Gingko trees are the last surviving species of an ancient line. They are not flowering trees, like maples and birches, but they do make seeds. Some individuals produce only male, pollen-bearing cones; others produce ova inside round seeds. Gingkos are extinct in the wild. They would have vanished altogether if they had not been planted in gardens and parks and along city streets. Gingko seeds have a nasty smell, so female trees are not planted and aren't even used for breeding. Baby gingkos are rooted from the cut branches of older gingkos without benefit of sex. All those you see are pollen makers.

each of these changes, climate changed, too: sometimes it was bone chilling, and other times sweaty hot or dusty dry or soaking wet. The weather in the barren open might have been anything: monsoons of rain followed by shriveling drought, a fine clear autumn day, a blizzard. The old-time swamp dwellers weren't prepared for times like these. Sedimentary rock, patiently recording, show a disaster for water life and a new opportunity for landlubbers.

PIONEERING PLANTS

As usual, it was plant pioneers that first pushed outward from steamy coal forests toward new frontiers. And as usual, they took their water with them, this time inside seeds. They did it by reducing their sexual stage to a size so small that you need a microscope to see it.

It's strange to realize that a pine tree or a peony bush is the asexual, not the sexual, stage in the plant's life cycle. The tree or bush is capable only of producing spores, like those that dot the underside of a fern leaf. It is the spores that grow into a mini-plant capable of reproducing sexually with sperm and ova.

Various spore-bearing plants of the coal forest produced their spores within cones that stood atop

rock of road cuts, even red roads themselves are the stains of that great rusting. The red dust that turned farmland to dustbowl during the 1930s was more than 200 million years old.

Emerging from coal forests into the redlands beyond in the days of the early amphibians, you would have been in nowhere land. Nothing lived there; nothing could. Even now, windswept, sunbaked barrens is no place for frog hunting and fern collecting.

An ice age gripped southern Gondwanaland. Glaciers came and went there for millions of years. Whenever they thickened and spread, they locked up water that would otherwise have rained into the ocean. The ocean shrank. By 230 million years ago, there was more dry land in the world than there had ever been.

Whenever glaciers melted, the water spilled inland again. The ocean flooded and stranded Pangea 20 times in 60 million years. With

the plant (ground pine and horsetail still have cones on top). When the spores were ripe, they, like fern and moss spores, were released to the wind. Some of them would land on ground moist enough for the little sexual plant to grow and do its thing.

One small change revolutionized this system. Instead of opening when spores ripened, cones remained shut. Protected within the cone, the spores grew into sexual plants right there; fertilization was safely accomplished, and the cone opened only when well-developed embryos were ready to dig their roots into the ground.

A number of different kinds of plants discovered how to do this. The first was a kind of fern that is now extinct. Others were cycads (the sago palms that are common in Florida), gingko trees (which survive along our streets and in our parks, but are extinct in the wild), and all the conifers.

A PORTABLE POT

The conifers—pines, spruces, firs, and hemlocks—were enormously successful. They comprise a third of all forests today, and they have barely changed in 300 million years.

The cone of a conifer is a specialized leaf cluster. Spores are made at the base of each leaf. While the cone is green and the spores are growing into microscopic sexual plants within it, the cone faces upward. Larger cones produce large spores that divide to become several multicellular plants that, in turn, make ova. Smaller cones on

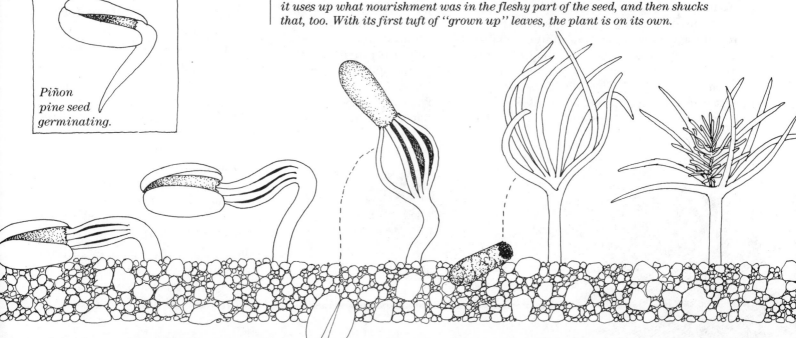

Piñon pine seed germinating.

The embryo plant that grows safely inside its seed is a tiny version of its parent, complete with root, stem, and leaf bud. The little baby is easy to make out inside peanuts, avocados, or other large seeds that split easily. Here, the embryo of a piñon pine reaches out root first to the soil. Water absorbed by the root swells the stem and the leaf bud, which causes the seed jacket to break. As the embryo grows, it uses up what nourishment was in the fleshy part of the seed, and then shucks that, too. With its first tuft of "grown up" leaves, the plant is on its own.

MOST YEARS AND MAST YEARS

Beneath their tough water-proof jacket, pine nuts are succulent, sweet, and fatty. They are the main course for squirrels and birds in many forests. During winter they may be about the only food around. By spring few are left to sprout into the next generation. Or so it goes most years—but not mast years. A mast year is one in which the weather has been particularly good for trees. Those are the years when you will have the best luck finding pinecones, for good weather fuels a baby boom. Pines (and nut trees, whose seeds are also eaten and digested embryo and all) take advantage of these good times to make huge crops. You can gather armsful of cones, squirrels and birds can eat themselves sick, and still there are nuts left to sprout in spring.

the same tree do the same thing, but on an even tinier scale. Their product is sperm.

Pine sperm, however, don't swim like fern sperm do. They gave up flagella and wrapped themselves in a tough coat that resists drying. Looking like that, they are called pollen. Tiny and tailless, but safe out in the air, pollen is released from the cone and wafted by the wind. The trip need be no longer than to the nearest large cone, by now filled with ripe ova and up-turned to receive sperm. Fertilization takes place within this snug housing.

At this point, a more primitive sexual plant would drop the fertilized egg onto the moist soil below it. Pines don't. They "plant" the egg in a portable pot, the seed, which contains all the moisture and food needed to take care of an embryo's growth. When the embryo pines have had a good start in life, the cones turn downward, open, and drop their seeds to the ground.

The adult plant also has improved water conservation. Very little moisture evaporates from conifers' narrow, leathery, resin-coated leaves. During dry weather, they shut down their thirsty growth, becoming dormant (inactive) until the drought is over. Dry-season dormancy proved to be a pre-adaptation for surviving cold seasons,

A female cone has an egg in each compartment.

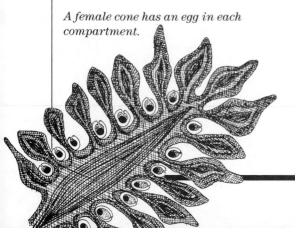

A male cone split lengthwise to show its pollen grains.

THE ALL-PURPOSE BAND-AID

When a conifer is injured, it bleeds sticky stuff called resin. This is its all-purpose Band-Aid. The resin quickly seals the wound and slowly hardens. It kills bacteria. That is why some floor cleaners and dandruff shampoos are pine scented: They used to be made of pine tar, a substance derived from the resinous wood, to kill bacteria on floors and on human heads. Now the active ingredient may no longer be the piney part, but people accustomed to associating the smell with cleanliness still like bacteriocides to smell like a pine forest. Best of all, conifer resin may be the only bandage that gets revenge. An insect that caused an injury by biting through a conifer's bark may not get away with its crime—it may get stuck. The most perfect fossils of insects are those trapped in amber, which is fossilized resin from conifers.

when the chemistry of growth is halted for lack of heat energy to run it. Fiercely protecting their sexual plants, carrying precious moisture in their seeds, and turning a tough surface to the elements, conifers marched over the red barrens of Pangea.

THE INCREDIBLE EGG

Amphibians did not follow them. They stayed close to water in the forests and evolved in their own damp ways. Some became robust carnivores as large as a human, but at egg-laying time, back they went to the water to see to the making of the next generation. Their need to keep their eggs from evaporating tied them to an endless repetition of their own evolution, pond to shore and back again. How far can you go if you can never go far from water? It was the reptile descendants of amphibians that had the freedom to follow the marching forest.

Judging from their fossil bones, the earliest reptiles were hardly different from amphibians. They were about the same size and the same shape; they lived in the same wet places and still had a sprawling walk. In fact, the steps involved in becoming a reptile were so small and so gradual, that had it not been for the discovery of fossil eggs, scientists would not have been able to draw the line between advanced amphibians and primitive reptiles. If you find a reptile egg, you know its mother must have been a reptile. The egg you eat for breakfast was the reptiles' great invention.

Like the conifer's seed, the reptile's egg is a completely self-contained life-support system. It carries its own pool of water—the white—and a store of food—the yolk—which the embryo uses up as it grows. A sanitary pouch, the allantois, handles wastes. The leathery shell lets oxygen in and carbon dioxide out, yet it helps to keep moisture from escaping this small and perfect world. Equipped with a better way to hatch a baby, reptiles were no longer tied to open water. Jelly eggs must be kept wet; leathery-shelled eggs need only warm dampness.

Besides inventing shells, reptiles invented hide. You won't find belts and wallets made of frog skin, but snake, lizard, or crocodile hide is tough. A creature with a slippery surface can safely slither along slimy ground. Rough rocks would scratch its belly. Like conifers, reptiles presented to the world a harsh surface that conserved water. Even on the living animal, reptile hide isn't wet or slimy. It is drier, in fact, than your own skin. It lacks the sweat glands through which you

THE ANATOMY OF AN EGG

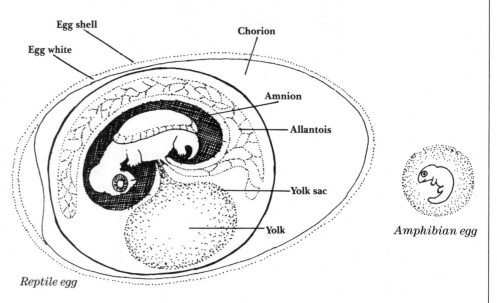

Egg shell

Egg white

Chorion

Amnion

Allantois

Yolk sac

Yolk

Reptile egg

Amphibian egg

The white of an egg, the tough membrane around it, and the eggshell are secreted by the mother in the course of preparing her eggs for laying, and are not part of the egg cell itself. The boundary of the true egg is the chorion, just inside the white. Within the chorion, the embryo itself floats in a thin bag called the amnion. Sprouting from the embryo's belly are two sacs. One, the yolk sac, holds the yolk that will nourish the embryo until it hatches. The other sac, the allantois, does double duty as lung and toilet. It exchanges waste gases for fresh air, and also stores urine. Since all four of these membranes—chorion, amnion, yolk sac, and allantois—are made by the embryo, you will not be able to find any of them in the eggs you eat. Those chicken eggs have not been fertilized, so there is no one inside to make the membranes.

A newly hatched reptile, like a newly hatched bird, has short stalks on its belly. These stalks are the stubs of the animal's prehatching food supply and waste-disposal systems. The remains of a mammal's prebirth supply and waste-disposal system is the stump of the umbilical cord, which leaves the scar called a belly button.

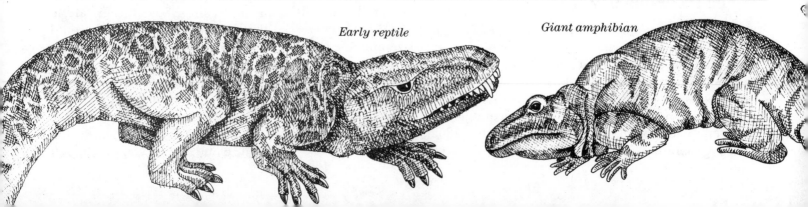

Early reptile

Giant amphibian

lose moisture, and it lacks the various glands of its amphibian forebears. Leathery eggs and leathery bodies allowed reptiles to invade the uplands and create there ways of life that had never existed before.

FROM HEAT SOURCE TO HEAT SINK

On the heels of conifers flew insect browsers, and right behind them lumbered their reptile predators. Life in blazing sun and chilling winds can't have been easy. Reptiles work best within a very narrow range of temperatures. Cooled below 33°C (91°F), the average lizard grinds to a halt. Digestion stops, movement slows, and the animal becomes a sitting lizard for someone else's meal. An overheated liz-

ard is also in trouble: Heated to over 38°C (100°F) it goes into convulsions and dies.

Living beside a swamp, a reptile's answer to a chilly morning is a warm soak, and its answer to a blazing afternoon is a quick dip. But as Pangea turned drier and cooler during the Gondwanaland ice age, staying "just right" must have caused no end of trouble to those whose bathtubs were drained.

There are many ways that modern animals regulate their internal temperature, and reptiles invented them all. The northern snake you find on the road is stealing heat from a sun-warmed surface. The desert horned lizard that you don't see at noon is doing the same in reverse: letting the cool earth in its burrow steal heat from it. Places where reptiles can warm themselves

ALL BALLED UP

The first thing you'll notice about lizards if you live in the North is that they're not there. There are no northern lizards, because there are no hibernating lizards. But there are quite a few species of snakes that remain unfrozen by descending below the frost line. At least one species of garter snake makes it through the winter by making like a pariesaur. As the weather cools, northern garter snakes head for dens deep below rocks. More and more garter snakes arrive at these winter hibernation camps until, at some, there are thousands crowded together. When snakes coil together into a solid ball, the outside surface from which heat is lost is reduced, and the inside volume in which heat is stored is increased. Even so, the mass of snakes cools so much that their blood congeals to the consistency of mayonnaise.

Pariesaur

OUTSIDE AND INSIDE

Snakes look legless from the outside, but a few betray a leggy past. Boas and pythons have remnants of leg and hip bones (boas even have a pair of hind claws), and the thigh bones of blind snakes show as knobs beneath the skin. The way of life of the blind snake may be a clue to the evolution of all snakes. Blind snakes are burrowers who snake along underground in pursuit of termites. Burrowing lizards move underground like that, and many have weak limbs or none at all. Like them, the ancestor of snakes may have burrowed itself into shape within the earth before venturing out onto it.

turn pink as they shed heat by dilating tiny blood vessels in the skin. That's called blushing; you can feel the heat of it when you blush. A hot anole lizard pants. The evaporating moisture removes heat. Some pythons shiver. The friction of jiggling muscles heats them up.

Another way to stay just the right temperature is to adjust the amount of surface exposed to air: Curl up to keep warm in a cold bed, stretch out to warm up in the hot sun. A snake sprawls to bask, coils to conserve heat.

A balled-up body shape is a more permanent way to stabilize temperature. Compare a huge snowball with the surrounding snow. When the sun shines and the air warms, the blanket of snow covering the ground melts quickly; its "skin" is large compared with the bulk of its "body." The snowball lasts much longer. It has the greatest possible bulk wrapped in the smallest possible surface. The most ball-like of the early reptiles was the immense pariesaur.

All these supplementary controls, however, are more like gadgety inventions than drastic redesigns. Reptiles still depend on their basic method, moving from heat source to heat sink. Since they must take frequent time-outs to warm up or cool down (and since there are inevitable times when there isn't

are called heat sources; places where they can cool off are called heat sinks. All reptiles spend considerable time moving from heat source to heat sink and back again, depending on their temperature.

They have also developed supplementary heat controls. The horned lizard changes color. By increasing the amount of dark pigment in its skin, it absorbs more heat; by paling, it reflects heat. Some iguanas enough heat to get them going, or there is too much heat to make the going safe), reptiles are inactive a great deal of the time. That's just as well, for their hearts aren't made for the athlete's life.

Lizard, snake, and tortoise hearts have three chambers, as do amphibian hearts. Blood chock full of oxygen arrives from the lungs to one chamber of the heart, and blood with all the oxygen used up arrives from the body to a second chamber of the heart. So far, so good. But then both kinds of blood are sloshed into the third chamber for repumping back to the body and lungs. Not so good. Reptiles just never get completely fresh blood to fuel their muscles. With their poor blood, sluggish ways, and short legs, reptiles lumbered through their finest age in slow motion.

SLOWLY, THE TORTOISE

Tortoises live a life of slow motion that approaches standstill. They have dragged on just about unchanged for 250 million years, the most ancient of the few reptiles that still exist. A tortoise, snug in its armor and safe from predators, can live for over 150 years.

Tortoises behave as though no time has passed since they began. They eat what they find on the forest floor, and part of the menu—fern sprouts, mushrooms, earthworms—is as old as they are. They hollow out nests for their eggs in warm sand or in rotting vegetation, but don't stay to see what hatches. When hot, they dig down to dump heat. When cold, they lie in the sun. And when winter comes, they dig in deep, come to a stop, and simply wait it out. Some have stepped backward in time, into the even-temperatured water of their amphibian past. They are called turtles. Tortoises and turtles have stuck

NOT TOO WARM, NOT TOO COLD

Our sex depends on our chromosomes, but the sex of a turtle depends on the weather. Turtles have no sex chromosomes; an embryo can become either sex depending on the temperature at which it is incubated. If all the eggs in a nest are kept cool, all the turtles may hatch out as male. If all the eggs are kept warm, all the turtles may hatch out as female. If the weather could be trusted, and if all turtle mothers went about their task scientifically, digging their nests just so deep, in a spot just so damp, with just a certain exposure to the sun, and covering their eggs with just so much rotting vegetation, all turtle babies would be of one sex. Only fickle weather and turtle sloppiness guarantees that there will be both male and female hatchlings in each new generation.

INSIDE AND OUTSIDE

A turtle's armor is ordinary reptile scales carried to an extreme. Other reptile scales, for instance those of snakes, are made out of thin bits of bone covered by a horny substance like fingernails. Each scale is separate; you can feel the soft skin between them. A turtle's carapace (its top shell) and its plastron (its bottom shell) are also made of scales, but with no skin in between. The bony parts are thick and have fused together to cover the whole back and belly under a thin layer of horn. In most species, the backbone and ribs are fused to the carapace, but in some species the skeleton of the animal is perfectly free, and the animal could be likened to a lizard stuck through a can.

Summertime, when the living is easy, is growing time for trees and reptiles. Just as you can count the years of a tree's life by counting the growth rings in a section of its trunk, you can tell a reptile's age by the number of growth rings in a section of its bone. Because a turtle wears bone on its back, its age is right out in the open. During each growth spurt, each plate in the carapace adds new bone around its edge and a new ridge of horn on the surface. Best guesses of age are made on young animals, and in hibernating species that don't grow

This giant tortoise (a terrestrial turtle) lived 10 million years ago in India.

at all during winter. Tropical and subtropical turtles might have more than one growth ring a year, and older turtles grow so slowly that the rings are too narrow to count accurately. Still, any particularly large specimen of any reptile species is almost certainly very old, for reptiles never stop growing, and they live surprisingly long. The record is held by a land tortoise who lived in captivity for 152 years.

Perhaps the most peculiar thing about turtles is the location of their shoulder blades. In every other four-footed animal, the shoulder blades are *outside* the rib cage. The turtle's

shoulder apparatus is *inside* its ribs. This ornery exception to the rule is the kind of thing that keeps evolutionists awake at night. If change is gradual, requiring hundreds of thousands of generations to be completed, how could turtles have walked or swam while their shoulder blades were gradually moving around or through the obstacle of their ribs? No, fossils don't give the answer. No, this is not a trick question. This little mystery is thrown in just so that you, too, can lie awake nights wondering how—or how fast—the feat might have been accomplished.

to the basics, and the basics have been enough for them.

SMALL SOLUTIONS

Other early reptiles pioneered brashly as sea monsters, globular herbivores, or huge toothsome carnivores, but all of them became extinct. The only survivors were those that remained small enough to escape extremes of temperature, or remained in the steamy jungle. Today there are only about 6,250 living species of reptile, and only the lizards and tortoises are remarkably old. Snakes branched off from ancestral reptilian stock only about 100 million years ago.

All snakes are carnivores: garter snakes are frog eaters, ring-necked snakes are worm and slug eaters, green snakes are insect eaters, black snakes are rodent eaters. But they spend little time hunting. Their energy needs are so low that they can go for weeks, even months, without a meal. Nor do snakes go far in search of food, or move from one hunting ground to another. A snake's hunting ground may be as small as 100 square yards—smaller than a basketball court—and it may live there all its life.

Within that territory it may have favorite basking places where it warms up to working temperature morning after morning. If the day is cool and the sunbath has just begun, the snake may be quite sluggish and easy to catch.

This need to bask just when they are the most sluggish has forced many snakes to camouflage themselves. Green snakes are green as grass, water snakes are a dull muddy hue, and many other species are patterned in a way that breaks up their snaky shape into blotches, bands, patches, and speckles that are nearly invisible against dried leaves or stony ground.

The rattle on a rattle snake's tail makes the warning very clear.

ADS AND LIES

Brightly colored snakes that don't match their background either have no need for camouflage (they are nocturnal or live mostly underground) or are dangerous, or are lying. Gaudy black, red, and gold banded coral snakes are poisonous. Their showy colors say "keep away" as effectively as a skunk's bold stripe. Scarlet snakes and milk snakes aren't poisonous at all, but use the same three-colored ad to lie about how dangerous it would be to bother them.

The threat posture of a snake, who may also vibrate its tail as a warning.

Just as an organism adapts to one environment and then, as circumstances change, uses old talents to meet new challenges, so behavior evolved for one use can be put to another. Ring-necked snakes colored red beneath their tails coil the tail and raise it as a red warning flag when another ring-neck snake enters their territory. You would be given the same warning if you were to disturb the snake, but in this case it would be a bluff. The snake doesn't know it's bluffing, and the gesture certainly didn't come about as a response to snake collectors. It is simply using an old gesture in new circumstances; often, the bluff works.

Behavior can itself act as the circumstance that drives evolution. Many snakes vibrate their tails to warn others away. By some genetic fluke, rattlesnakes have trouble shedding their skin completely. A snake's skin detaches first at its mouth, and is then peeled back down the length of the body as the snake slides forward, so that the skin slips off the tail inside out. The rattlesnake's skin breaks at the tail end, so that when the snake has slithered out of it, a cap, like the toe of a sock, is left in place. Each new shedding adds another cap. If rattlesnakes hadn't been in the habit of shaking their tails, those that burdened themselves with unshed skin would probably have been at a disadvantage. As it was, the dry caps shaken against one another gave a loud warning, and the snakes were attacked less often. So favored by their own behavior, rattlesnakes evolved their rattle.

The anole threat when competing for territory includes throat fanning and head bobbing.

BOASTS AND BLUFFS

In many species, from lobsters and lizards to moose and man, males compete for territory or for a female in contests that rarely wound and almost never kill. Claw clacking, throat fanning, antler locking, and arm wrestling are bloodless battles. There is good reason why creatures do not evolve dangerous contests. Take fighting lizards. Every fight leaves both with injuries. Can the injured winner mate? And will the female accept a damaged lover? Even if he can and she will, repeated injuries reduce his life span and, therefore, the number of offspring he will be able to father. Take the loser. If he is going to lose anyway, he would be better off admitting it before he gets hurt. The ideal contest is one in which both can predict who would be winner and loser by judging one another's size, strength, vigor, and determination without actually holding the battle. That way the winner wins in good health, the loser lives to win another day.

A LIZARD'S CHOICE

Individuals, by selecting one another, have a direct influence on evolution. By choosing a mate whose vigor, personality, and possessions are likely to benefit offspring, an individual increases its own reproductive success, and thereby the future of its kind. Such choices are easy to observe among lizards.

Fence lizards and Carolina anoles are territorial like snakes, but their territories are right against one another, forcing a degree of social life. Not all territories are equal. Insects may be more plentiful in one place than in another, or a particular area may be well protected from predators. Males compete for larger or better territories.

You may see two male lizards facing one another at their common boundary, engaged in a head-bobbing contest that will decide a boundary dispute. The western fence lizard spreads its sides out flat, making it look bigger than it is. The Carolina anole spreads a fan of skin beneath its jaw that shines ruby red.

Finally, one of the lizards, put down by the vigor of the other's display, gives up. His head lowers to signal defeat, he shrinks his sides or fan, and if he is a Carolina anole, his emerald hide fades to brown. The loser retreats to a second-rate landholding.

A female bases her choice of a mate on the outcome of this contest. She will choose as father for her offspring the lizard who makes the best show of himself, and who holds the best real estate. Such a "he-man" gets many opportunities to mate, and passes his genes to many descendants. The females who choose him benefit their own genes, which are mixed with those of an obviously superior individual, to produce superior offspring.

CATCH THAT TAIL!

Catch an anole by the tail, and that's all you get. The rest of the lizard keeps going. The tail end, detached bloodlessly and painlessly at a special joint, wiggles for a while, interesting a predator just long enough for the lizard to escape. The tail grows back, but never to as fine a shape or as long a length as the original. Male anoles pay a social price for their escape. Stumpy-tailed ones lose out to other males in contests for the best places to live, and females prefer a male with a long tail as well as a large landholding. There is logic to this prejudice: Although the special joint saves lives, a lizard cautious or nimble enough not to get caught in the first place may be a better bet for breeding.

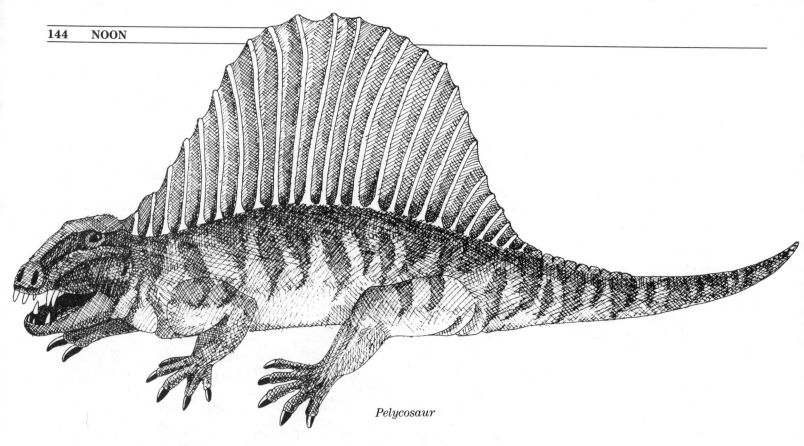

Pelycosaur

SAILS IN THE SUNRISE

The few reptiles on dry land today managed to come this far by keeping a low profile. But some reptiles that ruled the land when tortoises first withdrew into their shells were not such modest creatures. They were big and bold and full of promise. They were our reptile ancestors.

You wouldn't have known to look at a pelycosaur that it had anything to do with the warm and fuzzy mammals that were to descend from it. Its skin was dry and scaly like a lizard's, and its legs were no improvement. Some pelycosaurs carried atop their back a great sail of skin supported by long spines and networked with blushing blood vessels. No doubt the sail, like the anole's fan, made it look bigger to rivals and better to females, but it was also a solar heater. Turned to the rising sun, this contraption soaked up the first rays of warmth, making the finbacked pelycosaur the early bird of its day, who could catch for breakfast other reptiles still sluggish in the cool of morning.

To go with this clever way to start the day, finbacks developed a fine set of teeth with which to chew their food. Chewing doesn't seem like a startling skill until you watch an anole lizard struggling to eat a big bug. It chomps and chomps, but can't use its jaws in the grinding motion that would mash the bug to swallowable size. It can't even bite off a smaller chunk, for its teeth are stickers, not slicers. The anole might use its front feet to try to cram its prey into position for swallowing, but if the bug is too big to be bolted whole, the lizard must give up the meal.

The ability to take a bite with slicing incisors, to shred with canines, and to grind with molars, allows the eater more kinds of food to swallow. Full of energy and toothsome, too, the pelycosaurs successfully founded both vegetarian and meat-on-the-claw ways of life that made them the most impressive large land animals of their day.

TROTTING ON

Pelycosaur descendants did even better. One branch of the family spawned the therapsids, longer limbed trotters whose fossils are found all over Pangea from the far south to the far north.

And that is very strange. The far north and the far south of Pangea 250 million years ago weren't such hot places. In fact, they were cold enough to be blanketed with snow all winter. If the therapsid reptiles could live there, why aren't we treated today to the sight of lizards cavorting through the snow?

These days, there are no northern lizards at all. What few cold climate reptiles there are bury themselves for the winter. You won't find any northern snakes or turtles above ground after autumn. In those cold parts where therapsids made their home, fossils of a little fish-eating reptile have been found. They most likely hibernated.

But a therapsid the size of a rhi-

THE BETTER TO EAT YOU WITH

Open a lizard's mouth and you'll see a boring set of teeth—all the same size, all the same pointy shape. Look a fossil finback in the mouth, and you'll see a set of teeth that might almost fit your dog.

noceros would have had to dig a heck of a hole to hide in. Even medium-size therapsids were hefty animals. More likely, these reptiles were not cold blooded like their forebears, who never left the tropics. And they were probably not bare skinned like other reptiles. They were probably warm blooded, and they were probably hairy.

A warm-blooded mammal's annual food needs compared to a cold-blooded reptile's annual food needs.

BONY CLUES

There is convincing evidence that therapsids were warm and hairy. The bones of cold-blooded animals that live where there are wet and dry seasons, or warm and cold ones, show growth rings something like a tree does. Finbacks, for instance, did most of their eating and most of their growing during the wet season, and grew only slowly during dry seasons, when food was scarce. Wide and narrow growth bands al-. ternate in their bones. Therapsids, like warm-blooded animals, don't have growth rings, showing that they ate well all year long. Their bones show tightly packed channels for blood circulation, which only warm-blooded animals require.

Another way to guess from fossils whether an animal was warm blooded or cold blooded is to measure the amount of fuel it used.

Cold-blooded animals don't rely on food to keep their inside temperature high. Warm-blooded animals are like furnaces that must constantly be stoked with food to keep their inner fires burning. Although both are about the same size, the warm-blooded shrew needs 100 times its weight in insects every year while the cold-blooded anole needs only 10 times its weight in insects to meet its much smaller energy needs.

Looking at this ounce by ounce, 100 ounces of insects will support 1 ounce of shrew for a year. The same amount of insects will support 10 ounces of lizard. Even a large mammal like yourself, who loses heat less easily than a small one, uses 80 percent of the calories it consumes to keep itself warm. You have to eat five times more calories than a reptile your size. To figure out whether a fossil predator of a particular size

was externally or internally heated, scientists measure how much it ate. They count predator and prey bones and calculate the weights of the living animals they belonged to. The answer tells them how many pounds of that predator were supported by how many pounds of its prey. Pound for pound, therapsids were fueled by only about a third as much prey as a wolf needs today, but by a good deal more than was needed to support a finback. Finbacks were outside-heated sunbathers; therapsids were inside-heated furnace stokers, but their thermostat was probably set at a little over 30°C (86°F), rather lower than the 36 to 39 degrees (97 to 102°F) of modern warm-blooded animals.

As for therapsids' hairy hides, that's only a good guess. Hair doesn't easily leave a fossil record, but who can imagine any of these big animals rollicking naked in the snow?

THE BIG BAD WOLF?

Therapsids were the fishing otters, the thick-skinned rhinoceroses, the woolly bears, and the vicious wolf packs of their day. Other reptiles of that time were low to the ground and out at the elbows. Their jaws were made of many bones, only one of which held teeth. They could chomp, but only up and down.

JAWBONE TO EARBONE

When you were a young fetus, the jawbone that is now the hinge on which your mouth swings open and shut was separated from your skull by another small jawbone. As you developed, that small bone migrated upward to become the malleus, or hammer bone, of your middle ear. In moving from jaw to ear, the malleus of humans and of every mammal repeats a migration begun 265 million years ago in the skulls of therapsids.

Therapsids were way ahead of them. Their posture was better, and so was their bite. They were higher off the ground, and their knees and elbows were tucked closer to their body, letting them trot instead of waddle. The breathing space between skull and mouth was generous, the better to smell with. The toothed jawbone grew larger, crowding smaller bones at the rear of the jaw into the ears, the better to hear with. A joint developed between jaw and skull that allowed the jaw to move up and down, back and forth, and side to side, the better to eat with. You would think therapsids were practicing to become the big bad wolf, but that isn't what happened.

MILES AND MILES OF ALLIGATORS AND CROCODILES

Just about the time therapsids had moved as far as they could get from the watery homeland of their reptile ancestors, another group of landlubber reptiles was returning to the water. These were archosaurs whose descendants we know well in their modern suits of crocodile and alligator hide.

Crocodiles, including the smaller American ones called alligators, commute between the water, where they conduct their hunting business, and the shore, where they lead their domestic lives. At work, a crocodile chases fish or lies in wait

Hairy therapsid

THE HEART OF THE CROCODILE

When awaiting prey in the water, a crocodile floats with only ears, eyes, and nostrils above water, or waits entirely submerged among the bottom weeds. Holding its breath, it depends on a reptile heart. Fresh and stale blood mixed together are recirculated over and over again until the last of lungsful of air has been used up. When the crocodile surfaces again, a valve closes and—presto!—it has a four-chambered heart that works the same as yours.

Stale blood comes in from the body, and is pumped back to the lungs for freshening.

Freshened blood comes in from the lungs, and is pumped out to the body.

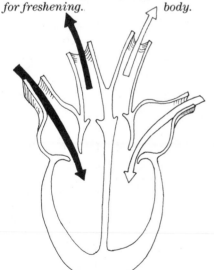

Mammal Heart

Reptile heart, in which fresh and stale blood mix.

Submerged

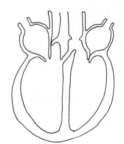

Crocodile heart, with valve in middle open so fresh and stale blood mix while the animal is submerged.

Surfaced

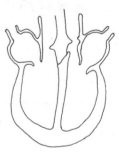

Crocodile heart with valve in middle closed so fresh and stale blood are separated when the animal surfaces.

for animals that come to drink at the water's edge. At home, crocodiles loll about basking in the sun, and there they mate, incubate their eggs, and rear their children.

Their archosaur ancestor chanced upon this short commute between bedroom and business sometime around 300 million years ago, and the crocodiles, evolved from archosaurs 225 million years ago, continue that life-style unchanged, and unchallenged by any other creature. They have been able to keep their traditions because they are so perfectly suited to their environment.

Crocodiles swim by folding their legs against their bodies and lashing the water with their powerful tails. Their unusually long and strong hind legs are thrust against the bottom to make sudden turns and are kicked beneath them for lightning sprints up the bank. By comparison, crocodile front legs are short and far less muscular.

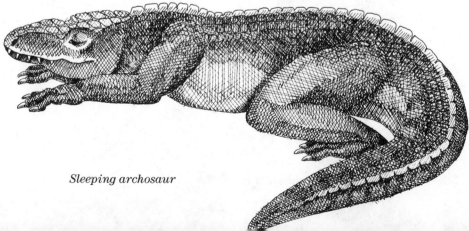

Sleeping archosaur

A modernized heart supplies generous amounts of oxygen to the crocodile's large brain, and energy for its many social activities.

MOMMY DEAREST

For those who have seen crocodiles only in their guise as logs at the zoo, it is difficult to imagine what fond parents they are. Our own American alligator mothers build large nests—six feet wide by a yard high—of mud and weeds. Bacterial decay provides the heat in this incubator, but mother handles the controls. She urinates on the nest from time to time to keep it damp. The mother alligator (and in some crocodile species, both parents) stays home during the several months of incubation to guard the eggs and to encourage the embryos with soothing grunts. As the babies become ready to hatch, they answer with twitters and chirps, which lets parents know it is time to attend to the hatching.

Parents of the largest, most feared crocodile species that inhabits the Nile River in Egypt open the nest, assist with the removal of shells, and gently carry the babies in their mouths down to the water for their first bath.

For the next year, or even for several years, the parents keep their babies in a nursery they hollow out at the water's edge. The babies feed on mollusks and other miniature prey, and mother and father prevent them from straying from the nursery and protect them from enemies.

When family affairs don't require all their attention, crocodiles in the neighborhood get together socially. They go for communal fish chases, swimming in a row to trap a group of fish, and then sharing the catch with one another. One neighbor will help another to drag into the water a large meal captured on the bank, or several friends may get together on the bank to have their picnic ashore.

Crocodiles' archosaur ancestors may have lived just such a life, coddling their young, cooperating in their business, and inviting one another to dinner. With their large brains, efficient hearts, warm natures—and especially their long hind legs—archosaurs were about to best the therapsids and take over the world.

200 MILLION YEARS AGO

A Great Extinction · Egg-Laying Mammals · Warm-Blooded Dinosaurs

By 200 million years ago, 95 percent of Earth's history was over. From the old seas where life began, across greening dunes, up muddy banks where fish first flopped ashore, through swamps crawling with amphibians and reptiles, and up into pine barrens trodden by the first creatures warm enough to nuzzle snow, almost all the ancient forms of life had died. The shallow sea had evaporated entirely; it was never to return. Ninety-six percent of all marine life had vanished, including half the species of jellyfish, sponges, mollusks, worms, echinoderms, crustaceans, and fish. Three-quarters of all amphibian species were extinct.

This extinction has been called the greatest crisis ever in the history of life. Of all the plants and animals of Pangea, only two species in ten were left to populate the planet. Every creature you now see is descended from those few survivors. Ways of life that seem to us the natural order of things—running in herds, hunting in packs, hiding through the night, flocking to the south—were to evolve with them. The archosaurs gave us the birds. The therapsids gave us ourselves and other mammals. But you wouldn't have noticed the little creatures becoming birds and mammals very much, back in those days of disastrous drying. This was the age of the dinosaurs.

FROM FOUR LEGS TO TWO

Some species of archosaurs responded to the great drying like yo-yos, bouncing back from their descent into the water to rise again to life on land. With less and less swamp available, that was the best way to go, and they had the wind and the legs to make the grade.

Lying down to nap in the sun, the beasts who left the swamp looked just like those that gave rise to crocodiles. But wake one up and you would have seen the difference. Their muscular legs had grown stouter still, their rear ones even longer. Hip and shoulder joints had changed, allowing an upright, high-bellied gait. Moving slowly, these archosaurs walked on all fours; picking up speed, they reared up and sped along on hind legs alone.

Rising archosaur

There occurred at this point an accident of engineering. When a crocodile strolls along, its gait is a sort of *ca-lump, ca-lump.* Muscles tense to drive it forward, then relax as the belly drops back to earth. But an archosaur standing on its hind legs must balance its body above the ground by keeping its muscles somewhat tense all the time, tightening here to avoid a fall to the right, there to avoid a fall to the left, or to stop a forward lurch or halt a backward lean. You, too, teeter whenever you are erect.

Muscle tension (muscle tone) and the tiny jerks, quivers, tightenings, and loosenings that keep an animal upright produce heat. The archosaurs, as they rose up off their bellies, warmed up. The more they reared up to balance on their hind legs alone, the warmer they became. And the warmer they became, the more they were dinosaurs.

AS DIFFERENT AS DAY AND NIGHT

As dinosaurs rose, therapsids declined. There was no fight. Dinosaurs were simply hot stuff. They had perfected the four-chambered heart. Their blood, warmed by exertion, supplied a rich mix of air and fuel. They cranked up their metabolism, set their thermostat to high, and became warm blooded.

Though nothing is so hot as the debate about whether dinosaurs were truly warm blooded (and therefore no longer reptiles at all), there may have been an evolutionary spiral as selection favored the more energetic individuals. More active muscles need more food; more food produces more heat; more heat favors a higher metabolism; higher metabolism provides more energy to get food; more food feeds more muscle, fuels more motion, makes more heat. According to some scientists, some dinosaurs could remain nearly as warm to the touch as you are regardless of the weather.

Early dinosaur

One more step took some dinosaur species beyond the trodden paths of their warm archosaur homeland out into the cold where only therapsids, bundled in fur, had ventured. They acquired insulation. At first, they just ruffled their scales. In the raised position, excess heat could be lost to circulating air. Lowered, warm air was trapped between scales and skin as insulation. Gradually, the scales grew longer and frayed to both sides. Before long, some dinosaurs were ruffling their feathers.

Dinosaurs eventually came in shapes and sizes suited to every corner of Pangea, and every way of living there. It used to be thought that there are only so many ways for an animal to earn a living, and those that do the job best, get to keep it, while those that are clumsy lose out. The theory suggests enchanting pictures: little dinosaurs, light-weight and long-limbed, sprinting two-legged after insects, snapping them away from therapsid competitors; big dinosaurs outdoing in size and toughness therapsids who had toyed with a rhinoceros way of life; herds of dinosaurs, helmeted with horns and clothed in leather, thundering past clutzy therapsids roaming in browsing groups; packs of carniverous dinosaurs hunting down therapsids that had been the hunters.

Feather

A scale with a raised keel in the center.

A keeled scale frayed at the edges.

Unhappily for those who love a good story, there is no fossil evidence that any such things happened. While it is true that there are only so many resources in the world, there appear to be an infinite number of ways to divvy them up. No creature's way of earning a living is quite like any other's. No dinosaur appears to have applied for a therapsid job; no therapsid appears to have lost its job to a dinosaur. All we can tell from their fossils is that dinosaurs grew in number, diversity, and size, while therapsids grew few and smaller.

Finally, therapsids were no more than little furry creatures, warm to the touch, whose clever noses and sharp ears helped them slip through each day unnoticed in a world of monsters. There came a time when the last of the therapsids retired altogether from the day's work and became nocturnal.

And that was to be their answer for 120 million years. Dinosaurs didn't take the night shift. But the remnant bands of small therapsids found themselves peculiarly equipped to do so. Their ears, enclosing three tiny, floating bones, could amplify the merest rustle in the dark. Their sensitive noses could sniff down prey through the blackest night. And come the dawn, little furry families climbed to treetop nests, or crept into their burrows.

While dinosaurs prowled the daytime world, the descendants of the last therapsids scurried toward their destiny in a cloak of darkness. They were the first mammals.

A REPTILE RIDDLE

When does a reptile become a mammal? The answer to that riddle

NIGHTWORLDS

S ome zoos reverse the hours of day and night for their nocturnal animals. At night, when your world is dark, theirs is brightly lit. There is not an animal in sight. As the sun rises in your world, the lights go off in theirs. The animals wake up. Then a trick is played. Since most of these night animals are unable to see red light, which we see perfectly well, red lights are turned on. Zoo goers get to see the nightlife of nocturnal mammals during the day, while the animals remain, in their eyes, in the dark. You can create a similar world of darkness to observe pets, such as hamsters, that are more amusing by night than by day. A red darkroom bulb, available at photography stores, will do the trick. Place a red darkroom bulb in a lamp near their cage. At night when the room is dark, turn on that lamp only.

is that there isn't any answer. You can say that at such and such a time that therapsid over there was certainly a reptile. And you can say that 100 million years later this descendant over here certainly was a mammal. But even if you had the skeletons of each generation in between, you still couldn't point your finger at one and say, "There! That's the first mammal!"

What would tell you? Not fur, because therapsids had fur even when they definitely were reptiles. Giving birth to live young, even if you knew therapsids did that, wouldn't tell you much either. There are fish and frogs and snakes that give birth to live young, and there are mammals that lay eggs.

Perhaps, if the fossil record had preserved them, you could point to the mammary glands for which all mammals are named. But even there you would be in trouble. Before mammary glands produced milk, they produced sweat. Other skin glands make oil. Wouldn't an animal that helped to nourish its babies and speed their growth by letting them lick needed salt or fats from its belly fur be "nursing" its babies? You can see the problem.

So all that can be said about the many remains of therapsids and their descendants is that at first they were certainly reptiles, and at last they were surely mammals.

An early placental mammal.

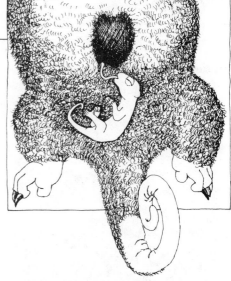

The nipple of this particular marsupial, a phalanger, is a long tube that reaches all the way down the infant's throat. The baby was removed from its pouch to have its portrait done.

HATCHED FROM AN EGG

The early mammals, animals that feed milk to their babies, came in three forms: the monotremes that laid eggs, the marsupials that gave birth to very young embryos, and the placentals that gave birth to well-developed babies. Some scientists consider that monotremes are actually therapsids—the only ones still alive—or at least animals that evolved separately from other mammals, from a different therapsid ancester.

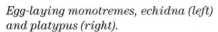

Egg-laying monotremes, echidna (left) and platypus (right).

There are now only three species of egg-laying mammals—the platypus and two species of anteating echidnas. Their body temperature of 30°C (86°F) is the lowest of any mammal (some placental mammals are as high as 39°C (102°F). Their thermostat is less reliable than that of any other mammal. Reptilelike, they cool as the weather cools and warm as the weather warms.

Reptiles that give birth to living young are actually more advanced than platypuses since they don't lay eggs at all. Even oviparous (egg-producing) reptiles often produce thin-shelled eggs that are not laid right away. While the eggs are inside the mother, there is exchange of oxygen, carbon dioxide, and nutrients between mother and embryo. The platypus has not gotten that far. Unable to nourish her fragile eggs, she must lay them right away, stuck to one another in a clump, in a nest of moist rotting vegetation. When the young emerge only 10 days later, they nourish themselves by licking and sucking milk as it oozes from pores and drips through the mother's belly hair.

Echidnas have gone a step further in infant care. They, too, pro-

D.O.R.

Is it safe to handle an animal found Dead on the Road? D.O.R. animals are safer to handle than those found dead elsewhere, because they have been killed by accident, not by disease. Nevertheless, it is wise to check with your state health department in case there is a local epidemic of any disease that affects humans. Look in the morning along a road you travel daily to be sure a dead animal was killed no longer ago than the night before so that it is still fresh.

Opossums are, of course, very interesting to examine because they are so different and because they are so like the possums that lived in the days of the dinosaurs. The rear toes have an opposable thumb with which possums can grasp branches. The tail is naked; like a monkey's tail, it is prehensile and can hold onto objects. Possums use their tails for climbing trees and for carrying dried grass to their nests. Babies sometimes curl their tails around their mother's tail and ride while hanging upside down. The female's pouch, low on her belly, is entered through a slit. Inside are 13 nipples arranged in a circle of 12, with one in the middle. Twenty newborn babies could fit in a teaspoon; it would take more than 200 to weigh an ounce.

duce sticky eggs. But in preparation for their delivery, the mother's belly skin folds into a temporary pouch. She lays the eggs into the pouch, where their sticky surface adheres to the fur inside. When the echidna eggs hatch, the young stay in the pouch to lick oozing milk.

POPPED FROM A POUCH

Marsupials like the opossum and most of the mammals native to Australia have a permanent pouch, and milk pores are surrounded by a nipple. The unborn embryos still produce the fluid-filled amnion (the sac that surrounds embryo and yolk) invented so long ago by reptiles, but the yolk is very small, and the mother doesn't package her embryos in a shell. She does contribute a tissue connection through which she and the embryo exchange gasses and food. This, too, has been done by reptiles. Some Australian lizards nourish their unshelled embryos through a tissue connection within the mother's oviduct.

In marsupials, the connection isn't elaborate or intimate enough to nourish the embryo for long; it is born still an embryo. The only well-developed parts are the front paws, with which the embryo pulls itself through its mother's belly hair and into her pouch, and the nostrils, through which the embryo sniffs its way to the nipple. There it fuses to a long, thin nipple all the way from lips to throat. Connected to this fuel line, it has little work to feed itself during the rest of its development into a real baby ready to pop from the pouch.

All other mammals have drastically modernized the reptile egg. The first to do so was probably very like a shrew. The egg yolk is too tiny to nourish the embryo at all. The allantois (the reptile egg's sanitary pouch) and the chorion (the membrane that encloses the egg itself) grow into a spongy mass of tissue called the placenta. The placenta invades the wall of the uterus, where the embryo's blood vessels intermingle with the mother's blood vessels. Between the two circulatory systems, what the baby needs to get is delivered and what it needs to get rid of is dumped.

The baby that results from this efficient supply system still needs milk after birth, but it is much more grown up than a newborn marsupial.

FUELING THE BABY FACTORY

All the marsupials, from the lukewarm opossum to the cool kangaroo, have lower body temperatures than placental mammals because

OUT OF THE EGG, INTO THE UTERUS

Like a reptile embryo, a mammal embryo grows its own support systems. The embryo still floats in fluid inside its amnion. It has a yolk sac, although it does not nourish itself with yolk, and the tiny sac disappears before birth. The blood vessels of the allantois, a reptile's lung and toilet, do similar work in mammals. They are the embryo's blood vessels within the placenta, where wastes are disposed of and oxygen and nutrients are taken in. The rest of the baby's portion of the placenta grows as fingerlike projections from one side of the old reptile chorion into the spongy lining of the mother's uterus.

An unborn baby is often pictured as growing inside the uterus, but actually it is not inside the uterine cavity. It is inside its wall. While the embryo and its support systems are still no bigger than a pinhead, the developing placenta erodes a tiny opening into the uterine lining, which then closes over the whole little package. Placental enzymes thin the walls of the mother's blood vessels so that the walls leak blood into small pools. The leaky area of the uterine lining is the mother's portion of the placenta, and it is at the pools that wastes are exchanged for air and food. The mother's blood itself never enters the baby, nor does the baby's blood enter her.

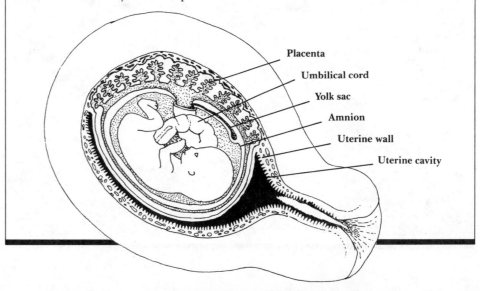

Placenta
Umbilical cord
Yolk sac
Amnion
Uterine wall
Uterine cavity

MULTIPLICATION

The placental white-footed mouse and the similar-looking species of marsupial "mouse" called *Antechinus minimus* are about the same size and might both have a litter of four babies, which are born after about the same length of time in the uterus. Baby mice are weaned at three weeks. Marsupial mice are not ready to leave the pouch until they are two months old, and are not weaned until nearly two months later. By the time *minimus* babies leave their mother, baby mice that share the same birthday may already be grandparents.

they don't burn food as efficiently. Low-geared metabolism limits the number of babies they can make in their lifetimes. Compared to them, placental mammals are a baby production line.

Animals that metabolize food efficiently have fuel to spare for babies. They can produce many embryos. The embryos can grow at a phenomenal rate. After they are born, the babies' own cranked up furnaces allow them to use milk so well that they can continue to grow fast into adulthood. Then the mother tools up for the next batch of babies.

Given the same amount of fuel, a marsupial mammal just can't pump the same amount of fuel into her young as a similar-size placental can. A slow burner, the marsupial doesn't have much energy to offer her embryos before birth (and the primitive placenta also carries less nourishment). The embryos are no better at getting energy from milk than their mother is at getting energy from worms. Growth is slower, adulthood is certainly longer in coming; the assembly line is literally not so hot.

These slowpokes were eventually swamped in the population explosion of placentals. Of all the early kinds of marsupials, only one survives in North America: the common opossum.   Perhaps none might have survived anywhere in the world had they not been saved by the secession of South America.

GOOD-BYE GONDWANA-LAND

By about 150 million years ago, Pangea began to break apart. First, Africa sailed majestically eastward, severing its connections with the rest of Gondwanaland, and with North America. Shreds of North Africa stuck to America at a few places where it and Europe had together joined with our continent. (There are fossil African trilobites in Boston subway tunnels.) What was left of Gondwanaland slowly drifted away from North America. A piece of it, complete with fossil bones of Gondwanaland animals, forms northern Florida and part of Georgia. Eventually, New Zealand broke away from Gondwanaland, followed by Antarctica and finally Australia.

The parting was slow: The breakup took a total of 100 million years. Wherever animals are when continents come apart is where they'll stay and where their descendants will be. A continent could end up having something as cute as a koala bear, or as plain as a possum. Africa came away without mammals (or at least none who left fossils for the record) and got none of its own until it again bumped into Asia and Europe much later. New Zealand came away with no mammals of its own either, and never did get any. South America left with a nice selection of mammals, including many placentals, but when Antarctica broke free, it took only marsupials along for the ride, so that was all Australia had when it, in turn, left Antarctica.

So away marsupials sailed on their private island, where they evolved into quolls, quokkas, and koalas, as well as cuscuses, numbats, wombats, wallabies, potoroos, kan-

Pangea is drawn as a jigsaw puzzle in which the continents are given their modern shapes since their actual shapes aren't known for sure. Drawn that way, there appear to be slivers of ocean dividing them from each other, although Pangea was a single landmass.

As the continents come apart, a new sea washed over the continental crust that stretched all the way from what is now Central America to what is now Central Asia.

By 50 million years ago, as the continents drifted further apart, the space between them was filled by a new ocean—the Atlantic—all the way to the abyss.

LOOK-ALIKES

An animal's shape tells how an animal lives, whether it is a dinosaur, a bird, or a mammal under the skin. This might look like a picture of a shrew, a striped dog, and a slightly peculiar monkey, yet all are marsupials who carry their babies in a pouch. Each resembles a familiar placental animal because its body has evolved to suit a similar lifestyle. The thylacine had a head like a wolf, teeth like a wolf, and feet like a wolf because it lived like a wolf, trotting after large prey for hours in open grassland, and using fangs to kill. The last thylacines were seen in the 1930s; they are probably extinct now. Marsupial mimics of shrews live in holes or tunnel through vegetation, hunt at night, and dine on insects. The cuscus, with its prehensile tail and handlike paws, spends its life in the forest climbing through the tree-tops. Like the true monkeys, it lives off leaves and fruit.

Cuscus

Marsupial shrew

Thylacine

garoos, and bandicoots. And all we got was possum.

WHAT POSSUM SAW

Ancestors of the old American possums saw with their own eyes the dinosaurs that we know only from fossils. What they saw, the fossils say, were animals that lived very much like animals live now, except that they were dinosaurs.

The typical early dinosaur was no monster. An early coelurosaur called *Saltopus* is a good example. It was about the size of a housecat, and weighed two pounds. *Saltopus* had five fingers on its hands, three toes on its feet. The body was sleek, and its slender neck and tapered tail were beautifully balanced on long, powerful legs.

All the coelurosaurs were built along racy lines and hunted small game. One, named *Coelophysis,* was about as big as a medium-size dog and hunted in flocks. Flocks, not packs, seems the right word: The smaller coelurosaurs almost undoubtedly had feathers. *Saltopus* and *Coelophysis* were probably lightly downed with feather-scales. The smallest two, a crow-size dinosaur named *Compsognathus* and an airy little thing called *Archaeopteryx,* had full-fledged feathers. That's for sure. They left them with their fossils.

...AND MORE LOOK-ALIKES

Triceratops was a look-alike of a rhinoceros: It, like the rhino, ate low, tough vegetation and relied on strength, horns, and sheer size to discourage predators. The ankylosaur here was a look-alike of a now-extinct armadillo: Both ate soft foods at ground level and relied on armor and a tail weapon to defend against predators. *Struthiomimus,* whose name means "ostrich mimic," lived like an ostrich on open plains, where speed and good eyesight protected it from enemies. It used its beaked jaw to eat a mixed diet of fruits, vegetables, and small animals.

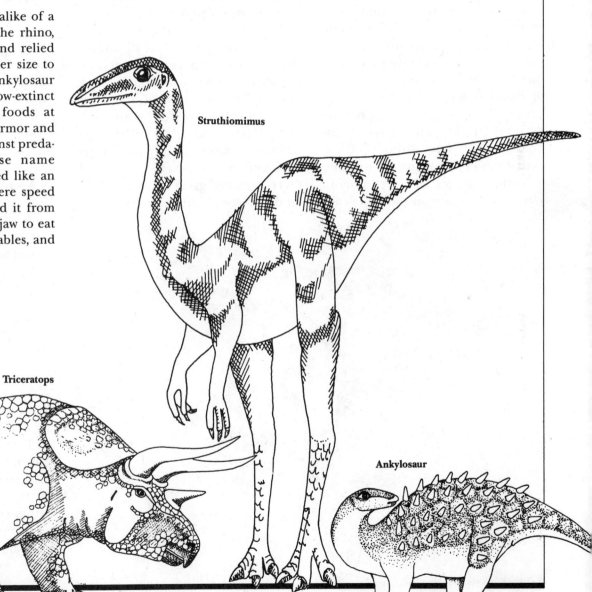

Struthiomimus

Triceratops

Ankylosaur

Much more is known about dinosaurs than bones alone can tell. An animal has only one body to offer the fossil record, and it must lay down its life at just the right time and place for fossilization to occur. But in its lifetime an animal leaves thousands of footprints that catch their maker in action. There are dinosaur nests, too, and eggs, and babies. Some eggs that have remained intact and have been opened only now after all these eons show embryos turned to stone at various stages of development. Where bones are found, they are not always of one life. Some fossil finds are the remains of many lives. Nesting sites, footprints, and groups of skeletons leave no doubt that dinosaurs were social.

As far as bones alone go, *Saltopus* was the basic plan. Most dinosaurs stuck with it. Others elaborated on the basics as they invaded new landscapes. The uplands of the time were thickly forested with redwoods, firs, and pines. The lowlands were moist with tender ferns and emerald mosses. Here and there stretched great dry plains covered with tough brush. In these various habitats, dinosaurs invented, as mammals were eventually to reinvent, the browsing lives of antelopes and bison, and the predatory lives of cats and wolves. Possum saw it all.

EATING UPWARDS

Think of sauropods as elephants weighing 20 times what an elephant weighs, and fed by conifer needles alone. As long as an animal can support itself, its size is limited only by the amount of food available to it. No one else had ever eaten conifers, and the great forests beckoned to the horizon. Sauropods ate their way to such a size that they were forced back down on all fours. They ate on to gigantism, and kept on

A flock of Coelophysis.

eating until they had reached their engineering limit. If they had been any heavier, their bones would have broken under their weight.

Apparently sauropods ate constantly. Their peg-shaped front teeth were badly worn from stripping branches. Lying by the thousands among sauropod remains are stones swallowed and stored in their gizzards as millstones to grind

FOOT MOLDS AND CASTS

A fossil footprint of a dinosaur comes in two forms: a hollow, called a mold, and a bump, called a cast. A mold is the footprint itself. A cast has been formed by sediment that filled the footprint mold.

You can make your own casts of actual footprints of animals and then make a mold from the cast to re-create the footprint itself. Look for footprints, especially on muddy shores where animals come to drink, or invite your pet to leave its footprints in the fine mud of a drying puddle.

You need:
Plaster of Paris
Water for mixing the plaster
Large spoon

Discarded plastic food container
Paring knife or pocket knife
Scissors
Shirt cardboard, or other thin cardboard
Freezer tape
Thick shampoo

1. Follow package directions, and mix the plaster of Paris in a discarded plastic food container.

2. Pour or spoon the mixture about an inch thick over the footprint. Let it

harden for several hours. Carefully lift the cake of plaster from the mud, and set it aside to further harden overnight. The next day, brush off any dirt that remains. You can now make a mold that will look just like the original footprint.

3. Trim the plaster cast to a roundish shape with a knife.

4. Use the scissors to cut a four-inch strip of cardboard long enough to go all the way around the cast. Wrap it around like a collar and tape it in place with freezer tape. Smear the surface of the cast with thick shampoo.

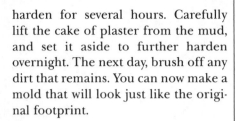

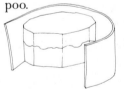

5. Mix another batch of plaster and fill the mold to the top of the cardboard strip. When it has hardened completely the next day, tear away the cardboard and carefully separate the two layers. Rinse off the shampoo after the plaster has hardened for another day or two.

Brachiosaur

their food. The stones are worn to a smooth polish.

Although belly stones added considerable weight to their already heavy bellies, having the muscular kind of stomach called a gizzard relieved sauropods of the need for having heavy grinding teeth. The light sauropod head was easily carried atop a long, slender neck. Braced upright against the trunks of trees, they stripped the needles from the tallest conifers of the time. Down on all fours, they easily reached low plants like cycads.

These plants became evasive and defensive. Short cycads toughened or became covered with spines. Tall conifers grew taller. Over millions of years, tree trunks lengthened to outreach necks, necks lengthened to overreach tree trunks. Finally brachiosaurs stood four stories tall, and redwoods stretched still taller.

The fast-growing, straight, and towering conifer forests of today were shaped by sauropods way back then.

Monstrous as they were, the sauropods were not nearly as heavy as an elephant the same size would be. Their bones were delicately hollowed out, more like trusses than solid beams. The bulk of the animal was hung like a suspension bridge atop the pillars of its hind legs. Air sacs throughout the body further lightened it. Still, at 90 tons, sauropods had grown as heavy as bone will support.

Sauropod footprints tell of gentle giants. One set shows a herd of 20 animals of various ages all walking together, youngsters are in the center of the group, protective grownups surrounding them. No sauropod nests, eggs, or hatchlings have been found, so these peaceable dinosaurs may have given birth to live young.

WHERE THE ANTELOPE DINOSAURS PLAYED

As sauropods gave up on toughened and thorny bushes, another group of herbivores, the ornithischian dinosaurs, moved into that browsing niche. Possum might have sat watching them from the branches of a gingko tree in what is now New Jersey. There ornithis-

RAISING WATER

To provide water for its leaves, a redwood must raise water over 107 meters (350 feet)—that's 35 stories—from its deepest roots to its highest needles. For a long time no one understood how a tree could do that lifting job, for it has no pump, muscles, or any other machinery for pushing water against the force of gravity. As it turns out, the tree makes no effort at all; the water lifts itself.

Each leaf has pores on its underside through which water leaves by evaporating, one molecule at a time. Right behind each water molecule is another, clinging to the first by the electrical forces between them. As the first exits, it tugs the next, and like a samba line, that one tugs the one behind, and it, in turn, tugs the water molecule behind it. The column of water is continuous from the leaf pore back down through the entire tube of water-containing cells all the way to the roots of the tree. The pull of each exiting molecule tugs the whole column behind it.

To feel how tightly water molecules hold onto one another, wet two pieces of glass (microscope slides or the round pieces of glass from flashlights) and lay one on top of the other. Although nothing but water holds them together, they will be very hard to pull apart.

The speed at which the column of water in a tree vein moves up and out depends on the weather. On a wet night, when few water molecules are evaporating from leaf pores, the column barely moves at all. On a hot, dry day, the water in a tree may be rising upward at 200 feet an hour.

chians grazed on dry upland plains bristling with spiny cycads and interspersed with groves of leather-leaved gingkos. Although they weighed several tons, they were the antelopes of their time. Their mummified corpses, dried out and covered by drifting sand before decay destroyed the flesh, include remnants of leathery skin without a trace of scales. Their toes were hoofed. The twigs and leaves of their last meal are still in their desiccated stomachs.

Ornithischian tracks show them living—and dying—in herds. A set of hadrosaur tracks catches a group walking side by side, their youngsters trailing to the rear. Another records a near spill: One hadrosaur turned and three others had to lurch sideways to avoid a collision. Sometimes the footprints record a disaster. A herd of *Iguanodons*, perhaps startled by a predator, stampeded to their death over the edge of a cliff in what is now a coal mine in Belgium. A group of 15 infant hadrosaurs and an adult guarding them were killed all at once by a flash flood in Montana.

Many species of hadrosaurs were marked by a head crest, horn shaped and arching back over the neck in some, more like a helmet in others. Very likely, they roamed in mixed herds and recognized their own species by its distinctive profile, as mixed herds of antelope do. The crest was often hollow, an extension of the nasal cavity. They may have sniffed the wind through this extended nose for the warning smell of predators. Fossil skulls also suggest excellent hearing. The hollow crest may have amplified the hoots and caws of hadrosaurs calling to one another across the windblown plains.

CERATOPSIAN SAWMILLS

If the hadrosaurs were the elegant antelopes, the ceratopsian dinosaurs were the thundering bison of the plains. No cycad was too prickly for them. Their beaked jaws were so powerful that they could bite wood and mash it to pulp in a sawmill of blade-sharp teeth. To support their massive skulls and work their immense jaws, they had a thick muscle attached to an arc of bone spread back over their necks. Their cheeks were thick with muscle, too. Almost

all had a horn mounted atop the muzzle, something like a rhinoceros, and some supported a pair of horns above the eyes as well.

Kindled on the equivalent of sawdust and newspaper, the largest of these beasts, *Triceratops,* grew to 7 meters (28 feet) and weighed 9 tons. Not even the largest dinosaur predator could have taken on a healthy adult *Triceratops.*

One of the early ceratopsians, *Protoceratops,* left fossils in every stage from egg to adult. Parents built their nests close to one another in a communal nesting area. Fifteen or more eggs were laid in each nest, and they were arranged concentrically, as if the mother had circled her nest while laying them. The hatchlings were cared for in the nursery until their chewing ma-

A hadrosaur eating a cycad.

Stegosaur

BAD LIFESTYLES, POOR POSTURE

Everywhere, textbook illustrations, museum exhibits, and plastic toys show dinosaurs slugging through swamps and dragging their tails. When the bones of huge dinosaurs were first recognized, little more than a century ago, it was thought that the largest four-footed ones, such as brontosaurs, must have been swamp dwellers who supported their weight by living half submerged in water. Giants like *Tyrannosaurus rex* obviously walked on two feet, but artists imagined them, and museums reconstructed them, as though they were three-legged stools, supported by their two legs and their heavy tail.

More fossil finds and more careful work has shown that these ideas couldn't be right. The stomachs of the giant sauropods contained coarse upland foods, not soft swamp vegetation. So these giants had to have left the swamps. As to the carnosaurs, their tails were rigid and couldn't have bent to the ground.

It finally became clear that dinosaurs were built like suspension bridges. The powerful hind legs of four footers and two footers alike bore the animals' weight like a tower of the Golden Gate Bridge or the George Washington Bridge bears the weight of the span. The weight of the animal to the front of its hips was

balanced by the weight of the animal to the rear of its hips, so the tail was actually a counterweight to the rest of the beast. But an awful lot of money had already gone into mounting skeletons, painting pictures, and making molds for plastic toys. Don't expect brontosaurs to rise from swamps or tyrannosaurs to lift their tails for a while yet. Better lifestyles and good posture cost money.

STONE PATHS

There are some dinosaur footprints preserved in what used to be a riverbank in Dinosaur National Park in Connecticut. For a fossil footprint to be findable, the sediment in which the print was made and the sediment that filled it must have different textures. If both layers are the same, the stone they become doesn't naturally divide into layers, and the fossil, although it is there, is unlikely ever to be found. When the two materials are different, the rock tends to come apart at their boundary. Sometimes the upper portion—the cast—is destroyed with time so that only the impression remains, as with these prints. Sometimes the opposite happens: The underlying layer crumbles away, leaving only the bump of a cast.

chinery was powerful enough for pulping operations. Until then they were probably fed prepulped pap by their parents.

TOUGH-SKINNED TENDERMOUTHS

Two final groups of ornithischian dinosaurs took advantage of the one food the others had ignored: mosses, tender seedlings, succulent ferns. They were stegosaurs and ankylosaurs, and their beaks and teeth were as modest as their habits. Mounted on four stubby legs close to low-growing greenery, they never grew to monster size.

No doubt they couldn't move very fast and would have been an easy meal for carnivores. But they saw to that problem quite well. The stegosaurs had a double row of bony plates marching down their spine, and spikes at the end of their tail.

The ankylosaurs, toward the end of their evolution, had completely covered themselves with an overlapping coat of mail something like an armadillo, but spikier. When threatened, they crouched low, ducked their heads, and presented an unappetizing exterior. If the predator insisted on sniffing too close, out lashed an axe of a tail that could have bloodied the snout and maybe bashed in the skull of its enemy.

TRACK TALES

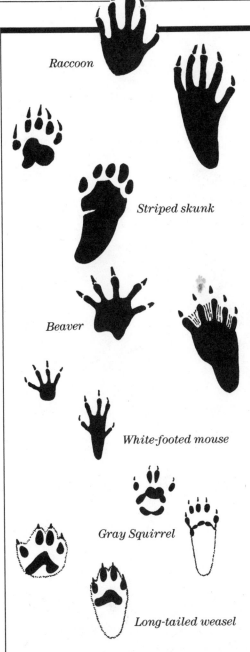

Raccoon

Striped skunk

Beaver

White-footed mouse

Gray Squirrel

Long-tailed weasel

Y ou will find the most tracks, and the most telling ones, in fresh snow. Snow is so fine and soft that even a mouse leaves its dimple-size tracks behind. Follow tracks forward to see where an animal goes to find its food, or backward to see where it lives or sleeps. You may come upon a story of violence: tracks that end abruptly between the twin brush marks of hawk or owl wings.

Tracks can tell you other things about the animal that made them. When moving slowly, an animal's feet tend to leave complete prints all the way from heel to toe, and the depression from all pads will be equally deep. When an animal is running fast, the hind end of each footprint may be shallow or may not be visible at all;

the front may be deep and show clear marks of toes and claws.

The four footprints of a jumping rabbit are set close together, and no footprints are ever on top of another one. A walking animal steps out first on one forefoot, then moves the hind foot on the same side, then repeats those steps on the opposite side. Front and back prints sometimes overlap. If you can tell the difference between forefoot and hind-foot prints, there is a way of figuring out the length of the animal's body. Measure from the midpoint between two hind footprints to the midpoint between two front footprints. That measurement is roughly the distance from the animal's hips to its shoulders.

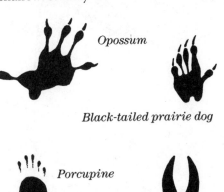

Opossum

Black-tailed prairie dog

Porcupine

Pronghorn "antelope"

Nine-banded armadillo

Mountain lion

Coyote

Black bear

White-tailed deer

Dromaeosaur

A TIMELY NOTE

Comic books and science fiction movies are understandably reluctant to leave out any of these marvelous beasts. All sorts of dinosaurs live cheek by jowl in fiction. In fact, dinosaurs inhabited the earth for well over 100 million years, new forms evolving as old forms died out. By the time there were ankylosaurs, there were no stegosaurs. Ceratopsians did not crunch cycads while brachiosaurs munched redwoods. But, at any one time, there were at least as many dinosaur species as there are mammal species today, so that if there were to be a field guide to the dinosaurs for any century 150 million years ago, it would be just as chockful of pictures and descriptions as a field guide to the mammals for our present century.

At another time—10,000 or a million years later—there would still be as many dinosaur species, but some might be as different as a woolly mammoth of a million years ago is from a bare-skinned elephant now. Lengthen the time between guides to the full 165 million years of the dinosaurs, and the pretty little dog-size coelurosaurs that run across the first pages of this chapter have become the dreadful tyrannosaurs that pound through science fiction. Of course, fiction may have the timing wrong, but *Tyrannosaurus rex* was real.

THE ENEMY

Whenever they lived, whatever their size, and however they protected themselves, the browsing dinosaurs were forever hounded by their enemies, the carniverous dinosaurs, coelurosaurs, and carnosaurs. Fossil footprints left in a layer of mud show a giant sauropod ambling along on feet padded like an elephant's to cushion its enormous weight. Hard on its trail are the three-toed, clawed tracks of a hungry predator.

Footnotes on a lake bottom show a sauropod, rear end afloat like a hippopotomus, swimming along by pushing front feet into the mud. The mark of a hind foot appears only once, when the sauropod kicked it hard at the bottom to make a left turn. But carniverous dinosaurs could swim, too. Eubrontes, a smallish meat eater, swam in shallow water by kicking its toes along the bottom. The tracks appear abruptly, go on for a distance, and then disappear suddenly. At either end of the track, the animal's swimming motion must have lifted it off the bottom.

The largest carnosaur was that Class B movie heavy, *Tyrannosaurus rex*, who grew so large that it could attack bulky ceratopsians from above, out of the way of their dangerous horns. Tracks of various species of tyrannosaurs show that they hunted sometimes alone and sometimes in pairs, running at four miles an hour, or about the speed of their fastest herbivore prey.

Eubrontes is a more typical dinosaur carnivore than *Tyrannosaurus rex*. These medium-size carnivores sped along as fast as you can sprint—about 6 kilometers (10 miles) an hour. And they traveled in packs. One set of footprints records the passage of 19 eubrontes not only traveling together, but marching abreast. In this pack formation they were probably able to round up a herd of sauropods and pick off the old and the weak as wolves cull a herd of caribou today. A few very rare tracks show one final horrifying picture: eubrontes had the ability to leap, perhaps from ambush, like a cat.

SCI-FI ALIVE

The agile, elegant little coelurosaurs were relatives of the carnosaurs. As time advanced, some of them grew to the size of ostriches. They evolved brains larger than any modern bird. Their eyes were huge—some species perhaps could see well enough at night to hunt for possums. The most advanced of the group, the man-size dromaeosaur, had forward facing eyes, which gave it 3-D vision. It had an opposable thumb to grasp objects in its three-fingered hand. This intelligent, grasping beast with 3-D eyes was armed with a huge claw with which it ripped its prey to shreds. What might it have done next if extinction hadn't put an end to its remarkable evolution?

But none of the large dinosaurs were to survive. Only the little feathered coelurosaurs, running the meadows after insects, themselves learned to fly from danger. They are the dinosaurs that are still among us.

How Dinosaurs Learned to Fly

The plumey fossils of *Compsognathus* and *Archaeopteryx* are practically identical and perfectly dinosaurian, complete to teeth and three-clawed hands. The only difference is that while *Compsognathus* was evenly feathered, *Archaeopteryx* had grown exceptionally long arm and tail feathers. Neither had the sort of shoulder that allows the flapping motion of flight. Neither was a bird.

But were they dinosaurs? That is a tricky question. Fossils don't come labeled with their name: somebody has to decide what makes a creature a bird or a dinosaur. In the past, scientists reasoned that if a creature had feathers, it must be a bird. *Archaeopteryx* became known in every biology textbook as the first bird. However, when this famous fossil is examined for 13 characteristics that differentiate reptiles from birds, 11 are reptile-like and only two are bird-like (besides feathers, the thing has a wishbone).

A great upheaval is going on among the name-makers. The most rebellious (and possibly the fairest) among them propose a whole new evolutionary address: a new class, *Dinosauria*, that is a warmblooded and therefore distinct from cold-blooded *Reptilia;* and three sub-classes—*Saurischia,* whose members had hips like lizards, *Ornithischia,* whose members had birdlike hips, and *Aves,* the birds themselves. With these new names, *Archaeopteryx* remains a dinosaur, but on its way to becoming a bird. And, with these new names, even birds are dinosaurs.

Suppose you were to come upon *Archaeopteryx* chasing grasshoppers in a meadow. It is running full tilt, arms held poised to grab its prey. Just as it is about to pounce, the grasshopper springs into the air right over the dinosaur's head, and lands behind it. The dinosaur screeches to a halt as its tail flips up

Archaeopteryx

like an air brake, veers about using feathered arms as rudders and, legs still beating in stride, takes off in the opposite direction after the grasshopper. Now the grasshopper leaps again, this time straight ahead and nearly straight up. The dinosaur, too, leaps into the air, elbows out and claws at the ready, and grabs an aerial meal.

Suppose the dinosaur lifts its elbows higher still, spreads its arms wider still. Perhaps much to its surprise, its feathery arms lift it like a kite on the breeze, and the dinosaur is momentarily airborne. And so the dinosaur learned to soar.

By the next page in the fossil record, you would no longer come upon a small coelurosaur draped in feathers chasing grasshoppers through the meadow. Had you been around then observing these little flapping things, you would have been a bird watcher.

THE SKY'S THE LIMIT

When the first birds took to the air perhaps 130 million years ago they were not alone. Just as the dinosaurs were racing onto the uplands, another group descended from archosaurs, the pterosaurs, were climbing into the trees. They leaped from limb to limb first by leg power alone, then with the added lift of a skin flap stretching

A MODERN DINOSAUR?

The shoulder joint of a bird is specially shaped for the flapping motion of flight. The breast bone is specially shaped for attaching large flight muscles. Otherwise, there is almost no difference between the skeleton of a small, running, insect-eating dinosaur and the skeleton of the first small, flying, insect-eating birds. Both had tails. If you peel skin and muscle from the rear end of a modern bird, you can still make out tail vertebrae, fused together into a spade-shaped stub. Feathers still stick out to either side, and birds can fan them as an air brake when landing.

Dinosaurs had air sacs that lightened their bodies; birds have them too. These air sacs connect with the lungs and the air birds breathe travels throughout their innards, even to their very bones.

The coelurosaur dinosaurs had scales on their legs. So do birds today. Birds don't have teeth anymore, but their DNA still carries instructions for making tooth enamel, just as the DNA in dinosaurs did.

DINOSAUR NESTS?

Many of the dinosaur eggs found in the West are upright in bowl-shaped nests, with only the bottom half of each egg buried in what once was mud. It's supposed that dinosaur mothers gathered vegetation with which to cover the exposed portions of their eggs. As the vegetation rotted, it would keep the eggs warm. This is how many reptiles and a few birds incubate their eggs today.

Most birds that don't use dead plants to warm their eggs nevertheless gather plant materials, form them into a bowl, and lay their eggs inside. Perhaps they have never lost the vegetable-gathering urge, or the notion that bowls are best. Maybe they are building dinosaur nests.

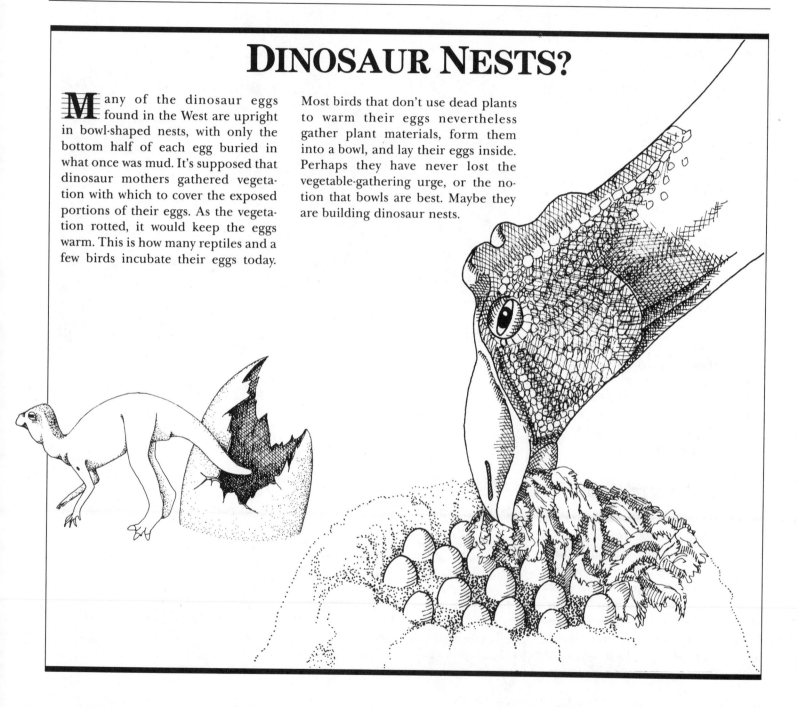

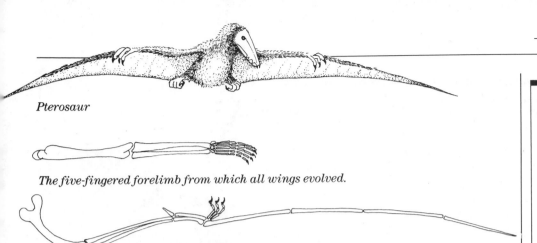

Pterosaur

The five-fingered forelimb from which all wings evolved.

A pterosaur's wing: the index finger is very elongated.

A bird's wing: most of the fingers are fused together.

from front leg to rear leg. Pterosaurs, like *Archaeopteryx,* finally flapped. But they weren't feathery. They were furry.

By the time birds ventured into their airspace, the pterosaurs ranged from the tropics to the arctic. They varied in size from ones as small as robins to ones with wings that measured 15 meters (almost 50 feet) from tip to tip, and who sailed the open ocean like fuzzy albatrosses.

Pterosaurs kept all their fingers and toes. One finger grew immensely long and became the frail support for the wing membrane. The other four fingers and all five toes remained as branch-clinging claws. Hind legs were short. Fossil footprints show pterosaurs walking on all fours, dragging their wing membranes along the ground beside them.

Pterosaur wing membranes, and their single-fingered support, were fragile. Any tear to the wing or fracture of the bone grounded these flyers, leaving them to hobble feebly along or cling, starving, in the treetops. Birds, however, kept their long, strong legs. When grounded, they run like dinosaurs away from enemies and after food. They fused their whole wrist and their fingers, too, into a thick, strong wing tip. The arm bones—not the hand alone—became the attachment for the wing surface. And instead of a thin, fleshy sail, birds' flight surface is of tough feathers that, when injured, are easily replaced.

FANCY STUFF

In the spring, when birds are building nests, leave out bits of colored yarn, string, ribbon, the cellophane "grass" used in Easter baskets, clippings from your dog, or your own hair. Watch what happens. Birds will soon be shopping in the fancy-goods store you have set up for materials to build their nests. As they come and go, you can observe their route and guess the nest's location. Later, when the nest is finished, it's fun to see woven into it the red yarn or the poodle fur you provided. At the end of the summer, as you see birds beginning to flock together for migration, it is all right to take the nest and keep it.

THE PRICE OF A MEAL

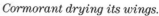

Cormorant drying its wings.

Birds that live in the same neighborhood don't necessarily shop in the same markets or pay the same price for their food. Take gulls and cormorants, common shorebirds whose out-in-the-open ways of life make them easy to observe. Both eat fish, but cormorants pay dearly for every mouthful, while a gull's meal is cheap.

Cormorants fly to their fishing grounds with effort. Gulls ride the wind with barely a flap. Cormorants' feathers aren't well oiled. They sink up to their necks when swimming, but the oily gulls bob like a cork in the water. Gulls grab fish from surface waters, while cormorants dive deep. Their wettable feathers are an advantage for diving, and they may find in deep water larger prey than gulls skim from the surface, but they can't keep it up for long. Waterlogged, they must stand on a rock and "hang" their wings to dry. Fish for fish, a cormorant pays more in energy than a gull does.

Then there is the kind of market gulls and cormorants know how to use. Cormorants can only dive for fish. Gulls stalk docks and ride boats with fishermen, stealing bait and eating leavings. They scoop up urchins and mussels at low tide, and break their shells by dropping them onto rocks. They walk the parks of coastal cities pecking at peanuts in the company of pigeons, eat leftovers from trash cans, and wheel inland to shop in garbage dumps.

While noticing these differences, notice also the result. There are many times more gulls than cormorants. When fish are scarce, cormorants lay no eggs at all, while gulls raise their normal number of nestlings and laugh on.

Birds are extraordinary flying machines. Engineers, however, still puzzle over how pterosaurs could fly at all. Did they flap strongly enough to lift them high or carry them far, or if they glided mostly, how did they take off or land on such skimpy legs? Perhaps they hardly ever landed, except on water, but if that is so, then where did they lay their eggs? One engineer is now trying to answer some of these questions with robot pterosaurs. Meanwhile, it is a mystery how pterosaurs flew through nearly as long a time as dinosaurs walked, including 80 million years in which birds were flying, too. They began to dwindle toward the end of the age of dinosaurs, but it can't have been because they failed to fly. Nevertheless, with their final extinction, the sky was the limit for birds.

BIRD BRAINS

As the last of the dinosaurs, birds may carry with them the circular plan of dinosaur nests, the open-mouthed signal to regurgitate food to dinosaur babies, and a few loud words in dinosaur language. Such things are written in the brain, and so long as they work, they last.

Bird brains have stayed about the same size throughout their evolution. Birds have no space left over in their brains for idle learning. A bird learns what it's got to learn—no more, no less. Yet what a bird learns—who its mother is and where home is—is necessarily different for each individual. It can't inherit such information. How does it know what it is supposed to find out?

Each bird comes pre-wired to look for cues that turn learning on and tell it what the learning means. A duckling's cue for learning "mother" is the first moving object it sees that requires a certain amount of effort to follow. If it's hard enough to follow, the duckling "knows" that the moving object is its mother—even if it is in reality a wooden decoy of a male duck, a box pulled along by a string, or a person strolling past.

Such a system seems to be wacky, but in the wild, it's very unlikely that the first moving object a newly hatched duck will see is anything but its mother.

Pre-wired cues take up very little space, leaving "empty" brain for learning those things for which the wiring is prepared. Once the duckling has learned what it needs to know, the pre-wired instructions are erased. If the cues remained, they would prove confusing—the duckling would continue to learn who its mother was over and over with any moving object that happened along. The cues begin to fade in about half a day, leaving that brain space free for other uses.

The learning itself, however, is put in place as another sort of cue to be tapped long after the duckling no longer needs its mother. Whatever "mother" was to the hatchling, that same sort of object will be "mate" in adulthood. The unfortunate duckling who has been

BIRD CALLERS

Nature centers and sporting-goods stores sell the Audubon bird caller with which you can bring songbirds out into the open. The device is twisted like a cork in a bottle to make various clicks, chirps, and twitters. Some can get a bird song out of it, but it is easier to try for "scolding" sounds. Nesting songbirds call *tut tut, tik tik,* or other simple worry notes when they believe their nest is threatened. Mimicking the sound brings them out to see what is wrong. To learn a scolding call so you can copy it, approach a bird's nest and listen to what its owners say.

mothered by a human will attempt to court humans when it grows up.

A crucial piece of learning in songbirds is the song that signifies a bird's own species. The female, although she may never sing herself, must learn the song in order to recognize a mate of her own kind. The male must sing the song to attract her, and to announce his ownership of property to neighboring males. Birds learn only their own song. Their brain comes equipped with instructions to pay attention to a few characteristics that make their song distinctive; they ignore songs that don't fit

Ringed turtle doves

those expectations. When what's supposed to happen doesn't, song learning fails. Birds can't learn their proper song unless they hear it sung.

On the other hand, bird calls are written out completely in the brain. Birds don't have to learn to scream

in fear, to cry out an alarm, or to summon other birds to mob a predator. Perhaps bird calls are similar to dinosaur language, for some birds understand the words for attack and flee as they are pronounced by other species. When you see an egg-stealing crow being mobbed by a crowd of smaller birds, they are often of several species that happen to live nearby. The alarm call of a jay will send sparrows into flight.

The fear scream is used by birds when they are attacked by predators, and is the equivalent of screaming bloody murder. Not all species of birds, however, fly to the rescue of the screamer. Some do nothing. The scream summons only other predators who then become distracted as they argue among themselves about who is to finish off the screamer. Meanwhile, the

RECORDING BIRD SOUNDS

Recordings of bird calls and songs are available in the shops of many nature centers and natural-history museums, but if you record your own, the sounds will stick better in your memory. The best season is spring, when males are loudly advertising; the best time is early morning, when they are all advertising at once. Use a cassette tape recorder and bring field glasses and a bird guide with you.

Advertising birds choose "announcing posts," often high in a tree that stands out against other trees,

on a rooftop, or on a fence post. While recording, locate the bird, get a close look at it with the field glasses, and use the field guide to identify it. Speak its name into the recorder after its song. If you're unsure the first time, try to find that bird again. It is likely to reappear at the same announcing post on other mornings. After several weeks of listening and collecting, you will be able to tell which of your local birds is nearby even when it is too distant or too hidden to see.

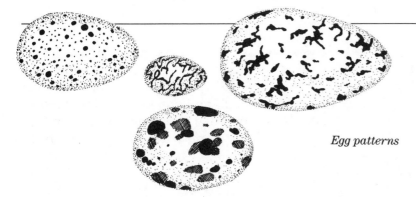

Egg patterns

screamer buys time for its own escape. Those who do nothing stay safe.

RULES TO BREED BY

Mental economy results in physical economy. Birds take action on cue, but waste no effort if the cue is not given. A male ringed turtle dove doesn't bill and coo unless he sees a female. The female's ovaries don't prepare eggs unless she sees him billing and cooing. The pair mates only if they find a hollow place and materials to build a nest with. Only if they have built the nest themselves will they incubate the eggs in it, and only if they have incubated will their throat glands triple in size to secrete the "crop-milk" with which doves feed their nestlings.

The system saves time, energy, and mistakes. No billing and cooing means the male hasn't produced enough of the hormone testosterone to make sperm. Why bother readying the eggs? Each step depends on some cue that makes it a sensible step to take. The cue might not be the simplest one you could think of. For instance, the simplest cue to incubate might be the sight of eggs. But the cue that is used is more clever. By the time the doves have finished the whole sequence of events that leads to a finished nest they have built themselves, the eggs they sit on are bound to be their own. If the cue to incubate were the sight of eggs, whether or not the rest of the sequence had been completed, they might easily nurture the genes of total strangers.

FOOLED BY PHEASANTS

Nevertheless, there is a loophole in the system. If an onlooker lays her eggs in the nest at just the right moment, when parents are cued to

Prairie chicken   *Pheasant*

BIRD DELI

You can attract particular kinds of birds to your home by offering them the particular kinds of food they like best. Put out tiny thistle seeds to attract finches. Cardinals can't resist an orange, served in slices or just cut in half. To bring in woodpeckers, tie a lump of suet to a tree. Mixed birdseed, which contains both tiny and large seeds, attracts a mixed group of birds, but often the larger or more aggressive species will crowd out shyer, smaller ones. English sparrows, pigeons, and starlings tend to take over bird feeders, which will hurt your chances of enjoying many of the more interesting species in your area. All three would rather peck seed from the ground, so mount the bird feeder high and tempt them away from it by tossing corn on the ground at a distance from the feeder. The corn will also bring pheasants to dinner in areas where they live.

sit on whatever eggs appear, it can leave the exhausting task of childrearing to the fooled couple. Gulls and other birds who breed in crowded nesting grounds avoid having to raise the young of others by laying eggs speckled or splotched in ways that appear unique to their owners. A gull that spots an unfamiliar egg will push it out of the nest.

Prairie chickens haven't evolved an egg recognition device, and they are being fooled into extinction by parasitic pheasants. Before pheasants were imported into North America, plump little prairie chickens were our most numerous prairie bird. Now, in the easternmost part of their range in Illinois, their population size has been reduced from millions to only 300. Part of the problem is simply that pheasants are big, aggressive birds, and their mere presence makes prairie chicken hens so nervous that they abandon nest sites before finishing the nest. No nest, no eggs. If the hen persists long enough to cue herself to take the next step, the finished nest seems to have the same meaning to the pheasant hen. She, too, lays her eggs in it.

The prairie chicken, pleased with any eggs at that point, incubates both her eggs and the pheasant's without noticing the difference in size. The pheasant eggs hatch out

THEN THERE'S THE PHALAROPE

An interesting case, the phalarope. The one with the black, rust, blue, and gold pattern is surely the male. Except she isn't. The dull one is the male. What's more, the father phalarope mothers the babies all alone. Although the female lays eggs, she then leaves the nest and never returns. The male incubates the eggs, warms the nestlings when they hatch, and does all the feeding too.

Behind this strange switch lies an interesting evolutionary yarn. The coloring and the reproductive behavior of birds are controlled by hormones. Both sexes produce androgens—the hormones that we call "male" and that cause us to grow whiskers—and estrogens—the hormones that we call "female" and that cause us to grow breasts. In birds, androgens are responsible for brightly colored feathers, while estrogens are responsible for incubating and feeding behavior. When the sexes produce similar quantities of both kinds of hormones, their coloring is similar, and both male and female care for the brood. Gulls are like that, so are most other shorebirds, and so, once, were phalaropes.

Then some hen was born with a defect in her ability to produce estrogen. She laid eggs, but remained "turned off" to childrearing. Her mate carried on—he had always shared that job—while she left the breeding ground.

Phalarope breeding grounds are dangerous places because they are open to predators. So this unmotherly nest deserter was at an advantage compared with females eager to incubate. So were daughters who inherited her hormonal disability. Low-estrogen females increased in the population.

That favored males with less androgen and more estrogen. The less there is of male hormone, the duller the feathers, and the duller the feathers, the less easily predators spot their prey. The more there is of female hormone, the greater the urge to care for babies, and the better that babies are cared for, the more survive.

Meanwhile, females with more male hormone and less female hormone gained another advantage. Their more stunning plumage attracted males and, like peacocks and roosters, these showy hens actively courted mates and aggressively chased away competitors. The new-fangled family was a huge success. In every species of phalarope today, the female is liberated and the male keeps house.

Female phalarope

Male phalarope

before her own. Now she notices: These are alien chicks. Disturbed by the changelings, the prairie chicken hen abandons the whole eerie business. The pheasant hen takes over the care of her own brood; the unhatched prairie chicken eggs are left to die.

Pheasants aren't parasitic anywhere else in the world. Here on our own farmlands we are watching a new evolution—and a new extinction.

GUESS WHO BABYSITS?

You can guess something about the sex roles of birds by their color. When both sexes of a species are colored the same, the male and female are likely to share equally in parenting. Usually such species—sparrows, for example—are dull-colored or mottled. The camouflage of these birds helps to hide them from predators while they are incubating eggs or feeding nestlings.

For species in which the male has bright plumage, such as goldfinches, parents don't share in raising the brood. The dull-colored female does that; the male specializes in brilliant displays that win him mates and put down competitors who covet his landholding. Brightly colored or boldly patterned males are avid suitors and fierce protectors, whereas their hens are shy dur-

Bluebirds, beautiful and once common birds of meadow, park, and yard, have now nearly disappeared from the East for lack of places to nest. Bluebirds make their nests inside natural cavities in trees, or in bird houses. But pushy house sparrows and cocky starlings get all the good homes first. Both of these foreign species were released in Central Park in New York City in the last century, and both have since become pests from coast to coast. They way outnumber bluebirds. But there is a way to outwit them. Build a house that only a bluebird can move into.

The house will stand less than five feet off the ground. This is lower than house sparrows like to live, so they will look elsewhere. Starlings will try hard to take the house over, but— Hah! The door is too small! Bluebirds will find it just perfect. In one case, a couple moved in 30 minutes after the house was up, as though they had been watching the workmen build their dream house.

You need:
Pencil
Ruler
6-inch-wide wood shelving, 5 feet long
Saw
Hand or electric drill with 1 ½ -inch paddle bit and ⅜ -inch bit
Hammer

Nails
Three-quarter round stair rail, 6 feet long
Spade

1. Follow the illustration and use a pencil and ruler to measure and mark

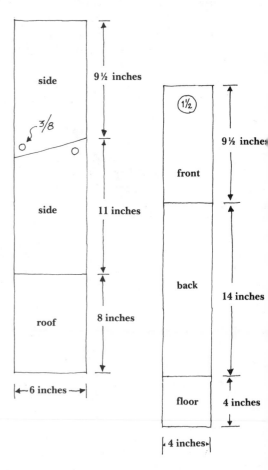

COME BACK BLUEBIRD!

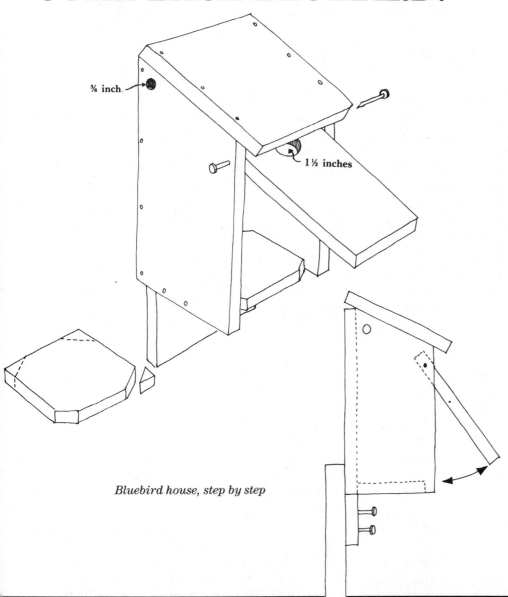

⅜ inch

1 ½ inches

Bluebird house, step by step

where the board is to be cut. Saw the board into pieces.

2. Drill the large entrance hole in the front piece with the paddle bit, and the small ventilation holes in the side pieces with the ⅜-inch bit.

3. Saw the corners off the floor piece to provide more ventilation.

4. Using the hammer and nails, nail all the pieces except the front together as shown. Be sure the rear wall doesn't stick up above the slope of the side walls, or the roof won't fit. The portion of the rear wall that projects below the house is for attaching it to the pole. When the rest of the house is assembled, attach the front by two nails about an inch below the roof line, and opposite one another so that the front swings up like a door for cleaning out the old nest each fall.

5. Now nail the assembled house to the top of the stair rail. No finish is needed, but you can paint the outside (not the inside) of the house in a pale color if you want to.

6. Choose an open spot for the house, with a tree no more than 50 feet away. With the spade, dig a narrow hole between one and two feet deep, or pound a hole with a crowbar. Put the post in the hole, jam stones around it to hold it steady, and pack the soil in hard around it.

ing courtship, and peaceable. A male and female with the same coloring mutually court one another and have similar temperaments.

But domestic relations between the sexes are always a compromise between the reproductive strategy that would give a male the most offspring and the reproductive strategy that would give the female the most offspring.

For males, who make billions of microscopic sperm, the more mates, the more offspring. So long as each mate is able to raise chicks by herself, a cock would do best to fertilize a whole flock of hens and then walk out on them.

For females, who make a limited number of large, lavishly provisioned eggs, there is no advantage to having more than one mate. Extra mates would not increase the number of eggs fertilized. Her best strategy is to get help in raising her chicks to adulthood.

In fact, the male rarely gets away with abandonment. His strategy is defeated by the fact that other males compete for females. Although each male requires at least one female to have any chicks at all, a whole flock of hens can share a single male. Other males have no opportunity to reproduce at all. Thus the cock who seems to enjoy for free the reproductive services of a harem pays for the privilege of a large family by defending a territory large enough to support them. Where food and safe nesting sites are plentiful, hens extract the costs in child care instead.

TELLING A COCK BY ITS COLOR

Like female anole lizards who judge a male by its tail, hens use esthetic judgments to choose a mate. Their tastes are no more frivolous than a lizard's, but in the end lead to false advertising.

A bird's skin color, weight, athletic vigor, and plumage indicate the state of its health. Birds with even minor illnesses have pale skin, are smaller, tire more easily, and have dull or shabby feathers. Females have only to observe these outward signs to choose a mate most likely to be a healthy, vigorous provider and defender. His health may also indicate that he is resistent to infection, and likely to pass a good immune system on to her chicks.

Naturally, it's in the nonresistent cock's interest to fool hens into thinking he's healthier than he is. If pale skin indicates disease, a male whose exposed skin is a ruddy billboard of health (for example, the turkey's scarlet wattle) will have a better chance of being chosen. If vigor indicates health, a male could assure a mate's approval by extraordinary displays of energy (for example, the mockingbird's aeriel acrobatics). And if feathers are signs, then dull colors like grays and browns will be less pleasing to females than bright colors such as the yellow of a goldfinch, the blue of a bluejay, and the red of a cardinal. So, even trickery evolves.

But that is not the end of this story. Once hen preference for colorful males has evolved, nearly all males will be colorful. What then? Well, then the males that exhibit color in more striking ways will win the hearts of admiring hens: the bluejay who displays his blue between white wing bars; the mallard whose iridescent neck is dazzling against a buff background; or the "eyes" of a male peacock's tail arranged in arresting patterns.

Such patterns are inheritable; a hen that mates with a dandy cock will tend to have sexy sons. Her sexy sons, like their handsome dad, will attract females easily. The flashy pattern will spread in descending generations.

Finally, flashy looks becomes disconnected from the question of health. What hens find beautiful drives evolution.

Scientists resist the notion that evolution means progress, that because something is new, it is better. That resistance is quite a struggle. Human intuition can't help but

NORTHERNERS OR SOUTHERNERS?

Nearly a quarter of the bird species that breed in North America migrate south for the winter, many to the tropical rain forests of Central and South America. In these wintering grounds, they spend more of their lives around toucans and parrots than around cardinals and jays. And there, insects, fruit, and nectar are available year-round.

Northerners have tended to think of migrating birds as fellow northerners who, like themselves, flock south for a winter vacation. But why, if the living is so easy in the south, do vacationing birds return? There must be a very good reason, for their wings are their own, not an airplane's, and the distance is thousands of miles.

The fact is that during spring and summer the living is easier in the north. Come the first warm days, hordes of insects hatch out all at once. The days are longer than in the tropics, and so are the best hunting times of dawn and dusk, when bird and bug alike bustle into action. With the spring rains, uncountable earthworms squirm to the surface. When the blueberries ripen, they ripen by the billions. When the grass goes to seed, there are seeds everywhere. In the tropics, there is never that much food all in one place, all at one time, and all laid out so conveniently.

And northlands are safe lands. Birds that breed in the tropics have to contend with frightening numbers of egg-stealing, nestling-eating snakes, monkeys, opossums, raccoons, and kinkajous. They tend to build tiny, hideable nests in which only a couple of eggs will fit, and still more eggs and young are lost than in the north.

So it may be that migratory birds are not northerners. Perhaps they are tropical species that vacation in the north where the living is easy and babies are safe.

---

find a peacock esthetically superior to the presumably dull fowl from which it originated. But here is the ultimate trick: Our intuition—our taste, our sense of what is fine and beautiful—has evolved like any hen's has. Why is a red cardinal more beautiful than a brown wren? Perhaps because we connect the color red with good things: red fruit is ripe fruit, and red lips belong to healthy people.

SUMMER SILENCE

Breeding over, birds begin to shuck their sexual apparatus. Brilliant feathers may be exchanged for drab disguise. Testes and ovaries shrink to almost nothing; no sense carrying extra weight or feeding unneeded organs. Birds whose high-protein insect diet built up their own tissues and that of their nestlings may now switch to energy-rich seeds for fat storage and heat production during the cold months ahead. The songs males sang to announce their presence fade away. Dawn now brings only a summer silence. The caged canary shuts up by destroying that part of its brain that knows its songs.

As a canary falls silent, the song area in its brain shrinks. Nerve cells shorten and lose communicating branches and their connections with other nerve cells. Some cells are lost altogether. The anatomy that knew how to sing is discarded along with that summer's songs.

To sing again, the bird must grow new brain material. Nerve cells lengthen and rebranch. New cells grow and new connections are created. With a song center as fresh as a baby's, the canary pulls from its hard-wired library the basic elements of canary song, then practices, elaborates, composes them into new variations. When spring comes, the canary sings again—using a brand new repertoire.

THE NUTCRACKER'S SECRET

No one knows whether brain economy has been carried quite so far in other song birds, but the hardwired inherited knowledge that runs a lizard as rigidly as a wind-up toy seems to be used in a thinking way in birds. Clark's nutcracker, a relative of jays and crows, buries as many as 33,000 piñon pine nuts for winter meals. Each hiding place is miles from the stands of pine it harvests, and each hole holds only four or five seeds, so there are thousands of hiding places. The bird refinds most of them; it would starve if it didn't.

There are various ways hidden food caches might be relocated without relying on memory. They might be sniffed out, but birds can barely smell. They might be marked with a signpost of some sort, but in fact the nutcracker camouflages each hiding place with whatever rubble is typical of the location. The caches might be hidden only in certain kinds of locations so that the bird could look, for example, only on south-facing slopes and find the seeds there by trial and

DOWN THE CHIMNEY

One spring day a California couple returned home from vacation to find their house inhabited by a flock of 800 swifts four deep on the windowsills, strolling beneath the kitchen stove, huddled in flower vases, hiding out in Kleenex boxes.

That's not fun, but it's also not rare. The mistake is a natural one: From the air, chimneys look like hollow trees. Apparently, a flock of migrating swifts ran into foul weather and took a nose dive to shelter down the nearest "hollow tree." After all, the pattern written on their brain is a lot older than chimneys.

error. But that isn't what the nut-cracker does.

Small brain or not, nutcrackers simply remember for nearly half a year the thousands of spots where they have hidden their winter supply of pine nuts. They do it much the same way you recall where you put a pocket knife or where a certain flower grows: by forming a mental map of the area. As a nut-cracker buries seeds, it notices the locations of landmarks such as boulders and trees, their distances from one another, and the general lay of the land. Move its landmarks, and it is as baffled about where to find its food as you would be trying to find a can opener on moving day.

MAPMAKING

As long-distance fliers, birds have probably evolved far better mental mapmaking abilities than any dinosaur would ever have needed. Even the daily flight paths of communally roosting birds like starlings, crows, grackles, and red-winged blackbirds are long. In Nanuet, New York, in an area of fast-food chains, parking lots, and shopping malls, nearly 8,000 crows congregate each night after the nesting season is over in their traditional roost in trees above a condominium's swimming pool. One flight path brings 1,500 of them from the

AFRICANS IN BOSTON

Fossils of tiny 600-million-year-old blue-green algae found when workers were tunneling for Boston's subway system have turned out to be foreigners. The blue-green algae had lived in Africa. Apparently, Boston is a bit of Africa left behind when Pangea broke apart. Boston is not the only part of the Atlantic Coast that comes from overseas. Tri-lobite fossils from the slate belts of Georgia and the Carolinas appear to be African too.

east over White Plains—a 14-mile commute.

That distance is nothing for a bird. The tiny ruby-throated hummingbird, the smallest bird in the world, travels all the way from New England to Mexico for the winter. The phalarope, a small shore bird, travels from the Midwest to the Amazon jungle in South America. The arctic tern holds the long-distance record. It makes a yearly round trip of 22,000 miles from as far as Alaska, across the Atlantic Ocean, down along the coasts of Europe and Africa, to the Antarctic Ocean, and back again.

The maps that guide birds on these long journeys are drawn from mere sketches with which the bird is born. The sketch for a night-flying migrator may be a map of several stars—not much, but enough to send it in the right direction. Day migrators may carry with

them the rough outline of a coast they are to follow. Pigeons are guided by a magnetic map—grains of magnetite inside their skulls act like a compass.

As with the pattern of song a bird is to learn, a map sketch gives cues for what to notice in order to complete the picture. An island, a playground, a parking lot, or your home might all be represented in some bird's brain as it learns its way around its local neighborhood, its flight path to a night roost, or sometimes in the company of learned elders but sometimes not, a thousand-mile journey to another continent.

IS THIS TRIP NECESSARY?

The trips birds make often seem excessive. Why go to the Amazon when Florida is so much closer?

Once in the Amazon, why return to Lake Michigan? Without understanding the history of the maps birds now follow, we will never know.

Perhaps the sketches for some birds' maps began all the way back when they still shared the air with pterosaurs. The trip might once have been a short seasonal journey from snow-covered uplands to fields where pine nuts lay exposed, or a crop-following circuit that took the flock no further than a crow's commute. But a hundred million years and more have passed since birds first coded these maps in the nerve cells of their little brains. Drifting continents have caused distances to stretch; climates have changed. A Canadian bird could once have traveled mere hundreds of miles to reach subtropical climate. It must travel thousands now. A bird might once have hopped from Georgia to Africa. Today the Atlantic Ocean stands in between.

Those distances stretched as slowly as they are stretching now. The movement of landmarks was never noticeable, not from year to year nor from generation to generation. A bird whose map said "follow the coastline until you get to the jungle" would have had to increase the length of its journey less than an inch a century. The changes in climate, even the coming apart of Pangea, would have been imperceptible, but may account for the strange places birds now find themselves as they follow their ancient maps over a land that, by 100 million years ago, was bursting into bloom.

100 MILLION YEARS AGO

Fruits and Flowers · A Multiplication of Insects · Chemical Warfare

A bird following the eastern coast of North America 100 million years ago would have seen the new Atlantic sloshing gently between drifting continents. South of the fragment of Gondwanaland that had remained attached to Florida, coral animals were building the reefs that would eventually lengthen the peninsula. To the north, the Appalachians had become middle-aged mountains, smoothed by time. Rivers that had once flowed westward off the sides of these mountains had found valleys low enough to break through. They changed course, and now flowed eastward, out to sea, carrying with them mountain crumbs that were to rim the coast with beaches.

Magnolias bloomed below. As time passed the green carpet that covered the Appalachians became dotted with their white flowers, and specked with the golds, pinks, and oranges of other flowering plants.

Swooping down over Delaware, the bird would have seen trees and bushes nodding with these brand-new ornaments, or bowing under the weight of fruit.

Fruit was a new meal for birds and dinosaurs, but it wasn't the main meal. A bird, alighting on a magnolia twig, would have more likely snapped up the flowering plant's constant companions: its pollinating servants, its leaf-eating enemies—insects like the ones we know today.

To see these insects close enough to understand them is to enter another world. It is a world in miniature, where a life can be measured in days, a stem can feed a herd, and the pull of molecules is stronger than the force of gravity. Yet insects are responsible for roses, maples, and all the flowering plants, for a skunk cabbage can't live without its flies.

MAGNOLIA TIME

Fossil grains of magnolia pollen dating from 110 million years ago are the oldest traces of flowering plants. Magnolias are the most

GREEN FLOWERS

T he first flowers were green. Some still are. The flowers shown in the photo are the green blooms of the tulip tree, a member of the magnolia family that is common in northern woodlands. Its green petals photosynthesize like the leaves they evolved from. The flowers of other magnolias have lost the chlorophyll from their petals and so are white.

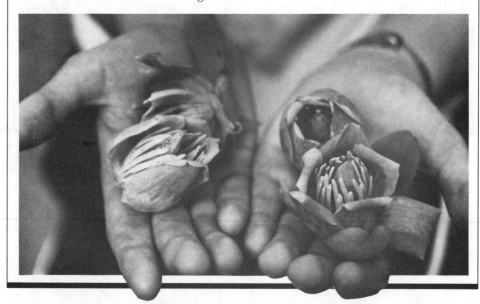

primitive flowering plant alive. Their blossoms are shaped like cups and turned to the sky—an old style, and a lasting one. At the base of the flower—above the petals in a magnolia, below them in many other flowers—is the ovary, which holds the ova (eggs). The ovary swells into a fruit when the ova are fertilized and become seeds. Magnolia fruits also hint at their ancient history. Their seeds are clustered together very like a cone.

But flowers and the fruits they become are very different from cones, and the seeds that fruits contain are not at all like pine nuts. In the endless conifer forests that sauropods browsed, pollen was produced in extravagant quantities. Sediments show the ground tinted for miles with a dust of windblown grains. The fallen pollen fed insects, but didn't do the trees any good. Whatever drifted to the ground was wasted, for it couldn't get to the cones in the treetops unless someone were to pick it up and put it there.

That must sometimes have happened. Pollen is a protein-packed food, too small for us to bother with, but just right for insects. Insects flying cone to cone, hairy legs dusty with pollen, might light by chance on ova bearing cones, and so get male and female together. Nothing forced insects to do that,

though; the female cones offered nothing to eat.

Flowers take the chanciness out of an insect delivery system. By packaging pollen together with ova in flowers, plants eliminated waste, hyped-up fertilization, and changed forever the relationship between themselves and insects. There are only 65 species of cycads still left in the world. Even the conifers face the future with a bare 450 species. There are, however, over a quarter of a million species of flowering plants.

EAT A FLOWER, BREED A PLANT

To most of the million species of insects, flowering plants are the main meal. For every sort of food a plant provides—root, leaf, stem, sap, and seed—there is an insect that eats it. Leaf miners eat away the flesh of a plant in the almost immeasurable space between the top and bottom surfaces of a leaf. Aphids suck plant juices by piercing through stems into sap-filled vessels rich in sugar. Beetles gnaw at living bark. Termites eat the wood itself. All this eating is harmful, yet flowering plants turned insect hunger to their own use by providing a banquet of flowers.

The feeding station was upturned for easy landing and well-

GHOST FLOWERS

Indian pipes look like funguses and live like funguses, but they are flowering plants. Their nourishment comes from a company of bacteria that live among their roots digesting debris and feeding their plant. Indian pipes have not only lost their chlorophyll, they have lost their leaves as well. What you see is nothing but the flower.

stocked with a display of pollen. The flyer landed, bustled about getting dinner, knocking pollen off. Some of the pollen fertilized that flower. Some, caught among the insect's bristles, fertilized other flowers as the insect continued to forage. The plant was fertilized, and the bug never knew it had been used.

Over millions of years, plants improved their flowers by stocking them with coveted sugars in the form of nectar, by advertising their wares with wind-borne fragrances and bright colors that stood out against the monotonous green landscape, and even by tricks and traps likely to capture an insect servant. The scent of rose, the nectar of honeysuckle, the extraordinary shape of the orchid please your senses by sheer accident. Those flowers evolved as insect exploiters.

ALL-PURPOSE OVARIES

The evolution of fruits was also selfish, for they are food for the embryo plants, and sometimes they are their boats, wings, or grappling hooks as well. The seed of a flowering plant isn't left naked to its fate as is the seed of conifer. It is well-clothed in an ovary that supplies many more of the embryo's needs than the mere pantry of a pine nut does.

The difference isn't apparent when you compare store-bought pignolia nuts, the nuts of a pine tree, with white almonds, the nut of a flowering tree. Both nuts are the naked seed. But the pignolia has merely been skinned; the almond has been removed from its peach-like fruit, then shelled, then skinned. Even nuts you buy in the shell do not come in their complete ovary. Like new-fallen hickory nuts or horse chestnuts, the shell of a walnut from the tree is surrounded by a thick, tough fruit. Such seeds are armored, as well as nourished, by their ovary.

The ovary of an orange packs a huge amount of food; so does a string bean. Leave a string bean on the plant and the pod—the ovary—will be slowly consumed by the embryos growing inside it. By the time beans are fat, hard, and ready for planting, the pod is as thin and as dry as paper.

Many ovaries also provide transportation for the seeds they contain. Jewelweed ovaries propel their seeds through the air with a spring mechanism. Others wait upon the wind. The fluff of a dandelion and the wings of a maple are parts of their ovaries. The coconut palm makes an ovary boat for its seeds to sail away in.

Live transport systems were exploited, too. Barbed ovaries may

BLOSSOM SHAPES

Even a small bunch of wild-flowers is likely to include an amazing variety of flower types. In some, it is easy to find and identify the different parts. Others are confusing. Green, leaflike sepals form the bud covering of a rose. When the bud opens, the sepals droop down below the petals. But in an iris flower, the sepals are the three frilly falls that form the blossom's "skirt." Flower petals may fuse, as they do in pea flowers. The foxglove's trumpet is five fused petals. What appears to be the flower of a Jack-in-the-pulpit is actually a leaf structure; the tiny flowers are inside, pressed tightly together in a spike. Each daisy or dandelion is actually a bunch of flowers. The yellow ones that form the center of a daisy are trumpets of fused petals called disk flowers. The row of outside flowers have what appears to be a single white petal each; each is fused from several petals and is called a ray flower.

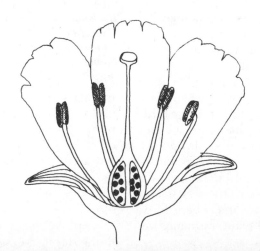

BIRD GARDENS

Each half of a lima bean is a cotyledon. The first true leaves form between them.

Beginning gardeners may be surprised to find that they must weed their garden of baby trees and bushes as well as crabgrass and dandelions. How could a wild cherry have invaded the pansies when there are no cherries in the yard? The birds are to blame. They have eaten berries of many kinds and from many places, but the seeds themselves are not digestible. When a bird defecates over the garden, it plants the seeds. This happens a lot if a tree where birds perch, plop, and plant overhangs the garden.

Weeding a garden is therefore a good way to learn what kinds of fruits the birds in your neighborhood eat. You may not be able to tell which plant is which from the first single or paired "leaves" that top the sprout. These are cotyledons, temporary structures that provide nourishment before the first true leaves sprout. Cotyledons are roundish to longish, and they tend to look much the same. Let seedlings grow their first pair of true leaves above the cotyledons, then use a field guide to identify them. You might find seedlings of juniper, rose, honeysuckle, cherry, hawthorn, dogwood, mulberry, blackberry, and many others.

To plant one, fill a small pot with moist potting soil. Poke your finger into the soil to make a deep hole. Dig under the plant carefully to free its roots, then transplant it to the pot quickly so the roots don't dry out. The seedling should sit in the soil at the same level it was in the ground, with dirt firmly pressed around its roots.

Keep the plant outdoors in the sun. Water it several times a week. By fall it will be big enough to transplant again, this time into its permanent place in the garden. Most bird-planted species are sun lovers. Clear grass and weeds from the place you choose. Dig a hole a few inches wider and deeper than the pot. Hold the pot upside down and bang the rim against your palm to free the plant. Carefully hold the plant in the hole at the same level it was growing in the pot. Fill in under and around it with loose soil and water it well. That first winter, protect the baby plant by heaping dry leaves all around it.

Roses, blueberries, and other small plants flower and fruit as early as their second summer. Birds will then come to your garden to eat from the plant they originally planted.

have been scattered about by downy dinosaurs long before your dog came home with burrs. Ancient birds may have planted indigestible seeds in their droppings after dining on the sweet ovaries that enclose them. Large, sweet, tender, and brightly colored fruit exploit their seed carriers just as flowers exploit their pollen bearers. Spit a watermelon seed, plant a watermelon embryo.

NAPPING PLANTS

Most of the species of magnolia are at home only in warm places. Very likely, the first flowering plants evolved in such comfort, for even today they are scarce at the cold heights of mountains and in the dry sandy barrens where conifers are comfy. The shortcoming of the first flowering plants was their leaves' short life. Conifer needles live for years protected by tough skins and resinous coatings. A tender, flat, widespread leaf is easily frozen by frost, torn by wind, and withered by drought. In even-tempered climates, damaged leaves are shed and new ones are grown as needed. But during an angry winter or a surly drought, new leaves are destroyed as quickly as the plant can make them.

Flowering plants eventually evolved a way of getting through

SEED SHAPES

Dried seed pods make interesting and pretty collections. Collect the seed pods just before they are fully ripe, while the pods still have some moisture left. If you wait longer, the seeds themselves will have departed and you will be left with empty pods—or even with no pods, if they also have left their plant. Cut the whole stem that holds the seed pods and hang it in a dry, airy place to finish drying. Some of the pods in the illustration are from common wild plants. Pods from garden plants are not often seen because, like peas, the seeds are eaten before they are ripe or, like poppies, the seed head has been cut off after the flower has faded. You may have to convince the gardener to let one or two plants mature their seed pods for your collection. A nice collection would include seeds that travel in different ways.

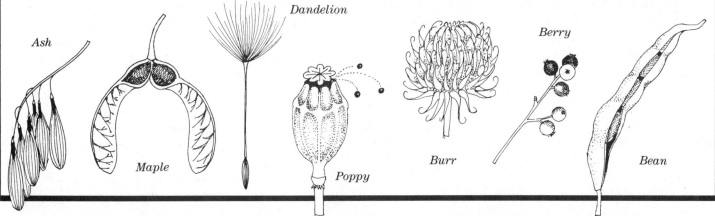

Ash

Maple

Dandelion

Poppy

Burr

Berry

Bean

hard times leafless. This they did, probably first through dry seasons and then through cold ones, by napping. Bring a bare apple branch into the house in December, stick it in water, and you will have a bare apple branch stuck in water. Do the same thing in February, and you'll see the branch will burst into bloom. The apple tree in December is in the napping stage called dormancy. Until its nap is over, nothing will tease it into action. Three months later, having counted the hours of winter by its own internal clock, it is "expecting" the spring you provide.

A dormant plant is really quite busy not only counting hours but also taking temperature readings, measuring day length, revising its chemistry, adjusting its output of hormones, even fussing with the construction of this and that kind of cell.

Trees measure light and temperature chemically. Some species are so delicately tuned to day length that their chemistry is measurably changed if the day is artificially shortened by only 15 minutes. A few plants, apples among them, pay no attention to light at all, but rely on their own built-in clock and the temperature. Most plants probably "expect" fall to arrive based on an internal clock and then fine-tune their responses based on both hours of daylight and changes in temperature.

Changes in the amounts of light and heat cause changes in the kinds and amounts of hormones plants produce. The hormones, in turn, direct the rest of the plant's chemistry. When a tree's leaves change color and drop off, the tree has taken its first chemical step in becoming dormant. The tree's branch tips form bud scales, where new leaves will sprout in spring. Inside the bud scales, tiny leaves or blossoms form. You can see them with a hand lens if you remove the scales carefully.

Other changes are invisible. Sugars that will protect cells from freezing are sent upward from the roots. Some plants make alcohol, their natural antifreeze. In case ice forms in spite of these precautions, cell walls are reconstructed so tiny ice crystals can be transported out before the cells are damaged. All this busyness and more is going on while the tree looks to us quite lifeless. By the time winter hits hard, the plant is prepared. A few species can live through temperatures as low as $-44°C$ ($-112°F$).

All through the coldest months the dormant plant counts the winter hours. If winter were to be shortened, as it is when you bring an apple branch indoors in December, the plant wouldn't be able to re-

A plant press like this one holds dozens of plants, and it is large enough that many plants can be pressed whole, from root to top. It is made of ventilators, which let air circulate, stacked between two pieces of plywood and weighted with stones. Three ventilators is a good starting size; the more ventilators you make, the more plants you can press at a time. If you can get the lumberyard to cut the wood for you, construction time will be only a few minutes. Plywood is tricky to cut for beginners; you may want adult help.

You need:
Ruler
Pencil
Saw
Two pieces of ¼-inch plywood, 16 by 24 inches
For each ventilator, six pieces of 2-inch lattice cut 24 inches long, and nine pieces cut 16 inches long
Carpenter's glue
Hammer
19-gauge ⅝-inch brads
Large sheets newspaper
Two web straps, at least 4 feet long, with non-slip buckles (available at art or hardware stores)

1. If your lattice hasn't been cut to the dimensions in the list, use the ruler and pencil to measure and mark the pieces to the correct sizes. Cut the lattice with the saw.

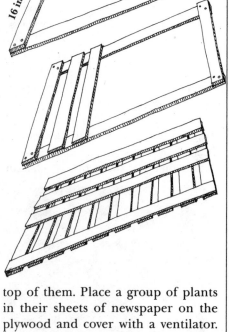

16 inches

24 inches

HOW TO BUILD A PLANT PRESS

2. Build the ventilators on the floor. For each ventilator, take two 16-inch pieces of lattice and two 24-inch pieces and construct a frame the same measure as the plywood pieces. First glue, then use the hammer and brads to nail the outside pieces together.

3. Evenly space the remaining seven 16-inch pieces of lattice along the frame. Glue, then nail them to the frame. Turn the ventilator over, and do the same with the four 24-inch pieces. You don't really need to nail anywhere except along the edges, but you can if you want extra strength. Do the same for each remaining ventila-tor. When all three ventilators are fin-ished, so is your work!

4. Press plants between three or four sheets of newspaper. The press is slightly larger than a full-size newspa-per sheet (like the *New York Times*) folded in half. Lay out three fully-opened thicknesses of newspaper for each group of plants. Place the plants on half the newspaper in just the posi-tion you want them to be in after pressing. Fold the sheets over the top of the plants.

5. Stack them in the press this way: Lay out both straps flat on the floor. Place one of the pieces of plywood on top of them. Place a group of plants in their sheets of newspaper on the plywood and cover with a ventilator. Add another group of plants in news-paper, and another ventilator. Repeat for as many plants and ventilators as you have. Finish with the second piece of plywood, then strap the press tightly.

6. Keep the press where air circulates well (not in a basement, for instance) and weight it with rocks. Most plants will dry flat in less than two weeks. If you open the press and change the newspapers every day, they'll dry faster. The faster the plants dry, the better they keep their colors.

1,2,3, GO

Trees begin to prepare for the winter as soon as they have finished that summer's growth. Look at a tree's branch tips in July. No more new leaves are unfurling, and leaves that earlier were tender and pale have become tough and darkened with chlorophyll. All these grown-up leaves are at work producing food, so much food that there are more carbohydrates than the plant needs. The surplus is being stored in the tree's roots.

By the end of August, the tree has stored a great deal of food, but not enough. As days shorten and temperatures drop, the plant begins to raid the leaves themselves to stash away in the winter larder whatever goodies they contain. Chlorophyll and many other kinds of leaf molecules are broken down for their valuable minerals and sugars. When the chlorophyll that makes leaves green is gone, other pigments that have been in the leaves all along to help the chlorophyll capture sunlight show their true colors— red, orange, yellow, purple. When almost all of the leaf flesh has been recycled back into the body of the plant, circulation is cut off. The leaves drop; it's fall.

spond to spring. A particular breed of apple may need 1,000 or 1,500 hours at a temperature below 5°C (41°F) before it can emerge from dormancy. Other plants have different requirements, depending on how long cold weather lasts in the plant's native area. For example, in an area where the temperature drops below 5°C (41°F) for 900 hours in a typical winter, native plants there will require 900 hours of chilling to complete their dormancy. Chilling requirements are therefore like a rough prediction: Winter *should* be about finished by the time the 900 cold hours are over.

A potted rose would certainly be as lovely a houseplant as a potted gardenia, and a pine would be more impressive than a palm. Why don't we grow our northern natives in our houses? We don't because we can't. Heated homes never get cold enough to throw northern plants into dormancy, and they can't live without their winter rest. Therefore there are no northern houseplants; they are all southerners.

CAUTIOUS SEEDS

Should an unusually warm week in March force an apple tree to sprout too soon, it could recover from its mistake by sprouting new shoots to replace frostbitten ones. Once a seed has sprouted, its stored food is quickly used up and harsh conditions will kill it. Therefore seeds of wild plants have particularly fussy requirements for sprouting. If those requirements are not met, seeds can remain dormant for extraordinary lengths of time. When two lotus seeds that archaeologists found buried in a bog were given the right conditions after a 2,000-year dormancy, they sprouted, grew, bloomed, and produced seeds of their own.

Many seeds that lie on the forest floor require a dose of red light—one component of sunlight—before they will sprout. The green canopy of a forest in full leaf absorbs red light, so that very little reaches seeds on the floor. Such seeds can sprout only in early spring before the leaves are out unless they happen to have fallen in forest clearings. Newly sprouted maples, cherries, beeches, and oaks are already inches high before their parent trees have begun spring growth. You'll always find more seedlings in clearings than in shaded portions of the forest.

Seeds of some desert plants have a hormone coating to keep them dormant; the coating will dissolve in water. The brief desert showers that sometimes fall out of season don't dissolve enough of the hormone to break dormancy. The seed will begin to grow only after a long rain, signaling the start of a reliably wet period, washes all the hormone away.

ANOTHER WORLD

From the very beginning, the evolution of plant eaters and eaten plants have gone hand in hand. These two oldest of land pioneers had already been living together for 300 million years by the time the first magnolia bloomed. The relationships between insects and plants are as intimate as the relationship between a termite and the bacterial zoo inside its gut, and as alien to us.

Insects live in another world. Gravity, the force that affects you the most, affects an ant very little. The force that affects an ant the most you can't feel. You cope with the force of gravity all the time. Your bones and muscles must be strong enough to hold you up against its downward pull; every step you take is an effort against gravity. If you fall, the force of gravity crushes and ruptures blood vessels, leaving you bruised and bleeding. Toss an ant from the top of the World Trade Center and it will land unharmed. It is so light that it fairly floats to earth.

On the other hand, you can touch the bark of a tree and feel no pull. To the ant, the pull between the molecules of the bark and the molecules of its own feet is a very powerful force. It makes no difference to the ant whether it walks on the upper surface or the underside of a branch. The adhesion between molecules is what holds an ant's feet to a surface, and that is the force the ant must overcome with every step.

Because they are so little bothered by gravity, insects are incredibly strong. An ant can lift a carcass 50 times its weight, and a bee can haul a load 300 times heavier than itself. If you had the strength of a bee you could drag 15 tons, and if you could jump like a grasshopper, each leap would take you 30 yards. Even on the moon, where gravity is much less than on Earth, people can't lift and leap like that. An insect is almost as weightless on Earth as an astronaut is in outer space.

Flying light, insects have made their way to every part of the globe. Even a heavy honeybee can fly for miles, and smaller insects like midges seem to hover interminably in the air. Up there is a world without obstacles, without the rub and bump of things, solid only in the sense that air is thick enough to beat wings against.

Alighting, an insect surfaces on solid food. Insects are so small that a meal is a pinprick of blood, a few dead scales of shedding skin, some grains of pollen. A single rose stem feeds a generation of aphids for their lifetime. Every cubic foot of meadow or woodland—above and below the soil, on the insides and outsides of plants—teems with insects. Yet we giants have trouble finding them. Too many are too tiny for us to see.

SOW PLANTS...

Vegetable seeds you buy in packets are ready to sprout whenever you plant them because either they are from tropical plants that don't require dormancy, or they have had that need bred out of them, or they have had their needs met by the grower before they were packaged. "Grand Rapids" lettuce seeds, for example, have been exposed to light to tell them the world is safe to grow in. Other seeds are dried, sometimes for several years, and chilled as well. Only if they have experienced "winter" will they agree with the gardener that it really is spring.

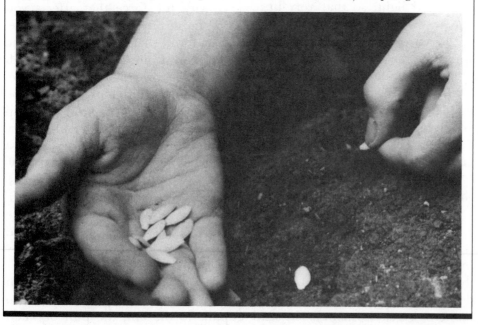

SMALL PACKAGES

An insect's body is wonderfully tidy. Its gut is a single tube from mouth to anus. Lungs aren't necessary because insects exchange oxygen and waste gasses through a network of tubes opening to the outside through pores. There is nothing you would recognize as a heart either, for there is no blood. Nutrients are distributed in a clear fluid pumped feebly from rear to head out the open end of a single vessel, and this fluid sloshes freely from there throughout the body, stirred up whenever the animal jiggles. If you see red blood when you squash a gnat, it is most likely yours.

Think of a computer the size of a gnat. An insect's nervous system is like printed circuitry, each input from the outside world leading to an automatic output that is programmed in the diagram of its inborn intelligence.

The input comes in bits. Each facet of an insect's eye relays a single bit of image. Hundreds or thousands of such bits create a picture, as dots create a picture in a newspaper.

Each bristle that pokes through a gap in an insect's unfeeling cuticle conveys only one bit of information through the nerve at its root. Some bristles work like switches: OFF when standing straight out, ON when bent. Other bristles are turned on by a change in temperature. Still others fire the nerve in response to a chemical signal: if the particular sort of molecule for which they have receptors land on them, they fire. Some chemosensory bristles have a firing threshold; they send their bit into the circuitry only if many of their receptors are filled with scent molecules.

The number of bits required to trigger a behavior is programmed. If a few touch-sensitive bristles on a fly's feet are bent by airborne debris when it is in flight it will con-

...REAP PESTS

Unfortunately, no sooner does a garden grow than its insect pests appear. They are not last summer's bugs. They are last fall's eggs laid, perhaps, in the ground just as last fall's seeds fell onto the soil. The insect embryo in its egg and the plant embryo in its seed spend the winter the same way—dead to the world. These insect eggs have dormancy requirements, such as chilling, just as seeds do. They, too, halt their growth completely during the winter, and measure light and temperature to time their next move. Come spring, insects hatch and seeds sprout at the same time because the pests have synchronized their watches with the plants they pester.

CLOSE UP

You can't use an ordinary snap-shot camera to take an insect's picture. The lens won't focus closer than several feet away, which is too far to get a good look at such a small creature. The camera must be equipped with a macro lens, one that focuses within inches of its subject. Many amateur photographers these days do have equipment for such close-up work. If you know someone who has this equipment, ask him or her to join with you in exploring the tiny world of insects.

The close-up above is of a katydid who happened to stand still for its portrait. Few insects are that coopera-tive. Therefore, choose a newly opened flower as the background for your insect portraits. Mounting the camera on a tripod will keep it steady, but if you sit comfortably next to the flower and prop your elbows on your knees or a bench, you can hold the camera steady enough. Set the shutter speed high enough to "stop action" (the camera owner will know how to do this), and focus on the inside of

the flower. Now wait until your first customer appears. Usually this will take only a few minutes. It may be a bee, a fly, a moth, an ant, a beetle—all sorts of insects eat pollen or sip nec-tar. Refocus the lens to make the in-sect itself the clearest part of the pic-ture, and snap fast. If the film is for color slides, the portrait will be the actual size of the insect. If it is film from which prints are made, the pic-ture will be bigger than life.

tinue flying. If many are bent, it will fold its wings and lower its feet: the behavior of landing.

The behaviors themselves follow in sequences: the act of folding wings and lowering legs will trigger probing movements of the fly's mouth parts. Probing in turn may result in signals that indicate sugar is present. If the amount of sugar is sufficient, zing goes another trigger, and the fly eats. The order in which behaviors can occur is rigid. Step B follows step A, and step C doesn't happen unless both A and B have come before it. Some choices are possible: A male fly that lands on a drop of jam being enjoyed by a female fly doesn't have to eat with her. Most likely he will choose to mate with her instead. Still, that is a narrow choice. Insects are strong, they are intelligent, but they act like robots.

ROBOTS AND MASTERS

Plants that are pollinated by a particular insect accommodate that insect's robotlike behavior. For instance, skunk cabbage is pollinated by flies, whose services it assures by triggering various fly behaviors that will result in pollination. In early spring, when snow still lingers, skunk cabbage is already blooming in the bogs. Around each bloom is a patch of open ground where snow has melted. The skunk cabbage blossom has melted it. Using last year's store of fuel, the plant burns starch to make heat and rises up through the melted patch of ground. With no other bloom in sight, skunk cabbage corners the market of early-hatching flies.

To a fly's eye, a skunk cabbage's mosaic of dark blooms against a white ground is like an oversize dinner plate. But the skunk cabbage blossom doesn't rely on its pollinator's appetite or vision. In both color and odor, the blossom masquerades as meat. Flies are programmed to seek out such a meal not for themselves, but for the maggots that will hatch from their eggs. The purply-brown flesh of the skunk cabbage blossom mimics the remains of a dead animal. So does the pungent smell.

It's not in the skunk cabbage's interest to carry this mimicry too far. Were it to mesh perfectly with the fly's program, it would have to host maggots. But, how is it to hold the attention of its pollinator once its meat disguise has been uncovered? The skunk cabbage hospitably offers the fly food and shelter. Sugary nectar, the "quick energy" food that ants, bees, butterflies, and flies eat, is made by plants solely to attract insect pollinators. The flower has no more need of nectar for its own nutrition than it has a need to smell itself. Landing gear down and sensors turned on to sugar, the fly walks in the direction of increasing concentration of sugar molecules. This direction, the blossom assures, is downward to the bottom of its peak-roofed cup.

Inside this warm shelter the fly lingers over its meal. The weather is still raw outside, making it difficult for the fly to get up enough heat to do what it's supposed to do: fly about, find a mate, copulate, lay eggs. Indeed a skunk cabbage blossom might be likened to a social club at which the meeting and greeting of the sexes is encouraged by good smells, good food, and warm shelter.

More to the point for the flower, its own reproductive needs are met by its guests.

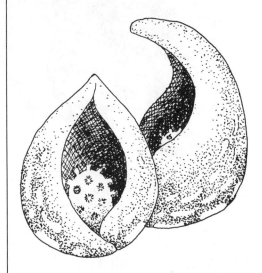

Skunk cabbage blossoms

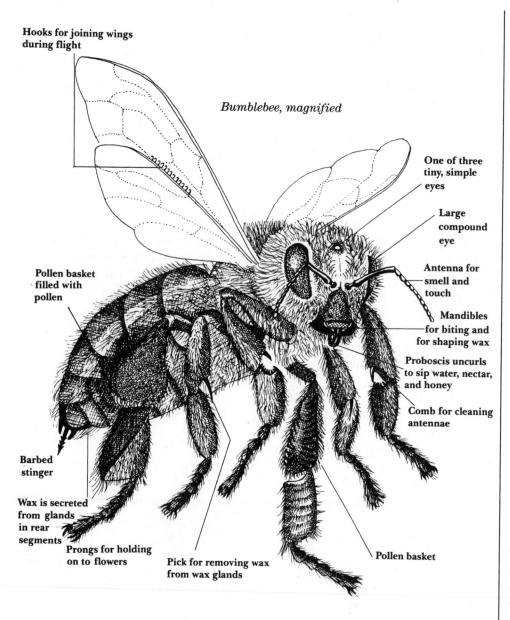

Hooks for joining wings during flight

Bumblebee, magnified

One of three tiny, simple eyes

Large compound eye

Antenna for smell and touch

Mandibles for biting and for shaping wax

Proboscis uncurls to sip water, nectar, and honey

Comb for cleaning antennae

Pollen basket filled with pollen

Barbed stinger

Wax is secreted from glands in rear segments

Prongs for holding on to flowers

Pick for removing wax from wax glands

Pollen basket

TURNING THE TABLES

Some plants that once catered to insects' tastes in flowers have turned the tables by developing a taste for insects. There are about 400 plant species that eat meat.

Being a carnivorous plant isn't as easy as living like a daisy. Daisies have only to spread their roots in the soil and bask in the sun; everything they need is close at hand. Carnivorous plants inhabit bogs and barrens where other plants would starve for lack of nitrogen and phosphorus, ingredients found in rich soil and in plant "foods" with which we feed our gardens. Carnivorous plants don't need to be fed good soil or fertilizers; they feed themselves with insects.

The pitcher plant feeds itself a liquid diet. Its leaves, red-veined or splotched as prettily as a flower, are cups into which glands secrete a watery pool. Other glands along the outside of the leaf secrete nectar in a trail that leads to the cup's lip. Insects follow the trail to its end

SEE THE BEE'S KNEES

Although a field lens (see page 27) is useful for examining insects, you need a more powerful lens to see all the extraordinary details of bee knees and butterfly wings. The most useful magnifier is a hand microscope, such as this one made by the Japanese company SKS, which magnifies 25 times actual size yet is only a few inches long. Hand microscopes can be ordered by mail from scientific supply houses. Your school's science department will have catalogs and prices. Although they are not cheap, they are less expensive than regular microscopes. They can be carried in a pocket, need no special lights or mirrors, and have lenses that are of top quality. Best of all, a hand microscope lets you watch a caterpillar's mouthparts as it chews a leaf, an aphid being born, or ants conversing by using their feelers. You can also see the shapes of pollen grains, the actual cells in plant leaves, the scales that color butterfly wings, and the texture of your dog's fur. A hand microscope is a gift worth begging for—or working for!

and fall over the slippery, waxed edge into the pool below where their drowned decaying bodies enrich the pool into a nourishing soup.

In other meat-eating plants, the leaf surface above the pool is covered with stiff, downward-facing hairs that prevent a meandering insect from walking upward. Some species secrete digestive enzymes into the pool.

In the pitcher plant, the leaves themselves act something like roots. They absorb nitrogen and phosphorus, and pass them on to the rest of the plant. Whatever is left of the decaying mess that accumulates in the cups over the summer sinks into the soil when the plant dies down in the fall. When the pitcher plant sprouts again in the spring, it uses last year's food until its new cups are ready for work.

The Venus flytrap snaps its "jaws" shut over its prey. The sticky-tipped tentacles of a sundew bend over their prey to ensnare it. Bladderworts suck in food and digest it in a temporary "stomach," the bladder for which these plants are named.

None of the features of carnivorous plants are unique in the world of plants. Many plants arrange for their own reproduction by luring and trapping pollinating insects. Plant glands secrete and absorb all

HOW TO MAKE

This insect net is light, strong, and a lot better made than the kiddy ones for sale in stores. Making it involves some cutting and whittling with a pocketknife, so be careful.

You need:
Roll of 12-gauge galvanized wire
Grease pencil
Hacksaw
Tape measure
Pocketknife
Bamboo garden pole, with stout walls and no splits, ½ inch wide by 5 feet long
Masking tape
Roll 20-gauge galvanized wire
Pliers
Small scrap of lumber or kindling wood
Vise
Cloth rag
Hammer
1 square yard fine muslin
Yard stick
Scissors
Needle
Thread (or sewing machine)

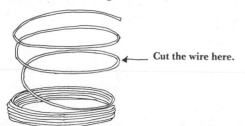

← Cut the wire here.

1. Pick up two full loops of the 12-gauge wire. Using the grease pencil, mark the second loop where it meets the free end of the wire. Cut the wire halfway through at that point with the hacksaw. Then bend it to break off the double loop from the rest of the roll.

2. Open out the wire loops into a single, large loop. Bend the first six inches of one end sharply to form a prong. Starting at that bend, use the tape measure to measure around the loop for 34½ inches and make a second bend at that point. This will give you a single loop about 11 inches across, with two prongs for attaching the rim to the handle. Cut the second prong the same length as the first.

3. With the pocketknife, cut a small notch in the bamboo pole about six inches from one end. Enlarge the notch with the point of the blade

until you have a very small hole into the hollow part of the bamboo pole. Use masking tape to tape the prongs

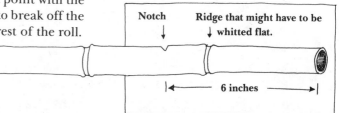

Notch   Ridge that might have to be whitted flat.

|← 6 inches →|

into place at that end of the pole as shown (if the ridges in the bamboo prevent the prongs from lying flat, whittle them down).

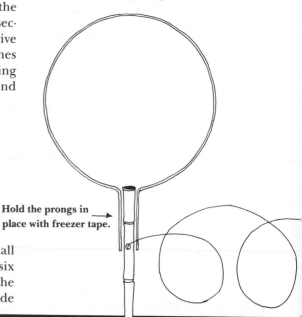

Hold the prongs in → place with freezer tape.

AN INSECT NET

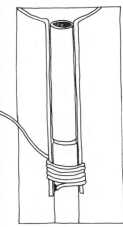

4. Stick one end of the 20-gauge wire several inches into the hole to hold it in place. Wind the wire around the prongs and pole, removing the tape as you go. The winds should touch each other and be as tight as you can get them all the way from the bottom to the top of the prongs. When you get to the top, cut the wire with the cutting portion of the pliers, leaving an extra eight inches. Poke that free end under the last four winds, and pull it through them with the pliers. Then cut off the end of the wire.

5. With the pocketknife, pry off a couple of small wedges from any scrap of wood. The wedges should be about 1½ inches long and ¼ inch wide at the top, and they should taper to a point at the bottom. Lay the loop end of the pole in a vise (wrap it in a cloth rag if it slips), and tighten the vise. Push wedges into the open end—two or three is all that will fit—and hammer them in snugly to hold the wire rim firmly in place. Take the pole out of the vise and lay it aside.

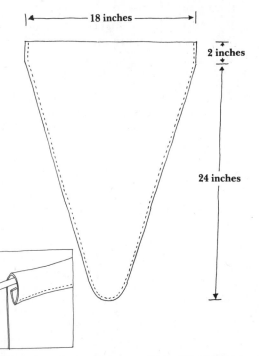

|← 18 inches →|

2 inches

24 inches

6. Follow the pattern to cut the muslin net: Fold the cloth in half lengthwise, so that it is 18 inches wide folded, or the width of the top of the net. Mark with the pencil the center of top and bottom edges, and with a yard stick draw a line between the two points. Measure 26 inches from the top of that center line, and make a mark there. That's the bottom of the net. Draw the rounded bottom, then use the yardstick to draw slanted sides that begin two inches from the top. Cut through both layers of cloth with the scissors along your penciled pattern lines. Stitch the sides of the net first, turn it right side out, then fold the top over the wire rim and stitch that into place.

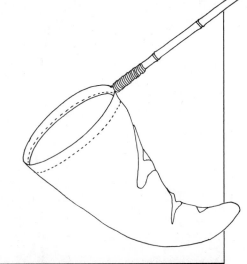

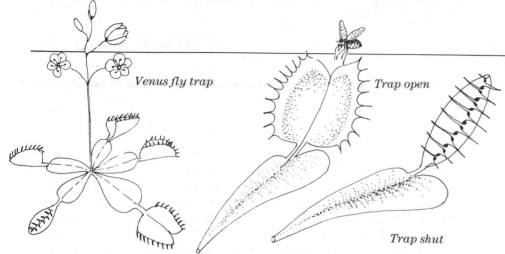

Venus fly trap

Trap open

Trap shut

sorts of products, including glues, sugars, oils, waxes, and enzymes. The flower heads of sunflowers turn to face the sun, grapevines wind ensnaring tentacles around supports, sensitive plants whip their leaves away from harm's way. What makes carnivorous plants so strange is that they have put all these features together in a way that is so animal-like.

BUG BRED

An ordinary flower of today is shaped like the primitive magnolia: an open cup formed by a circle of

petals. Carnivorous plants still make their flowers that old-fashioned way.

Other flowers, such as the heavy-lipped lupines and the trumpet-shaped honeysuckle are less open to the world. Nectar in these flowers is not available to all comers. Lupine mouths can be opened only by insects heavy enough to push down the lower lip when landing. Honeysuckle nectar can be sipped only by those with a straw long enough to reach it. These fancy flowers were bred by insects.

When plant breeders create a

Plant breeders control who the parents of the next generation will be by doing their own pollinating. Try it yourself with daylilies. You won't see the flowers of the next generation until the summer after next. That will be worth the wait if you try a half dozen different combinations, inventing six new varieties of daylily that may never have been seen before. If you have no daylilies of your own, neighbors may let you breed theirs.

Daylilies get their name from the fact that each blossom opens for one day only; that is when both its pollen and its ova are ripe. Fertilize in the morning after the dew has dried so pollen won't be soggy, but while blossoms are still fresh.

Gather the pollen first. Just pluck a few anthers from the plant or plants that are to serve as "fathers." Breeders keep the anthers in aluminum muffin pans with each compartment labeled with the father's name. If you don't know names, write down color and other interesting characteristics on a self-adhesive label for each compartment or container of anthers you gather. Then choose the 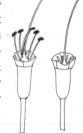 "mother" blossoms—plants whose blossoms are a different color, size, or shape from the blossoms on the fa-

Sundew   Tentacles extended   Tentacles bent

TRY IT YOURSELF

ther plants. Fertilize the stigma in the center of the blossom by dabbing it with the pollen end of an anther. Again, breeders keep track of their crosses by immediately labeling the stalk of that flower with a plastic label

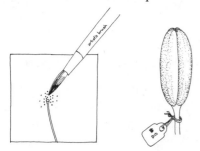

held in place with thin wire, available from garden centers. Use a soft lead pencil to write on the label what cross you have made. The female's name or description comes first: "Susan Elizabeth with pollen from the variety Hudson Valley"; or you could write "large yellow x small red." Always label the mother flower at least with the date, for that is how you will know when to gather the ripe seed.

Check the ovary a week later. If it is swelling, it has been fertilized and the seeds inside are growing. About 50 percent of daylily crosses work. The seeds will be ripe five weeks after fertilization, or, if you forgot to write down the date, just as the pods begin to crack open.

Pluck off the ripe seed heads and

split them open to harvest the seeds. You can store the seeds in envelopes with their label to plant outdoors later, or you can plant them indoors right then.

To plant, fill a plastic or clay pot with potting soil. Poke a 1-inch hole into the soil and stick in the seed. Cover with soil, and keep moist. Plant the same way outdoors in the garden, but not until mid-October in the North. If planted too early, the newly sprouted babies won't survive freezing; planted late, the seeds will wait out the winter and sprout next spring. Plants grown indoors over the winter

should be transplanted outdoors in the spring. Label the plants with plastic labels that stick into the soil. They should have the same information about the parents written on them that was on the original label.

The plants won't blossom their first summer. They will blossom the second summer, and then you will see the new flowers you have created.

new form of flower, it is called artificial selection, as opposed to the "natural" way nature does things. Artificial selection means choosing to reproduce individual plants that are the most pleasing or useful, and preventing the reproduction of those that are less pleasing or less useful. Plant breeders have chosen corn plants that give the best harvest and have refused aid to less productive ones. As a result, "wild" corn is rare compared with the giant cultivated varieties.

Bees and other insects have also "bred" flowers although it took them thousands, not hundreds of years. Heavy bumblebees prefer flowers with a solid landing platform and a heavy pollen crop, while butterflies look for flowers that hold in their depths the greatest amount of nectar. Each individual plant produces flowers slightly different from the flowers of neighboring plants of the same species. Those that are visited by more pollinators tend to produce more seeds; those that have fewer pollinators usually produce fewer seeds. Plants visited mostly by butterflies are selected for deep cups, which can hold more nectar, while those visited mostly by bumblebees are selected for lopsided construction. A lupine of today can't be entered by a butterfly. A bumblebee can't sip from a honeysuckle. The "wild" flowers that lupines and honeysuckle are descended from are now extinct; the insect-bred varieties are common.

There is another way to look at this: Perhaps the plants bred their pollinators. Who is responsible for the butterfly's super-size straw if not the blossoms from which it sips? Flowers that make their food available only to long-strawed butterflies are also selecting for reproduction those individuals most useful to them. For both plant and pollinator, the advantage of selective breeding is reliability. The butterfly has a store for its own exclusive use; the plant has a pollinator it can always rely on. The system has worked so well that there are many plants whose flowers are designed not even for one major group of insect, but for a single species.

Lupine and bee.

Honeysuckle and butterfly.

HAND IN HAND IN HAND

The evolution of flowering plants and insects goes so closely hand in hand that it is sometimes difficult to tell which is which or who is doing what. The "spittle" found on many meadow plants is not produced by the plant. Hidden inside safe from predators is the nymph of a small insect called a froghopper that produces the froth as a cover for its juice-sucking activities. But the large, hollow bump on a goldenrod stem *is* made by the plant in response to the injury made by a gallfly in laying her eggs. The bump serves as a shelter for the egg.

Decorative knobs and points on the undersides of leaves also contain eggs, and also are made by the plant in spite of its better interests, since the eggs may hatch into larvae that will eat its leaves. The lacy patterns within some leaves are, on the other hand, made by insects called

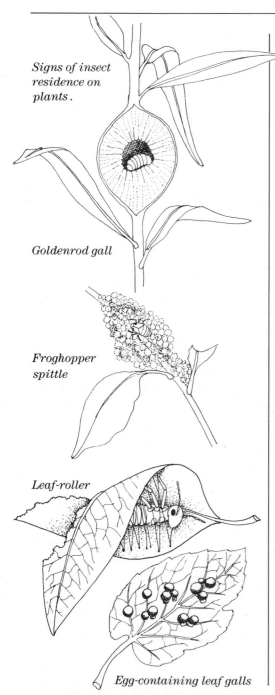

Signs of insect residence on plants.

Goldenrod gall

Froghopper spittle

Leaf-roller

Egg-containing leaf galls

HOW TO USE AN INSECT GUIDE

A million species of insects are known, and 100,000 of them live in America. This has created something of a problem for those who make field guides and for those who use them. In the past, you had to know a bug was a bee to find its picture, and if it happened to be a fly masquerading as a bee, you were out of luck. The Audubon Society's *Field Guide to North American Insects and Spiders* has a neat solution. It groups species according to 23 basic shapes, which are pictured as silhouettes and are used as thumb tabs in the color-photograph section. If the insect you find is shaped like a bee, its picture will be in the bee-shape section even if it is a fly.

leaf miners that spend their entire lives eating away the flesh of the leaf from between its upper and lower surfaces. Within almost any curled or folded leaf you'll find insects in some stage of their development. Some have forcefully curled the leaf by pulling its edges together with silk; others have induced the leaf to curl for them by injuring it. Katydids look like leaves themselves. Green cabbage worms masquerade as the leaf ribs of cabbage (they avoid purple cabbages).

The goldenrod gallfly and the cabbage-green caterpillar go hand in hand only with their own plant. The gallfly can't lay its eggs elsewhere. It can't even lay its eggs further up or lower down on the stem; all the galls on a patch of goldenrod are at the same height. The cabbage moth can't lay its eggs on a plant that doesn't smell like a cabbage, nor will its caterpillars eat a plant that doesn't taste like a cabbage.

For each insect, the sequence of inputs that lead to a behavior may be so rigid that the insect is tied to a single plant family or to a single member of that family. The ties that bind the insect and its host plant are coded in their genes for a perfect match: cabbage green skin to cabbage green leaf, veined wing pattern to veined leaf pattern, ability to stimulate the growth of a gall to the gall-growing response to stimulation, the nutritional requirement of the insect to the nutritional content of the plant. Even the timing is exact: moths' eggs

A Collecting Bottle

The cyanide that professional insect collectors use to kill insects is extremely dangerous. But some sort of poison must be used. The collecting bottle described below uses household ammonia, which would also poison people if they were trapped in a bottle with nothing else to breathe. *Don't breathe the fumes.* If ammonia gets on your skin, wash it off under running water.

You need:
Roll of cotton (available in
   drugstores)
Wide-mouthed quart jar with a
   screw top
Tablespoon
Household ammonia
Waxed paper

Stuff cotton an inch deep into the bottom of the jar. When you're ready to go out collecting, pour a tablespoon of ammonia onto the cotton.

Don't soak the cotton; you want fumes, not liquid that will spoil the looks of your specimen. Cover the cotton with a piece of crumpled waxed paper so the insects won't touch the cotton.

Long before the insect dies, it will be unconscious. Each time you open the bottle to drop another insect in, some vapor will escape. Work fast, and screw the lid on fast and tight. Leave the insects in the jar overnight after you have finished the day's collecting. Otherwise you might pin them up passed out only to find them waving at you from the display case an hour later.

hatch into caterpillars just as the host plant breaks into leaf.

The Evolution of an Embryo

Plant evolution encourages intimacy with pollinators, but discourages closeness with pests. The smell of marigolds will repel insects, and so they are often planted among vegetable crops. The vapor from an orange contains a pesticide. These are only two weapons in an arsenal of chemicals that plants have been concocting ever since the first leaf was chewed. Many are brewed specifically for caterpillars, perhaps the world's most impressive eating machines.

If beings who had known insects only as they were in coal-forest days were able to see a caterpillar now, they would not know what the caterpillar was. Primitive insects such as grasshoppers and roaches change gradually through many molts from babyish to adult form, but they resemble the adult all along. A caterpillar looks nothing like the adult moth or butterfly it will become. It does not even look like an insect; it has a head, but where is its chest? It has legs, but they lack the joints there seem to be too many of them.

The larva of a moth is more like the tadpole of a frog than it is like an infant that will change only a little as it grows. The cells that will develop into wings and antennae have not yet been instructed to do that. Fly maggots are arrested at such an early stage of development that they lack legs altogether. These larvae are strange in other ways: Caterpillars have biting mouth parts, though adult moths can't eat at all, and butterflies are sippers, not biters. What looks like legs along the rear portion of a caterpillar's body aren't. They are freshly evolved appendages not even derived from the many pairs of legs sported by worm ancestors. Maggots and caterpillars don't go through gradual changes to become adults although they do grow enormously, molt skins that have become too tight, and emerge from each molt with, perhaps, brighter colors, bolder patterns, and bigger bristles. When they become adults, it is all at once in a single molt. Only within their cocoons do caterpillars revert to their original, primitive, winged body plan. (This is as strange as if we, while tailed embryos, were to specialize in some non-human way to get along in the outside world and were only to return, at the age of twelve or so, to the human form.)

Before it wraps itself in its cocoon, the caterpillar eats. Concentrating on growth and specialized as an eating machine, it fattens to adult weight much sooner than insects that change continually and have evolved no special mechanisms for fast feeding. Many moth caterpillars complete their growth in weeks. A grasshopper requires the entire summer. A housefly can be super fast: Eggs hatch into extremely immature larvae within a day, the maggots complete their growth within a week, and they have finished their metamorphosis to become sexually mature adults in two more days. There can be three dozen generations of houseflies every year, but there is only one generation of grasshoppers.

Yet adult flies may not have changed their shape as their larvae changed shape; there may have been flies before there were maggots. Genes dictate development at every stage; natural selection works at any age. Circumstances can favor those larvae that eat the best and grow the most. Caterpillars and maggots have been under different evolutionary pressures than adult moths and flies, although larva and adult are the same species.

THE PLANTS FIGHT BACK

Periodically, there are outbreaks of gypsy moths in the Northeast. When full grown, the caterpillars of gypsy moths are nearly three inches of bristling ugliness. They can strip the woodlands bare as winter. You can hear them chewing; their droppings falling like rain. When caterpillars are ready to pupate (change into their adult form), they blacken the ground and the walls of houses in their search for surfaces where they will spin the cocoons within which they will transform their bodies. You can't walk outdoors without killing a cupful at every step.

People fight the caterpillars with everything from burlap wrapped around tree trunks (the caterpillars

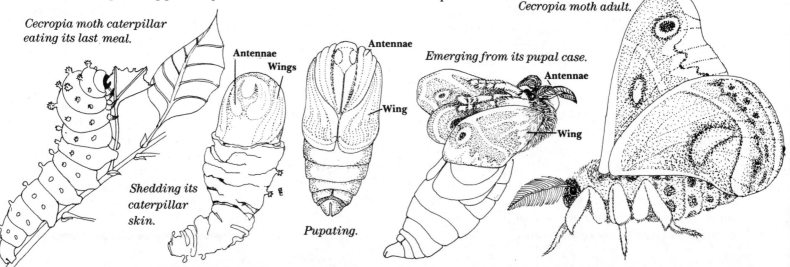

Cecropia moth caterpillar eating its last meal.

Antennae
Wings

Shedding its caterpillar skin.

Antennae

Wing

Pupating.

Emerging from its pupal case.

Antennae

Wing

Cecropia moth adult.

TREE TALK

When a leaf is damaged—whether it is bitten by an insect or torn by you—it releases a special chemical. The chemical vaporizes and is detected by other leaves as it spreads in the air. The plant "knows" it is injured. Some plants also know when another of their species is injured. When an alder attacked by tent caterpillars releases its damage signal to the air, it and its neighbors all pile up pest poisons in their leaves. They have no brains or nerves, yet they learn and they talk.

get lost in its folds) to clouds of viruses sprayed from an airplane (the viruses infect newly hatched caterpillars).

After the third year, gypsy moth caterpillars vanish—but not because of traps and sprays. Their own dinner is their downfall. The trees fight back.

Oak trees are the gypsy moth caterpillars' favored food. Once an oak tree has been stripped, its next crop of leaves is tough, less nutritious, and unusually high in chemicals harmful to insects called phenols and tannins. Caterpillars raised on these leaves don't grow as fast or become as large as those that move into an area that has not been stripped before. Many of these affected caterpillars die before they can pupate, either because tannin and phenol are toxic to them in such large doses, or because they are undernourished and so succumb to disease.

Trees stripped one year produce "inferior" leaves the following year as well. By the third year, the insects, overcrowded and undernourished, are hit by an epidemic of the very same viruses that failed to get rid of them when used by humans. The population collapses.

CHEAP TRICKS

Chemical warfare is expensive to the plant that conducts it. Normal leaves cost less energy to make. Pest-resistant leaves would be too costly unless the tree were really under attack. Sugar maples play a kind of Russian roulette. They produce some leaves high in toxins and others low in nutrients; they scatter these two kinds of "bad" meals among leaves that make a perfect diet for insect pests. To insects that can't tell which leaf is which, every meal is a gamble. Those that can tell which are the "good" leaves must search for them—a waste of the insects' energy, and an invitation to insect-eating birds.

Some of the toxins plants make to foil pests are wickedly clever. Tomatoes and potatoes make a chemical that blocks the manufacture of digestive enzymes. Their pests starve to death. The wild potato (though not the cultivated one) pretends to be a frightened aphid by producing a chemical these insects use to signal fear to one another. Certain that fellow aphids must be in danger, these pests run away.

Citrus fruits defend themselves with limonoids. To us limonoids are

FLEA KILLER

Look closely at an orange skin. Each dot on its surface holds a droplet of oil inside. That oil when released carries a tingling orange aroma delicious to us, deadly to insects.

Sniff the orange, then damage its skin with your fingernail as if you were an insect trying to eat the fruit inside. Sniff again.

Release a lot of oil by grating the whole surface of the skin off with a kitchen grater. Put some of the grated skin in a collecting bottle. It can kill flies and many other insects within two hours. It can also kill fleas. Rub grated orange skin into your cat's fur for an absolutely safe, deliciously scented insecticide.

only the bitter taste in grapefruit juice or in orange skin, but they stunt the growth of insects, or kill them outright. One tropical plant interferes with growth by producing a chemical that prevents molting, so that the insect is squeezed to death in its own cuticle.

Members of the carrot family—Queen Anne's lace as well as the carrots you eat—produce a devious poison. A pest chewing leaves in the shade of the plant is safe. But out in the cheerful sun, the chemical it has eaten is transformed into a lethal poison. The insect dies.

LEARN TO LIVE WITH YOUR PINE

In spite of their little brains and rigid behaviors, insects easily keep up with change. Like any other life form, each insect is genetically unique, its body not quite like any other, its behavior programmed slightly differently. Because of the short time between generations and the huge number of eggs insects lay, evolution can be very rapid. The black pineleaf scale insect can evolve noticeably within the lifespan of a human.

This scale insect is a wee bit of a thing that sucks the juices from Ponderosa pine needles. It lives in constant battle with the tree's chemical defenses. Each Ponderosa pine

WHY MEDICINES ARE POISONS

Aspirin, caffeine, nicotine, quinine, curare, opium, mescaline, cocaine, digitalis, and hundreds of other drugs have evolved in plants as chemical weapons against pests. That explains why some are useful as medicines, yet all are also poisons. Drugs work because they change the body's chemistry. When a small creature such as a mouse or a beetle eats a drug-laced meal, it gets a big enough dose to make it "crazy," ill, unable to reproduce, or dead. We are so very much larger than the intended victims that if we take a mouse-size dose, our own chemistry, though changed, is less deranged. Aspirin, for instance, interferes with our manufacture of a substance necessary for inflammation, and so it is a useful medicine for reducing fever and swelling. But every medicine is by nature a poison, and even aspirin can kill.

has an arsenal somewhat different from every other Ponderosa pine, so the scale insect could not evolve once and for all the best way to get along with its particular host. For any population of scale insects newly inhabiting a pine, some in that generation will get along okay, many others will be stunted or die. It would make no sense to migrate to a different tree; the next pine might prove to be more lethal still. But natural selection automatically adjusts pest to host.

Ponderosa pines live for a century and more, while each generation of scale insects lives for only a season. Since the individuals who don't get along well with their tree die or reproduce poorly, the tree is left increasingly to those who find it fine. In time, all descendants of the original settlers are a specialized race of fellows unlike other races on other pines in the neighborhood.

All other forms of life evolve continually, too, but most so slowly that the change is imperceptible and immeasurable within the lifetime of a human. Yet within the lifetime of a human, every individual that has been born is a combination of genes never born before, and some genes are new ones that no one else has ever had. Every person lives a life never lived before, under selection pressures that also are unique.

SOMETHING NEW UNDER THE SUN

Daisies also produce a poison that works only when the insect who has eaten it is exposed to light. One insect has found a way around that trick awful poison. Look on daisy plants for rolled-up leaves. Inside each is a leaf-rolling caterpillar. That one leaf is its lifetime meal. Since it never steps into the sunlight, it is never poisoned.

Our own species is evolving, right now, this very minute.

COURTING A CARNIVOROUS FLY

Behavior also evolves. The evolution of behavior is particularly clear in insects because much of what they do represents an inherited instruction rather than a spur-of-the-moment decision. In a group of species that includes both primitive and advanced members, the very steps of behavioral evolution may be visible.

Females of the dance fly family are so anxious for meat and so careless when hungry that they are likely to eat the male as he attempts to copulate. One species of dance fly appears to have solved the problem by an incomprehensible gesture: The male presents the female with a pretty little balloon of woven silk. For some reason, she doesn't eat him.

What is there about a balloon that announces courtship instead of mealtime? The puzzle is solved by looking at how the males of other species of dance fly manage to mate without being cannibalized.

In the most primitive species, the male catches an insect that will make a nice meal, and offers it to a female. While she eats, he mates. That direct, honest offering is the original solution.

The male of a more advanced species decorates his offering with little strands and blobs of silk to capture the female's attention. Competing in the gift-giving department, a still younger species wraps the present entirely in a silken bag. Then comes the cheater: a species of dance fly that offers a smaller insect, but in the same generous wrappings.

If female flies are taken in by small offerings in large packages, then won't they be fooled by the trappings alone? Yes, indeed. The most recent species of all offers his

SETTING BOARD

The wings of dragonflies and other flying insects will not lie flat for display in an insect collection unless they are set that way on a setting board while the insect is still fresh and limp. The setting board used to dry their wings in the right position isn't a fancy piece of equipment; you don't have to be very accurate.

You need:
Pencil
Ruler
Scrap of Styrofoam about 6 inches wide by 1 foot long, and 1 inch thick
Hobbyist's knife
Two pairs of tweezers, preferably with pointed ends
¼-inch-wide strips of paper
Dress pins

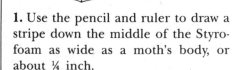

1-inch thick Styrofoam

1. Use the pencil and ruler to draw a stripe down the middle of the Styrofoam as wide as a moth's body, or about ¼ inch.

2. Using the knife, cut out the stripe to make a groove about ¼ inch deep.

3. To set the insect, let its body rest in the groove. Handle the insect with two pairs of tweezers, one to hold the body while you position the wings with the other.

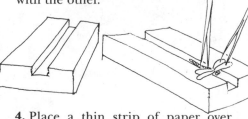

4. Place a thin strip of paper over each wing. Pin the ends of each strip to the Styrofoam to hold it in place. The pins go through the paper strip, not through the wing. After the paper strips are in place, you can adjust the wings so all four show by teasing them into position with the tweezers. Allow the insect to dry for several days and the wings will stay the way you set them.

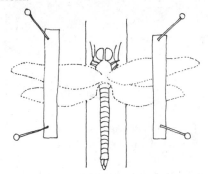

To Display Insects

There are several ways to display insects. They can be kept in transparent plastic boxes (available in hardware, sports, and novelty stores) so that you can see them without opening the boxes, or they can be stored in larger cardboard gift boxes, which can be opened when you want to show them off. Fit either kind of box with a piece of corrugated cardboard or Styrofoam at the bottom to hold the pins on which insects are mounted.

Insect pins are the best mounting pins because they are so thin, but if you can't get them, bead needles also work. The science department in your school will have mail-order catalogs from scientific supply houses that sell insect pins. Bead needles are very thin needles used for stringing or sewing tiny beads. They are sold in craft stores and notion departments. Insert the pin where it will be least noticeable and do the least damage, usually right between the wings. A nice touch is a tiny label held in place by a pin beneath the insect's body. Write a number on each label, then use the number to identify each insect by name on a larger label stuck on the box.

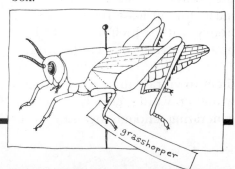

grasshopper

silk balloon to the female, and it is quite empty.

This is how insect talk evolves. A direct action (distracting with food) is made more distinctive (the food is decorated with silk). Food might or might not be understood as courtship, but decorated food appears only during courtship, and signals what is about to occur. The signal is then made even more compelling. A completely wrapped piece of food can't be misunderstood. Finally, the signal becomes a showy symbol that stands for, but no longer is, the original action.

HOUSEHUNTING HONEYBEES

By such steps, some insects have come to exhibit what strikes us as uncanny intelligence, judgments that to us would require conscious thought, languages that to us would require learning.

Honeybees have evolved in a way that allows them to live in cold climates where, below 10°C (50°F), they are too cold to fly. To survive the winter, a colony of honeybees must store at least 10 kilograms of honey with which to fuel their bodies during the cold months. That good supply of food allows them to vibrate their wing muscles while crowding closely together, generating enough heat to warm

HONEY MONEY

Beekeeping is a good deal. The bees work, and you get honey and money. Call your local cooperative extension agent to find out a source for bees and beekeeping equipment in your area. They, and the 4-H Club, will also be able to tell you where to get how-to information. The boy here raises bees in a suburb of New York City. Each hive, with bees, costs about $100, but with reasonable care you should get 100 pounds of honey, which can be sold for at least $2 a pound, in your first summer.

the hive even in desperately cold weather. But only if their shelter is a snug one. The African honeybees from which our species evolved build their hive out in the open. Our wild honeybees build their nest in the cavity of a decaying tree. The quality of the cavity is the difference between a colony's survival for as long as five years, and a cruel death the very first winter.

Honeybees carry in their brains the "ideal" hive plan: a cavity with a volume of 45 liters (47 quarts), large enough to hold the amount of honey they will need, but not so large that it will be difficult to heat. The ideal entrance hole is small enough to keep out wind and rain, and is at least 2 meters (over 6½ feet) up the trunk, where predators can't easily reach it. This entrance is ideally located toward the bottom of the cavity so warm air doesn't escape from it and faces south to give the bees a sunny spot for warming themselves before taking flight on cool days.

Each spring the previous year's queen and a swarm of about 30,000 workers leave the old nest to youngsters and set out to find a new home. A few hundred workers scout the countryside for likely sites. Each works individually, traveling sometimes for miles, poking into knotholes and among tree roots for a suitable cavity.

There is seldom enough light inside a cavity for the scout to see for herself how large it is or where the entrance hole is located. She judges these dimensions by pacing out the measurements from one end of the cavity to the other, around its circumference, and to various points from the entrance. The job takes hours.

Even after the first thorough inspection, a scout rechecks the cavity under other weather conditions, and at other times of day. The better a cavity matches her preconceived notions, the more pleased she is.

This pleasure is expressed by the enthusiasm with which scouts report their find back to other scouts at the swarm. The report is in the form of a dance—the same dance by which workers inform their fellows of the location of a patch of flowers—and the liveliness of their movements reflects how good a find they have made.

Scouts that have found an inferior cavity move sluggishly. When they notice another scout reporting better news, they join her livelier dance and, as they learn the promising location, fly off to see for themselves. If they, too, are pleased with this find, they return to repeat the location to still other scouts. And so, perhaps after several days, the most enthusiastic scout gradu-

ally converts the others to her point of view. The decision is made.

WHISTLING IN THE DARK

Communication between species also evolves; in fact it is commonplace and the two species don't have to speak the same language. You know to back off from a barking dog, although people language doesn't include barking. The message one species receives may even be an unintended message conveyed by the other species. You back off from buzzing bees, although the buzz is simply the noise their wings make, and the bees mean nothing by it. When any such sound (or sight, or smell) arouses a predictable response in another, it is communication.

An example is the noctuid moth who eavesdrops on bats. Bats locate insects by beeping sound waves into the night, and listening for the returning echoes as the beeps bounce off their prey. Like any hunter, they intend to go unheard—and their beeps are too high for most insects to detect. But noctuid moths are attuned to bat frequencies. Using only four nerve cells, two in each ear, noctuid moths evade bats' sonar, and thus avoid being eaten by them.

Each ear of this moth is just be-

ON BEING AN ARROW

When you lead friends to a place they don't know, you light out ahead of them and they follow. You are their arrow. A bee might also fly like an arrow to lead a few friends to a new place. Leading 30,000 followers is not so simple. Some will lag behind, streak ahead, turn aside, or go backward, and the leader will soon be lost among the milling crowd. Honeybee scouts show their fellows the way to a new hive by becoming arrows over and over again, first in one part of the crowd and then in another. They streak through the swarm in the direction of the new hive, then they circle back to streak through again. The pattern of their movements is not a straight line, but a series of short loops and longer, more energetic forward runs.

This is interesting to think about because it may explain how the figure-eight dance of honey bees evolved. Bees were originally solitary, not social, insects, and most species still live alone. Others are mildly social, living in very small groups. Maybe early ancestors of honey bees were straight arrows to their few followers. Maybe as they evolved larger colonies, scouts became looping arrows, as they still are when leading the way to a new hive. Maybe the dance worker honeybees use today to give directions to a patch of flowers is an abbreviation. The loops of the figure eight, like a scout's loops, are ignored. It is the energetic forward run, emphasized by a waggle, that points the way.

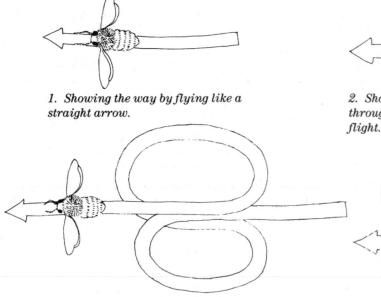

1. *Showing the way by flying like a straight arrow.*

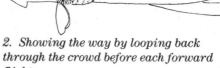

2. *Showing the way by looping back through the crowd before each forward flight.*

3. *The loops come together as a figure eight.*

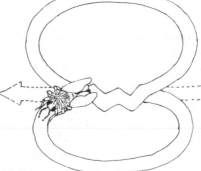

4. *A waggle is added to the middle of the figure eight to emphasize direction. Now a dance instead of a flight, the rest of the arrow is no longer necessary.*

hind the rear wing and has two sensory hairs, each connected to a nerve cell. The "A" nerve fires when hit by weak sound waves such as the squeak of a bat still yards away. Using the "A" nerves alone, the moth can tell whether the bat is above it, behind it, to the right, or to the left. Its strategy is to fly in whatever direction keeps the bat directly behind it. From that position, the bat can't bounce its signal off the moth's wing surfaces. It loses its target.

When the moth and bat are closer than eight feet to each other, the "B" nerves, which are triggered only by loud squeaks, go into play. Firing the "B" nerves jams the moth's steering mechanism. It goes into a crazy series of loops and dives. It has no idea where it is going, but neither does the bat. Often a dive dumps the moth in grass or shrubbery, from which echoes are so confusing that the bat can't distinguish those of the moth from those of leaves and twigs. Communications are disrupted; the moth is safe.

Moths that eavesdrop on bats, bees that talk house with one another, live to see another day, another spring. They, more likely than bat-deaf moths or inarticulate bees, live long enough to reproduce. In the end, every kind of communication, whether between cells in an

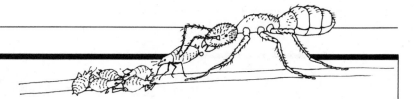

ANTS AS BABYSITTERS

If a species becomes able to signal to another species, as when dogs bark to us or we call to them, wonderful things can happen. An ant begs another ant to regurgitate a drop of food by stroking its face with its feelers. Using the same gesture applied to the other end, ants make the same request of aphids. When an ant strokes an aphid's abdomen with its feelers, the aphid exudes a sweet drop of honeydew. Honeydew is a waste product, excess sugar that aphids must get rid of continually if they are to process enough sweet, but protein-poor, plant juice to meet their protein needs. Ants meet their protein needs from other foods, but those foods are poor in sugar. This is a case where one's waste is the other's feast.

Many species of ants depend on the sugar they get from herds of honeydew-producing insects. They keep the herds together and guard them from predators.

One kind of herd animal is a leafhopper who, in turn, depends on ants as babysitters. No more than 3 percent of leafhopper nymphs survive to adulthood without someone to care for them. With their mother's care, 10 percent survive. But with ants to herd them, nearly 30 percent make it to adulthood. As though she knows that statistic, a mother leafhopper whose nymphs are being cared for by ants will leave that brood and lay another clutch of eggs. Because there are ants, she can make more babies. Because she can make more babies, more ants can be fed. And because everyone benefits, it is not really so surprising that herds and herders, even tiny ones like aphids and ants, should have come to an understanding.

individual's body, or between similar organisms or between total strangers, has evolved because it has aided reproduction. Flies that have not "understood" our gestures have not escaped our swats, and are no longer among us. Noctuid moths that are around now represent an unbroken line of descent from moths that have laid their eggs before the bat got them.

Or before the dinosaur got them. Fossil noctuid moth eggs 75 million years old have been found in Massa-

AN OVERSIGHT

Sit outside in the dark of a summer night with a flashlight. Before long, moths and other night flyers will appear, circling in the light's bright beam. They seem to be attracted to the shine and to be unwilling to leave it. But when you think about it, the idea doesn't make much sense. What lights shone at night a hundred million years ago? Only the stars and the moon.

Moths make a mistake when they blunder into the beam of your flashlight. It is, in their tiny brains, a celestial light—the moon or a bright star—and they are using it, as they have for millions of years, for navigation. Turn your flashlight off to navigate by the moon and you will find it an easy thing to do. As long as you guide your steps in such a way that the moon is always to the same side of you, you will be walking in a straight line. Now turn the flashlight on, prop it upright on the ground, and try to navigate by its beam. If you keep it in front of you, you will bump into it. If you keep it to one side of you, you will circle it. Evolution can't predict the future; moths arrive at your flashlight for no better reason than that they evolved in the absence of flashlights.

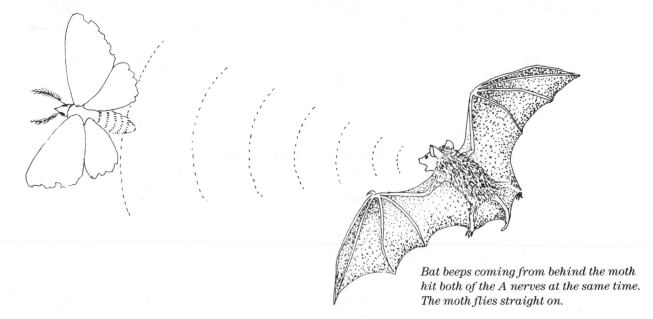

Bat beeps coming from behind the moth hit both of the A nerves at the same time. The moth flies straight on.

chusetts. There were no bats back then. Who might the moth have heard whistling in the dark? Or perhaps they had no "bat-busters" back then.

We will never know. If there was a mammalian predator, a not-yet-bat already speaking in ultrasonic, we couldn't tell from its fossil what its voice sounded like, any more than we can tell from a fossil moth egg what sort of ear it had. If there was a moth-eating dinosaur, they are all gone now. The noctuid moths and other members of the midget multitude, the birds that flew, the mammals that hid, the plants that napped and their seeds that patiently waited out hard times are the only ones still around whose genes, programmed with an understanding of an earlier world, might hold such secrets in them. The end of that earlier world was about to come.

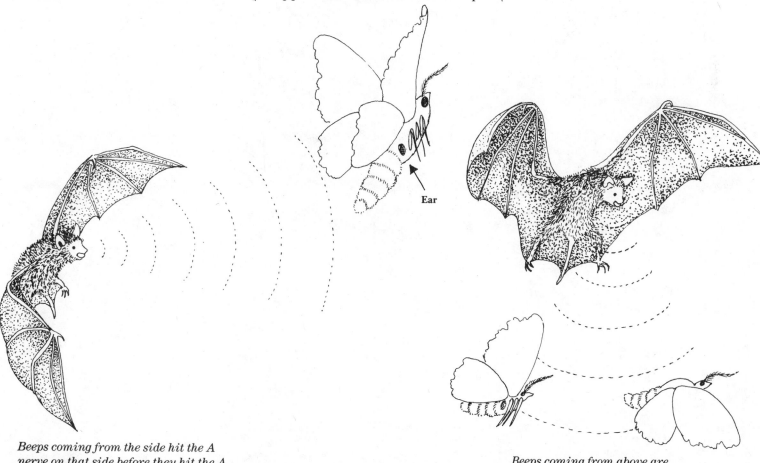

Ear

Beeps coming from the side hit the A nerve on that side before they hit the A nerve on the opposite side. The moth turns away from the bat.

Beeps coming from above are interrupted with each beat of the moth's wings. The moth dives.

DUSK

60 MILLION YEARS AGO

A Cosmic Collision · Shrews and Bats · Creodonts and Condylarths

One day, about 65 million years ago, something terrible happened. There are tantalizing clues as to what it might have been: a dusting of the rare element iridium in sediments that come from that time; a horrifying emptiness in ocean sediments; minute shells that formed soon after at 5°C (9°F) above normal ocean temperatures; the last fossils of dinosaurs in any sediment anywhere.

What the clues add up to is an awesome extinction, and few mysteries have ever excited the imagination of scientists as much as it has. The event wiped out all dinosaurs on land, all pterosaurs in the air, and almost all large reptiles of every sort on the land and in the sea, as well as many mammals, birds, and some trees and flowers. It also exterminated nearly every kind of plankton at the surface of the sea, and all but a few of the mollusks and crustaceans that browsed the upper pastures as larvae, and their predators, and the predators of their predators. All the many foraminifera whose shell- and leaf-shaped bodies can be admired today under a microscope, are descended from a handful of survivors.

The central mystery is how any one event could have made life impossible both for monstrous dinosaurs and for tiny plankton over the vast reaches of continents and over the vaster surface of the oceans, and clear around the globe. Some think the dinosaurs died from the cold as the climate chilled. Frigid polar waters spilled into the gaps as Pangea pulled apart, and that was certainly chilling. But plankton thrive in chilly water, yet hardly any survived. Some think the culprits were volcanoes. They were tumultuous then, but if they were mass-murderers, they were surprisingly selective, for all pterosaurs were killed, but only some birds; small dinosaurs, but not little possums; swimming mollusks, but not swimming fish. Polar waters and volcanoes also fail to explain why, after whatever it was that happened, the ocean heated up. Only one bold guess explains the unearthly dusting of iridium: Earth's collision with an extraterrestrial body. Whatever the nature of the catastrophe, it speaks more for the vigor than the weakness of life, for within a few million years, the survivors had refilled the world with as many species as there had been before.

It is dusk, 60 million years ago, and the mammals are coming out.

CRASH

Dinosaurs, the largest animals, may have died because phytoplankton,

CRASH!

Few creatures are as critical to as many different other species' survival as phytoplankton are, but any species can be important. Sea stars, for example, are what is called a keystone species in their community, for if they are removed, the whole community crashes. Along northern coasts, sea stars prey on mussels, the most abundant mollusk there. If sea stars are removed from the community, the mussel population explodes at the expense of other mollusks that reproduce more slowly. What was once a rich community becomes nothing but a mussel bed.

Right now, acid rain and other industrial wastes are killing conifers. Nearly half of the Black Forest in Germany is dying; conifers that crown the old Appalachians are dying, too. Those forests that met the challenge of dinosaurs by growing so majestically tall are now home to hoards of insects that evolved hand in hand with them, to the bird descendants of dinosaurs that eat their seeds and nest in their branches, and to mammals that first climbed them to safety long before the great dying. If they go, the animals that depend on them will go hungry and homeless. It doesn't take long to destroy what took so long to build.

CHALK BUBBLES

Drop a piece of chalk into vinegar and watch the bubbles rise as it dissolves. The bubbles are carbon dioxide, the gas that forms when calcium carbonate dissolves. The chalk is undissolved remains of shelly phytoplankton, for in a normal ocean some calcium carbonate escapes dissolution as it sinks, and falls like snow over the ocean floor to form layers of white sediment. The chalk, however, is either from phytoplankton that lived before the great dying, or from phytoplankton that lived after it, not from any that lived during it. For reasons still mysterious, the calcium-bodied plankton that became extinct 65 million years ago dissolved entirely. Nothing of their chalky shell remains. There is a blank in that layer of the seafloor.

the smallest plants, died. Extinction can occur like a chain reaction because each species depends for survival on other species, which in turn depend on other species.

Phytoplankton are the first and most important link in a very long chain. Depending directly on tiny photosynthesizing plants are the thousands of species that eat them. If they die, browsers that eat them

die, and so do predators that eat the browsers. The surface of the sea can become nearly lifeless. So can the bottom. The rain of nourishing corpses from the top dwindles and bottom dwellers—plants and animals—starve. Large creatures can topple along with small ones. But what might cause the ocean's rich crop of phytoplankton to fail?

Scientists who discovered the dusting of iridium laid down about 65 million years ago have figured that this rare element could come only from an extraterrestrial object. Earth's rocks and soils contain very little iridium, but certain meteors, including comets are rich in it. A mere flyby, such as when Halley's comet loops past the Earth, leaves very little dust on the Earth. These scientists think a very large object, probably a comet as large as Halley's, must have hit our planet to account for the dusting of iridium. Their estimate shows the object to have been at least six miles in diameter, large enough to have caused an almost unimaginable explosion followed by a "nuclear winter." There has been much talk recently of nuclear winter. Calculations predict that dust from nuclear explosions or from collision with an extraterrestrial body would blot out the sun for weeks, maybe for months. Under the dark sky, steamy jungles would cool and sum-

mer would change to winter. Plants would starve for lack of the light they need to photosynthesize, or they would freeze to death. Such explosions may also pollute the air with substances that cause acid snow and rain, stressing plants and phytoplanktons still more.

When organisms die, their corpses release the substances they were made of. Normally, living organisms recycle these substances as quickly as they are released by dead ones. The rotting fleshy portions of plants release carbon which, combined with oxygen, becomes the carbon dioxide from which living plants manufacture food. The dissolving shelly portions of limy phytoplanktons also release carbon. Besides being used for photosynthesis, this carbon is combined with calcium (instead of oxygen) to build the calcium carbonate skeletons of living phytoplanktons, mollusks, and crustaceans. But continents-full of rotting vegetation and oceans-full of dissolving plankton would overload the system. Scientists who developed this theory believe that when the skies finally cleared over land and sea, an excess of carbon dioxide may have been building up in the atmosphere. Many species that might otherwise have cleared the air of carbon dioxide were not to survive the short-run stresses to which they had been

A TERRESTRIAL FOOD WEB

Terrestrial plants support a web of life similar to that supported by plankton in the sea. This food web might occur in a suburb. The arrows point from the eaten to the eater. Plants are eaten by rabbits, squirrels, mice, seed-eating birds, and herbivorous insects. The smaller herbivores, in turn, are eaten by a variety of small predators: spiders, beetles, toads, birds, and snakes. Both herbivores and small predators are eaten by large predators such as foxes and owls.

No food web is really as simple as this one. A suburban acre or a city park may have voles, moles, and chipmunks, as well as mice (of more than one kind) and squirrels. There are not one, but dozens of species of seed-eating and insect-eating birds. Insect relationships anywhere are much more complicated than the eating exchange shown here among spiders, carnivorous beetles, and herbivorous caterpillars. Only two large predators are shown here; that leaves out hawks, dogs, and the family cat. Even the food web of our own backyard is too complicated to draw—but you could have a good time trying.

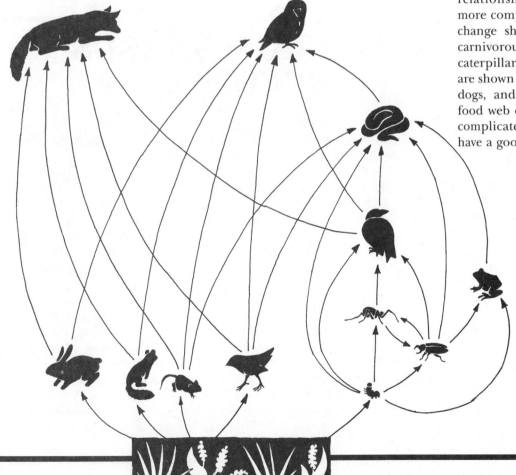

subjected. Many others were to become extinct in the long run because the air could not be cleared fast enough to save them.

Carbon dioxide gas is transparent, like window glass, and, like window glass, it is an insulator. Carbon dioxide lets in sunlight, which heats the surface of the Earth, but it doesn't let that heat escape. After the brief cooling, temperatures seem to have gradually risen worldwide over thousands of years until summer days were routinely scorchers. The ocean temperature rose, even at the bottom.

Long-term heating explains the mass extinction of dinosaurs and large reptiles more easily than short-term cooling. Cold-blooded reptiles too large to shed their heat in burrows could die of heat prostration. The problem may have been worse for warm-blooded dinosaurs, for they produced extra heat, and may not have evolved efficient ways to pant or sweat extreme heat away.

Mass dying, however, doesn't always mean mass extinction. As long as there was refuge anywhere for any band of survivors, they might have made it through the worst of times. To become extinct, an organism must fail to reproduce. Phytoplanktons fail to reproduce if the chemistry of the water they inhabit isn't just right. It cannot be acidic, or for that matter, too warm.

In the larger world we inhabit, extinction could be caused by oaks with no acorns, pandas with no mates, mates with no sperm, eggs without life. But, what about the dinosaurs? Perhaps the sex of a dinosaur was determined by incubation temperature, as it is in reptiles, and whole generations of giant beasts hatched in open, unprotected places and were therefore all male or all female. They would have been a unisex population unable to reproduce. Sperm die easily of overheating, and if dinosaurs kept their sperm inside their hot bodies, they may have become sterile, another cause of reproductive failure. Or perhaps there were just too few left, and they could no longer find one another over the emptied land-

DEATH VERSUS EXTINCTION

The scene of the dying dinosaurs in Walt Disney's *Fantasia* is fantastic: Gasping for breath in the hot air, vainly trying to drink from drying mud puddles, one after another of the great beasts bites the dust. But dying doesn't cause extinction. There are always individuals immune to plague, adaptable to change, saved from catastrophe.

Survivors quickly begin to restore the population. All forms of life overproduce—lay more eggs, form more seeds, give birth to more babies than are needed to replace them in the population. Each species is prevented from overrunning the world only because every other species also overproduces, and there is only so much world to go around. When there is mass dying, more living space is created, and the survivors and their descendants quickly refill it with offspring.

So the only way a species can become extinct is to fail to make more of itself. The greatest dinosaur mystery isn't how they died, but why they made too few baby dinosaurs. What if the sex of dinosaurs was determined by temperature, as it is in turtles? An unusually high incubation temperature in eggs too well-buried and too large to cool off even at night might cause a unisex generation of all males or all females. And that would be that. Without being there to see for ourselves, we'll never know for sure, but that scenario for the end of the dinosaurs is more fantastic than the one in *Fantasia*.

scape. Therefore, if only the phytoplanktons had held out 65 million years ago, feeding their browsers and recycling their carbon dioxide, we might still have had dinosaurs. We would not, however, have had ourselves.

THE SURVIVORS

Big beasts no longer bounded along the riverbeds, tramped the forests, browsed the plains, or swam the coastal waters. No bellows broke the silence, no thundering feet whipped up the dust, no spray from bathing dinosaurs glistened in the scorching air. But the world was not completely empty.

Plants can survive months of dark and cold as seeds, and get through heat waves by going dormant. Generation after generation, animals that by nature or habit had ways to cope with the difficult times now upon them, held on. Snakes, lizards, and turtles, who need so little to eat and know so well how to get out of the sun, survived. Birds can fly to cooler places; most of them, too, survived. And little mammals who don't mind darkness at all, who can live on modest rations and have such clever ways of dumping extra heat, looked out upon a world where opportunity beckoned.

Over the next 350,000 years, plankton survivors spread again

THE NUMBERS GAME

Right now, there are about the same number of species in the world as there were in the days of the dinosaurs. There are about the same number of species as there were in the days of the coal forests. In fact, there are about the same number of species as there were in the ancient seas over the craton.

There is room on Earth, it seems, for a certain amount of diversity, and no catastrophe has yet made more than a temporary dimple in the wonderful variety of life. Mammals, for instance, waited in the wings as long as dinosaurs held center stage. Then, when the dinosaurs made their exit, there was space for mammals to step into the spotlight, don new costumes, perform new acts, evolve the modern roles of ape and ass and panda. This is strange to think about. Catastrophe is creative: We would not be here if the dinosaurs were.

over the surface of the sea. The water gradually lost its acidity, the air recovered its balance, temperatures went back to normal.

For every spot that the dinosaurs had vacated, there was somebody poised to fill it. Over the next 5 million years, some birds grew to gigantic sizes, gave up on flying, and turned to browsing. Flocks of *Diatryma* roamed the plains as ostriches do now. Some birds that had specialized as ocean fishers also gave up on flying. As penguins they took over the small marine reptiles' place. Other birds filled in as coelurosaur-size carnivores, becoming eagles, hawks, and owls. But for birds, who had long ago given up their hands in favor of wing tips, there was no going back to that more useful plan. Only mammals had the four little paws that were to become the horse's hoof, the whale's fin, the elephant's pad, the lion's claw—and the human hand.

LITTLE BROWN FURRY THINGS

The number of mammal species in the world today is just over 4,000 according to the two-volume *Mammals of the World*.

Flipping through the 3,000 illustrated pages of this work is strange, for almost all the mammals are strangers. All those that you can name, or have ever seen, take up less than a tenth of the book. The others are little brown furry things that look so much alike you feel

A WHALE OF A TALE

Why did the whale become a whale? The answer seems to be: Because water got deeper. The earliest about-to-be whale that has been found waded the balmy, briny Tethys Sea 50 million years ago. Its skull says it was a fish eater, and other fossils say the fish it ate were herring. But nothing says it didn't have four feet like any other mammal.

The Tethys was at that point scrunched narrow and shallow, possibly with no outlet to the ocean on either side. A four-footed not-quite whale would have had little trouble cornering a school of herring in the shallows without so much as a dive.

But as the continents drew apart, the seaway opened and deepened all the way from Texas to India. Little by little, would-be whales were tempted farther from the shallows. Finally, those that could bid good-bye to the land forever had become whales.

A strange thought comes to mind. Someone is showing a movie of a fish swimming in the sea. The sea becomes shallow, just puddles. The fish's fins turn to legs, and the animal climbs ashore. Then the reel is run backward. The animal wades in shallow water. The water deepens, becomes a sea. The animal's legs turn to fins, and it swims away.

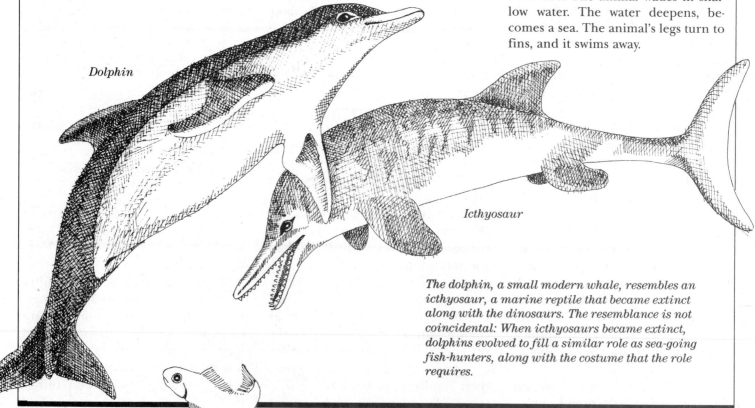

Dolphin

Icthyosaur

The dolphin, a small modern whale, resembles an icthyosaur, a marine reptile that became extinct along with the dinosaurs. The resemblance is not coincidental: When icthyosaurs became extinct, dolphins evolved to fill a similar role as sea-going fish-hunters, along with the costume that the role requires.

you're looking at the same page over and over again. The whole picture of what a mammal is begins to change. Hardly any are giants like bisons and bears. Few are even as big as a rabbit. Only a handful have anything as special about them as horns or hoofs. Most are shy, mysterious creatures about which almost nothing is known, because hardly anyone ever sees them. The world of mammals 60 million years ago must have looked very much like the pictures in *Mammals of the World* today—one little brown furry thing after another.

All the early mammals walked flat-footed like shrews and possums walk, and like you would walk if you got down on all fours, on the palms of your hands and the soles of your feet. All paws had five toes splayed out from one another. This basic design was very useful for many things, but not especially useful for any one thing. Getting about flat-footed, an animal can run as fast as a raccoon, but not as fast as a dog, which runs on tiptoe. You can check out the difference by sprinting flat-footed, which will get you nowhere fast. To speed up, you automatically raise your heel off the ground and push off with toes alone.

Try digging. Splayed fingers don't make as good a shovel as fingers held closely together; you'll

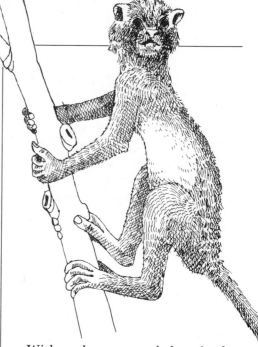

wish you had longer, stronger nails, too. Try climbing a tree without using your thumbs. Try swimming with and without flippers on your rear paws.

With old-fashioned paws, the small mammals that lived to see the dinosaurs die could catch an insect, reach a berry, dig a worm. They could leap a bit, climb a bit, run a bit, burrow a bit. But not one of them could do any of these things as well as this or that brown furry thing today, even though they didn't look very different. The differences are in the little things—the fingernails, front teeth, eye sockets, snouts, and thumbs.

FOSSIL FINGERNAILS

Flat fingernails in the fossil record signal the evolution of the first primates, the family of monkeys and of man.

Primates are ancient mammals, related more closely to the ancient tree shrews than to any other sort of animal alive today. Our ancestor seems to have been a tree shrew of a sort long since extinct. It was snouty like a modern shrew, and scurried in trees like a squirrel. A squirrel can scurry along the surface of a branch, but can't grasp it between thumb and fingers. It can go high up in a tree, but not out to

its very edge. It can pick up a nut between two front paws, but can't pluck it with one paw.

The first primates that evolved from tree shrews solved all that. The oldest fossil primate foot that has been found has a big toe that veers way off to one side and, when bent, closes neatly against the sole of the foot. Using this big opposable toe, the animal could grasp branches and pluck fruits. Instead of claws, which aren't necessary when toes and fingers can cling to trunks and branches, this animal had flat nails that protected the top surface and also helped avoid stubbed toes.

Small as these innovations were, they created new opportunities. The first primates probably ate leaves. Leaves are within easy reach of any tree dweller, but they are among the poorer diets nature has to offer. Energy-loaded, starchy, sugary fruit is a much more efficient diet. Grasping onto branches rather than padding along their surface, small primates could get out even onto the very small twigs at the tips of trees. As anyone who's ever climbed for apples knows, that's where the fruit is. Fruit is still the staple diet of almost all the tarsiers and lemurs, primitive, often nocturnal primates; and the more advanced daytime primates, monkeys, and apes.

Without long, curved claws in the way, toes and fingers could better feel their way around, peel fruit, gather nuts, or pick up a bug and pop it in the mouth. With an opposable big toe and thumb, there was new strength and nimbleness for everything from combing fur to making nests.

With a firm grasp on a branch, primates were safer than pad-along-the-surface tree shrews had been. First, the animal was less likely to fall. Also, it didn't have to use the tree trunk as its vertical highway, but could climb further out among the branches and hoist itself up or let itself down from limb to limb. Finally, the very tips of tree branches, which are slender and fragile, are just where clawed predators fear to tread.

A HEAD START

Pressure to find food and evade predators may have been the cause of the evolution of primates' feet, but the effect was way beyond becoming the acrobat of the forest. Change itself creates new pressures: to have a surer sense of touch for judging handholds, to gauge distances better when plunging through the treetops, to have a sharper eye for the shapes and colors of ripening fruit, to have brain space for memorizing where crops will ripen and when.

Primates' eye sockets moved forward, giving them 3-D vision. The snout, with its now little-needed smelling surface, shrank, along with the long jaw that supported it. With the muzzle squashed in and the eyes pulled forward, the skull was pushed into a roomy, almost globular shape. Portions of the brain that processed visual information and the sense of touch in hands and feet increased at the expense of the smelling centers. The monkey's face was in the making; so was the most expensive brain around. Rats use only about 4 percent of their energy to support their brain; humans use 20 percent. But the cost is worth it if you can afford the luxury. Primates are the whiz kids of the animal world.

Primates supported their bigger brain with their better diet. In fact, having thumbs meant easier, faster harvesting of food, and easy eating meant having time and energy to spare, and having time and energy to spare meant being able to afford a better baby, too. Once primates switched to a fruit diet, they didn't have to work as hard or as long to load themselves with energy. Energy didn't have to be wasted in producing dozens of babies either, because babies tightly clutching their mother's fur out on the swaying twigs were safe from predators. Parents could afford to spend their savings on raising fewer babies more carefully, and for longer lengths of time.

The longer an infant spends with its family, the more time it has to learn the family's ways and the less it must rely on inborn know-how. The brain can give up some areas devoted to automatic circuitry and build instead large areas that will be shaped by education and experience.

Longer childhood, too, creates pressures: Once a group of mammals is committed to a long childhood, those that use it best are at an advantage. There is a spiral in evolution: Selection favors those individuals that have a larger brain in that globular skull, that have a still longer childhood to stuff it full of knowledge, and that have a longer lifetime altogether so that enough of these big-brained, slow-growing babies can be born and grow to adulthood. Evolution isn't one event: It's a web of events that all push and tug at one another, making a monkey out of a shrew.

MIGHTY MITE

Primitive shrewlike mammals gave rise to primates, and probably to all the other modern types of mammal within the first 10 million years after the great dying. Shrews still very like the grandparents of us all are still among us, leading the same sort of life that got them through the catastrophe. Tiny as shrews are—the smallest weighs a sixteenth of an ounce, no more than a penny—they are the mighty mites of the animal kingdom. They de-

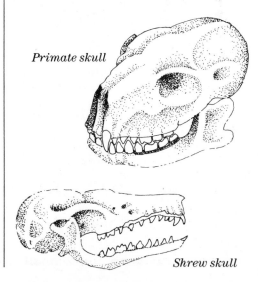

Primate skull

Shrew skull

HAND DUG

Moles can get out of hand. Although their little pointy teeth can't gnaw through roots, their powerful digging feet lift turf in lawns and plow out hollows around flower roots in gardens. The roots dry out; grass and flowers die. That's okay if there's only one mole around—the small damage it does is more than made up for by the number of root-gnawing grubs it eats. But a clan of moles can dig up the whole yard.

Poisoned corn and grain pellets are sold for killing moles, but they don't work. Moles don't eat corn or grain.

Trapping moles is tricky. Two kinds of traps are used, either a special mole trap that spears the creature from above, or an ordinary rat trap. A mole trap is set above a feeding tunnel; a rat trap is set inside the tunnel,

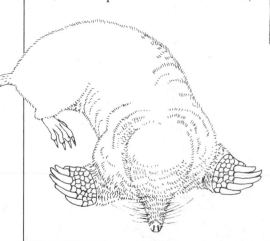

and the portion that has been dug out to get the trap in is covered with a board or a rock. The mole is supposed to blindly blunder into either kind of trap.

The catch is: Which tunnel is the feeding tunnel? Moles use each feeding tunnel for only a few days. Most of the tunnels in a lawn are not in use anymore. The only way to find out which tunnels are active is to stamp

everyone of them down flat, then watch for newly raised ones in which to set traps. The more moles there are, the more confusing this becomes, and the more time it takes.

A better solution than killing moles may be to kill their food. Special insecticides made for grass-eating grubs are sold in garden supply stores. When food becomes scarce, most moles will simply move on.

serve to be noticed as something more than what the cat drags in.

Yet the corpses the cat drags in are likely to be the only shrews you'll ever see. (Even that opportunity to notice one is only because cats don't eat shrews—musk glands along the flanks make them smell unappetizing.) Shrews hug the ground so closely that they are almost within it—beneath leaf litter, under snow, between the stems of grasses. Their burrows are so small they can be mistaken for the tunnels of earthworms. And they are fast.

The shrew is cranked up to such a high energy level that its heart may beat 1,200 times a minute when it is alarmed. It must eat every three hours, day and night, summer and winter. Shrews die of starvation after less than half a day without food. To satisfy their voracious appetite, shrews are always on the go at top speed rummaging for worms, snapping up larvae, darting after scuttling beetles, biting at funguses, and attacking small mammals. Some hunt down their prey by using their long snouts to burrow and to sniff underground. Others find prey in the dark by sonar, beaming squeaks into the night and listening for the echo that will tell them where to turn. Shrews eat at least their weight in food each day; some consume twice that.

Screaming with rage, shrews will attack anything that threatens them, biting at face and throat with razor sharp teeth. A shrew may eat its prey or its attacker while it is still alive. Our most common shrew, the short-tailed shrew, paralyzes small animals with poisonous saliva.

The high-speed, daredevil shrew burns out its life in about a year. But there's something grand in its brief accomplishments. A one-ounce shrew may have eaten 11½ kilograms (25 pounds) of insects, produced 30 babies, and taken 446,760,000 breaths in its short burst of life.

BROTHER MOLE

Although the mole is a heavy-handed beast, it is brother to the shrew. The relationship is easy to see. A mole has a pointy snout, blunt rear, and short legs. But the animal has evolved in special ways to suit its underground life. Its small ears have been pinched until they are just holes invisible beneath the fur, where they can't get clogged with dirt. The mole's eyes are only dots that can see light, but can't tell a toadstool from a toad. The front legs are pushed forward so far that the toes line up with the nose. The bones are thick; the toes form shovels; the nails are heavy-duty rakes.

Moles can travel a foot a minute in loose soil. You can watch the tunnel moving ahead through a garden, usually at dawn or dusk. Some species of mole shovel by using one front foot and then the other and pushing the dirt along behind with the rear feet; other species use a breast stroke to swim through the dirt. The part of the tunnel just below the surface of the ground is a feeding tunnel in which the mole hunts by touch and smell. A mole feels with its whiskers the vibrations of earthworms that have stumbled into this unexpected cavity in the ground. Then, having learned which way to go, the mole sniffs down its favorite food.

Way below the feeding tunnel is a more complicated construction in which the mole lives. There are sleeping rooms, rooms where earthworms, paralyzed by a sharp bite, are stored for times of food shortage, perhaps a large nest, lined with leaves or grass, for raising babies, and long tunnels that connect upper feeding grounds.

The mole can move quickly through this permanent construction. The nap of its soft fur is directionless—whether the mole is moving forward or backward through a tight spot, it can slip smoothly along. The mole's body is so streamlined that it is almost neckless and hipless. Changing its mind about which way to go, the

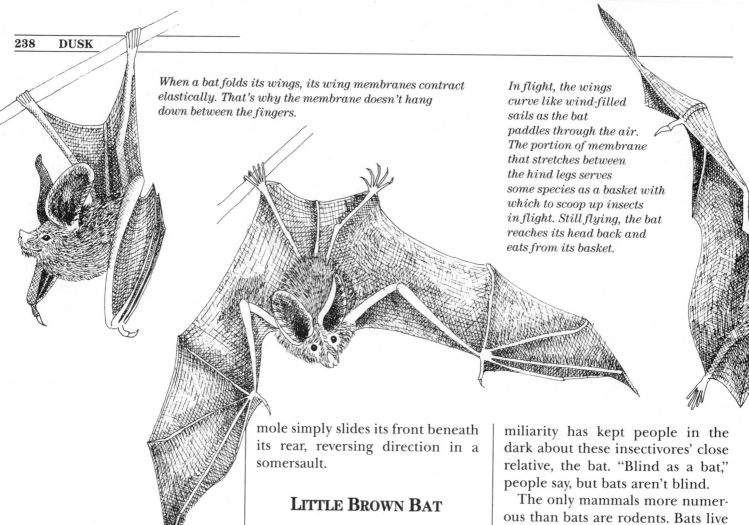

When a bat folds its wings, its wing membranes contract elastically. That's why the membrane doesn't hang down between the fingers.

In flight, the wings curve like wind-filled sails as the bat paddles through the air. The portion of membrane that stretches between the hind legs serves some species as a basket with which to scoop up insects in flight. Still flying, the bat reaches its head back and eats from its basket.

As a bat prepares to take off, it spreads arms and fingers, stretching its wing membranes into sails from which nothing sticks out but the bat's feet, head, and thumbs.

mole simply slides its front beneath its rear, reversing direction in a somersault.

LITTLE BROWN BAT

The early insect eaters never grew very big or very noticeable. People spend their lives surrounded by shrews without ever meeting one face-to-face. They can draw a picture of a mouse, but not of a mole. Many know these creatures only by reputation. A "shrew" is a woman with a nasty temper and a shrill voice. A "mole" is a spy, afraid to come out into the light of day. The same lack of eyeball-to-eyeball fa-

miliarity has kept people in the dark about these insectivores' close relative, the bat. "Blind as a bat," people say, but bats aren't blind.

The only mammals more numerous than bats are rodents. Bats live everywhere we live: in cities, steaming jungles, dry deserts, and cold forests as far north as the Arctic. In our climate, most bats hibernate through the winter, after adding so much fat to feed themselves that their weight may be doubled. Most of the thousand or so species of bats occupy the tropics, where they evolved from primitive insectivores perhaps 45 million years ago. North American bats are still rather like

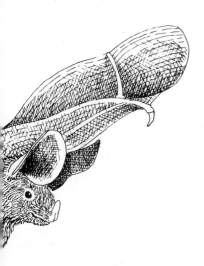

their ancestors—miniature eaters of insects, and hunters in the night.

FLAPPING ON ALL FOURS

Bat flight isn't like bird flight. Instead of the up and down flapping motion that carries birds smoothly across the sky, bats use a swim stroke that plunges them erratically through the air in the jerky way of a person doing the breaststroke through water. The stroke most likely evolved from a leaping motion that at first took its ancestor on a glide from branch to branch, for the wing surface is attached to the rear legs as well as to the front legs, something like the flap of skin on a gliding squirrel. Bats still flap all four feet to fly.

Flying under one's own steam has been invented only four times in the history of the world: by insects, by pterosaurs, by birds, and by bats. Except for the insects, animals have had to flap their arms to fly. Pterosaurs used their arms and a single finger; birds used their arms and three fingers, which form the wing tip; bats used their arms and all their fingers except the thumb.

The fingers act as ribs to hold aloft a sail of skin that spreads between them and along the bat's sides all the way to its ankles. Like the fingers of your own hand, the bat's fingers spread from the palm, stretching the wing membrane between them. When the bat relaxes its fingers, the elastic web between them snaps taut. Even with fingers tightly shut, there are no drooping folds of wing between.

SOUND PICTURES

Bats use their nearsighted eyes to avoid collisions when crawling close to one another in their crowded roosts. Outside the roost they get around in complete darkness by ear alone. Their ears are finely tuned, not to the rustlings and flappings that other animals listen for, but to the echoes of their own voices bouncing back to them from their surroundings much like a submarine uses sonar to locate its target.

Ultrasonic beeps are sent out through the nose or half-opened mouth. While the beep is being sent, muscles close the bat's ear so it can't hear its own noise. Between beeps, ears open to catch the echo bounced off even the thinnest twig or fluttery moth. Sound waves bounced back from nearby surfaces hit the ear sooner than those from faraway surfaces, so the sound pictures the bat forms of its surroundings are three dimensional, complete with the bumps and hollows of the landscape, and the shape of an insect flying about.

Just as our eyes fill in the lay of the land by turning here and there, a bat gets a full picture of its surroundings by turning its ears. And just as we can plot the course of a moving object by noting where it is from one glance to the next, a bat can tell the speed and direction of an insect by comparing each beep's echo with the next one's echo, and "seeing" the movement against the unmoving background landscape.

However this image looks to a bat inside its own brain, it is wonderfully accurate. Bats can easily avoid entangling in tree branches, and can zero in on an insect no bigger than a mosquito. Yet bats sometimes collide with one another when they are reentering their roost. Apparently they know the way so well that they don't bother to

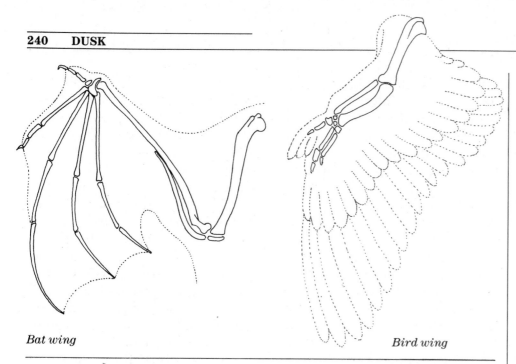

Bat wing

Bird wing

pay attention to the echoes they are receiving, or to look where they are going.

BAT BIRTH CONTROL

Bats living in cold climates keep to an odd sexual schedule. They can't mate during the winter, because they're asleep. Males can't mate in spring, because all their stored fat has gone into keeping them alive over the winter, and they are in no shape to produce sperm. They can't mate in the summer either. Large testicles hanging down in the scrotum would throw the bats off balance during flight, so for the summer hunting season bat testicles are small and are tucked up inside the body, where the temperature is too high for sperm to survive.

That leaves autumn as the only time for sperm production—and that leaves females out of luck. Females can't get pregnant in the fall because their babies would be born in winter when there's not a thing for bats to eat.

So, ignoring one another's predicaments, each sex does what is best for it. The male mates in the fall. The female doesn't get pregnant until the following spring. She stores the sperm safely in her cooled body during the winter, and becomes pregnant just as she is ready to emerge from hibernation to gorge on insects that hatch in spring.

A female bat feeds her baby milk from two nipples placed nearly in her armpits, where the baby can be warmly nestled under its mother's wing. The mother makes a quarter of her weight each day in milk. If a human produced milk that well, a mother could make about 14½ kilograms (32 pounds), or just over 14 liters (15 quarts), or enough to feed a litter of five babies. The bat gives all that milk to a single infant, and for good reason. Bats too small to fly die in great numbers, usually by falling from ceilings.

Since most bats have only one baby at a time, and only one pregnancy each year, and chances are high that the baby will fall from the cradle before it is old enough to fly, you'd think there wouldn't be a lot of bats in the belfry. Other tiny mammals, such as shrews and mice, live only three years or less. If a bat had the normal life span of other animals its size, it couldn't reproduce in its lifetime the minimum of two babies needed to replace it and its mate in the population, and so bats would become extinct. Bats, however, have an incredibly long life span. Adults live for 20 years or more, and each year each female brings a new baby bat into the world.

CREODONTS AND CONDYLARTHS

Of all the little brown furry things in ancient forests, only two groups

THE HAND AND THE FOOT OF IT

T he embryos of all mammals look about the same in their early life. The bumps, called limb buds, that will end in hoofs on a horse embryo look the same as limb buds that will be wings on bats, flippers on seals, and hands on you. As the weeks pass, cells in one part of the limb bud divide faster or slower, more toward this direction than that one, and the hand or foot or wing begins to take shape.

The plan that cells are following as they "decide" whether or how fast to multiply is not contained in a "hand gene" that acts as a blueprint of the final product. Scientists think the patterning of a limb is the final result of the local conditions in which each cell finds itself. The chemical environment close to the body, where the upper arm will take shape, is different from the chemical environment farthest away from the body, where the hand will take shape. So the rear of the limb bud has a different chemical environment from the front of the limb bud. The particular chemical environment around a cell determines which instructions in the cell will be turned on and which will be turned off. This means that the cells in one place will grow, for instance, into the bulges of fingertips, but the cells anywhere else will not be able to do that.

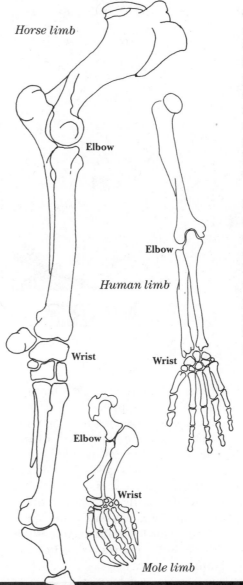

Horse limb

Elbow

Elbow

Human limb

Wrist

Wrist

Elbow

Wrist

Mole limb

Once a clump of cells is doing its thing, it lets loose still other chemicals locally. These chemicals turn off instructions in nearby cells. For example, for a certain distance in every direction, no other cells can bulge fingerlike. In this way, local conditions not only control the shape of a finger, but also how close fingers can be to one another, and in what direction they can grow.

Thinking in this way about how a limb is shaped makes evolution easier to think about. There need not be a drastic change in genetic plans for a drastic change in shape to happen. Instead, small changes in the instructions for how much of a chemical to produce, and when, and for how long, can make the difference between five fingers and one, a hoof and a fingernail, a flipper and a wing.

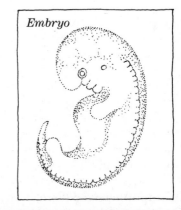

Embryo

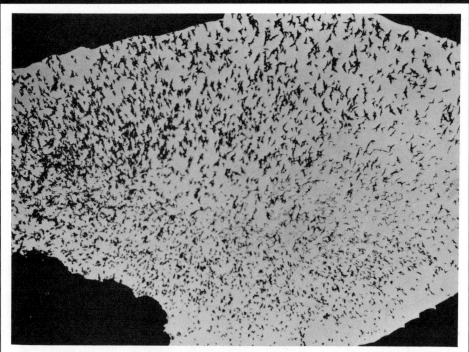

AND MORE AND MORE AND MORE

To see our common little brown bats, which weigh in at 5 grams (¹/5 ounce), watch at dusk, when they first come out of the roost to feed, and while your eyes can still make them out against the darkening sky. Little brown bats usually start the evening with a drink of water taken on the swoop along the surface of a pond or swimming pool.

Always alert to prey, they turn abruptly here and there as one insect after another attracts their attention. A single bat will appear as a flutter of darkness often seen only from the corner of the eye. The effect of several bats is something like leaves blown crazily by a gust of wind: You see the moving shapes, but you can't follow any particular one of them. Occasionally a bat will come quite close to your head. It has no designs on you, but is interested in the mosquitos you attract.

were destined to become the large, noble beasts that people think of when they think of mammals. The creodonts were going to become the carnivores with wicked fangs; the condylarths were going to become the herbivores with thundering hooves. But you'd never have known it to look at them.

These days, a herd of cows strikes us as about as different as you can get from a pack of wolves, but those days, the eaters and the eaten looked about the same. They were all blunt-faced, short-legged, slow-moving, small-brained, and no bigger than a bread box. Wandering through the forests of the Great Plains 60 million years ago, you could best tell which was which by who was following whom. Ahead: the hunted, chewing leaves. Behind: the hunter, licking chops. Together, creodonts and condylarths were a push-me-pull-you of evolution: Neither one could make a move without the other moving, too.

You could have told that a race was on by looking at their footprints. To keep ahead of creodonts, condylarths stood up on tiptoe and surged ahead on thick, blunt claws that were really small hoofs. To catch up with condylarths, creodonts stood up on tiptoe—and grew hoofs. The copycat strategy didn't work for long, however, because the condylarths then acceler-

CLEAN AS A BONE

There is a story about a visitor in a foreign land who was served a strange meat stew. The bits of meat contained small bones, which the visitor removed as he came upon them, and idly arranged beside his plate. Only as he pulled the last bone from the last morsel of flesh did he realize he was arranging the skeleton of a bat.

That's one way to clean bones for a skeleton collection.

The other way is to serve the stew to carrion beetles (also called burying beetles) and let them clean the bones. Small meals, such as a bird or mouse, are cleaned fastest. (Before handling a dead animal see page 270.) Wrap the carcass in ½-inch mesh hardware cloth; that will keep the larger beetles from dragging a small corpse away, and will keep the corpse safe from dogs. With metal shears cut the piece of hardware cloth wide enough to roll all the way around the carcass, with several inches of overlap, and about twice as long as the carcass. Roll the hardware cloth around the carcass like a tube, then flatten both

ends of the tube and bend them over to make a closed container.

Dig a shallow hole in a protected place, such as under shrubbery. Cover the bottom of the hole with a rag so that no bones will be lost. Put the wrapped carcass in the hole and cover it loosely with soil and leaf litter. You might put a rock or a board over it for further protection from dogs, or tie it to the shrub.

It's hard to say exactly how long it will take for the beetles to finish their job. That depends on the size of the skeleton to be cleaned, the number and kind of beetles in your neighbor-

hood, and the time of year (winter, for instance, isn't beetle season). Check every few weeks to see how the work is progressing.

The skeleton is likely to have fallen apart by the time the beetles have finished, and it's very difficult to glue and wire bones together as museums do. Instead, sort the bones as they are in this photograph, and glue them with white glue to paper, cardboard, or wood to display them. You could also glue them to a piece of Plexiglas using a glue intended for plastic. That would allow you to see the bones from both sides.

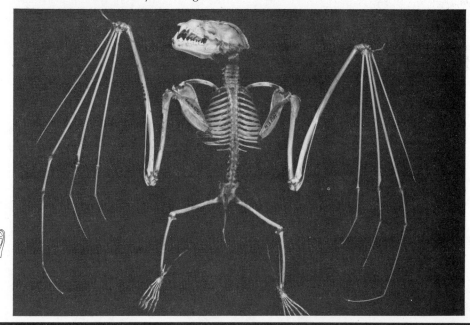

DEPEND ON YOUR FUNGUS

The lichens that crust rocks and bark are funguses living so closely with algae or cyanobacteria that the two are a single organism. The fungus delivers the raw materials—minerals and water—and its partner supplies the energy. Together, they can eat rock.

This way that funguses have of getting along with green plants is very old. Funguses lived among the roots of land plants 400 million years ago. Today, four-fifths of all land plants depend on funguses at least to forage phosphorus for them. In return, the plant provides its funguses with carbon. Orchid seeds can't sprout unless their funguses feed them. Beech trees, pines, and willows have given up their own root hairs, and instead depend on funguses to absorb everything they need from the soil, and from greater distances by far than roots reach. In the soil of the tropics, less than one-one thousandth of the nutrients ever penetrates below the top 5 centimeters (2 inches) of the forest floor. Funguses digest every-thing edible before it sinks any further.

They are almost as active in northern woods. For every mushroom that you find in a walk through the woods, there are thousands upon thousands of funguses that don't happen to be fruiting, though their mass of hyphae is growing out of sight below the ground. Each hypha is digesting the forest floor along its entire length. There may be hundreds of thousands of hyphae extending for many yards in every direction from each individual mold and mushroom, and there are countless individual funguses in every yard of soil. A walk in the woods is a stroll across a vast digestive system.

Yet strangely enough, there is almost no nutrition in a fungus. A heaping handful of edible mushrooms has one-fifth the carbohydrate, less than half the protein, and only a quarter the calories of a whole head of lettuce. Mushrooms are 90 percent water.

ated by lengthening their stride (longer legs will do it every time) and by launching themselves like pole vaulters on narrowed feet.

This left creodonts in a situation of diminishing returns. A dinner of condylarth flesh was a slender meal, and the energy to catch it by simply running after it increased as the prey accelerated. One tribe of creodonts gave up being copycats, and began to be cats.

Within a few million years, creodonts with sharp claws and long teeth crept, hid, waited for their prey to stray close enough, and then pounced from ambush. To become more effective at snack attack, creodonts were forced into more slinky catlike and weasellike shapes. To avoid creodonts, condylarths were forced into more rangy catch-me-if-you can horse shapes, just-you-dare rhinoceros shapes, and grovel-in-the-underbrush pig shapes. Their push-me/pull-you evolution was by no means over, but by 55 million years ago, you could at least have told the eaten from the eaters.

INHERITING PARADISE

The world that all the little brown furry things inherited from the dinosaurs was a paradise. The climate was so mild that redwoods, unable now to live much farther north than

Creodont   *Condylarth*

WASTE NOT, WANT NOT

Our North American trees enjoy a measure of privacy. They may house a crust of lichen on their bark, some Spanish moss on their limbs, or a vine, but on the whole they keep themselves to themselves. Trees have no privacy in the rain forest. They are draped in other plants. Many of these are epiphytes—plants such as orchids, bromeliads, and staghorn ferns that get their fair share of light by rooting on trees instead of in the ground.

Epiphytes get light, but they also get problems. Rain falls, but it falls to earth. Minerals are down there, too, way out of reach for tree dwellers. Any organic food, such as leaf litter, must be caught on the fly.

So epiphytes are quite a crew. Some hang out aerial roots that are like the compressed sponges you sometimes see in hardware stores. Give them a little water, and they swell right up. Tank bromeliads are shaped in such a way that rain falling anywhere on their leaves flows to the center of the plant, where it is hoarded in a reservoir. A whole world of microorganisms, insect larvae, and the tadpoles that eat them may live there. As they digest each other and the litter that falls into the tank, their waste products nourish their host. Other epiphytes grow hollow parts for ants to nest in. Ant garbage is their food.

Most epiphytes eat and drink so efficiently that they get along on little more than rain, dust, and whatever debris falls into their laps.

Epiphytes can be more than a nuisance. The combined weight of wet epiphytes is enough to topple their tree. Trees have evolved various strategies to avoid getting overburdened. One is to have smooth bark, another is to have oval leaves that end in a

drooping tip; both help the tree to shed water fast. A dry tree can't easily be inhabited by algae, lichens, and moss, and the tiny dustlike seeds of epiphytes can't easily get a start in life without those nutritious surfaces to cling to. Palm trees continually drop their oldest, bottommost leaves, along with any epiphytes they carry. Some trees shed great strips of bark, thereby peeling their burden off.

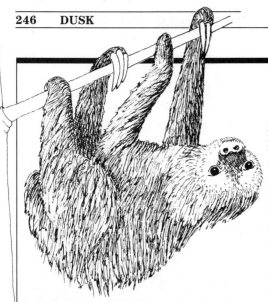

FAITHFULLY, THE SLOTH

The sloth is such a slow animal, and moves about so little, that algae grow in its fur, hiding it in green. For months it may browse lazily on only a dozen or so trees, of which several are special favorites. A sloth may eat as much as 10 percent of its favorite tree's leaves each year.

That may explain a curious thing about sloths. When other tree-dwelling animals defecate, they just let it fly from 30 meters (100 feet) up. Some nutritious manure is captured by epiphytes as it falls; the rest scatters over the forest floor. Sloths don't do that. Each time they have to go, they laboriously climb all the way from the safe treetop to the dangerous ground, dig a hole with their short, thick tail, and bury their feces at the base of their tree. Perhaps they are feeding it.

California's pleasant coast, grew in Alaska, Greenland, Sweden, and Siberia. There was no ice in the Arctic. Palm trees grew as far north as 50 degrees latitude, roughly the boundary between the United States and Canada. Below that subtropical zone—that was similar to Florida's landscape today—was a broad band of tropical rain forest.

Since then, the band has narrowed, and has been broken up here and there by patches of drier jungle, and then, as heavy year-round rains returned, coalesced again. Rain forest has thus moved with the rain, spreading and retracting like an ameba, pinching off pieces of itself and reconnecting them once more. Yet, with all these changes in shape and place, the environment within the rain forest

has been unchanged these 60 million years. On that 6 percent of Earth's land, there are today more kinds of plants and animals than have existed anywhere on land at any time in the history of the world. Two-thirds of all terrestrial plant and animal species inhabit the rain forest. Almost the entire remaining third may have originated there.

The temperature of the forest floor varies by only a few degrees from night to day, from season to season, and from year to year. As much as 200 inches of rain falls every year; the ground is always moist. Except where a tree has fallen, creating a clearing, mere pinpoints of sunlight penetrate its depths. Only the treetops 200 feet overhead bask in the sun.

The rain forest floor is nearly as

sterile as white scrubbed sand. Anything nourishing in it is washed away by rain. Even after millions of years, only a couple of inches of soil can accumulate over clay that supports no life at all. Life in the rain forest depends on a steady rain of debris from above, just as bottom dwelling marine plants and animals rely on a rain of corpses. So in a way, the rain forest is like the shallow sea where the world's other explosion of life forms took place 500 million years ago.

Every scrap of food in the rain forest is recycled into life before it can be washed away, and this ability to get what one can while the getting's good is the fundamental way of life in the rain forest. Over its entire expanse, there is more to eat than anywhere on Earth. But in any one spot, there is never enough of any one sort of food to go around. In northern woodlands, beeches grow in groves and hemlocks fill whole forests. In rain forests, a seedling can't grow near its mother tree because the mother plant is already draining the nutrients from her area. Trees therefore depend on birds and mammals to transport their seeds to a distance, often miles away. If trees of the same species can find enough nutrients only by living far from one another, then birds and mammals, too, must spread out to harvest their fruits, and insects to sip their nectar.

THE STRANGER THE BETTER

When individuals of a species are spread over huge expanses of forest, they lose track of one another. In a whole lifetime, they meet only a few potential mates who inhabit their neck of the woods, and the genes they carry become isolated from the mainstream of their species. Those that live on the fringe become less and less like their ancestors. And it pays to be different in the jungle.

If all plants were to flower or fruit at the same time, there would probably not be enough pollinators or seed dispersers to go around. It's better to be different: a plant that blooms and ripens seeds a little earlier or a little later than others in the neighborhood has a better chance of attracting insects to fertilize it or birds or mammals to carry off its fruit. And if, like the skunk cabbage, it can become so different that it has a monopoly on one kind of pollinator or seed disperser, it no longer has to compete for these with other plants. And for the insect, bird, or mammal it is better to

TRAITOROUSLY, THE FIG

One member of the fig family, *Ficus benjamina*, has become a popular houseplant. It can get along with no sun, and it grows into a handsome tree. As the young tree becomes too large for its pot, it may sprout roots from its trunk. It is showing its true colors: It is a strangler fig.

Of all the aggressive jungle plants that have evolved to make their way in a hard world, the strangler figs are the most ferocious. The seed of a strangler fig, dispersed in bird droppings, sprouts high in the litter-filled crotch of a tree, where there is nourishment, water, and light. It begins to send aerial roots downward. Eventually, the roots hit soil and dig in.

With this new source of minerals, the strangler fig grows, and grows, and grows. Its roots completely cover the tree on which it began its life. They grow strong, like a tree trunk. The branches are long and spread out. Finally, the nurse tree dies. It has been strangled within the fig it harbored as a baby.

MONSTERA

Vines get to the light by climbing on other plants. Once they have reached the heights, they spread out and bask in the sun. They have various ways of clinging while they climb. Pea and grape vines cling with tendrils that curl around whatever they touch. Climbing beans and honeysuckles twine their whole stems around whatever support they can find. Poison ivy clings with rootlike hairs, and Boston ivy with tiny bulbous growths that swell to wedge themselves in crevices.

The ways vines move can be positively creepy. Most plants grow toward light. *Monstera deliciosa,* a tropical vine sometimes called split-leaf philodendron, actively seeks dark places; the darkest place is likely to be beneath the largest tree. The largest tree, towering above the others, provides an avenue to the sunlight at the top of the forest. To reach the top, *Monstera* switches strategies and grows up toward the light.

You may know *Monstera* as a handsome houseplant with huge, glossy

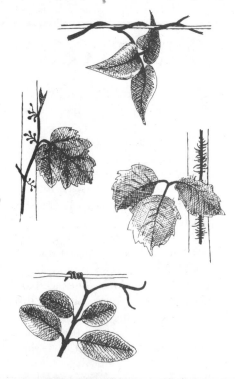

leaves that are deeply indented and grow in a generous clump. The plant can prove disappointing. Once settled into an apartment, it seems to degenerate into an ordinary vine with one long, spindly stem that sprouts an occasional small, heartshaped leaf.

Monstera is a clever plant. Not only can it switch from being a dark seeker to being a light seeker, but it can switch from being a climber to being a basker. In low light, such as in an apartment, it behaves as it does in the jungle when it is climbing a tree straight, fast, and without bothering much with leaves. Once out in the light, the plant stops creeping and throws itself into making gigantic, sun-greedy leaves. Unfortunately, the normal sequence of events is reversed when you buy a *Monstera*. It was happy to make those wonderful, gigantic leaves in the bright greenhouse where it was raised. Moved to the relative darkness of your home, it switches gears and behaves like a creepy vine.

have a private plant than a public one. To be on the fringe—to become unique—is perhaps to found a new species.

Therefore, the rain forest is almost the opposite of our northern woodlands. Where we have thickets and groves, flocks and herds, the jungle has loners. In our forests, there are perhaps a dozen species of trees on an acre of woodland, but an acre of rain forest may have as many as 200 tree species. We have pigeon flocks, bison herds, prairie dog towns; in the rain forest, birds of a feather don't flock together, and the largest group of animals is likely to be a mother with her babies. We have multitudes of individuals and a small number of species; the rain forest has a multitude of species, each made up of a scant number of individuals.

From the time the dinosaurs

died, Earth's climate has gradually cooled and the rain forest has shrunk. To the north and south, its richness of mammals has been squeezed out of paradise. The mammals that now live to the north and south of the rain forest—the deer and the antelope, pigs, cats, rats, and people—all began as jungle beasts.

EATING TOUGH

One of the oldest jungle beasts around in our climate today is the sewellel. In fact, it's the oldest living rodent in the world, a remnant of some ancient population that left no other descendants. Its home is as junglelike as a temperate climate has to offer: the rain forest of the Pacific Northwest, where at least 40, and sometimes as much as 80, inches of rain a year greens the

AN EYE FOR COLOR

Visitors to the tropics are bowled over by brilliant scarlet, red, and orange flowers, colors rare in northern blossoms. These bright flowers are almost all designed to attract hummingbirds, which are their pollinators. Bees are colorblind to red, so a red rose is black to them. Hummingbirds, themselves often splotched with red, like our own ruby-throated hummingbird, see and love the color. They are so attracted to it that a person sitting quietly in a jungle clearing dressed in a bright red shirt will soon attract a buzz of hummingbird admirers. But the birds will not stay. They are looking for nectar, the reward their red flowers hold out to them in return for pollination.

The ruby-throated hummingbird, only 9 centimeters (3½ inches) long, is the smallest bird in the world. It weaves its nest out of plant down and spiderweb silk. Its eggs are no bigger than peas.

Yet hummingbirds are not particularly shy, and they are easy to attract to a garden. Garden stores sell red plastic vials that you can fill with sugar water and tie to plants in the garden. You can also use a small medicine bottle brightened with a red ribbon and wired to a plant with a garbage-bag tie. Better yet, plant hummingbirds' favorite trumpet-shaped, nectar-filled flowers: orange trumpet vine, red lilies, scarlet bergamot, and pink petunias.

Late in the afternoon, as the summer day cools and darkens, hummingbirds will come to sip the nectar with their superlong beaks. To perform this stunt, hummingbirds hover motionless in the air like helicopters. They are the only bird that can fly backward.

ground with moss and bracken, and softens the soil to muck. Breezes blow balmy air from over the ocean. Winter in that forest is not very cold at all. There, and only there, the sewellel still swims its flooded burrows.

Like all rodents, the sewellel isn't much to look at until you look in-side its mouth. There you'll see what makes a rodent a step above a shrew: an extraordinary set of teeth. The menu enjoyed by primitive jungle mammals was varied—ripe fruit, succulent leaves, squishy insects, tender corpses—but it was all soft. Not one of the shrews, bats, primates, creodonts, or condylarths

WHY AVOCADOS ARE NOT EXTINCT

Fruiting plants produce fruit so that someone will eat it and, failing to digest the seed, will plant it in a pile of manure. The larger the seed, the larger the animal that must be invited to eat. Avocado pits are big enough to choke an ape: Who could eat one? Apparently, the original avocado eater was a giant sloth, two stories high on its hind legs, that became extinct about 10,000 years ago. That should have meant extinction for the avocado, too. But just then, Stone-Age humans wandered into avocado country. Of course, they knew enough not to choke themselves on huge pits, but they also knew enough to gather good food when they found it. From then on, avocado pits were spread about by hand instead of by bowels, and were planted in garbage heaps instead of in manure piles. They not only escaped extinction; they evolved further. Sloths endured tough, skimpy, bitter avocados. Humans were fussier. They chose to carry home only the largest, fleshiest, oiliest, sweetest fruits, whose descendants are in supermarkets today.

of the old jungle had the dental equipment to crack nuts, grind seeds, or chew tough vegetation. That left a lot of food on the plate. It was inevitable that some animal should get its teeth into the problem.

The sewellel may be very much like the first mammals that did so. Its front teeth are upper and lower pairs of incisors that are chisel shaped and chisel sharp. "Incise" means "cut," and the two pairs of incisors all rodents have come together in a scissors action that can cut through wood. The blades never wear out or need resharpening. They grow throughout the animal's lifetime, continually rehoning their edges against one another.

Behind the incisors is a gap of bare gum: There are no canine teeth, and there are no premolars. The animal easily slides rough food along this smooth curve of gum to the rear of the mouth where it is ground up by molars.

Using this workshop of a mouth, sewellel ancestors dug in and chewed on through the ages. A scarcity of tender greens? They ate them brown and hard; they ate pine needles and bark. Season after season, age after age, sewellels and the more advanced rodents that came after them chewed out for themselves a bigger chunk of the world than any other mammals. Half of all mammal species are rodents; there are more rats than people. They have gnawed their way along through jungles, forests, woodland, brushland, and out of the woods altogether into the grasslands that at last swept the mammals across the new-laid plains of North America.

Porcupine skull split through the jaw to show how long the incisor teeth are. The bottom ones grow from behind the molars.

Sewellel

40 MILLION YEARS AGO

The Spread of Grass · Rodent Hordes · The Rise of the Rodent Eaters

Where sewellels now nibble needles high in the Cascade Mountains, the coast was flat 40 million years ago. There were no Cascades, or any of the coastal ranges. Mountains raised in the West more than a hundred million years before had been worn down and washed away. Their rock was the dirt of the Great Plains. Wide rivers wandered through broad deltas to the ocean.

Subtropical forests, mossy and fern-filled, spread eastward like a continent-size green carpet. Moist winds and mild showers swept in from the warm Pacific. With nothing higher than a hill to stop them, they misted clear across North America—the weather report for Oregon would have been about the same as the weather report for Nebraska, Illinois, and Connecticut. It hardly ever snowed.

But underneath the soft, damp forests of the West, the crust was moving again. The Pacific plate pushed under the continent, bringing with it part of California, Oregon, and Washington. Volcanoes erupted all along the plate's edge from Alaska, clear through Central America. The Rockies were nudged upward, the Andes grew. The Great Plains were gently lifted to new heights. Over the next 20 million years, and all over the world, other collisions raised other mountains, lifted other continents. Winters grew colder and summers drier. Trees died. Grass grew. The prairies were born.

Far from retreating with the palmy woods, rodents with their chisel teeth stayed put as grass invaded. They ate the grass. Everybody else ate them.

The Universal Food

Grass is a newcomer in the world. There wasn't any for the first moles to line their nests with, or for noctuid moths to drop into as they evaded the first bats, or for condylarths to graze. Common as grass is now, in drylands and wetlands, tropics and tundra, sprouting in pavement cracks and stretching in waves to the horizon, the world didn't have a blade of it until about 50 million years ago. Now grass is everywhere and, one way or another, feeds almost everyone on land.

Rice, corn, wheat, rye, barley, and oats are grass. Sugar cane is grass. Grass can make a cow, and the cow's milk. Cookies made of flour, butter, and sugar are nothing but grass. A hamburger is grass. Cats that eat mice that eat grass are grass. Birds that eat bugs that eat grass are grass. Dogs that eat rabbits that eat grass are grass. That's a lot of grass.

Actually, it's even more than you think. Of all the energy in a meadow of grass, some is wasted as heat in the grass's own life processes, and some is not available because it is in undigestible portions of the plant. A steer grazing a meadow can get only 10 percent of the energy contained in the grass it eats. The same loss of energy happens when you eat the steer's hamburgers. You get only 10 percent of the total energy the steer had harvested from the meadow, or the equivalent of 1 percent of the energy in the grass it ate. Every time food is passed along from one life form to another, only a tenth of its energy is captured.

If you live on hamburgers, there has to be 10 times more steer than you to support you, and 10 times more grass than steer to support it. Thinking of that in pounds, it would take 100 pounds of grass to make 1 pound of human; 5 tons of grass to make a 100-pound human. And that's only one hamburger eater.

Please Walk on the Grass

You'd think that all the grass would have been eaten off the earth long ago. The reason it has not is that it grows in a peculiar way. Other plants grow from their tips. Snip off the tip of a daisy stem, and the stem stops growing. Cut the lawn today, however, and the clipped

HAYWIRE HAYFEVER

Every spring, when the grass begins to bloom, millions of people begin to rub their itchy eyes and wipe their drippy noses. They are suffering from hayfever, a misnamed allergic reaction not to hay, but to one or more sorts of pollen, including those from trees and ragweed as well as from grasses. Sometimes, people claim to have "rose fever," or claim that goldenrod makes them sneeze. Not so. Both of those flowers are insect pollinated, and their pollen grains are too large to float into eyes or noses. Only wind-blown pollen grains are small enough to blame.

But, really, you can't blame them. Allergy symptoms are caused by the body's own immune system. Watery eyes, runny noses, coughs, and sneezes are the body's attempts to rid itself of the "bad" guys, such as disease-causing viruses. There is nothing virulent about pollen. Hayfever is a case of mistaken identity.

ends of the grass stand higher off the ground tomorrow, higher still by the following day, and high enough by the weekend to need cutting again. Grass blades grow from the crown of the plant just below the soil. Growth can be astonishing. One species of bamboo, the tallest grass, can grow 41 centimeters (16 inches) in a week.

Grass grows sideways, too. Many grasses send shoots outward underground to colonize new territory. The more the plant is attacked from above, the more it shoots out to all sides. Cutting multiplies it. Turf grasses such as those used for lawns and many others that are considered weeds, can grow a whole new plant from a mere fragment of underground shoot.

The trampling of thunderous herds is good for grassland. Trampling hurts bushes more than grass, and the more bushes that are injured, the easier it is for grass to take over—not to mention how grateful grass is to receive manure.

Fire can't permanently injure grass. Flames spread so quickly through former years' dried blades that the fire soon passes, leaving the crowns ready to sprout again, and the whole plant invigorated from a thorough fertilizing with its own ashes. In fact, fires started by lightning are as necessary to a prairie as a lawn mower is to a lawn. Without burning at least once a decade, prairie gradually turns back to forest.

What about the wind, then, which stunts the growth of trees? No problem; let it blow. Grasses are pollinated by wind. Dry seasons?

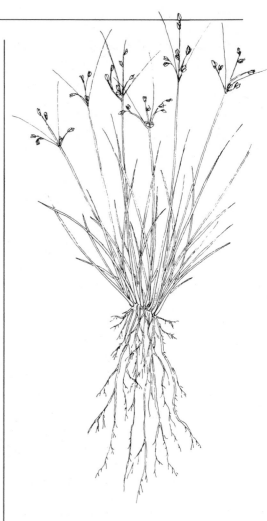

READY OR NOT, HERE I COME!

Given a good road, a grass plant can travel yards in a single summer. A good road might be a flowerbed; the vehicle is the grass plant's runner; an underground stem called a rhizome; or an overground one, called a stolon, such as the stems that reach out from spider plants. New plants grow at intervals along the runner, and each of those plants in turn sends new runners to invade new territory.

Look for a grass plant that has invaded a garden. With a garden fork, loosen the soil under it until you can carefully lift it without breaking its roots. The white, pointed shoots sticking out below the crown are rhizomes. Feel the point; some rhizomes are so stiff and sharp you could almost prick your finger on them. You can see that the runners have no trouble boring through even hard soil.

Now use the fork to loosen the earth along one of the runners that continues away from the plant. If the plant has been growing for some time, some runners may have grown three or four feet long, and may have sprouted new plants all along their length. The grass that covers many square feet of a garden may be connected to one plant.

Seeing you so interested in this investigation, your parents may ask you to get rid of the grass in their garden while you're at it. Be careful. Every fragment of every rhizome you leave in the ground, even ones no more than an inch long, can grow a new grass plant and travel on.

Harsh winters? Spring floods? Grasses have all the answers.

Marsh grasses grow in clumps that raise the blades above the water; rice blades grow longer as the water rises. Grass gone dormant during drought sprouts green within a day of the first rain. Greening grass signals spring when the snow still lies in melting patches.

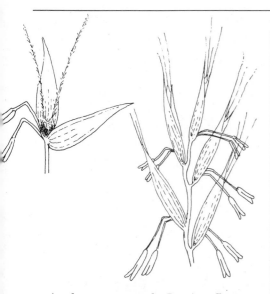

And grass spreads. Its tiny flowers produce pollen in huge quantities and lift it to the wind to be carried across wide-open spaces to even the most isolated plant at the very frontier of a grassy invasion. Seeds travel everywhere: spiked ones are caught in an antelope's fur and galloped away, tasty ones are squirreled away by a chipmunk and then forgotten, ones still clinging to the seed head are flown away to a bird's nest, there to fall to the ground and sprout anew. There are about 10,000 species of grass, and no amount of eating has been able to keep them back.

It took tens of millions of years for the prairie to become the smoothly rippling carpet you can see now. At first bushes grew among the grasses, stands of trees interrupted it. But once grass began to spread through thinning woodlands 40 million years ago, there was no stopping it, or the animals that ate it.

THE GUTS OF THE GRASSEATER

Perhaps the first animals to come out to play in open grasslands were the squirrels—rodents every one. The squirrel family, *Sciuridae,* is large and confusing. Squirrels are squirrels, and so are chipmunks, prairie dogs, and beavers. The family is mostly down to earth—and often in it. Only a few members scurry squirrel-like in the trees. A woodchuck, for instance, is a typical squirrel, and a grass eater to its very gut.

Without specialized guts, a woodchuck would starve to death on all the grass its rodent teeth could chew. Each nutritious grass cell is jacketed with stiff cellulose, a substance so indestructible that no animal enzyme can break it apart. Only bacteria can ferment the jacket off a grass cell. All grass eaters, from mice to elephants, provide permanent housing for cellulose-digesting bacteria and give those bacteria a long time to do their job.

A glance inside a meat-eating weasel and a grass-eating woodchuck would show one method grazers evolved to hold onto their

WUCHAKS

The name woodchuck comes from the American Indian word wuchak, which was used for a number of nondescript brown animals. It has nothing to do with chucking wood. The wuchak's other names in the East are groundhog and momax. In the West, a wuchak is a marmot.

food long enough for bacteria to work it over. They give it a long road—a long intestine—to travel. Any squirrel has more guts than a weasel.

Woodchucks and other rodents provide their bacteria with a special office off the intestine in which to conduct their digestive business. Just before entering the large bowel, food is waylaid into a pouch called the caecum (our appendix is the remnant of a caecum from our vegetarian past). There it is brewed to digestibility for several hours before continuing its journey.

BURROWING DOWN

Even though grazers have special guts, they still have to spend many hours eating in order to get enough nutrients. But grazing is a dangerous business. There the animal is, busy stuffing its belly, with nothing better to hide behind than a bunch of buttercups. Woodchuck evolution has therefore been shaped as much by the possibility of being eaten as by the opportunity to eat.

A woodchuck eats grass, clover, alfalfa, and dandelions growing in the area near its burrow, from which it seldom strays more than 50 yards. The burrow is quite something. It may go 5 feet underground and extend for 30 feet. It comes complete with a nest room lined with grass and a separate toilet room. The front entrance is usually obvious. It's often alongside a fence, boulder, or stone wall, and is marked by a large mound of earth and stones that have been exca-vated from it. Usually there's a se-cret back entrance that isn't at all obvious, and which is used by curi-ous woodchucks for spying on curi-ous people.

In New York State, woodchucks excavate 1.6 million tons of soil each year to make a "home" bur-row, a hibernating burrow, a burrow for each baby as it grows up, and a new burrow whenever the location of the old one no longer pleases them. Sometimes they move be-cause the noise of traffic worries them, or because they have heard the bang of guns.

Winter finds woodchucks holed up and out cold. Out cold isn't an exaggeration. When hibernating, a woodchuck lowers its body temper-ature from nearly 37°C (98°F) to just a few degrees above freezing. Its heart beats only four times a minute; it takes a breath only once in six minutes. It stores no food at all, living from fall to spring on its fat alone.

MOMS AND SUPERMOMS

Woodchuck babies are curious and unafraid. They have to be taught to be cautious. Mothers differ in per-sonality, and therefore in the way they teach their youngsters to be-have. A chummy mother may make a game of caution. She encourages her children to follow her a few feet from the burrow entrance, then suddenly dashes back into it with her young tumbling in behind her. In a few seconds, she pops out onto the mound sniffing, looking, and listening for pretend enemies as her babies peek out to watch her performance. She repeats the game time after time, until her children know it so well that they beat her to cover. When they emerge, they, too, stop to sniff the air, and scan the horizon.

A cooler sort of mother teaches the same lesson in a less playful way. She leaves her babies grazing a few feet from the burrow, then without warning charges toward them and chases them into the den. She doesn't follow them in, but goes

THE LONGEST MEAL

The time it takes to get food into your belly is nothing compared to the time it takes to get food into your body. You may bolt down a pizza in a minute, but it takes hours for your digestive enzymes to break the pizza down into molecules small enough to pass from your hol-low gut into the real interior of your body. The time can be roughly mea-sured by counting the number of hours that pass between swallowing a meal and defecating the undigestible leftovers. To clock digestion time, in-clude a generous helping of beets in your meal. Their red pigment is not digested. The number of hours that elapse between eating beets and ex-creting beet-colored leftovers is a pretty good measure of how long it takes to process a meal. You can clock your dog's digestion by adding beet juice to its meal.

A dog's meal moves out in 12 hours. We, who eat both meat and vegetables, hold onto our food up to twice that long. A meal of hay takes two and a half days to get from one end of an elephant to the other.

DOUBLE DIGESTERS

Cows, deer, antelope, and sheep digest their food twice. So do rabbits. A cow swallows unchewed grass into a fermentation chamber called a rumen. There it is churned and squeezed to a pulp, and worked over by bacteria. The pulp is regurgitated a mouthful at a time for fine grinding by the cow's molars and for moistening with nitrogen-rich saliva that bacteria need to make their own body proteins. Each mouthful is called a cud. A cow that has finished chewing a cud reswallows it into the rumen for more processing, and begins chewing the next cud. After a second and final chewing, cuds bypass the rumen and arrive at the stomach proper. There the meal is digested again by the cow's own enzymes. But what is the meal by that time? It is no longer grass. Cows digest the bacteria they have nourished on grass and spit, and not the grass itself.

Rabbits double digest in a different way. They give each meal two complete trips through the digestive system. The first time through the gut, greens are digested as much as they can be by the bacteria's and the rabbit's enzymes in the time available before the meal reaches the end of the intestine. The undigested portion is molded into soft pellets, which are excreted in the rabbit's burrow. The rabbit then eats these pellets, and round they go through the digestive system a second time. This time the rabbit treats the excreted pellets as the real thing. They are deposited outdoors as worthless dung.

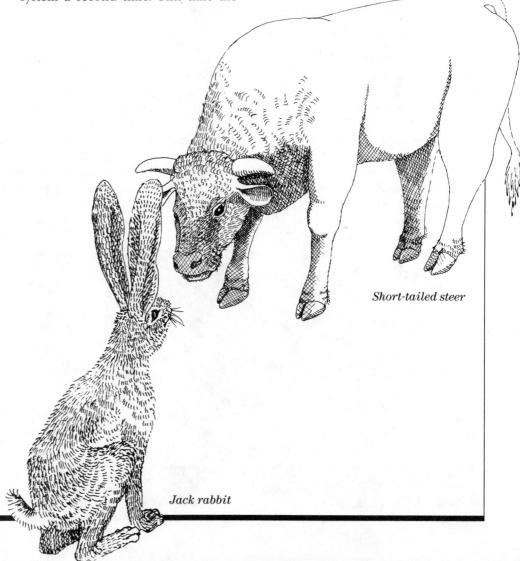

Short-tailed steer

Jack rabbit

ANYBODY HOME?

Even if you find a woodchuck burrow, it doesn't mean there's a woodchuck living there. Rabbits, possums, skunks, and raccoons enjoy the convenience of these spacious quarters. Almost all foxes live in woodchuck burrows. So there's no way of knowing what's down there—or whether you would want to meet it.

The best way to meet woodchucks is to watch for them during their grazing times, bright and early in the morning (when they also drink their only drink of the day—dew) and again in the late afternoon. Favorite spots are the grassy parklands along old-fashioned highways, and in pastureland.

Once you've found a woodchuck, look for a "blind," a clump of bushes or the crotch of a tree from which you can see it without it seeing you. The blind should be downwind of the woodchuck. Field glasses will let you see the animal closely even if your blind is at some distance. When the woodchuck finishes eating, it will return to its burrow, which you may be able to locate by following the direction it takes. If you can set yourself up close enough to the burrow, you may get to see the woodchuck sunning itself on the entrance mound, and, if it is a mother, you may get to see her charming family life.

back to her own grazing at a distance. The babies come out, and again she runs them to ground. These woodchuck youngsters, too, learn to dive for cover when danger threatens and to check things out before leaving the safety of the entrance mound, but their relationship with their mother is not as close.

These different mothering styles continue as Mom moves each baby into its own den and visits it until it is settled in. A warm mother moves her children close by, and may even keep one at home. She visits often, wagging her tail and rubbing noses with them in affectionate greeting. A cool mother moves her babies farther away, visits less often, and isn't as affectionate.

Before the summer is over, the children move once again, this time to burrows of their own choosing where they will spend the winter. Warmly mothered children may choose to remain close to home. Coolly mothered children may move quite far from where they were born.

Which is the best kind of woodchuck mothering?

IT TAKES ALL KINDS

Whether the best strategy for a woodchuck is to encourage children to live close by or far away depends on the lay of the land.

Woodchucks living in North America a few hundred years ago, before farming changed the landscape, were forest dwellers. The forest floor has fewer grazing areas than open pasture or meadow, but it offers many more places to hide from predators such as foxes. A woodchuck living in a woodland was better off as a loner defending its eating ground from others.

Out in the open it pays to be more social. Woodchucks give a shrill whistle of alarm when they see a hawk, fox, or hunter, and those that live nearby all dive for their holes when they hear it. If neighbors are also kin, the death of an individual doesn't mean the death of all its genes, for many of the same genes are carried in close relatives saved by the whistle.

The situation of each individual would further improve if each could recognize its kin. That way, in times of danger family members could be offered the safety of the nearest burrow. There are as yet no such communities of woodchucks, but out on the treeless prairie,

GIANT SQUIRRELS

The biggest squirrel, and one of the biggest rodents, is the beaver. Beavers run to 65 pounds—as big as a Labrador retriever—and a few grow to over 100 pounds. Some millions of years ago there were beavers here as big as bears.

As a beaver submerges to swim to the underwater entrance to its burrow, it becomes as watertight as a submarine. Valves close its ears and nose. Membranes slide over its eyes. A skin flap seals its mouth, leaving only the incisor teeth exposed.

Using those incisors, a beaver can cut down a willow tree 13 centimeters (5 inches) thick in three minutes, and can fell a tree as much as 84 centimeters (33 inches) in diameter. Beavers' only food is bark stripped from branches. Stripped branches are cut into convenient carrying lengths for building and repairing the dam.

Carrying a 1½-meter (6-foot) branch clutched in its teeth or held against its chest by its front paws, a beaver can swim at 9½ kilometers (six miles) per hour, about twice the speed of jogging. It can stay under water 15 minutes before surfacing for a fresh breath of air. Babies can swim from birth.

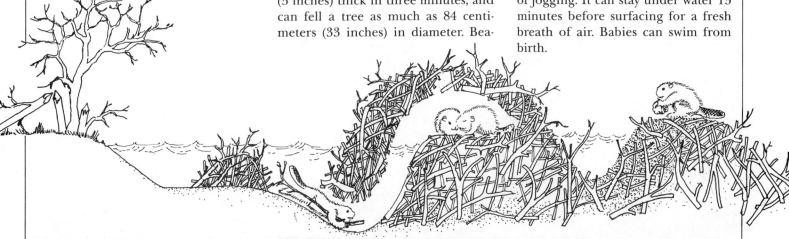

where there is not even the shadow of a boulder to hide them from hawks, eagles, coyotes, snakes, and badgers, a similar squirrel lives in just such a way. Prairie dogs have perfected talents that woodchucks have not been forced to develop.

SQUIRREL TOWN

Prairie dogs live in small groups, called coteries, of several females, their young, and a single male. Like woodchucks, the mother and her young wag tails to greet each other, and exchange open-mouthed kisses, rub noses and cheeks, nibble, and lick each others' fur. But unlike woodchucks, daughters seldom leave the coterie in which they were born, and they seldom outgrow babyish ways. Mothers continue to visit their children after they have moved to burrows of their own, and the habit of visiting never stops. In fact, all the adults visit with one another continually, greeting enthusiastically, lolling in the sun together, and even perching side by side on their mounds with arms about each others' shoulders.

The result is a kinship group made up of grandmothers, mothers, daughters, and sisters as well as youngsters of both sexes and their daddy—all of whom behave literally as "kissing cousins." Every baby born to every female in a coterie will be the male's own flesh and blood; half their genes will be his genes. Since all the females are related to one another, all youngsters will be brothers, sisters, first cousins, nephews, nieces, aunts, or uncles. A mother's own youngsters will share half their genes in common with her. By never growing out of showing fondness for one another, this large family remains emotionally glued all through their lives.

Unlike woodchucks, prairie dog families permanently share burrows with one another. A woodchuck watcher once observed an eccentric woodchuck family in which the children were fanatical diggers. They dug a dozen holes tunneling to the home burrow instead of the usual two. Before they could get any further, the mother escorted them to homes of their own. But what if she hadn't? The woodchuck children might have gone on to add

KISSING COUSINS

The boundaries of a coterie, a prairie dog's own neighborhood, are traditional; they are handed down to each new generation by kisses. It works this way: Within a certain area, any adult that a young prairie dog approaches will greet it with tail wags and kisses; beyond that area, any adult it approaches will chase it away. Where you're kissed is your coterie.

Numbers of coteries form neighborhoods called wards. Wards have natural boundaries, such as a ridge, stream, or patch of shrubbery, just as neighborhoods in our towns are often separated by parks, avenues, or shopping areas. The prairie dog town may have quite a few wards. Some towns are as big as our towns. They may cover a hundred acres and house several thousand individuals.

nest rooms and toilet rooms to their creations, all interconnected with the original burrow. This is what prairie dogs do, and their communal burrows may be the result of a dig-crazy family whose eccentricity paid off.

Each has a burrow of its own, but it connects to other burrows. When danger threatens, any member of the coterie is allowed to dive into any nearby escape hatch, and may emerge at some other hole altogether. Often, prairie dogs help each other to dig burrows. Cooperation may be their way to learn the whole underground layout of rooms and tunnels.

RUNNING AWAY FROM HOME

By living socially, prairie dogs have populated the plains in spite of having few protections and many predators. Nevertheless, somebody must leave home. With prairie dogs, it is the males who do so. They get an urge to run away from home just as they reach adolescence.

At first thought, there doesn't seem to be any reason why a group of prairie dogs can't continue to live as one big happy family. Between predators, illness, and old age, the population might remain at a steady number, and their communally protected genes might go on and on and on. The trouble is

ALBINISM

Albinism is an example of a harmful trait that tends to happen more often when close relatives breed than when nonrelatives breed. A few individuals of every sort of mammal lack a workable gene for the pigment melanin that colors their skin, fur, and eyes. Since mammals have pairs of chromosomes, there are two genes for each trait. If the other chromosome carries a working gene for the production of melanin, the animal will have normal coloring. Its "hidden" defect, however, is likely to be carried by its close relatives as well.

If two who carry the defective gene mate, some of their babies could inherit the defect from both parents, and would not inherit the normal gene. They would be albinos like the rat shown here, white furred and, with nothing to color their eyes but blood vessels, red eyes, too.

Unpigmented eyes have poor vision and are oversensitive to light. Unpigmented skin is easily burned by sunlight. A white animal in a dark landscape is very conspicuous to predators. Albino prairie dogs, sunshy and prone to predation would quickly perish. There's much less risk of doubling such harmful genes if mating is done beyond the family.

that mating between close relatives tends to give offspring a double dose of any harmful trait that, handed down by only one of the two parents, would be harmless.

Animals don't, of course, know about genetic risk. But any sort of behavior that, in the course of their evolution, has tended to keep brothers and sisters and parents and children from breeding with one another, has also improved their chance of avoiding the doubling of harmful traits, and has therefore increased their reproductive success.

Where there is space to begin a new coterie of his own, a young male prairie dog may do that. Once he has some burrows underway in a nice area and appears able to defend his territory bravely, a few females from adjoining neighborhoods move in. If no new land is available, the young male has two other choices. He can take over a coterie in which the defending male has died, or he can challenge a male to a fight, and win the territory along with its resident females. In this way, there is a rapid turnover of males, who bring "new blood" to the family, and prevent inbreeding.

There is another advantage to outbreeding, or mating with an unrelated individual: It maintains the variability of the whole population so that, while most members of the

group are sociable in a way that helps each individual to rear babies successfully, there will also be the occasional oddball whose eccentric behavior may work out better for itself and its descendants in changing times.

Changing times are all times. Both the woodchuck and the prairie dog were once forest animals that lived as loners. If woodland creeps back over grassland, it's nice to think that some weirdo might know what to do about it.

WEIRDO WOODCHUCKS

You might be startled to come upon a woodchuck sunning itself in an apple tree. But some woodchucks do. They even climb for the apples, sit on a limb, and hold the ripe fruit between their front paws to eat it. One woodchuck, chased by a dog, climbed 65 feet into an oak tree.

Picture it eating acorns, and you have a klutzy version of its relative, the elegant tree squirrel, which most think is the only squirrel worthy of the name.

Actually, tree squirrels are rare compared with ground squirrels. To be the real McCoy, the fluff-tailed acrobat, the favorite of park goers and peanut givers, requires a change not only in behavior, but in anatomy.

When cats or people climb trees, they keep their heads up whether they are going up or coming down. Tree squirrels climb up trees head first, but they head downward with their head downward. They can do this strange stunt because of a joint shaped to let the hind foot turn both backward and forward. Coming down head first, a tree squirrel's toenails grip the bark like hooks from which the animal hangs as it descends. Tree squirrels' front feet are also flexible. They turn sideways, allowing the claws to grip around furrows in bark or, on a small tree, to grasp the trunk like a pole. Using this technique, squirrels can scamper down trees as easily as they scamper up them.

Occasionally you'll see a squirrel leap from branch to branch—and fall. Gliding squirrels (some call them flying squirrels) are much better at this sort of thing. They leap the greatest distance with the fewest bruises by spreading flaps of skin sailwise between their stretched out limbs. Buoyed up on air, a gliding squirrel can leap as far as 73 meters (80 yards) from the top of one tree down to the trunk of another. They soar only slightly less amazing distances from treetop to treetop.

While in the air, a gliding squirrel can bank and turn, hold a steady horizontal course, or descend in a dive. To land, it pulls its rear feet forward, curving its sails into a parachute to land on all four feet as lightly as a feather. The instant its feet touch down, the squirrel scurries around to the far side of its landing limb in case an owl has followed it. Oddball behaviors have gotten squirrels from burows to treetops, but there's no getting away from predators if you're a rodent.

MOUSE MEAT

If grass is the basic diet of rodents, rodents are the basic diet of snakes, owls, hawks, eagles, foxes, coyotes, badgers, weasels, ferrets, raccoons,

SPREADING OUT AND HUNKERING DOWN

Gliding squirrels are seldom seen because they are nocturnal. They often build nests in "woodpecker trees," tall, rotted stumps hollow at the top and covered with the holes woodpeckers peck in search of insect larvae. Sometimes, if you tap on the stump, a gliding squirrel will peek out to see what's going on. Captured young, they make wonderful pets. Maybe that's because they are good at making the best of bad surprises. A naturalist, investigating a woodland after a forest fire had destroyed most of the trees, found gliding squirrels had moved into burrows underground.

martens, wild cats, and pussy cats. This list is just of the North American predators. Worldwide, the basic diet of 99 percent of all the carni-

PLAIN AND FANCY

No matter where you live, there's almost bound to be a ground squirrel that lives there, too. But it's hard to tell you exactly what it will be like. Those in the desert dress in dry-earth colors, those in damper areas wear darker pelts. A particularly dark brown ground squirrel of the Midwest seems to be colored to match the soil itself: It spends 90 percent of its time in burrows. Chipmunks, which live in sun-splotched woodland, match the pattern with spots and stripes.

On the other hand, it's not hard to say what a ground squirrel will be doing when you see it. It will be collecting food. A single ground squirrel was found to be carrying in its cheek pouches 162 oat seeds, 140 wheat seeds, and almost a thousand seeds of wild buckwheat. On chipmunk stored a whole bushel of chestnuts, hickory nuts, and corn kernels in only three days. Another stored up 67,970 items for the winter, including 15 kinds of seeds and one bumblebee.

A pair of pet store mice fill an aquarium with offspring in a couple of months.

vores is rodents. The reason is that rodents are the most plentiful meat around.

No mammal can multiply like a mouse. Unlike squirrels, which often can't breed until they are two years old, and then reproduce at the sedate rate of one litter of four babies a year, a female house mouse may mate at the tender age of 35 days, turn out her first litter as little as 18 days later, mate again the same day, shoo the first batch out of the nest in three weeks, and give birth immediately to the next batch. A single litter can have as many as 16 pups. The mother can produce half a dozen litters in each

NATURE'S NONCOMPETITION CLAUSE

When the fact of evolution was first discovered, people assumed that the winners had hung in there at the expense of the losers, who became extinct. Evolution came to be thought of as a struggle for existence, in which the game of life was won through competition. Now, after a lot of looking, it doesn't look that way anymore.

Think of two house mice—one wild, one pet—both living in your home. They are of the same species. They eat the same diet. They have both thrown in their lot with humans. But they don't make their living in the same way.

The wild mouse makes its living by stealth under cover of night. It does best by avoiding meetings with you. The pet mouse does best by meeting you night or day, tamely and openly. The two mice live in the same place, but they don't share the same niche.

Separate niches are what makes it possible for there to be so many different kinds of creatures in the world. If creatures all competed with one another for the same way of earning a living, one kind would be better at it—would win—and there would be few species in the world. In fact, creatures do just the opposite. They evolve, as house mice raised in laboratories and homes are evolving, by taking advantage of unique niches.

Pet mice and wild mice don't confront one another; each gets more by getting it its own way.

SAFE TRAPS

You can find out which small mammals live in your area by setting live-animal traps. Hardware stores sell a brand called Have-a-Heart. Remember though, that even live traps like these can turn into death traps; the mammals you catch may be so small that even a day without water or sufficient food is long enough to kill them. Put your traps out in the evening. The following morning, check the traps and free any animals you have caught.

Look for protected places to set the traps, such as in heavy meadow grass or nearly buried under leaf litter in a woodland area. Bait them with dry dog food.

A second way to trap small animals safely is to make pitfalls for them. Use a plastic 2-liter soda bottle. Cut off the top with scissors about 5 inches below the cap. Bury the bottle in soil up to the cut edge in a place where there is heavy vegetation, and bait it with dog food. The animal will fall in and not be able to get out. Don't set pitfalls when rain is expected; small mammals can drown in an inch of water.

Coffee can

2-liter plastic soda bottle

of the six years of her life.

Whether a house mouse multiplies at her maximum rate depends on how well she is fed. She can, however, live on soap, glue, and wallpaper paste if roots, seeds, stems, leaves, insects, and garbage are scarce. Times of plenty can bring plagues of house mice. Twice in this century, house mice swarmed the Central Valley of California. Someone counted them. There were about 82,000 mice per acre.

That house mouse plagues are rare is due to the long tradition of mouse eating. Most creodont descendants dropped out of the race with condylarths, and lined up for the rat race instead. Today, if you want to see a typical carnivore, look for a weasel.

THE BASIC WEASEL

The weasel body plan goes back to the days before grasslands, but the first fossils of close relatives of the weasel date from about when rodents began to live on grass, and carnivores to live on rodents. The body plan is best described as burrow shaped: A weasel can weasel through any hole it can stick its head into. A weasel-size hole is no bigger than the circle formed by your thumb and index finger. The hole doesn't have to be round. A weasel's skull is flat. Creeping with elbows high and belly to the ground, it can follow a tunnel less than an inch high.

Weasels also climb trees. They can scurry quickly through the underbrush, as could their creodont ancestors. And they have perfected a flat-footed, bouncing gallop that covers a lot of ground fast.

These talents make weasels the all-around carnivore, and one of the few carnivores that live up to the name flesh eater. Weasels eat nothing but meat, whether it is to be found tree high, burrow deep, or at ground level. A weasel is one of the few predators that can bring down prey larger than itself. A six-ounce weasel can slaughter a four-pound hare.

Weasels kill to eat, and they kill for fun. A weasel in a chicken coop may kill dozens of birds, although one hen is a meal. If that seems unnatural, it probably is, but only in the sense that weasels didn't evolve with caged animals as prey.

Pleasure is biological. An animal feels happy when an actual place in the brain is "turned on," and exudes good feelings in the form of certain molecules called endorphins. "Fun" is whatever sense of pleasure it takes to keep an animal doing what it has to do to keep alive. Prairie dogs get a bang out of digging, weasels get a kick out of killing. If weasels had evolved in circumstances where overkilling wiped out their prey entirely, only those whose pleasure in killing was quickly dampened by boredom would have survived. But prey on the loose was scarce enough that mass killing wasn't possible. A killing binge was no more than a night's meal.

THE BETTER TO EAT YOU WITH

Carnivore teeth point to a fierce beginning. All carnivores, including the weasel, have long, sharp canine teeth that can inflict a killing bite into the base of the skull, sever a leg tendon, or rip open a belly. Front premolars work like scissors to shear flesh from corpses. Rear teeth lock onto meat to tear it off in chunks. The jaw works only up and down, not side to side in the grinding motion of plant chewers. Food is bolted down a carnivore's stretchy throat in chunks that would choke a chewer. The lack of slack in the jaw joint makes a carnivore's bite very powerful. But for all their fearsome teeth, fierce ancestors don't necessarily mean bloodthirsty descendants.

The fact is that most flesh eaters are about as carniverous as a human in a delicatessen, or Yogi Bear in Jellystone Park. Even when eating flesh, carnivores usually go first for the stomach and intestines, including whatever predigested food is in them. That alone is a varied diet, and the carnivore is spared the work of grass digestion. The red fox, in spite of its bloodthirsty reputation, eats corn, berries, grapes, cherries, apples, acorns, crickets, beetles, grasshoppers, and even grass, as well as crayfish, mice, rabbits, and birds. Bears add to that list honey, mushrooms, fish, frogs, and apparently any sort of food we eat. Raccoons are no fussier, but are particularly fond of eggs. Fierce flesh eaters are rare, and big ones are rarer: There's not enough meat to go around.

By the time the grasslands had begun to appear, carnivores came in basic bear, fox, and badger shapes. Forty species of a carnivore called a bear dog once lived in North America, some as long as 35 million years ago. One kind included individuals weighing as much as 100 pounds. Fossils of a mother and her baby were found in one of many ancient dens that lie along what was then the floodplain of a broad river in Nebraska. They died, probably in a flood, about 20 million years ago.

Those ancient dens used by the bear dogs had already had a long history. Before the bear dogs took them over, foxy carnivores had raised their young there, and so had a thick set badgerish carnivore.

FUNNY AS A FERRET

Ferrets are weasel look-alikes that make wonderful pets. Until recently, they were kept as vicious ratters, caged, and handled only with heavy leather gloves. Now they are bred to be pets—comical fellows with plenty of spice but no bite. They are small enough to nap in socks, playful enough to chase stuffed mice and chew soft balls, social enough to ride around in pockets, polite enough to take to school, and long-lived enough to make them worth the inflated price charged for them in pet shops. Most ferrets live at least a decade.

Here is some good advice for would-be ferret owners. If you want a small ferret, choose a female. Males are nearly twice as big. Both sexes must be altered, males for the sake of their temperament, females for the sake of their health. (Unaltered females go into heat and remain in heat unless they are bred.) At the same time, the scent glands at the base of the tail are usually removed to cut down on their musky smell. They get the same shots cats get, and eat dry and canned cat food.

Some people cage ferrets, others don't. A perfect cage can be made of ½-inch mesh hardware cloth stapled to a simple wood frame 6 inches high and slightly larger than the largest size of disposable aluminum roasting pan. The pan, filled with cat litter, is the ferret's bathroom, entered through a hole in the wire mesh floor.

Ferrets will not soil their own sleeping quarters; they prefer to mess in corners, and in litter. You can keep a ferret uncaged in a small room with few corners to choose from, and put a litter pan in the corner (or corners) it prefers. Keep the pan clean, or the ferret will move its bathroom elsewhere. Those who travel with their ferret carry a small aluminum baking pan and a plastic bag of litter.

Although a cage or cage/room is convenient, ferrets are pets, not wild animals. Let your ferret out. Here are some things ferrets do: come when they're called, follow you around the house, explore inside dishwashers, lick ice-cream cones, play tug of war, steal small objects and lose them under beds, roll over for a treat of liverwurst, ride on your shoulder, pounce on cats, tease dogs, take splashy baths in a pan of water, make everybody laugh.

These early carnivores wouldn't have looked much more peculiar to you than the wolverine, a large and ferocious weasel relative found in northern forests, or the coatimundi, a small and peaceful raccoon relative found in Central America. But the primitive mammal had to undergo many changes beneath the surface before it could become a modern one.

ONLY FLESH DEEP

There are no longer living any truly primitive carnivores with which to compare modern ones. But you can compare the possum—a primitive

A quartet of curious raccoons.

STAMP FEET

Between corpses of animals killed by cars and corpses dragged in by cats, you may be able to get a close look at most of the mammals that live in your part of the country. You might start an unusual collection: footprints on paper. (First, see A Warning About Handling Dead Animals, page 270). You will need nothing but large index cards and an inked stamp pad, both available in stationery stores. Wipe the pads of the foot clean. Press the foot hard and evenly onto the stamp pad. Place the index card flat on the ground, then press the inked paw onto it. The most complete collection would include all four feet, labeled "right rear," "left front," and so on. You'll find a collection of footprints helpful in learning to identify mammal tracks.

A WARNING ABOUT HANDLING DEAD ANIMALS

There are not many diseases that are shared among different species. You can't catch parvo virus from your dog, for example, and your dog can't catch a cold from you. But the few diseases you can catch from wild animals can be serious. Therefore, take the following precautions when handling dead animals needed for the skeleton cleaning project (page 243), making paw prints (page 269), skinning (page 346), tanning (page 348), and any of the other investigations that you do on your own that use dead animals.

1. Do not approach an animal that is behaving peculiarly or that in any other way appears to be sick. Do not handle an animal you know to have died from a disease. Choose instead an animal found freshly killed on the road or one that has just been killed by a cat. They are the safest because you know what caused their death.

2. It's safest to wear latex gloves, sold in hardware stores and garden centers when handling a dead animal. Discard them afterwards.

3. Do not handle a dead animal if you have an open sore or cut. Germs can enter the body through and open wound.

4. Do not handle animal feces. They are the greatest source of germs and parasites.

5. After handling a dead animal, and before touching your fingers to your mouth or nose, or eating food, wash your hands with soap and hot water.

6. Some diseases are carried by fleas or ticks. If you see fleas on an animal, discard it. You are more likely to pick up ticks by walking around the countryside than by handling a dead animal, but still, if you see a tick, pluck it off with tweezers and kill it by dropping it into alcohol. Fleas and ticks spread disease only by biting.

7. Call the Health Department in your area to check whether there are other precautions you should take. They will know of any epidemics among the wild animal population that could be a danger to you.

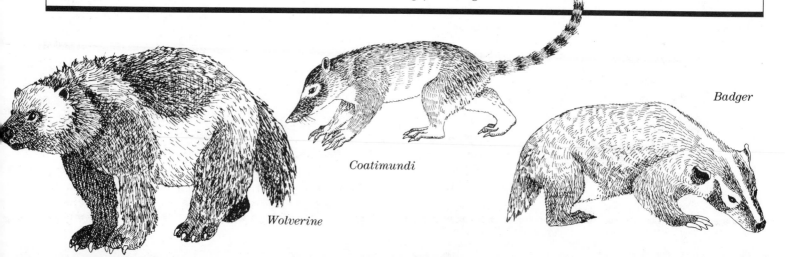

Badger

Coatimundi

Wolverine

marsupial—and the raccoon—a modern carnivore. On the surface they are not very different from one another, nor do they lead very different lives. Like the original mammals, both are nocturnal, smallish, five toed, and furry. Either one can make a nest in a hollow log, climb a tree, or open a garbage pail. They eat anything. Both handle their food as though they had hands. Their shape is nothing special: just a hump on four legs with a short, pointy snout poking out from a flattish skull. Peel the skin off the skull and the differences still aren't much. But peel off the muscles and you'll be surprised to see the differences beneath the flesh.

Almost all of a possum's head is muscle and bone. Almost all of a raccoon's head is brain. You could hold the possum's brain in an iced-tea spoon; you would need a quarter-cup measure to comfort-

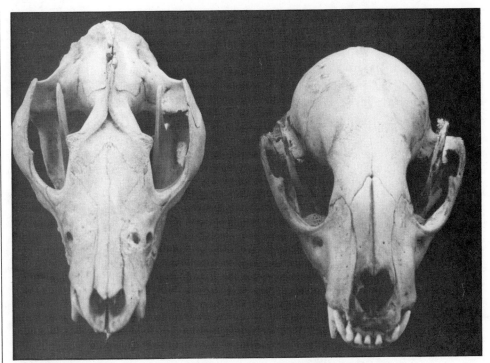

The brain case of a possum (left) is tiny compared with the brain case of a raccoon (right).

Fox

ably hold the raccoon's brain. Bigger brains also mark the difference between early carnivores and later ones; bear dogs were less bright than bears or dogs.

No Trivial Pursuit

Even after the prairie had been around for 20 million years, it didn't look like it looks now. It was still bushy. Under cover of the shrubbery, there were new mammals that were to lose their own hiding places by eating them up. They were only bush high, and were nothing much to look at. Little camels had no hump. Little elephants had no trunk. New carnivores, cat-like and doglike but not much bigger than a weasel, stalked them. What would become saber-toothed tigers and giant bison with horns ten feet across were then pussy cats and cows by comparison.

Over the next 20 million years, shrubbery was chewed away. Predator and prey became less and less able to play hide and seek. Grasslands became more like a chessboard; the players—predators and prey—played the game of where to go and how to get there, and the smartest were the winners.

Lonesome little hoofed animals teamed together into high-speed, horned herds too large, strong, and smart for dull predators. Carnivores evolved the brains to hunt in packs, to make plans, work together, and teach the rules of the game to their young. Even little primates, the second most primitive of the placental mammals, raised their forepaws from the ground and stepped out onto this new playing board.

High IQ became the name of the game, and it was all because of the weather.

20 MILLION YEARS AGO

New Mountains · Great Migrations · Horses, Cats, and Canines

Herds and packs of smart new mammals evolved in a bustle of activity. It was as though time itself speeded up, and even the rocks were in a hurry for change.

Old Gondwanaland came completely apart. Australia had already shaken loose from Antarctica; now Antarctica broke away from South America. There were new collisions. India, at sea for ages, docked against Asia and raised the Himalaya Mountains. Italy, a splinter of Africa, set sail for Europe. That docking of Africa's plate is marked by the Alps, the world's newest and still rising range. The whole West Coast was added on to North America.

Elsewhere, new volcanic island arcs arose out of the sea, or were added to the edges of continents, or were torn off them. Japan was torn off China. Hawaii arose from the Pacific. The Cascade Mountains were erupted onto North America.

Inland, the Rocky Mountains started a new spurt of growth. The Sierra Nevadas rose from the plains. Rivers that, when the West was flat, had flowed straight out to the Pacific, cut their modern, tortuous courses around mountains to the sea. Even land that stayed flat was lifted high. Rivers cutting through the swollen Colorado plateau carved the Grand Canyon.

All these changes redirected winds and ocean currents. The whole world, already drying and cooling, got colder and drier still. Antarctica once had forests filled with animals. When surrounded by icy ocean currents 20 million years ago, it froze. Clouds caught by the new mountaintops in other parts of the world dumped all their rain on the windward side. Land on the far side of the ranges turned to desert. Grasslands spread, becoming the prairies of North America, the savannas of Africa, the steppes of Asia, and the pampas of South America.

As fast as the weather changed, mammals changed with it. Land and life were becoming the world as you see it now.

MAKING HAWAII

The first photographs of Earth taken from out in space showed a planet more beautiful then we had imagined, but gave no surprises. There was the familiar schoolroom globe, with its familiar continents that children the world over are taught to draw.

Rain shadow

Seafloor spreading

Those shapes, however, are less than 20 million years old. The original small rafts of granite around which they grew are 4,000 million years old. Continents took on their modern shapes only in the last one-half of one percent of their history. They are now many times larger than the old cratons at their cores. New pieces of land, built without the benefit of a craton at all, have arisen in the ocean. Where did all that extra land come from?

Earth's crust circulates. New material seeps to the surface through rifts. Old material slips back down again through trenches. Think of a plate of ocean floor as a conveyor belt, with a rift at one end, and a trench at the other. At the rift edge, ripples of lava ooze up from the mantle, nudging older crust along toward the trench as the lava hardens to rock. New upwellings in turn push those ripples along, so that the older each ripple is, the farther it has moved away from the rift, and toward the trench.

The newest ripples are underwater mountain ranges lifted high by the heat below them. As they age and move along the conveyor belt, they cool and subside. By the time a strip of ocean floor has reached the opposite end of the conveyor belt, it is flat, and slips easily into the trench.

Conveyor-belt pieces of ocean crust simply recycle themselves. The oldest ocean crust is no more than 200 million years old, the length of time it has taken for it to ride its conveyor belt from rift to trench.

But now imagine a conveyor belt that moves over a particularly hot spot in the mantle below. Once in a while, the hot spot melts a hole in the crust passing over and new material bursts out, building a volcano. When a volcano grows tall enough,

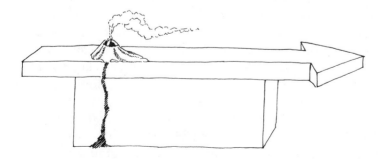

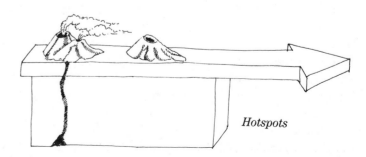

Hotspots

it sticks out of the sea as a volcanic island.

The ocean plate keeps right on moving across the hot spot. The volcano rides along with it, but the hot spot stays put. Eventually the mantle breaks through again, and there is a second volcano. In this way whole chains of volcanoes are made. That's how the Hawaiian islands were put on the map.

Hawaii's hot spot is still active. To the southeast of Hawaii itself a new volcano is growing on the ocean floor. It is Loihi, now about 3,046 meters (10,000 feet) high, but still about 913 meters (3,000 feet) below the water. It will one day add a new island to that state.

BUILDING HEIGHTS

Volcanic arcs can also be built smack up against a continent. Picture the trench end of an ocean conveyor belt at the edge of a continent. Instead of slipping down easily, it has to jam in under a great thickness of crust. Tremendous friction generates heat which expands and melts a portion of the mantle. The hot stuff bulges up, breaks through overlying crust, and builds a new volcanic edge. The Cascades were built that way.

The heat generated this way spreads way inland beneath a continent expanding rock as though it were a cake rising in an oven. That's

how the Colorado Plateau got so puffed up. As rivers cut through to the ocean, they carved the Grand Canyon through layers of sediment all the way to the craton, which had been deeply buried.

At the Columbia Plateau in the northwest, land has been lifted and cracked all over its surface. The plateau is built up from layer after layer of lava that rose through cracks and spilled over the land for thousands of square miles.

Heating also lifts old mountains into new spurts of growth. The old Rockies were warped upwards, humped, and folded into brand new mountains. In some places they are topsy-turvy. Folds rose up and toppled over.

The Himalaya Mountains were formed when a "conveyor belt" carrying India tried to dump itself down a trench next to Asia. So much of India's plate plowed under Asia that the crust there is 70 kilometers (43½ miles) thick, the thickest crust in the world. The narrow strip of mountains along much of the West Coast from Southern California all the way into Alaska is not so high or thick, but it is a strange rock. Here and there, the ocean plate seems to have carried chunks of alien land to our shore, exotic islands from somewhere in the Pacific—no one knows just where. But mountains are more than

chunks colliding. Besides the scrunched-up edges that have nowhere to go but up, material from the mantle bulges up where bodies of land collide, and hardens into new rock. Ocean crust that the continents or islands rode is added, too. There is ocean floor at the top of the Alps and on Mount Everest in the Himalayas.

SPREADING SHORES

Even as they grow upward, high places spread outward. Mountain ranges and volcanic arcs erode in rain and wind nearly as quickly as they are raised. Stones, pebbles, and sand wash down their sides and accumulate all around them. What you think of as a whole mountain is only part of it. The bottom of the mountain is deeply buried in material that used to be on the top.

Although the Alps are still being pushed up as two plates continue to collide, they are eroding as quickly as they rise. The whole coastal plain along most of the eastern seaboard is composed of material from the eroded Appalachians. The continental shelf that extends miles out to sea is made of rubble from those mountains, and from every mountain that came before them.

Just as a rift can form in mid-ocean, a rift can form beneath a continent. New material seeps up through the rift, wedging the conti-

THE SOURCE

In many places wells can be drilled a few hundred feet into solid rock, and water will spurt out. The water comes from way below the level of local ponds and streams. It has sunk that deep through porous rock.

Water sinking through porous rock heats up the deeper it goes. As it heats up, it dissolves minerals in the rock.

Finally, deep within the Earth, the mineral-rich water may hit a fissure, a crack in the rock above it. The superheated water expands upward through the crack. As it rises, it cools. The dissolved minerals in it begin to crystallize, forming a crust in the crack and then filling it. When that rock is later heaved up during mountain building and exposed by erosion, the mineral seam is exposed—as a streak of quartz, a vein of silver or gold.

These round trips usually occur where a continent is rifting and is filled with cracks. Between Salt Lake City, at the foot of the Rocky Mountains, and Reno, at the foot of the Sierra Nevada, our continent has pulled apart 50 miles in the last eight million years. There, in basin and range country, water completing its round trip bubbles to the surface in hot springs and spurts out from geysers. But the streaks of silver and gold that took tens of millions of years to make were mined out in the space of a single century.

Water is also responsible for diamonds, but they come from much deeper, are formed explosively in seconds, and are made of nothing precious, only carbon.

About 120 miles under the craton, right now, somewhere, water and carbon dioxide are leaking from the mantle, forming a bubble. The bubble of hot gas and water is expanding, forcing its way, very slowly, upward into the overlying plate of crust. As it moves, it pushes before it a column of boiling magma, molten rock. Some day, the column will pick up speed, go faster and faster, shoot up through the continent, and burst through the surface at supersonic speed, like a bullet. Pressure relieved, temperature subsiding, the molten material will quickly harden. One out of a hundred columns will crystallize into a pipe bejewelled with garnets, jades, and olivines, and set with chunks of diamonds.

Diamonds are carbon atoms pushed into a densely packed, tightly glued arrangement in the enormous heat and pressure of their birthplace. To stay packed tight, they must be "flash frozen." If the column of magma takes its time reaching the surface, cooling gradually instead of all at once, the carbon atoms will slip away from one another and take on the more relaxed, looser arrangement of graphite. Instead of diamonds they are pencil lead. Or they can evaporate into carbon dioxide. The substance that might have become the hardest substance on Earth disappears into thin air.

nent apart. The basin and range landscape of the Sierra Nevadas lies along a rift. At the rift, the eastern margin of the continental crust tipped upward, forming the Sierra Nevadas in California. The western margin was depressed into a basin that now holds the rubble from the mountains.

Such rifts may form a crack in a continent that reaches all the way to its shore. When that happens, the ocean fills the rift valley. The Red Sea was formed when the Arabian Peninsula split from Africa, opening a rift valley that was flooded by the sea. Still unflooded is the rest of that rift valley, which extends from the southern shore of the Red Sea all the way to the tip of the African continent. A rift is causing the Gulf of California to break away from the continent the same way Gondwanaland came apart, or New Zealand split off from Australia, or Japan tore itself away from Asia. Baja California is halfway to becoming an offshore island. The Gulf of California will open up and become a sea between it and the mainland. So brand new shores are added, too.

Seas change shape as the land around them moves here and there.

When Pangea began to come apart, ocean water filled the widening gap between the northern and the southern continents, forming a broad ribbon of water called the Tethyan Seaway that nearly encircled the globe. There was only one ocean then, on the side of the world opposite the continents; the Tethyan Seaway opened into it at both ends. Then, the Atlantic ocean formed, and the map was changed more radically. The Tethys is hardly recognizable now. The eastern portion was carried halfway around the globe as a narrowed but still sizable body of water that flowed between

SPILLING MOUNTAINS

The cracks that develop as crust is stretched thin are called faults. The first picture here shows a hunk of land faulted in two places. In the second picture, crust between the two faults has slipped downward, forming a basin, or valley. The basin is beginning to fill with sediments from the eroding highlands. The third picture shows how mountains are made when blocks of crust topple. As one edge of the block tips downward, the opposite edge tilts up. Sometimes, such slips happen suddenly. A 20-mile section of Tobin Range in Nevada jumped 16 feet in moments one day in 1915.

Mountains in basin and range country erode about an inch a century, so it will be the 212th century before Tobin Range will be cut back down to size after this latest growth spurt. The coastal range is going faster. Every mud slide you hear about after spring rainstorms in California is a mountain coming apart and washing out to sea.

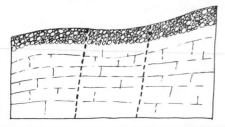 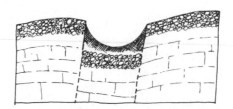 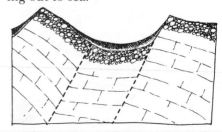

Africa and the combined continents of Europe and Asia as they traveled eastward in tandem. By 20 million years ago, Africa had touched base with Eurasia. Now that part of the sea dead-ends where the three continents meet. The great Tethys has become the scrunched up Mediterranean, and its adjoining seas, the Black, Aral, and Caspian, and, an ocean away, part of the sea floor below the Caribbean.

By such grand glidings, collidings, and uprisings, the world came to look like it does today. If it hadn't, you might not be here to appreciate it.

MOVING DAYS

There is a great movement in evolution that is almost like a tide. It begins in the belt of tropics that encircles the world, and it flows northward and southward, carrying the rain forest's many species toward the poles. In northern and southern temperate zones, where challenges are greater, many species become extinct. Those that survive evolve, not just into new species—more kinds of mice—but into brand new groups as different from one another as a mouse is different from a rabbit. A reverse tide disperses the latest models around the globe to multiply and speciate anew.

Animals in the past migrated from continent to continent over the poles when they were still forest lands.

The tepid Tethys, tropical and lush with life, thronged with species that spread over both shores and in the water throughout its length.

The Atlantic became a tremendous barrier to the movement of species from the Eastern to Western hemispheres. What remains of the Tethys is now on a much more Northern latitude and therefore colder and much less lush.

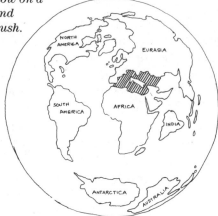

For ages the raw material of primitive mammals, crowded from the shrinking tropics, had wandered southward and northward toward the poles. From these vantage points, which are now much changed, mammals migrated over the face of the earth.

Maps of today usually show the continents of the world in two hemispheres, east and west, separated by the Atlantic and Pacific oceans. The centers in which some of the most important mammals evolved are out of the picture, and the routes they followed as they became modern species aren't obvious.

To get a better picture of mammals on the move, look down on the top of a globe at what is now the icy Arctic, and peer up at it from underneath, at what is now frozen Antarctica. Both were once temperate woodlands where hoofed animals in the north, and marsupials in the south, began to change into more modern forms. The polar land masses were connected to the continents of the northern or southern hemispheres by land bridges and island chains. Picture the radiating lines of longitude as two-way paths leading from warm middle latitudes where species were generated, toward the poles, where they evolved most radically, and back again over the globe, where they became the mammals you can see today.

Marsupials that had evolved in Antarctica migrated north into South America and Australia before those continents drifted too far apart for travel. After the separation, Australian marsupials had nowhere else to go.

North American and South American mammals hadn't met up with one another since Gondwanaland sailed away. Now an arc of volcanoes raised Central America. By 12 million years ago traffic was opened beween the two continents for the first time in over 60 million years.

That route was nearly a one-way street. First by island hopping from volcano to volcano, and then by walking along the completed isthmus of Panama, the rodent ancestors of rats, the cat ancestors of jaguars, the camel ancestors of llamas, and the primate ancestors of monkeys moved south into South America. Only sloths, armadillos, possums, and finally porcupines moved in the other direction, north to North America (armadillos are still traveling, a little farther northward each year).

Mammals stepped onto African soil only about 40 million years ago, as it bumped into Europe and Asia where the Tethys Sea now dead-ends among the three continents. Early elephants wandered in from Asia and rhinoceroses came from Europe, and both also went south into India and north over the pole into North America. Horses went the other way, from North America south into Siberia, down through the Middle East and on into Africa. Camels made the same trip. An ape that may be our ancestor meandered through Greece, Turkey, Pakistan, and India, as well as into Africa.

The history of each group of mammals in whatever spot it moved to depended on local circumstances. Antarctic mammals became fossils in rock buried under ice. Their Australian descendants got along fine until very recently, when humans brought in rodents, cats, dogs, and sheep. Practically none of the mammals that had evolved in South America survived the invasion by northerners. Most present South American mammals

The Isthmus of Panama was formed by volcanoes. At first molten lava pushed up shallow domes below the sea (1). As those domes ruptured, lava spilled out, building volcanoes (2). Repeated eruptions built the volcanoes higher until they rose above the water (3). Finally, so much material erupted that the whole area became land (4).

are descended from the invaders.

On the other hand, none of the northerners stayed the way they had been before they became world travelers. Cameloids became llamas in South American mountains; they became camels in Asian deserts. Horses thrived in Siberia, became extinct in America, and became zebras in Africa. Some primates that crossed the isthmus into South America became monkeys, but none of them became the same kinds of monkeys that evolved on the other side of the world, none became apes, and only one ape in Africa became human. If continents looked different then, our zoos would look different now.

LOSING TOES

Grasslands evolved from brushlands as grazers evolved from browsers. Someone had to nibble back the bushes and trample the saplings before the grass could overtake the landscape. The ancestors of today's hoofed animals that now are asses, horses, zebras, sheep, goats, bison, buffaloes, yaks, oxen, elands, kudus, bongos, oryxes, and addaxes all helped to eat the brushlands down to grass. The horse, descendant of condylarths, was among the first to do the prairie that favor.

The evolution of horses is known from numerous fossils that first appear 20 million years before the horse made its debut on the grasslands. These earliest horses were jungle animals. They probably lived the same way small, hoofed mammals live in forests now, alone or two by two, shy, nervous, alert to the merest crackle of a twig, and set at any moment to dash from sight. The first of them had toes that padded quietly along soggy jungle floor—four toes on the front feet

BLOWING ITS STACK

Most of Yellowstone Park is a caldera, the rimmed remains of the most catastrophic kind of volcanic explosion. Yellowstone blew up only 600,000 years ago, but it was one of a series of unimaginably violent events that had occurred at intervals for some tens of millions of years. The explosion of Mount St. Helens to the west of Yellowstone, in 1980 released 0.6 cubic kilometer of magma from the Earth, and left a crater 2 kilometers (about 1 mile) wide. Yellowstone's crater measures 70 kilometers (42 miles) at its widest point; it spewed out 1,000 cubic miles of magma.

There have so far been no explosions as great as Yellowstone in recorded human history. What would one be like?

The series of volcanic eruptions that include the Yellowstone eruption occurred over a hot spot below the continental crust. The volcanoes form a chain, just as the Hawaiian Islands do, and for the same reason: The hot spot stays put, the crust moves. A chamber of magma, as hot as 1,000°C (over 1,800°F), forms 4 or 5 kilometers (about 3 miles) below the surface. As it grows and rises upward, it melts the solid rock above it. The crust bulges into a dome.

The eruption begins when the dome breaks along its rim, and

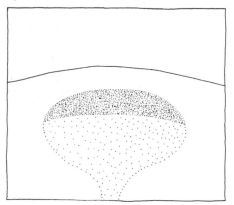

Hot magma accumulating in the crust lift it in a dome.

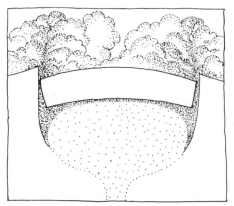

The center of the dome collapses, forming a caldera.

columns of magma escape through the ring-shaped fracture. Within a few hours—sometimes only minutes—the dome roof collapses into the chamber below, leaving the caldera, a sunken piece of land of perhaps 500 square kilometers.

Magma can flow from a volcano as red-hot liquid lava, as it does in Hawaiian eruptions, or it can explode out as red-hot fragments that range from dust size to boulder size, as it does in calderas. The exploded material streams outward over the countryside as a fiery blanket moving as fast as 100 meters (330 feet) a second, covering hills that are as high as a kilometer, and traveling as far as 150 kilometers. Everything in its path is simply burned to a crisp.

By the time the eruption is over, possibly only days later, an area up to 30,000 square kilometers has been covered with volcanic ash, dust, and

rock—more than 100 meters deep at the rim of the caldera, several meters (a few feet) deep even at the farthest reaches; everything beneath the flow is dead. Beyond that central disaster area, wind-borne dust spreads centimeters thick over millions of square kilometers, choking plants and animals alike. The ash from the yellowstone explosion blanketed all of Wyoming, Colorado, Utah, Arizona, New Mexico, Oklahoma, Kansas, Nebraska, and South Dakota; blanketed most of North Dakota, Nevada, and California; and blanketed parts of Montana, Idaho, Louisiana, Arkansas, Missouri, Iowa, and Minnesota.

Will it happen again? Luckily, eruptions this disastrous are very rare. Besides Yellowstone, only two other giant calderas, Long Valley in California and Valles in New Mexico, have erupted on this continent in the last million years.

and, for an extra push when escaping carnivores, three on the rear. The animal was so small and undistinguished you might have guessed it was a horse only by looking carefully at its middle toe. There the nail had thickened into a tiny pointed hoof that gave it better traction when startled into action or forced to turn at top speed.

Gradually the horse became taller, like a medium-size dog instead of a small dog. The front feet lost the fourth toe. The hoof on the middle toe became larger, but all three toes still touched the ground, leaving behind crow-feet footprints. This horse was a browser and had rounded molars good only for chewing tender vegetation.

By 35 million years ago you might have seen a tiny horse poised on dainty toes on the fringes of the forest, still nibbling leaves, but also sniffing the good green grass.

Over the next 10 million years, the horse gingerly stepped out of the woods to eat. No doubt it took only a step or two at first, grabbed a few quick mouthfuls of leaves or grass, and dashed back to cover. But the northern prairie was an endless banquet for mammals that could live there without looking back over their shoulders toward the safety of the forest, and the horse was an evolutionary pioneer.

Compared with rodents, who

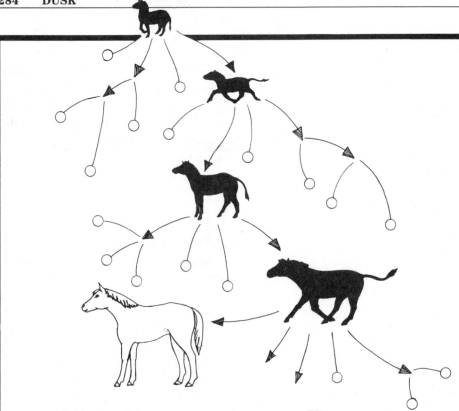

NO STRAIGHT LINES

Horses create a wrong impression: Because there are fossils of their evolution nearly every step of the way, it is easy to think that eohippus turned into *Mesohippus*, who became *Merychippus*, who was transformed into *Pliohippus*, and so on through all the hippuses to the modern horse. That's not how evolution works. If you trace all the species that arise from each ancestral one, you get a branching diagram, not a straight line. Many, not one, species can trace their descent from a common ancestor, and these species may in turn found still other species. Even the most recent common ancestor is the stock from which evolved asses, zebras, and quaggas, as well as old Dobbin. When the descent of horses is represented as a straight line leading from eohippus to *Equus*, the artist has ignored scores of other descendants that became extinct, and has saved himself a lot of lines.

never changed their anatomy or their behavior enough to keep them from coming and going freely between woodlands and grassland, the horse revolutionized its body and rediscovered a way of living that had been lost since the days of the dinosaurs. It evolved a one-toed foot protected by a broad, thick hoof that could take the pummelling of long trips at a trot, and of

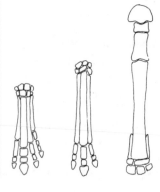

Horse feet evolved from four toes (left) to three toes (middle) to one toe (right). Mesohippus had three toes on its front feet. Two of them remain as the small splint bones visible to either side of the big toe bone of a modern horse.

stampedes from predators at full gallop.

Rounded teeth flattened and grew bigger, the better to eat grass. Grasses built their blades with harsh silica, the better to avoid being eaten. Horses responded with teeth that grew as fast as they were ground down, and that were hardened with enamel. They kept on eating; grass kept on growing.

By 20 million years ago, grasslands were looking more like grasslands, and horses were looking more like horses. With food spread as a solid green salad, horses had grown bigger. Teeth had grown larger still, the jaw had grown longer to make room for them. The eyes, originally set well forward of the ears, had moved back along the skull well behind where the long roots of molars might press against them. The new position let the horse see over grass even when grazing head down.

The two side toes hadn't disappeared, but they were too short to reach the ground. They have not quite disappeared yet. Feel for the narrow splint bones in a modern horse's lower foreleg (which is, in fact, a foot bone). They are the remnants of side toes. Once in a great while a horse is born with side toes dangling, hoofs and all.

JOIN THE CROWD

There are certain defenses against predators that are commonly evolved by prey animals who adapt to open places. These animals defend themselves with horns, they use sharp hoofs for a good swift kick, and they toughen their hide as a shield against others' weapons. Those details vary depending on what spare parts there are to work with, and how the animal must otherwise get along. But all prey animals that live where they are easily seen by predators go the way of flocks of dinosaurs and towns of prairie dogs: they team up.

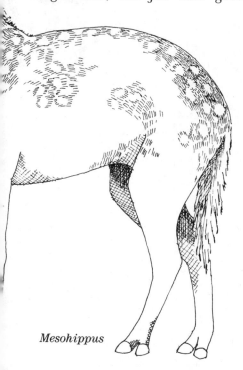

Mesohippus

NO MEN ALLOWED

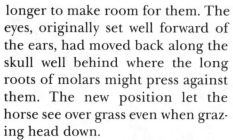

On late-night television, elephants rampage through jungle camps, screaming bloody murder and trampling everything in their path. They sure look bullish, but they must be cows.

Bull elephants aren't allowed in elephant herds, which are the exclusive clubs of mothers, daughters, and sisters.

Of course, cows can't keep bulls out altogether, but they do their best. Boy babies can stay until adolescence, then out they go. One adult male—and only one—can visit while a female is in heat, then he must leave. Reluctant bulls are pushed and chased—they are outnumbered by the cows, which are perhaps 50 strong, weigh 5,000 kilograms (11,000 pounds) each, and are united by ties of family.

Every elephant in the herd is related. And since elephants can live into their fifties and sixties, great-grandma, grandma, ma, and daughter may all be around, along with all the sisters they have ever had. Females never leave the family at all. There's a matriarchy for you.

Horses herded together as they left the shadows for the sunlight, and so has every other prey mammal that has made the same trip and is too large to hide. You can therefore tell where a prey mammal lives by the company it keeps. A moose walks by itself—in the shadowy forest. A bison walks with friends—along the sunny plains.

Relative visibility to predators also explains the difference in how our deer and our antelope play. Deer play a nervous, lonesome game of hide and seek.

White-tailed deer

Pronghorn

White-tailed deer are not adapted to open country. If caught in a cornfield, they make a dash for their home base of light woods or brush, where they are hard to spot. Full grown bucks play hide and seek solo; females are accompanied by their most recent set of twins, and sometimes by a daughter from the previous year. Yearling males have already left the family, and may pal around with a couple of other bachelors for a while. But no group is ever large.

Antelopes play a bold game of catch me if you can. Our only "antelope," the pronghorn, is the last remnant of a family that is unrelated to true antelopes and that dates back 20 million years, and has probably played in the open for about that long. Unlike deer, pronghorns live in desert, scrubland, and prairie in herds that may number a hundred—and sometimes a thousand. The larger the herd, the less likely that an attacker can single out an animal to attack, and the less likely the attacker is to remain unnoticed long enough to try.

SEEING WITH A HUNDRED EYES

In a way, a herd is a giant organism. Its surface is covered with sense organs—a hundred eyes scanning the horizon, a hundred nostrils sniffing the wind, a hundred ears listening for enemies. Picking up the sight, smell, or sound of danger, the warning movement of one unit can trigger the escape of the whole body. Startled herds of pronghorns have been clocked at a speed of 72 kilometers (45 miles) per hour. The

SHOO FLY

To a person unused to horses, they can be unsettling animals. They do sudden, noisy, nerve-racking things, like stamping their feet or snorting or swishing their tails. These gestures make them seem impatient and rude. That is just how they are intended.

Imagine that you are bundled up in winter clothing in a stuffy house waiting to go outside with your family. Everyone else is taking forever to get ready. Finally, in exasperation, you say "come ON!" Did you stamp your foot? That's what a horse is saying when it stamps its foot, and it is just as exasperated.

It may also snort. Snorting is a way of blowing dust from the nose, and a horse clears its nose before it sets out on an excursion as you might clear your throat before you set out on an explanation. But snorting is something like spitting. You might spit to get rid of a bad taste in your mouth, or to express the idea that someone is as disgusting as a mouthful of rotten meat. A horse may snort to get rid of irritating dust, or to express the idea that someone is as annoying as dust up the nose.

Tail swishing, in its literal sense, is just a way of shooing flies from the buttocks. But if it's apparent to you that flies are not the target of the horse's irritation, the animal might mean the gesture metaphorically, and for you. A fair translation would be "Get off my rump you pesky fly!"

highest speed recorded was 86.5 kilometers (54 miles) per hour. Yet it's a safe guess that only some of the hundred units in a pronghorn herd know what their body is running from.

Herd babies are born equipped to stick to and move with their herd practically from birth. A human baby can't walk for about a year; even a puppy can't get far on its four legs for several weeks. A newborn horse stands within seconds, and runs an hour later. A pronghorn can outrun a human when it is only four days old.

Infants and puppies, when they do stand and walk, toddle away from their mother. Foals behave as though they were attached to their mother by a tether exactly 5 meters (16½ feet) long. When she turns, her colt or filly turns; when she runs, it runs. Even at half a year old, foals spend a quarter of their time less than 5 meters from the mother, and are seldom further away than 25 meters (82 feet) even when they are approaching their first birthday.

ODD BODIES

The body of a herd changes with the seasons, breaking apart and then rejoining. During the summer, when female pronghorns must eat well while they are nursing their young, males move off, and eat elsewhere. The organism recombines for the winter. Single units of white-tailed deer clump together when they've lost their cover. During the winter, when they are more easily seen in the snow-white, leafless woods, they may form sizable winter herds.

Males break away from their clumps as breeding season approaches. One may establish a territory of his own, and fight to keep it from others. A new organism forms: the winner and his harem of females. Then it comes apart again. As the time of birth approaches, the females kick out the male. He moves into the bachelor body, which goes its own way to other grazing grounds, while the mother body swells with that year's babies.

There are other patterns. The herd may be composed always of female relatives and their young, with male visitors allowed to mate and then made to leave. Or the organism may always be of both sexes, with the tender young kept to

EXHIBITION GAMES

Stags of white-tailed deer have antlers; does don't. If antlers were for protection against predators, surely both males and females would need them. In fact, antlers aren't weapons at all. The points curve inward, not forward, so they are no good for goring. Antlers fall off by late winter, just when predators are hungriest and deer weakest.

Stags' antlers are used only during mating season, and only for pushing matches with other stags. As two rivals lower their heads in combat, their antlers interlock. They are used as wrestlers use arms, not as murderers wield knives. The loser may leave the field exhausted, but will seldom be injured.

Antlers are also used to avoid even ritual combat. We are not alone in admiring most the largest antlers with the most branches or "points." A doe gauges a stag's fitness, and other stags judge his power, by his headgear. Although stags grow their first set of antlers when they are yearlings, their antlers don't reach maximum size until they are four or five years old. Until then they usually know better than to challenge a male with a showy set of points. That makes sense both for youngsters and for mature stags. Winners risk more the more battles they endure; losers risk defeat time and time again.

Antlers are made of bone and are always shed annually. Horns are more like fingernails, and they are permanent. In many horned species, females as well as males have horns, but they are different: Males' horns are curved inward, backward, or round and round; females' horns often stick straight out. They are just what they look like: weapons to gore with. Females don't hold exhibition games—they get right to the point.

RIDE A RING OF HORSES

Novice riders circling the ring chafe at the bit: They don't want only to ride around in circles. But there is a good reason to fence them in. The horse solution to every problem is to run. Don't like it where you are? Run. Don't like that noise? Run. Don't like this thing on your back? Run. What's more, their reaction time is measured in microseconds, and the darnedest things strike them as ominous. A falling leaf can accelerate a horse to racing speed before you've noticed that it's fall.

Worse yet, running is the fundamental word in the equine language. It's something like shouting "FIRE!" in a crowded theater. It causes a stampede, except that instead of everybody making for the nearest exit, everybody follows the leader. Without a ring to ride in, one haywire horse heading madly for the horizon may take all the other horses with it as though they were glued together. A ring is very clever: It has no end. The horses play follow the leader with no place else to go.

the inside, while the outside bristles with the horns and hoofs of the adults.

HORSE SNOBS

A herd of horses is actually made up of smaller bands of from three to perhaps a dozen horses. A band might be a group of youngsters, all the same age and of both sexes, who became friends as babies. Or, as these friends get older, they might split into all-male and all-female bands. Most common are family groups of several mares and their offspring of various ages, herded by a boss stallion who left his friendship group to establish his own herd.

Stallions guide and guard their band, but they aren't always the head of the family. Mares can have a high social position, too, and a dominant mare, sometimes along with her best friend, may be followed as she chooses when to drink, where to graze, and in what direction to travel.

There is a certain snobbishness in horse social life. Cliques of high-ranking horses exclude others from friendship. Since they associate only with those of their own class, their colts and fillies are introduced early to the sons and daughters of the best families, who in turn may become their lifelong friends.

Even though life in barn and pasture is not the same as living free on the prairies, you can see traces of class distinctions and close friendships in domesticated horses. Only so-and-so can be stabled next to what's-his-name. If so-and-so is saddled up to go to the ring, what's-his-name will whinny complaints until so-and-so is returned to his side. In leaving the barn, there may be a certain order that must be followed if there are not to be sly kicks and nips of protest. On the trail, a dominant horse forced to follow a lower ranking one may take protocol into its own hoofs, charging its way to the front of the line. Or, the lower ranking horse may balk, obstinately stopping in its tracks until a higher ranking horse steps into the lead.

IT'S SMART TO BE DUMB

This obstinacy of horses is equalled by the mulishness of mules and the sheepishness of sheep. They're not what we consider bright. But intelligence is better measured by how well it serves its animal. A horse that wants to stop and think things out for itself before stampeding with the crowd becomes wolf meat, and is a dumb horse. IQ in herd animals is bigger than a brain. Because of its advanced social organization, the whole herd acts more

WHY THE CAMEL HAS ITS HUMP

Maybe you've heard that camels store water in their humps. A more scientific version of that notion is that they store fat in their humps, and by combining the hydrogen atoms in fat molecules with oxygen, they can manufacture H_2O. A few years ago a scientist set out to see for himself. He rented a camel, measured how much water it needed during the hottest desert weather, and then calculated how much oxygen it needed to make that amount of water. Then he figured how many lungsful of air that was, and how much water would evaporate with each breath. His calculator told him an odd thing: The camel would lose more water by evaporation than it would gain by manufacture.

Humph, said the camel.

Then what is the hump for, said the scientist?

Camel hair is good insulation. During the hot desert summer, camels shed most of their woolly insulation in order to better lose heat from their skins. The hump, however, keeps its heavy load of wool. Fat is also good insulation. In most animals, fat is deposited evenly all over under the skin. The camel keeps it all in its hump. Humps, the scientist could easily see, are kept on the back. The camel's fat filled, wool covered hump, he concluded, is an insulated sunshade.

Hmmmm, said the camel.

Then how does the camel get along without water, wondered the scientist.

As a human loses body water by evaporation, blood thickens and becomes too gluey to pump outward to the skin. Without blood flowing near the surface, little heat can escape through the skin. By the time a person has lost an eighth of his body's water, he has cooked to death.

In the hottest weather, the scientist's rented camel was able to survive on dry food and no water for two full weeks. After losing 220 pounds of water, a full quarter of its supply, it had perfectly normal blood. But the animal looked hideously shrunken. After more tests, the scientist had his answer: Water is lost from a dehydrating camel from muscles and other internal tissues that are better able to get along with less.

The camel had nothing to say. It was too busy drinking 27 gallons of water in ten minutes, after which it plumped up immediately as though it were a sponge.

LAMBIKENS

An animal can be born knowing what its species does without knowing who its species is. A lamb or a goat raised by humans knows to follow the herd, but it assumes its herd is human. The mistake is natural—whoever nurtures it must be its mother, and it must be its mother's kind. It tries to follow its mother and its herd into the house, the bedroom, the bed. It bleats inconsolably when locked out and left alone. People have said that there's no such thing as a single sheep because its "self" is its herd. A single sheep is like an arm or leg in search of a body.

On the other hand, there is a simple solution for those who want herd animals for pets. Even two sheep or goats (or one of each!) make a herd, so raise two babies.

intelligently than any of its members do.

Whether a species of herd animal can live on a farm has to do with the particular kind of group intelligence that species has. You won't see caribou in the barn, but you will see sheep in the meadow. Herds that invest brainpower in long-distance travel can't be convinced to stay put. The best that can be done with caribou, for instance, is to follow them around. Animals that shrewdly defend territories don't work out either. Roe deer, the common European species, know better than to share their land with other deer, or to move beyond their own boundaries. Herd animals that are smart to be alarmed are no fun on the farm. Antelope startle and run at the least disturbance. They hate crowding. If they are penned, they batter themselves against the barrier, and injure or kill one another in panic.

Sheep, on the other hand, were farm-smart before there were any farms. Generations grow up and stay together their whole lives on a home range they never leave. Food may be more plentiful in one area or another, according to season. The areas and the routes between them are taught by the elders to each year's crop of lambs. Sheep just naturally crowd. Lambs stick together as a group. Females are all friends and equals. The adult male with the largest horns is the leader. That's the sheep the crowd sheepishly follows.

Substitute pasture for home range, and a shepherd for a ram and elders, and you have a farm animal. Shepherds, like elders, show their flock the boundaries of the home range and how to move about it. Like the big-horned chief ram, they lead them to green pastures.

THE RACE CONTINUES

From about 20 million years ago, horses began to share pastureland with the ancestors of today's families of pronghorn, camels, cattle, sheep, and goats. All joined herds. The prairie thus laid out on its platter as rich a meal for carnivores as it had for herbivores, the difference being that while grass stays put, a herd is a movable feast. In fact, as these hoofed animals grew larger, their legs grew even longer in proportion to their bodies, and their escape speed accelerated. The race between creodont and condylarth was continued by carnivore and herbivore on a faster track than ever.

A baby crawls and a horse walks the same way therapsids did. Lift a front foot, put it down. Lift the rear foot on the opposite side, put it down. Switch to the other front foot, and repeat. You're one step forward. Since three feet are always on the ground, walking is steady, but slow.

When a walk is speeded up, it's a trot. The sequence of foot lifting is the same, but now the second foot is lifted just before the first one touches ground, so the animal is balanced on a right front and a left rear foot, or a left front and a right rear foot, during every step. That's faster.

Third gear is a gallop. Now the front feet work together as a pair, and so do the hind feet. The gait is like a series of leaps or pounces. The front feet lift off either at the same instant, or just after one another, and even before they have hit the ground, the hind feet lift off. At full speed, there are times when a horse has only one hoof touching the ground, and times when it is completely airborne. In a modern horse, the distance between hoofprints of any one foot may be 25 feet, or four times the length of the horse's body.

The speed a horse can gallop depends on the length of its stride, and the length of its stride depends on the length of its legs. The leggy horses that went to pasture 20 million years ago could outrun any carnivore around—in the long run.

In the short run, there's always a carnivore that can keep up. The few cats who slunk from the jungle in their own evolution toward a more open life did it by bending their backs to the job. When a cheetah sprints after its prey, it humps its back, tucks in its rear end, and reaches way forward with its rear legs while they are still in the air. That bend adds several inches of backbone to the length of its stride. In the middle of each leap, the cheetah bends its backbone the other way, so that legs are stretched out nearly horizontal. That adds

Cheetah in mid leap with back and legs fully extended.

Cheetah as it begins the next leap, with back humped and legs tucked.

inches, too. The result is a stride even more than four times the length of the cat itself, and speed enough to catch a horse. But there is a catch.

The cat has to put so much muscle into every leap that it tires quickly, while the horse, with its rigid backbone, uses only the large muscles of its legs. If a cheetah can't get a meal on the hoof in one short sprint, its dinner gallops tirelessly into the sunset. The cat goes hungry.

For this reason, there are few cats in the grass, few who hunt on the run, and few who eat anything larger than a rabbit. Mountain lions seek rocky, wooded, or brushy country, where they sneak up on their prey from ambush, trying to get within 30 feet before pouncing. Twenty of those 30 feet are covered in a single bound. If there are plenty of deer around, it may manage to bring down one a week, but mountain lions are forced to live mainly on coyote meat and porcupines, beavers, raccoons, rabbits, mice, and grasshoppers. The bobcat, our most common wildcat, eats mostly rabbits, enjoys chickens when it can get them, but will resort to squirrels, mice, and even bats.

Cats must roam enormous areas to find enough to eat. A mountain lion may travel 25 miles in one night's hunt. Even in so large an area, it can't afford to share the game with others of its kind. All our wildcats walk by themselves.

FELIX AND SYLVESTER

Domestic cats are descended from a wild species called *Felis sylvestris*—cat of the woods. Whether or not that's how the cartoon cats Felix and Sylvester got their names, that's

where pet cats—*Felis catus*—got their behavior. The two are so alike that where the wildcat survives in Europe, Africa, and Asia, the two interbreed without difficulty. Where house cats have been left to their own devices in the wild, they simply have taken up their wild way of life where it was left off 8,000 years ago when cats first became pets.

Therefore, mountain lion watching isn't necessary to see for yourself the hunting strategies of the cat family. Watch your cat, or, in particular, your kitten. The separate moves practiced by a kitten at play will eventually be strung together and used to kill small animals.

The hide-under-the-chair-and-dash-out-at-your-ankle game is a simple sprint from ambush, followed by a pounce onto prey and a bite into whatever is the narrowest area between two bulges. On you that's an ankle; on a mouse that's the neck.

More complicated is the scoot-across-the-floor-swiping-at-a-crumpled-paper-ball game. That's for when the mouse isn't captured at the first pounce. The swipes with claws extended, first on one side, then the other, prevent the mouse from turning away from its attacker. Sooner or later a swipe will hook the mouse in the cat's claws. A leap into the air and a swipe of the claws can bring down a bird.

A full string of moves begins with the kitten crouched low in ambush. If the "prey" isn't close enough to be reached in a single pounce, the cat gets closer by creeping low, as though it were hidden in underbrush or grass. Its body is very flexible. Elbows and heels are held so high that the cat's belly touches the ground. When close enough the cat lifts its rear, humps its back, shifts its weight between its two rear feet, and ready, set, GO! Bent backbone whips like a bow as the rear legs push out to their greatest length, and the cat lands on its prey with front legs fully stretched. Paws, claws extended, are faced inward as it lands, and the prey is locked between them.

Prey that struggles after it is caught—your hand struggling to get out of the cat's clutches, for instance—is fiercely held. The cat tries to turn its prey so that it and the cat are belly to belly. Holding the prey about the shoulders in a wrestler's grip, it rakes the belly with its hind claws, and bites the throat. Hard-wired for these maneuvers by inheritance, and well-

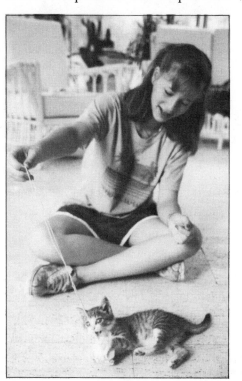

THE FIRST DOG?

Of all the dogs there are today, the ones most similar to the wolf are the huskies, the sled dogs of the Arctic. Even today, breeders in the Arctic sometimes cross their sled dogs with wolves to refresh the dogs' wolfish qualities. There are several wolf traits besides these dogs' tremendous energy, strength, and endurance.

The legs of huskies are long, the toes are arched, the nails are thick; they are made for running. The teeth fit against one another in a grip that locks flesh between them; they are made for holding onto prey. Huskies, like wolves, have two coats of hair, a short, dense, insulating coat and a longer one made up of coarser guard hairs that wear well against abrasion.

The pelt is most interesting for what it has to say. The head has wolf markings that emphasize facial expressions. Lips are black against a pale muzzle, so you could hardly miss a snarl. The dark rim of the ear contrasts with the pale inside, so the ears stand out like banners. Black-tipped hairs on the dark forehead gather together when the brow is furrowed. The belly is as pale as any flag of surrender, and is used that way when a dog flops over in defeat. The black-tipped tail carries pointed messages—wagged greetings, lowered deference, uplifted superiority.

practiced through such kitten games, grown cats can kill animals as large as themselves.

THE WAY TO GO

You can engage a kitten in hunting games for a long time inside the house or among shrubbery. Out in the middle of the lawn, where there is no cover, the cat will soon lose interest. Grasslands aren't its natural habitat.

The grassland stars are the dog family: coyotes, wolves, jackels, dingoes, and other wild members of the group. They run the open country; there are no jungle dogs.

Before rising mountains changed the climate, dogs and cats were similar, for they share a common ancestor. Both had claws like those that cats have now. Maybe both landed their meals by pouncing from ambush. But instead of specializing in the flexible skeleton that gave cats their long leap, dogs went more the route of horses. They evolved longer legs and a stiffer skeleton that gave them endurance as well as speed.

Killing methods changed, and so did killing weapons. A cat leaps on its prey's back, grips its hide with its claws, and kills with stabbing fangs that can neatly sever the spinal cord. Dogs' bodies are built for running, not leaping; their claws grip

GANGING UP

When a litter of pups is about two months old, they begin to gang up against one another. One pup will play-attack another. In seconds, all of the other pups will have piled into the game. They will even gang up on their mother; they will even gang up on you. You might think the excitement is merely catching and that they all join the melee, growling, biting, and tugging at one another. But they don't. Only one dog (or one human) is their play victim. On second thought, they appear to be cooperating, for they harass the victim from every side. Although the pups are more a nuisance than a danger at this point, they are practicing to kill prey together.

WINNING CHEMISTRY

R esearchers have noticed that the more contests with rivals that a male animal wins, the more likely he is to win again. The opposite is also true: Every loss tends to reduce an animal's chances of winning in the future. In some species, at least, the experience of winning increases the amount of the hormone testosterone that the winner produces. Testosterone production falls off in the loser. Testosterone heightens aggressiveness and competitiveness. Chemistry may account for the observation, "Nothing succeeds like success."

ground, not hide. They are biters, not stabbers.

Dogs developed long jaws with teeth that lock onto flesh. A wolf may close in on its prey from any side and grab it anywhere it can get a toothhold. For large prey, no one bite is a killing bite. Dogs kill large animals by using the same strategy used by large animals to keep themselves from being killed: they team up. The pack attacks from every side, and the dogs leap all over the prey. The animal dies not from any one wound, but from many wounds together.

This strategy is used not only by wild wolves, but by packs of pet dogs who, after mauling a deer, trot on home where they behave like perfect gentlemen. Wolves are the same. A wolf pack practically follows the Boy Scout oath, and for good reason. Dangerous animals that can get a meal only by relying on other dangerous animals of the same species can't afford to be dangerous to one another.

WHO'S WHO IN THE PACK

Each wolf in a pack knows its place. Social positions have been named according to the Greek alphabet: alpha, beta, gamma, delta, and on down to the last, the omega wolf. The alpha is boss, the beta is the alpha's best friend, and the omega gets to do the babysitting when the others go off to hunt.

Puppies scrap among themselves to decide who is who in the litter. By the time they are several months old, they have worked out their social standing from alpha to omega. Toss some new object into their midst (it has to be something a little alarming, like a rubber Halloween mask or a toy that squeaks). The one that approaches to investigate it first is the alpha. The others will approach in order of their social

The biggest dog doesn't necessarily have the highest rank. Here, the dog on the left lowers its tail and droops its head and ears to "salute" its superior, who is showing its rank by upright posture, pricked ears, and lifted tail.

THE SNIFF TEST

Dogs constantly leave urine samples at many spots outdoors, and continually check out the samples left by other dogs. Judging from their concentration as they sniff (and sometimes taste), and the carefulness with which they choose prominent places to pee, they are reading messages and leaving replies.

Humans also learn many things from urine. Using smell and taste alone, doctors in the past have diagnosed from urine various diseases, including, for example, diabetes, which makes urine sweet. Using more sophisticated chemical sensors than human tongues and noses, we can now analyze urine for hormones and many other bodily products to understand a person's physical condition. If we wished, we could also tell a person's sex from that person's pee.

Now think: On a scale from one to ten, the dog's sniffer rates a ten, while ours scores only two. Dogs can smell smells that are several hundred times more faint than the ones we can smell. They can distinguish by smell every human or canine individual and every species of prey animal as easily as we can distinguish by sight individual people and different species of mammals. It is perfectly reasonable to assume that, for a dog, a urine message tells the sex, age, health, and very possibly the mood of the dog that left it.

position in the litter's hierarchy, and each will signal its position with its tail. The highest ranking pup holds its tail highest, the others hold their tails lower than their superiors, but higher than their inferiors. The omega tucks its tail between its legs.

SAY IT WITH YOUR BODY

When we call "Hey, come on, come here!" to someone of our own species, we may beckon with hand and arm, and with our head, too. When we call "C'mon, come here!" to a dog, we behave very differently. We bend our legs, crouch forward, and clap our hands or slap them on our knees. Partly, that may be the built-in human way of summoning something small: We lean down to encourage a baby to toddle into our arms, and clap to urge it on. But, partly, we may have learned from dogs how to say "Come here." When a dog invites another to play, it bows," rear end held high, and slaps its front paws on the ground. And, when you think about it, who would slap and clap to call a cat?

STATUS SIGNAL

Puppy fights settle things only among puppies. As they mature, wolves in a pack and dogs in a neighborhood also have to sweat out their position among their elders. This they do less by scrapping than by proclaiming their status and convincing others to agree.

Subordinates state their position by lowering themselves somewhat, and turning their heads aside. Dominant wolves stand tall, and dare to stare. The signals speak of size. The dog that assumes it is superior makes itself look bigger with pricked ears, wide open eyes, and a high tail. The underdog lays its ears back, droops its eyelids, and lowers its tail. Two dogs may be of nearly equal rank in their own view. To decide which has an edge on the other, notice how high one holds its tail compared with the other.

You can tell that dogs agree with one another's statements if both wag their tails and greet each other. Greetings begin with a nose sniff, then a sniff to the hind end. The one that sniffs first is dominant. Males may end the meeting by leaving their calling card: peeing on a post. The smell states rank, too, and to a dog's sensitive nose, is almost as indelible as the printed word.

Dogs that don't agree with one another repeat their claims louder.

A dog that thinks another is challenging its rank will make itself look even bigger by raising the fur along its back and tail. It may remind the challenger of its willingness to defend its position by raising its lips to show its white fangs, and by growling. The challenger then had better lower itself. Otherwise, it is asking for a fight.

BULLIES AND WIMPS

Differences of opinion are usually settled by these dog versions of boasts, threats, and saying "uncle." But dogs are fed and bred by humans. They are no longer kept in line by living where the only meal is one hunted together, and where babies can't be raised alone. A pekinese can make an idle boast to a great dane. A terrier can keep on fighting when its opponent has said "uncle." Whether they are wimps or bullies, someone will come to their rescue.

Wolves evolved under circumstances that favored both leaders and followers, but didn't favor bullies or wimps. Leaders were favored because, supported by followers, they had a better chance to produce offspring. Bullies got a double whammy. They got hurt by fighting, and they lost friends. Bad health and no help meant fewer babies.

Followers were favored because,

In response to his owner's annoyance, this dog had turned belly-up, a "don't harm me" posture signaling defeat.

protected by leaders, they, too, had a better chance to reproduce. The alpha couple is the pack's mother and father. As they age or die, betas move into alpha position, or there is a scramble for the top. Social climbers are favored, wimps are not.

An alpha must be tough because he takes the greatest risk in hunting, but he must be kind because big-game hunting is risky to everyone, and subordinates need reassurance in order to keep their courage up. Subordinates are like members of a team. Brave biters, like star pitchers, may have high status, but there is no position, tracker or batter, that the team can do without.

Wolves love and obey their alpha for the same reasons a team loves and obeys a good coach: because he or she teaches them how to play the game, calms them when they're worried, and peps them up when they're discouraged. Watch dog trainers and you'll see that as they guide a dog with hand and leash, they also pat it, and cheer it on. That's the way to be an alpha to your dog. That's how to win its love.

BABY TALK

Love is the glue that holds a pack together. It's not a common emotion. Love evolved only among animals whose babies need their care. A tadpole needs no care, and a frog doesn't love its tadpoles. Mice need care for 21 days; the mother loves them for just that long. Among wolves, love is forever because dependence on the family is forever, and so, in a way, wolves must stay babyish.

Newborn pups urinate and defecate only as their mother licks their belly. As they grow older, pups invite cleaning time by presenting their belly for a licking. A grown wolf that turns its belly to another is claiming the love a baby gets, and admitting that it is socially inferior to the standing wolf. The gesture prevents dangerous fights. No wolf harms a belly-up opponent.

Other kinds of baby talk become grown-up language, too. Licking the mother's lips to make her disgorge recently swallowed meat for her pups is translated into a greeting to social superiors. The subordinate wolf licks the dominant one's muzzle. That's why your dog tries so hard to lick your face. The dominant wolf replies by briefly holding the other's muzzle in its mouth. That's why, when you pet your dog's face and hold its head, it feels so

happy. All adult wolves are babyishly loving toward superiors, and the alpha wolf finds all its pack mates lovably babyish.

SHEPHERDS OF THEIR FLOCKS

Predators can't afford to gobble their prey to extinction. It is in their interest to do just the opposite: to keep their herds healthy and numerous. Although wolves don't plan together how to care for prey, or even think about it at all, those behaviors that in the past have tended to keep an individual alive and preserve game from year to year for the next generation have been favored over behaviors that would cause injury and starvation. So, by accident, wolves have become the shepherds of their prey flocks.

Wolves take care of their flocks in several ways. Each pack lives in a large territory surrounded by a no-man's-land in which neither that pack nor neighboring ones hunt. Prey animals know where these safety zones are and seek them out. Each no-man's-land is therefore a game preserve, though it is also a pantry that can be raided when starvation is the only alternative.

The pack chooses only certain animals for slaughter. It won't attack an animal that refuses to run. A moose or caribou that stands its ground is in effect saying that it knows it is strong enough to put up a heck of a fight. Risk of injury or death makes that meal not worth the battle. The wisdom has been inherited by some dogs, whose en-thusiastic attack may be brought to a screeching halt by a cat that won't turn tail.

An animal in the prime of life and pink of health is almost never chosen. Meals are made from old animals, the injured, sick, or weak. By culling sick animals, the shepherds halt the spread of disease among their flock. By weeding out those that slow its progress, they speed the herd along its way. The pack even saves herds from starvation in times of famine. Where deer have become numerous, an entire population can starve to death over a winter. Culled by wolves, the remaining smaller herd survives.

If wolf etiquette and ethics sound familiar, that's no coincidence. Only two cooperative hunting societies evolved among mammals: dogs and us. Animals that do similar work tend to evolve in similar ways. The animals that were to evolve status symbols, corporations, and conservation were, 10 million years ago, apes. They had never eaten venison.

10 MILLION YEARS AGO

A Food Shortage · An Ape Solution · The Evolution of Humans

The scene is a waterhole in Antelope County, Nebraska, 10 million years ago. Tortoises and alligators lived there then. There wasn't any snow. Grass spread as far as the eye could see over flat land, broken here and there by shallow valleys with pretty streams and clumps of trees.

The number of hoofed animals was stunning. There were horses, camels, pronghorns, and dozens of other species, now extinct, on the plains. In wooded valleys tapirs browsed on leaves and twigs, and so did deer, as they still do. Strangely, there were more rhinoceroses than anything. They were grassland mammals then, and so they lived in herds. And, of course, there were meat eaters, from basic weasel to lumbering bear dog.

The scientist who found this waterhole said that the horizon 10 million years ago was so level that a stabbing cat could have watched the sun rise between the legs of a distant camel. But not on the day these animals died. Somewhere to the west a volcano erupted. A blizzard of choking ash blew over Antelope County, suffocating and then burying all the animals that had come to drink at the waterhole.

It was breeding season. Rhinoceros mothers were nursing babies that died trying to suckle for comfort. Some babies hadn't yet been born. Their fossils are still inside their mothers' fossils. Two kinds of horses died: the old, three-toed ones that still browsed the wooded valleys, and the new, one-toed ones that ate nothing but grass. One fossil was a turkey.

The mammals that would one day ride horses, celebrate Thanksgiving with a turkey, dig for fossils, and cry over rhinoceros babies lost 10 million years ago were yet to come.

A PROBLEM IN PARADISE

On the other side of the world and back in the jungle, the monkey business had prospered. Monkey troops skimmed over the canopy, long-armed gibbons swung along at dizzying speeds, and there were more kinds of apes by far than there are now. Theirs was a life of luxury, lolling in the noonday heat, dandling their babies, combing out each other's fur, cuddling, bickering, and fooling around for the fun of it.

For these monkeys, however, luxury was a necessity. Monkey mothers have a hard time raising their helpless babies without help in finding food and escaping enemies; almost all of them live at least in family groups, often in large bands. Families and bands can't stay together without social ways to win affection and soothe squabbles. Not everyone knows everything: Babies learn love in their mother's arms, rough and tumble with their fellows, respect for leaders among their elders, and all sorts of cautions, lore, and language from members of the band that have special knowledge. Chimpanzees need that kind of care for 10 years; they seldom have children before they are 13 years old. When they do, their survival and that of their babies depends on their education.

A vervet monkey learns "words," and also what to do when it hears each word. It learns to look up and clamber down when someone cries the vervet sound for "Eagle!," and to look down and scamper up when someone calls the vervet sound for "Snake!" An ape learns what foods to eat, when each is available, where to find it, and what routes to travel to get it. You may know only a few dozen fruits and vegetables; a gorilla knows 450.

Such careful childrearing takes up everybody's time and can't be done if the troop has to spend all day hustling for a living. So the business of producing high-quality babies works best in a jungle paradise where the living is easy and adults can afford the time and energy to raise babies that have so much to learn and take so long to grow up.

THE MONKEY BUSINESS

Y ou'd think baboons had bugs, the way they pick at one another all day long, but it's unlikely that anything is crawling on a baboon in a well-kept zoo. Still, they can't stop: Grooming keeps the group together.

As babies, we get loved by getting diapers changed, hair combed, faces washed. A hint of that original meaning may still linger in adulthood in the form of the lift we get from having our hair cut, or the urge we feel to arrange others' hair. But the equation between grooming and loving is much more limited in humans than in other primates, to whom picking through hair means much more than "I love you."

Notice who gets groomed the most in a band of baboons. He is the leader, and usually the only adult male. To groom him is not a duty, but a privilege allowed to those he most favors. It has the meaning of a badge of special status, a blessing of sorts. The female grooming the leader expresses to him deference to his leadership, as well as personal affection.

When the leader allows one particular female to groom him most often, it bespeaks her status among the others: chief groomer, a princess among commoners. Individuals of very low status—youngsters, for instance—

don't get to groom the leader at all.

Other pairs, or perhaps threesomes, of females and juveniles will also be involved in grooming. Although the groomer is often of lower rank than the groomee, the ritual expresses their closeness more than their social distance. Grooming cements friendships; it is a pledge of allegiance and a nonaggression pact

rolled into one, for the groomee won't bite the hand that grooms her or him, or vice versa.

Grooming defines what a band is, for everybody in a band grooms somebody, and no one grooms anybody outside the band. Among the baboons, you might say that grooming is belonging.

But ever since the world began to get cooler and dryer, the monkey business has been getting harder and harder. As trees became sparser at the edges, paradise got smaller, and monkeys and their relatives had to squeeze into an area that couldn't support as many of them, or they had to find new foods to add to their usual treetop menu. Most of them squeezed; some turned to foods at ground level. Today there are macaques that catch crabs at the seashore, gorillas that dig roots out of the ground, baboons that hunt young goats, and chimpanzees that use sticks to fish termites from their nests. But even wiping the platter clean, all but one modern primate is today a threatened or endangered species. That is every primate except us, who left the forest.

BABY BUDGETS

Part of the primate problem now is us, for we are cutting down the tropical paradise where we once lived at a terrible rate. But the large apes, of which there used to be so many species, began their long decline while our ancestors were themselves apes. Whatever threatened them, threatened us, too. For a species to dwindle or become extinct, the death rate (the number of individuals that die each year) must be greater than the birth rate (the number of individuals born each year). Those apes from which we are descended must have been able to make up for any unusual losses in the population by producing more than the usual number of babies. That is very hard for an ape to do, because each baby costs so much.

The more it costs to raise a baby, the fewer children a couple can afford to have. We figure costs in dollars; we could also figure the baby budget on work done to earn the food, shelter, care, and schooling each child requires. A chimpanzee mother must travel such-and-such a distance for food, work so-and-so much to gather it, spend

this much effort building noonday and nighttime sleeping nests, that much energy carrying the baby, this much more nursing it, and more still to protect, scold, comfort, and educate it. Thirteen years old when her first child is born, a chimp mom can't usually afford a second child until she is 18, when the first-born is a five-year-old able to gather food for itself under her supervision. At that rate, the most babies she can produce in her lifetime is six.

Of those six, several will die. The mother herself might not live long enough to produce so large a family. The baby budget is so tight that any bottleneck—an epidemic or a temporary decline in the food supply—may cause a decline in numbers from which the population can't recover.

WHERE WILL THE MONEY COME FROM?

Perhaps an ape facing this predicament could get a raise. For instance, if a mother were paid more food for the same amount of work, she might be able to raise two children at the same time, nursing one and gathering meals for the other. But there is no easier eating than in the jungle.

Maybe an ape could stretch the budget. Why not gather food in groups, so that one could keep her

A chimp family.

eye on several children while the other mothers worked? That's been tried. Chimpanzee mothers and older daughters forage in nursery groups, and still the budget is too small.

Work could be done more efficiently. Males, not tied down to children who must be nursed and carried, could find their food at a greater distance and leave what's close to home to the women and children. That's been tried, too.

Male chimps go their own way, gather food far from home, and hunt for young pigs and monkeys. When they find more fruit than then can eat themselves, they call through the woods for nursery groups within earshot to come and get it. Still, the budget is too skimpy to raise more than one expensive baby at a time.

Well then, if the males have so much energy that they can hunt pigs, why don't they bring home the

A human family.

bacon? Maybe that's what our ancestor apes did, and maybe from that generosity evolved the two-income family and the two-footed way of human life.

A PUZZLE WITH FEW PIECES

Unfortunately, any apes likely to have been our ancestors have left in the fossil record nothing but their unapelike teeth. One candidate, called *Ramapithecus*, lived some 10 million years ago. For the next 8 million years there is no record at all of how apes evolved, for most bones in the jungle are dissolved by acid soil and decayed by bacteria too fast for fossils to form. There is a 6-million-year gap between *Ramapithecus* and fossils of the next man-like mammals, the australopithecines—not really apes but not quite people either—that began to live on the African savanna 4 million years ago. They had walked there on their own two feet.

Our history is therefore like a jigsaw puzzle with almost all of the pieces missing. To figure out where the few pieces that are left belong, what the missing pieces might have been like, and how they all fit together, we have to use what evolution gave us: our enormous brain. Using our brain, we can make up theories about how we came to be the way we are.

A theory is a possible explanation; it is like the various scenarios a detective might make up to explain a crime, and thereby solve a mystery. One detective might come up with several ideas, and several detectives might come up with different explanations. Among these competing theories, the one that best explains the facts—the evidence—is the one most likely to be true. If there are many facts, only one theory is likely to fit them all. If there are few facts, several theories might account for them equally well. There are few facts in human evolution, and therefore there are many theories. The one that follows fits the evidence nicely, but it is not the only possible explanation, and all the evidence is not yet in.

WHAT TEETH CAN TELL

First, the teeth. *Ramapithecus* had evolved larger molars, with stronger enamel, than other apes of its day.

That puzzle piece is easy to place. It was eating tougher foods—fewer mushy fruits and more of the chewy vegetation that grows on the ground. With that piece, we can place *Ramapithecus* with its feet—probably all four of them—on the ground more reasonably than in the treetops.

Ramapithecus's canine teeth were small; the ape got along without large fangs. But why did it no longer need the snarly fangs all other apes still have? That puzzle piece is harder. But since modern

NOAH'S ARK

Would Noah really have been able to save animals from extinction by rescuing a pair of each species from the flood? In theory, that seems possible. Each couple routinely produces more offspring than are needed to replace the father and mother in the population. A pair of cats easily produces 10 kittens a year for a decade, or 50 times what is necessary to replace themselves in the population. The only thing that prevents a species from multiplying enough to cover the face of the Earth is competition for limited resources. With only so much to go around, one offspring per individual (two per couple) survive on the average. In a world emptied of competition by the flood, each pair of animals should have been able to repopulate its species by doing what comes naturally—that is, by overproducing. But modern rescuers—zoos and wildlife groups who work to save endangered species—have not had an easy time.

Disasters that kill off many individuals, squeezing the population through a time of lowered numbers, are called bottlenecks. Passenger pigeons, kin of the dove that brought back to Noah an olive branch of good tidings, were once the most numerous of all birds with a population of 5 billion. They were forced into a bottleneck when hunters' greediness decimated their flocks in the last century. Even though pairs survived in the wild and in zoos, passenger pigeons proved unable to breed unless crowded in large flocks. The last individual died in 1900; the species is extinct.

Pandas went through a bottleneck only a few years ago when the arrow bamboo on which they feed all bloomed, went to seed, and died. Arrow bamboo plants all do that in unison every hundred years, and apparently pandas have in the past recovered from these once-in-a-century famines. But in this century, the spread of farmlands has cut off groups of pandas from one another, lessening the choice of mates among survivors. As zookeepers have discovered, pandas are choosy about partners, reluctant to mate with strangers, and fertile for only a few days once a year. Pandas remain endangered in spite of a worldwide effort at matchmaking.

Cheetahs met a bottleneck of an unknown kind perhaps a few thousand years ago. Whatever that disaster was, it seems to have left alive only closely related individuals. Inbreeding among these kin resulted in various defects: Most of the males' sperm are incapable of fertilizing eggs; most of the females' babies die. Cheetahs are becoming extinct because their genes lack variety. That would have been the fate of any pair rescued by Noah, since the next generation after the flood would have been siblings, and the only possible matings would have been between the saved couple, or between the father and his daughters, or the mother and her sons, or between sisters and brothers.

Noah, as his modern heirs are discovering, would have had to have understood the fine points of reproduction to save species, for extinction is less a matter of dying than of breeding.

apes use their fangs mostly to compete for females, sex might be the clue.

Humans are sexually peculiar animals. Ovulation, the ripening of a female's egg, occurs in secret, unannounced by the smells and swellings that let male dogs and apes know when a female is fertile. Other mammals are sexually attracted to one another, and mate, only during fertile periods. Humans mate all the time.

The relationship between human mates is also unlike that of our closest living ape relatives. A male gorilla mates with a group of females with which he lives, and which mate with him alone. Chimpanzees are promiscuous: females mate with several males, and males mate with several females. Humans commonly choose a single partner with the intention of mating only with that person, and for the rest of their lives.

Just as strange, compared with the behavior of apes, is our peaceful way of conducting courtship. Apes snarl and bare their fangs to show how dangerous they could be; if pushed too far, they bite each other to settle who will mate with whom. We don't. We can't. We have no fangs.

Ten million years ago, those apes that were already losing the large fangs with which all other apes compete for females must have found some other way to decide who was going out with whom.

THE ODD COUPLE

Every once in a while an odd chimpanzee couple gives a hint of what might have happened. The female chimp becomes sexually attractive some days before an egg is ready to be fertilized, and she remains willing to mate even after she has become pregnant. A male may convince her to slip away to a secluded spot, just the two of them on honeymoon. The couple may become more than usually attached to one another, and that male may father several of that female's babies over the years. Among pigmy chimpan-

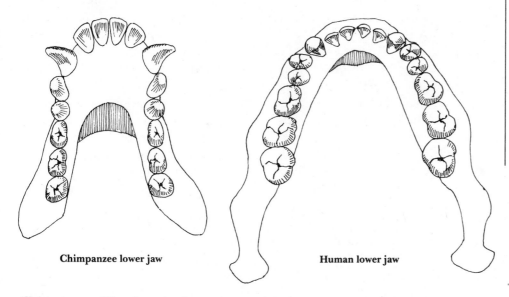

Chimpanzee lower jaw   **Human lower jaw**

Chimpanzees, like other apes have a squarish jaw; the two rows of molars are parallel. Humans have an arched jaw; the teeth are curved in an arc. Apes have a space between incisors and canines that isn't there on humans. The space is where the points of the other set of canines fit when the mouth is closed. We don't need that space, because our canines are so short.

Chimp incisor   **Human incisor**

zees, a species that lives only in a small area of Africa, this kind of behavior is more the rule than the exception.

The longer the period of sexual attractiveness, the less either of the pair can know exactly when the female is fertile, and the more easily a male can miss his chance of fertiliz-

The in-between jaw of an early australopithecine.

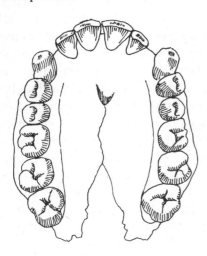

The earliest australopithecines had a jaw that was somewhere between that of apes and modern humans. The jaw is squarish, and the molars lie in two straight lines except for the last one, which is kicked in a bit, forming a bit of a curve. The canines, though very worn in this fossil specimen, are pretty big, and there is the space between them and the incisors where the lower canines rested when the mouth was closed.

ing her egg—unless he can keep her for himself the whole time. Fighting to keep her would be costly because it would injure him and disturb the whole band's peace. A better solution is to go steady. The more couples that are going steady within an ape band, the fewer fights there will be, and the less need there is for fangs. Small canine teeth begin to fit into place.

The next canine teeth to appear in the fossil record, those of australopithecines 6 million years later, are no more fanglike than your own. Some scientists think that during the gap between ramapithecines and australopithecines, honeymoon evolved into marriage. Among humans, the honeymoon is not over when the couple returns from seclusion after their wedding. A human female ripens her eggs in secret. Neither she nor her husband nor any other male knows for sure when mating can make her pregnant. For reproduction to occur at all, mating has to be frequent, and to mate frequently, the couple has to find one another attractive all the time. Sex among australopithecines may have taken on its modern human has meaning: love and faithfulness.

So far, so good. But the next pieces of the puzzle, only 4 million years old, show australopithecines walking on two feet. How come?

STANDING ON THEIR OWN TWO FEET

Chimpanzees, our closest relatives, stand up to see over the underbrush, and are able to walk a few steps at a time. They strip leaves off twigs to make termite-fishing probes, weave branches to make sleeping nests, crumple leaves to make sponges, and use sticks and stones as weapons. Ramapithecines might have used tools about that well, and it isn't hard to imagine a very smart descendant sharpening a stick to a point, or weaving branches into a container. Such a super-ape would need its hands free to use and carry tools, so evolution would favor those individuals that could spend more time upright.

If this is how our ancestors began to stand up on their own two feet, however, they had to be smart enough to invent tools first. Therefore scientists trying to piece together this part of the puzzle of human evolution at first expected to find fossil ancestors in the form of a super ape: big brained but ape bodied.

Australopithecines came as a shock. Instead of having a human brain in an ape body, they had an ape brain in a human body. No tools have been found. The theory that intelligence and invention drove human evolution could not be true.

The fact that australopithecine fossils are found in open country only added to the mystery. A two-footed gait, especially in its early, shambling stage before new joints had been perfected, would have been slow and tiring. Apes evolving an upright posture would certainly not have been fast enough to run after game or away from predators over the African savannas. The theory that human evolution, then, was driven by our ancestors moving into an open habitat is also doubtful. Walking upright had to have happened earlier. Those pieces of the puzzle, when nearly every bone in the body was being reshaped for the two-legged life must be lost in the woods where fossils are vanishingly rare.

Scientists re-sorted the known pieces and tried them a different way. There was still the problem of too-costly babies. If a male were to bring home extra food, family income would be boosted and more children could be raised. The more he could carry, the more help he would be. Two hands are better than one, and walking on two feet is the only way to carry with both hands.

Chimpanzees do carry food for short distances, using one hand while walking three-footed. They share occasionally. When a male chimpanzee is courting a female, she may beg food from him, using the same open-palmed begging gesture we use, and he will hand her some of the food he is eating. But that female also mates with other males, none of which can be sure he is the father of the baby she gives birth to. It does a father's genes no good if he feeds another father's child. The more certain the child's paternity, the more profitable it becomes to the father to assist in its rearing. Food sharing evolves with faithfulness, and two-footedness evolves with food-sharing.

"Lucy," an Australopithecus afarensis.

EAT YOUR JICAMA, DEAR

O f the 80,000 plants thought to be edible, we stock only a handful on our grocery shelves. Our ancestors may well have eaten more, not fewer, kinds of plants than we do. A real food adventure is to sample some of the crops that people—and not-yet-people—may have known about for millions of years, but that aren't common in our menus. You can find many unfamiliar fruits and vegetables in ethnic markets; ask the proprietor how to prepare them. A few, like the kiwi fruit imported from New Zealand, have made it to the supermarket league.

Tubers, the sugar-and-starch-storing roots of certain plants, must have been a staple among australopithecines. Hispanic markets are a good place to gather many kinds of tubers unavailable in most chain stores, and also peppers, and squashes, and bananas of all sorts (many of which are eaten fried). Look for a jicama, a tuber as big as a turnip, and as sweet, juicy, and crunchy as an apple, or an oca, pink on the outside, white on the inside, with flesh that is a combination of sweetness and tartness that has been compared with sun-ripened tomatoes. Manioc is the root from which tapioca pudding is made. There are also many more kinds of yams more interesting in flavor and texture than the usual sweet potato.

Oriental markets stock a multitude of fruits and vegetables: winter melons, lotus roots, bamboo shoots, water chestnuts, gingko nuts, and dozens of greens and funguses. Health-food stores are good sources for unusual grains and beans.

Think, as you experiment with these "new" foods, how many experimenters there must have been in the past. Somebody sometime must have been the first to eat a jicama. Of course, somebody somewhere must have been the first to be poisoned by pokeberries, too, so if you're tempted to experiment with wild foods, see the box on page 364, or read any of the books about foraging by Euell Gibbons.

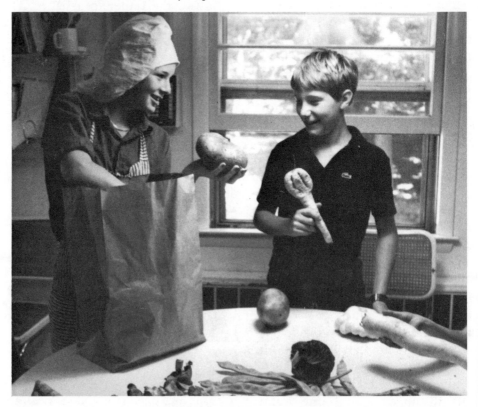

Wild as this theory sounds, it may solve the puzzle. Somewhere during the missing 6 million years faithfulness may have assured that a food-sharing male was most likely feeding his own children. A male who chose a devoted mate and a female who chose a good provider favored their own faithful food-sharing traits, and the physiology that made their unique sex life possible, and the anatomy that lifted their hands from the ground. Males were fathers now. It made sense to bring home the bacon—in both hands and on two feet.

THE DELUGE

People of various races and religions who lived around the Mediterranean Sea in ancient times tell the story of a great flood. No one knows how old the story is. But there was such a flood in that part of the world, and in no other part has such a story originated.

Land swells and shrinks as things go on beneath it. The levels of oceans also rise and fall as their basins change in shape and depth. About 5 million years ago, land at the Strait of Gibralter may have been at a high point, or water in the Atlantic Ocean at a low point. The part of the old Tethys sea that is now the Mediterranean was cut off from the ocean at Gibralter. It became an inland sea.

NO, THANK YOU

There seems to be a rule of human behavior that probably comes to us from our very distant past. The rule is: If a food is not eaten by your family, it must not be good. When presented with strange food, we take a tiny nibble (if we take it at all).

That made sense to those who had to discover by trial and error whether a strange food was safe. If an unfamiliar plant were poisonous, a nibble might sicken, but wouldn't kill. (A further protection is the nausea we feel when we smell a food that once made us vomit.)

Our caution is so ingrained that we must "cultivate" a taste for unfamiliar foods. Only after we have eaten them in increasingly larger doses over a period of time are we convinced the food is one that can be eaten heartily. Even the taste seems to change with time. At first, the flavor was suspicious. At last, it becomes delicious.

The dried-up Mediterranean.

Gradually, the sea evaporated. Rivers cut deeper into their beds as the sea level lowered. After a thousand years there was no sea at all. Under the present Nile River valley there is a narrow, deep gorge, carved when the Mediterranean was dry (it is now filled with sediments, and the present Nile flows above it). Even though this ancient gorge was a mile deep, the dried-up sea floor was still a long waterfall below.

The depth of that seafloor is almost impossible to imagine. Because the Tethys was originally a slice of ocean that opened as the northern and southern continents were rifted apart, the Mediterranean wasn't the shallow sort of sea that washes over continental rock as did the old seas of North America. The Mediterranean basin was 10,000 feet deep. The floor became a vast salt desert. From the desert, the former shores of the Mediterranean rose nearly two miles high.

Then the Atlantic rose and breached the Gibraltar dam. Water poured over a two-mile-high cliff into the empty basin. The waterfall spilled 10,000 cubic miles of water a year, 1,000 times more than the flow over Niagara Falls. In a single century, the basin was refilled to the brim.

There were repeat performances. Cores drilled from the seabed seem to show that over the next million years or so, the Mediterranean dried up 40 times. Each time it reflooded, the deluge lasted for a century. The roar of falling water could have been heard for many miles. Any australopithecines in the area would surely have heard it, and have come to see it. Could the story of the flood have been their story?

LUCY AND THE FIRST FAMILY

The earliest known australopithecines are a woman, called Lucy by the scientists who discoverd her fossil, and a group of at least 13 of her

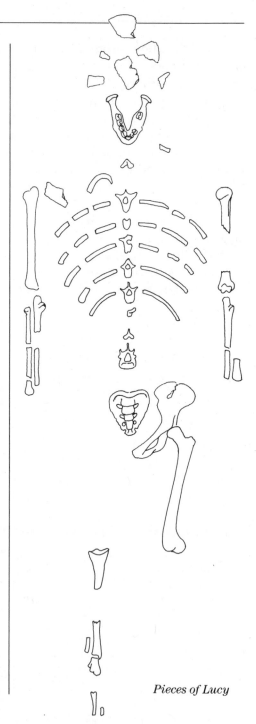

Pieces of Lucy

contemporaries, called the First Family, who died about 3.5 million years ago in what is now Ethiopia.

They could walk and run as well as we can. Their hips were totally unlike ape hips, and very like our own. They no longer had ape feet. They had grown bigger and lost the apes' opposable big toe. Fossil footprints left by somewhat more recent australopithecines look the same as ours. Their arms were rather long, as though they might still have climbed into a tree for safety overnight. But their hands were so like ours that they could have picked up a grain of sand between thumb and index finger. Lucy was tiny—107 centimeters (3 ½ feet) and 60 pounds. Others were as tall as 5 feet. With their heavy bones and muscles, they must have weighed up to 150 pounds, and been as strong as a chimpanzee, which is much stronger than we are. From a distance they might easily have been mistaken for humans.

Up close, there could have been no mistake. Lucy and the First Family had the skulls and brains of apes. Except for a set of teeth that would look at home in a dentist's office, Lucy's head looks like a gorilla's. She had no chin. There is no hint at all of the smooth brow and roundly bulging skull that was eventually to hold a brain four times ape size. The First Family left be-

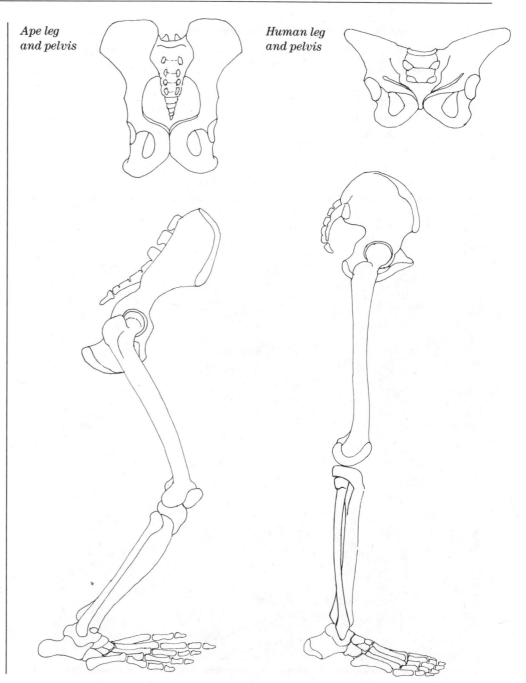

Ape leg and pelvis

Human leg and pelvis

RELIVING THE PAST?

Children do the darnedest things, and grown-ups can't see why. Why do they climb trees, swing on vines, toss stones, leap walls, fight with sticks, and make strange noises?

The urge to climb and swing may go back all the way to australopithecines (and beyond), whose long arms may have hoisted them to the tree-tops for safety. Throwing, jousting, and leaping are good training for a hunter, as *Homo habilis* might have been. The best mimics can bawl and moo to goats and bison, and call waterfowl down from the sky. Toddlers seem to think it's important to learn those noises; one of their earliest games is the one that goes "What does the dog say? Bow-wow!"

hind no campfires, and no tools; no hearths or hand-worked stones that old have yet been found. But if the story of how our ancestors evolved is correct, their solution to the tight baby budget that has forced every other ape toward extinction had worked: Australopithecines may have walked out of the forest because they were getting crowded there.

VERY GREAT GRANDMA?

There were three species of australopithecines: Lucy's kind, called *Australopithecus afarensis* after the Afar Triangle in Ethiopia where her fossil was found; a more recent species called *Australopithecus africanus;*

All mammals that have fingers are able to spread them to support their weight when standing or walking.

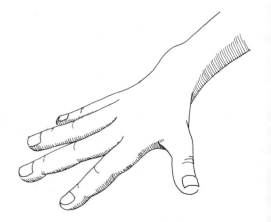

and an even more recent kind called *Australopithecus robustus* after its very heavy bones and massive jaw. All three species, and with them the whole line of australopithecines, became extinct sometime before one million years ago. Unless Lucy lives on in us.

The most primitive fossils considered to be human, and therefore given the genus name *Homo*, date from just short of 2 million years ago. Although Lucy's kind had by then been extinct for about a million years, *Homo* (man) is more like her than like the two other australopithecine species that were still alive when the first humans appear in the fossil record.

Both *Australopithecus africanus* and *robustus* grew large molars. Apparently they specialized in a vegetarian diet of tough roots, tubers, and grains. Lucy and the First Family had small molars that were grooved, chipped, and dented from eating many different foods, probably meats as well as vegetables. Our molars are small too, and get worn in similar patterns as we age. When still-missing pieces of the puzzles are found, they may turn out to be the many-times-great-grandchildren of Lucy, becoming the many-times-great-grandparents of us.

HANDY MAN

The first humans are called *Homo habilis,* "handy man"—handy because they were toolmakers, man because their brains were beginning to expand a little. But only a little.

Brains are measured by the volume of the skull that holds them. Australopithecines had brains that ranged from 430 to 550 cubic centimeters (26 to 34 cubic inches); handy man's brain was from 500 to 800 cubic centimeters (31½ to 49 cubic inches). Small human brains today are about 1,000 cubic centimeters (61 cubic inches), large ones are about 1,800 (110 cubic inches).

These people's tools were simple and easy to make: a hand-size stone from which flakes were chipped off one side to make a sharp edge. Such stones were used to cut carcasses into manageable pieces for

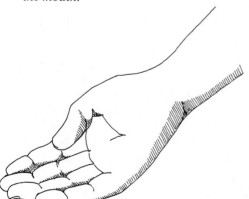

Most are also able to press their fingers against one another. With the fingers of both hands closed, the hands can be cupped and used together to bring food to the mouth.

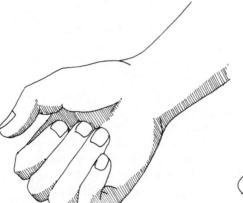

Mammals such as rodents can also close their hands to grasp objects between fingers and palm.

Primates can hold objects between thumb and forefinger, but only in humans is the thumb long enough to grasp even tiny things precisely between the tips of those two fingers.

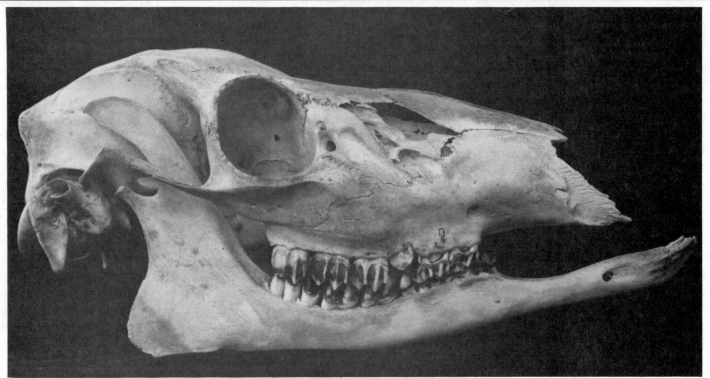

A deer skull found in the woods.

SKULL BONES

Skulls are harder than other bones, and teeth are harder still. They don't dissolve or decay easily. That's why there are more old teeth and skulls to be found than any other parts of skeletons. Almost anyone able to explore the countryside comes upon skulls—gull skulls washed up on a beach, bone-dry sheep skulls in the desert, deer skulls in the woods. They aren't the sort of thing you look for; they just turn up from time to time.

If you can get a few skulls together, it's interesting to compare them. People think of a skull as a single thing; actually, heads are formed of many bones, joined along zigzag lines. In humans, the bones of a newborn baby's head are not yet joined together. You can feel the largest of the spaces right on the top of the head, a soft spot called the fontanel.

No matter how different the shape of your head from a horse's or a mouse's, each is made of exactly the same bones—eight that form the brain case, and more than a dozen that form the face. Comparing these bones gives an idea of how the overall shape of skulls can change.

more than a million years by all people, up to perhaps 500 years ago by many people, and are still used today by some people. There were probably other tools: stones casually picked up to break open an ostrich egg or split a bone to get at the marrow, but too like other stones to recognize as tools. And there must have been perishable tools such as wooden spears, grass mats, hollowed gourds, and animal bladders. This is spur-of-the-moment equipment, easily found and as easily discarded.

Fossils of *Homo habilis* have been found only along East Africa's Great Rift Valley, where many australopithecine fossils have also been found, some living side by side with the first humans. The valley marks where the plate on which the African continent rides is coming apart all the way from the north, where the Indian Ocean has flooded the deepest part of the rift at the Red Sea, down through Ethiopia, southward through the continent, and beyond it all the way to the Antarctic Ocean. Huge lakes have settled into the widening rift. Though the climate is dry, the land flows with rivers.

River and lake shores are good places to live. There are all kinds of edible plants, and turtles, water birds, and their eggs to eat. Neighboring mammals come there to

EASY CUTTERS

The first stone tools were made when people's brains were still small. Their hands were very powerful, but their thumbs were possibly too short to meet the tip of the index finger for the pincer grip used in precise work. It follows that you don't have to be either smart or nimble fingered to make stone tools. If they could do it, you can do it.

The simplest tools were made by banging one cobble against another to break it. A cobble is a stone that has been worn to a smooth oval shape by water. Cobbles are found in streambeds, and also on pebbly beaches. Hard, fine-textured stones produce the best cutting edge. The ones below, for instance, are basaltic cobbles. The one on the right is a hammer stone, used to break the one on the left. The broken portion is the cutting edge; the tool was held by its smooth, unbroken portion.

You'll find that even this crude a stone tool is sharp enough to cut raw meat, to scrape a hide, to peel the bark from a sapling and sharpen its end to a point.

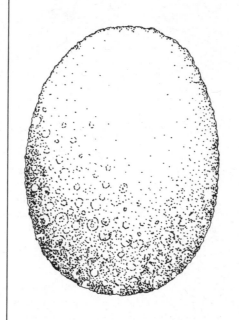
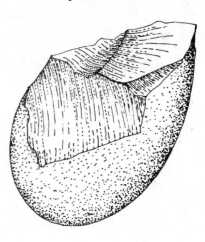

EASY CONTAINERS

Although the most beautiful baskets require a lot of skill to make, crude ones are easy. This one is made of grapevines, a supple material that's easy to find along country roads in most parts of the country. Choose strands of vine that are less than ¼ inch thick, and that are as long as possible. Cut them from the vine with pruning shears. It's hard to estimate how many feet of vine you'll need—cut lots, enough to loosely fill the trunk of a small car. Don't worry about hurting the grapevine; no amount of pruning will discourage it from growing back. Trim off leaves and side branches. Use the strands fresh so that they bend easily. They can be made even more flexible by soaking them in a bathtub of the hottest tap water for 15 minutes.

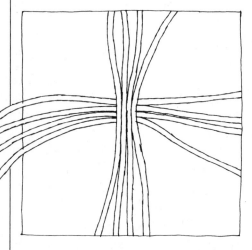

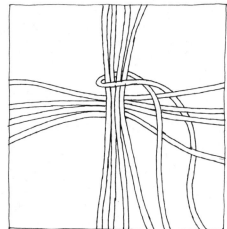

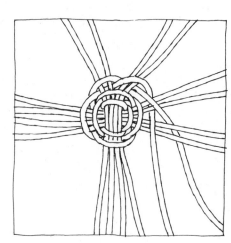

1. To form the ribs of the basket, cut eight pieces 3 feet long from the thickest strands. Lay four of the pieces crosswise over the other four, and tie them together with string. The string is removed when the basket is finished.

2. Loop a long, thin strand. Place it over one arm of the cross, and twist it once clockwise. Catch the next arm of the cross between the two strands, and twist again. Do that over and over until you have woven twice around the four arms of the cross.

3. For the next rounds, until the base of the basket is about 6 inches in diameter, divide the ribs into eight groups of two ribs each as you weave and twist the strands over and under these groups.

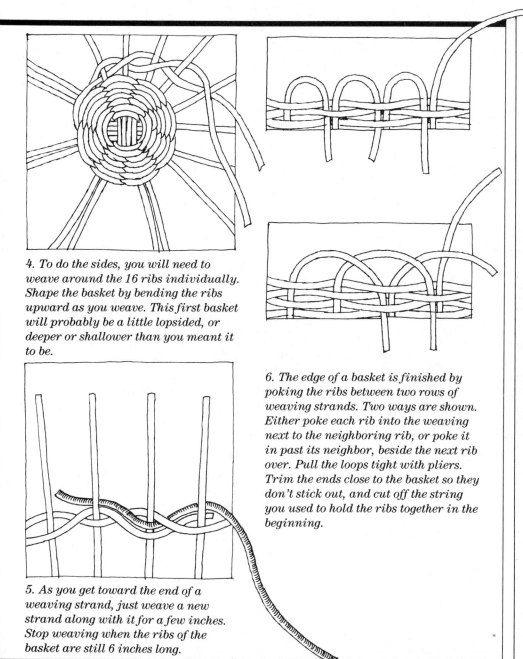

4. To do the sides, you will need to weave around the 16 ribs individually. Shape the basket by bending the ribs upward as you weave. This first basket will probably be a little lopsided, or deeper or shallower than you meant it to be.

5. As you get toward the end of a weaving strand, just weave a new strand along with it for a few inches. Stop weaving when the ribs of the basket are still 6 inches long.

6. The edge of a basket is finished by poking the ribs between two rows of weaving strands. Two ways are shown. Either poke each rib into the weaving next to the neighboring rib, or poke it in past its neighbor, beside the next rib over. Pull the loops tight with pliers. Trim the ends close to the basket so they don't stick out, and cut off the string you used to hold the ribs together in the beginning.

drink. *Homo habilis* shared waterfront with camels, horses, elephants, hippos, giraffes, antelopes, ostriches, and lots of pigs.

For about half a million years, *Homo habilis* gathered wild foods, hunted small game, and scavenged feasts from the occasional corpse of an elephant or a hippo in the Great Rift Valley. Time laid down pages of history to be read one day by his descendants. Volcanoes left ash. Flooding rivers left sediment. Generations of pigs, steadily evolving from primitive to modern forms, left their bones. Here and there are human teeth that may have bitten last into a fine ripe fruit, jaws that may have closed last on a fat tuber pried from the ground with a digging stick, and chopping stones that may have been grasped last by a hunter carving a pig to share with his family.

NEW PAGES

Then, suddenly, the pages open to a new chapter. *Homo habilis* fades out, and *Homo erectus* enters the fossil record. He enters as a strapping boy, 12 years old, who died of unknown causes. Nearly his whole fossil skeleton was found where his body washed into a marsh 1.6 million years ago in what is now Kenya. His third molars (they are sometimes called "12-year molars") had not yet grown in completely. But already the boy was 168 centimeters (five feet six inches) tall. Had he not died, he would have been a six-footer. Other *Homo erectus* fossils have also been found, perhaps not quite so old and nowhere near that complete, but certainly impressive.

Homo erectus's skull held a brain that at its smallest was like that of *Homo habilis,* but at its biggest was 1,250 cubic centimeters (76 cubic inches), 250 cubic centimeters (15 cubic inches) larger than a small modern human brain. He left word of his intelligence right away.

There were caves where he lived, hearths where he warmed himself, whole communities where he lived in homes built of wood or stone, and where he left skillful tools that he used not only for chopping meat, but for scraping hides and cutting skins for clothes.

Over the next million years, *Homo erectus* walked on, out of Africa, over Asia and Europe, after herds of deer and families of elephants that only an expert hunter could have trapped or slaughtered. Those were drastic times. Mammals, like the dinosaurs before them, grew gigantic. Vast glaciers, unknown since therapsids frolicked in Gondwanaland, crept over North America and

The Great Rift Valley (shaded area) extends from the northern tip of the Red Sea through most of the African continent to its southern coast.

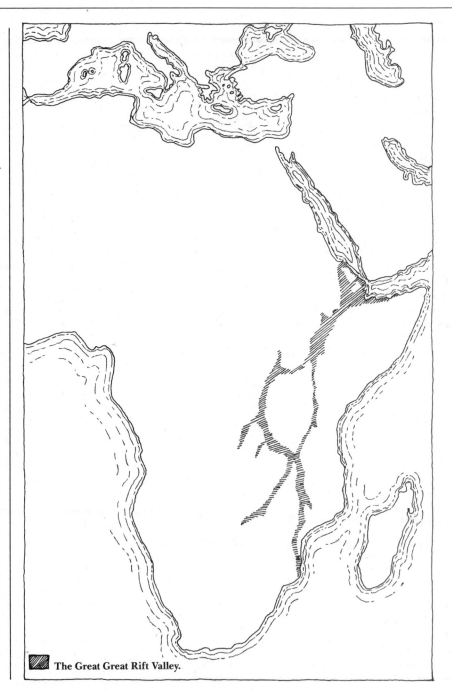

The Great Great Rift Valley.

Europe. During the ice age that was then underway, most of the giants on the earth were to become extinct. In the final million years of Earth's history, man populated the world with as many living descendants as there are years in the geological record.

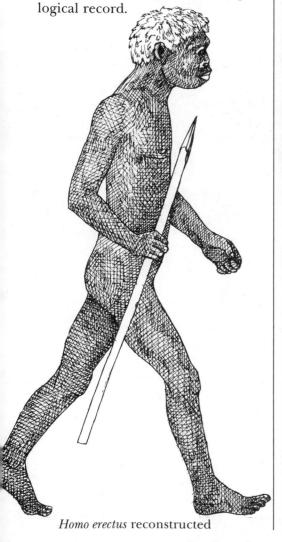

Homo erectus reconstructed

1 MILLION YEARS AGO

The Great Ice Age · Real Cavemen · First Pets · The Meaning of Being Human

You are living now in an ice age that started while *Homo habilis* lived in East Africa. It is a rare time. The last ice age before this one was 300 million years ago, when therapsids lived in snowy Gondwanaland, and the one before that was 410 million years ago, when algae were greening the shores of North America. There was another 450 million years ago, when armored fish swam the muddy bottoms, and still another 700 million years ago, when worms were the most complicated creatures around. Only the oldest was as great as the latest, which is called the Great Ice Age.

Normal climate is the worldwide mildness dinosaurs enjoyed, and that has been typical of Earth for most of its history. What seems mild to us is actually an interglacial period when ice has retreated to the poles and mountaintops, and winter snows are followed by spring thaws. There's no telling if that will last. If less snow thaws than falls, the glaciers will come again and the Statue of Liberty might stand torch-deep in ice. If more snow thaws than falls, she will be drowned in the ocean.

During the height of the Great Ice Age, glaciers covered a third of all the land on Earth. Standing on the 1.2-kilometer (2-mile) thick New England ice, your head would have been above the tops of fluffy clouds. Ice was piled five miles thick over Labrador—that's as high as a jet plane flies. The last retreat of ice as glaciers melted away was only 10,000 years ago, when Indians were here to see it, and woolly mammoths were not yet extinct.

COMING AND GOING

Whether you would have slipped on ice or sunk in water along the North Atlantic coast over the last million years depends on when you were there. Glaciers advanced and retreated quite a few times. Coming and going, they changed the map.

On the move, glaciers bulldozed the tops off the old Adirondacks, clawed out the Great Lakes, and strewed over the Midwest diamonds and gold nuggets carried all the way from Canada. The ice that covered New England weighed it down so heavily that its coast sank below sea level. So much of the ocean's water was trapped in glacial ice that the sea itself shrank. Forests grew over the continent's sandy shelf a hundred miles from the present Atlantic shore. There are elephant teeth there, now under water 120 meters (394 feet) deep.

Melting glaciers filled a bowl they had scooped out of the middle of the continent with more water than is in all the Great Lakes put together. When the meltwater broke through the bowl's rim, it formed a wall of water that raced outward at 31 kilometers (50 miles) an hour. In only weeks, the flood scoured out the scablands of the Columbia Plateau. The whole Northwest plain was left studded with buttes and mesas, all that remains of its original height, with the rest a network of channels bared of soil. Other lakes tore out canyons in their escape to the sea. The emptied lakes are now dried-out dimples, like the Bonneville salt flats in Utah, whose only water is the puddle called the Great Salt Lake. Some of the canyons still carry rivers; most are dry.

You can still see how far the glacier advanced. Its southernmost boundary is marked by a line of hills, called a moraine, clear across the land, where rubble that was trapped in the ice as the glacier advanced was left in heaps at its melting edge. Nantucket is such a rubble heap. So is Long Island.

Boulders as big as houses were transported hundreds of miles, and now lie scattered in the glacier's wake. Where they were dragged over rock, grooved scars called striations still show. Both boulders and scars can be seen in New York City's Central Park. Kettle holes, round ponds that have neither inlet nor outlet, like Lake Ronconcoma on Long Island, mark places where giant ice balls lingered. They were so

DROWNED COASTLINE

Physiographic maps, found in any atlas, show a part of North America not usually visible: the continental shelf, the edge of the continent that is covered by ocean. The map would look different in other times, for the coastline changes as the ocean rises or falls. Our eastern coastline is particularly interesting right now.

South of New York, most of the coastal plain is above the ocean, and the continental shelf is narrow. But northward, a broader and broader portion lies below the sea. From New England on, there is no coastal plain. The rocky coast rises abruptly from the Atlantic; the coastal plain is drowned.

In fact, New England would be twice as big if all its shelf were shore. During the Great Ice Age, the granite raft of our continent was tilted downward under the weight of the glaciers, and the whole Northeast was sunk deeper into the mantle below it. That sunken coastline is flooded over now. But when weight is removed from any floating raft, the raft rebounds. Ever since the ice melted, the edge of the continent has been rebounding. New Englanders will be glad to know that they are being lifted to new heights.

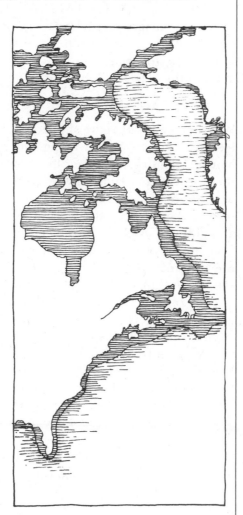

 **Continental shelf**

heavy, and so slow to melt, that they pressed the ground into hollows now filled with water. They are ice-age-old puddles.

GIANTS IN THE EARTH

As the Ice Age opened, mammals seemed to be following the dinosaurs into gigantism. Beavers grew to half the size of bears. There were elephant-size elephant relatives: mastodons with straight hair and long, straight tusks, and mammoths with woolly coats and immense tusks that curled inward like a pretzel. A swamp-dwelling, root-scooping elephant had tusks in its lower jaw that formed a flat shovel sticking out beyond its stumpy trunk, and two spiky tusks as well. Elephants evolved springy foot pads that cushion their weight, as had brontosaurs before them. And, as the tyrannosaurs had done, elephants lightened their huge skulls by developing air pockets that network the bone like cavities in a giant sponge.

There were glyptodonts that looked like ankylosaurs—armadillo-shaped vegetarians with backs humped in leather armor and a powerful tail that ended in a bony mace. They measured 3½ meters (12 feet) from snout to spikes. Sloths, now dog-sized mammals that lead their slow lives suspended upside down in the canopy of the

South American jungle, heaved their five-ton bodies overland. They reared up dinosaur style to their full two-story height to browse on trees.

Horns grew as fancy and various as the head crests of hadrosaurs. A deerlike creature that ran the Nebraska plains carried a large, forked prong atop its nose, as well as an ordinary pair of horns between its ears. Bison had horns 3 meters (10 feet) across. Irish elk grew fan-shaped antlers that measured a little over 3 meters (11 feet) from tip to tip and weighed 35 kilograms (16 pounds). Dog-size rodents poked double-horned snouts from their prairie burrows.

The great carnosaur of the day was the saber-toothed cat, whose teeth were so long they could not have been used for biting. Perhaps they stabbed their prey to death.

These mammals are like dinosaurs in another way besides their gigantic and exotic forms: They are known to us as fossils, giants in the earth. In all, 200 genera—all the species in 200 groups of mammals—became extinct within about a million years as ice carved out a new look for North America and Europe. No one will know why they died until someone knows how they lived, for some disappeared in the coldest times, as you might expect, but others thrived through the Ice Age only to vanish at its end.

Those that lived until the end— woolly mammoths insulated from the cold with fat and fur, Irish elk adapted to foraging the frozen tundra, giant ground sloths that survived by retreating to South America—were contemporaries of man. So were the stabbing cats and cave bears bigger than grizzlies.

Bones, skin, and long, reddish strands of hair from a giant ground

A boulder carried to its present location by Ice Age glaciers.

GOLF ON THE GLACIER'S EDGE

The full-of-surprises landscape of a golf course seems like a good invention. But, although people invented the game of golf, they didn't invent its game board. Golf was invented in Scotland, right smack at the glacier's edge. The original water traps were kettle holes. The original sand traps were pitted portions of eskers—winding rims of sand deposited by meltwater streams tunneling through or under the ice. Roughs were also debris dumped by rushing meltwater—lumpy hills called hummocks, knolls, braes, and kames. Rippling fairways were moraines.

These days, bulldozers heap up the hills. Trucks bring in sand for sand traps. Backhoes and dredges dig holes for water traps. That brings the game to the most unlikely places—Florida coral, Mississippi silt—but if you want to play real golf, go to where a glacier's been.

sloth were found in a South American cave along with man's stone tools. Indians in Alabama lit their cave homes with torches made from the leg bones of cave bears, hollowed out and stuffed with the bears' own fat. Early Europeans painted pictures of woolly mammoths on the walls of caves. Peat bogs where Irish elk met their end are also a burying ground of human remains. Man, the hunter, may have finished off the last of the monster mammals.

WHY SO SMART?

There are no human fossils that date from before the Great Ice Age. Our wonderful brains evolved from ape size to human size just then, and seem not to have evolved since. Brains that figured out how to get

Woolly mammoth

Stabbing cat

through an ice-age winter were the same size as brains that now figure out how to get to the moon. That seems like overkill. Why does our brain have the capacity to learn so much more than a caveman would have to know?

The answer must be that the size and complexity of our modern brain *was* needed by cavemen. Human history from the Ice Age on is a social story in which families joined together in tribes, tribes settled together in villages, villages became cities, cities controlled kingdoms, kingdoms united into nations, and nations involved themselves in world affairs. The urge to live in conglomerations of people, and the intelligence it takes to keep order among them, evolved together. Some sort of pressure must have favored those who were able to think about themselves and their relationships with others in more

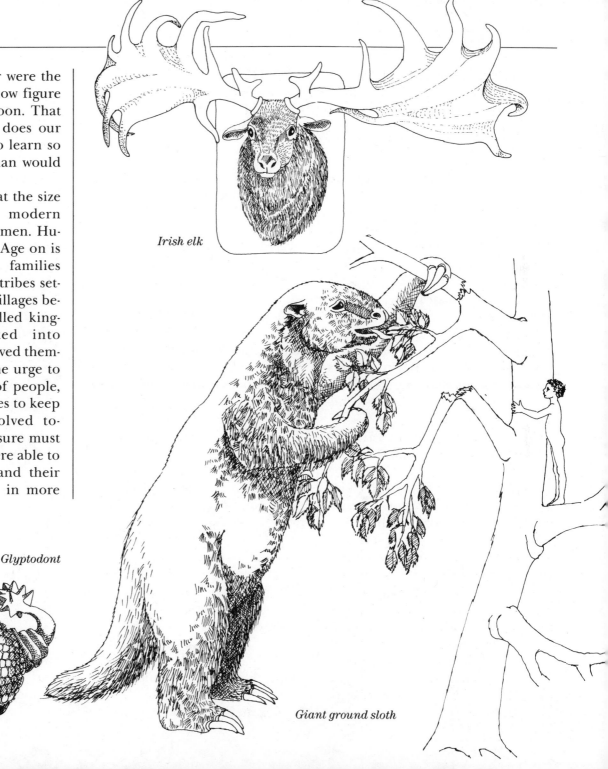

Irish elk

Horned rodent

Glyptodont

Giant ground sloth

complicated ways. The pressure itself may have been simple. There was the matter of getting food.

SCRAMBLE VERSUS SHARE

Deteriorating climate during the Ice Age tended to cause a clumping of food. Beyond the tropics, more and more land became like it is now, and worse. Vegetable crops clumped into the particular areas where they could manage to grow. Fruit clumped by season: berries in the summer, nuts in the fall. In winter, even clumps dissolved. No vegetables grew. Schools of fish hibernated below the ice, flocks of birds flew south. For humans, the most reliable food year-round became large, hoofed animals.

When food is plentiful and evenly scattered, the smart way to get it is to scramble for it, grabbing whatever is closest at hand like kids let loose in a candy store. Scrambling doesn't favor minding anyone's business but your own. Why should a weasel compete or cooperate for mice when they're all over the place anyway? No animal competes or cooperates for plentiful, scattered resources—air, for instance. Weasels are food scramblers, and weasels aren't social.

Clumped food—a single moose per square mile compared with hundreds of mice per acre—doesn't favor scramblers. How can a wolf scramble for the most moose when every other wolf is scrambling for the same animal? The cost of a free-for-all is too high. Clumped food favors obeying rules for sharing it. Wolves do eat moose, and wolves are social.

The food-getting strategy of chimpanzees is a combination of a little share and a lot of scramble. Everybody scrambles for fruit every day; a few share a piglet once in a while.

Homo habilis probably worked it the other way around: more share than scramble. But they may have lived only among close family who relied more on foods that could be gathered than on meat, and more on small game that a couple and their children could round up than on large game a whole hunting party would have had to bring down. Only as the Ice Age deepened during *Homo erectus*'s migrations did large game become a staple. Then families had to team together to hunt. They may have become more intelligent because they had to become more social, and they may have had to become more social because they had to eat.

THE CAVE

Fifty kilometers (31 miles) southwest of Beijing (once spelled "Peking"), in China, there is a large cave. Its rock was laid down as shelly debris in a shallow sea 450 million years ago, before there was much land, and before any life could live ashore. As the sea shrank back, the debris surfaced as a rounded hill, limestone through and through. The cave itself, formed by groundwater seeping into the rock and dissolving it from inside, began to form only five million years ago. That's about when what were to become cavemen were beginning to walk on two feet. A small entry into the hollowed-out hill was opened three million years ago during a flood from a nearby river. Lucy's kind *(Australopithecus afarensis)* had evolved by then.

The floor of the cave was at first ragged and sharp; its high, curved ceiling bristled with jagged points. Over the next couple of million years, occasional floods from the same river leveled the floor and silted it over. By 460,000 years ago, the cave had become a smooth and spacious room 140 meters long by 40 meters wide (460 feet long by 131 feet wide). That's when *Homo erectus* moved in.

WANDERING

People had come a long way from the pleasant valley of their origins. Small bands had spread from Africa into Spain and Turkey, and beyond into northern India and the interior of China. These migrations seem too far for people without horses to ride or wagons to ride in. But if each generation moves only 32 kilometers (20 miles)—that's 1 ½ kilometers (1 mile) a year—a century later their descendants will be 160 kilometers (100 miles) further. A million years will take them 1,609,000 kilometers (a million miles), or 39 times around the globe.

Wandering was typical of humans. Even a small family group, perhaps a dozen people, needed many square miles in which to gather, hunt, and scavenge food. One place might be best for fishing at a certain time of year, but then the family might move elsewhere to harvest tubers, to another place to gather nuts, and farther still to follow herds of game. When a group grew too large to support itself in an area that could be harvested on foot, it split up and moved on. In that way people spread outward

The Beijing Cave

The limestone hill.

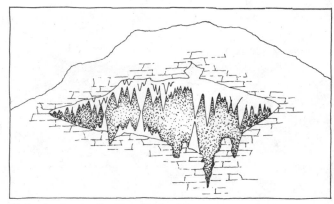

Water begins to dissolve the inside.

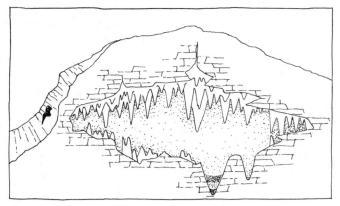

A flood opens an entrance.

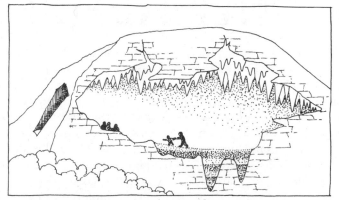

Five hundred thousand years ago, man moves in.

ETERNAL FLAMES

President Kennedy is honored by an eternal flame at his grave. The Olympic Games are opened with a flame passed hand to hand clear across the world. The Jewish holiday of Hannukah, Christmas Eve services, and many of the most serious religious events of people everywhere are marked by flames that are handed on candle to candle, torch to bonfire—and generation to generation. if you could trace these traditions back through human history, you would probably find that they evolved in an unbroken line all the way from those who first captured fire. Think of that the next time you blow out your birthday candles. The ones you fail to extinguish predict—of course!—the number of children you will have when you grow up.

from where they began; there were no other people to stop them.

During all this wandering, people seem not to have changed the way they lived. Apparently, their simple tools had served them well; tools hadn't changed for a million years, nor had the brains of their makers.

When the *Homo erectus* group discovered the limestone cave in China, the world was between glaciers, as we are now. The climate near Beijing was about the same as it is today, or about like that of Michigan. Uplands were covered with pines and spruces. Maples, oaks, birches, and nut trees grew in the valleys. There were many deer. It snowed in winter.

In spite of the cold, the band settled into the cave and moved no more. Remains in the layers of the cave floor show that *Homo erectus* lived there for more than 200,000 years, and that during that time their brains began to grow again. Bones from more than 40 people were found in the cave. At the lowest layer, on the original flood-smoothed floor, lay the typically small skulls *Homo erectus* had gotten along with for his first million years. In newer layers, the skull size gradually increased, until by the end of his stay 200,000 years later, the average brain was 70 cubic centimeters (4¼ cubic inches) larger.

KEEP THE HOME FIRES BURNING

The layers that accumulated over the original floor in the Beijing cave are of ash and charcoal from family hearths. Starting fires by rubbing sticks and striking sparks from flint came later: *Homo erectus* stole his fire from the wild.

After it was captured as a flaming torch or smoldering embers, *Homo erectus*'s home fire had to be kept burning, perhaps for decades. Either the flames had to be fed continually, which meant gathering firewood every day, or embers had to be kept hot beneath a layer of dirt or ash, and bared, refueled, and rekindled by blowing when flame was needed. Generations of children may have been warmed by a home fire stolen by a hero of the past.

Wildfires in any particular forest area are started by lightning on the average of once every seven or eight years, and sometimes only four times a century. They can be awesome things. A recent forest fire in Montana burned 14,000 acres (about the size of Manhattan island in New York City). The flames were visible at night 48 kilometers (30 miles) away. Smoke hung so thick that cars had to use headlights during the day. Firefighters said the fire was as loud as the roar of a 747 jet taking off. The heat melted glass bottles. Rocks exploded like cannon shots. The fire burned for two months.

The Montana fire was hotter and more destructive than most because the forest had been protected from burning for so long that a great deal of flammable debris and underbrush had accumulated to

RISING FROM THE ASHES

The longleaf pine of the Southeast thrives on fires. Its seedlings, sprouting in forest, don't even try to reach for the light until fire has burned a clearing through the canopy. The infant stem merely sprouts a topknot of needles that looks more like a clump of grass than a pine tree. For the next several years, or however long it takes for a fire to start, the seedling puts all its growth into a huge root system, where it hordes food.

When the fire comes, the seedling's needles are burned, but its central bud is protected by stubble, and its roots are safe underground. Fire over,

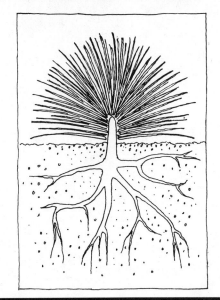

the seedling grows with all the hoarded energy of its huge root system. A young longleaf pine can grow as much as six feet a year for the first three years after a fire.

As though made bold by that success, young trees begin to prepare for the next fire. In fact, they kindle it. Having protected their own stems by growing corky insulation, they lay kindling in the form of a thick layer of dropped needles. That kindling will do away with the competition. When the second fire comes, it is so hot that longleaf pines are the only survivors. They have the forest to themselves.

ROASTING THE OLD WAY

Try roasting potatoes, un-husked cobs of corn, or chestnuts in ashes the way cavemen did. You will need a good accumulation of ashes in a fireplace (either indoors or outdoors) and, for your own safety, adult assistance. Build a new fire over the old ashes. When it has burned down to a bed of coals, rake a clearing off to one side and circle it with coals.

Prepare chestnuts by slashing a cross through the skin of the flat side with a small knife. Potatoes don't need any preparation except rinsing; corn should be left unhusked.

Shovel a layer of ashes into the clearing, then add the potatoes, chestnuts, or corn. Cover them and the circle of coals with a heap of ashes. Chestnuts and corn on the cob will be cooked through in as little as 15 minutes. Potatoes take longer, depending on their size, and you may have to heap more coals around the "oven" from time to time.

Rake your meal from the ashes, and let it cool until you can handle the food without burning yourself. Brush the ashes off the potatoes, shuck the corn, peel the chestnuts, and eat.

fuel the flames. When fire occurs more frequently, flames race quickly through smaller accumulations of debris, and temperatures

don't rise to such ferocious heights. Many large trees survive, and grass roots are unharmed. Throughout the history of forests and grass-

lands, these smaller fires have burned them so regularly that some species of trees and grasses depend on being burned. Many species of pine have cones that don't open to release their seeds until they are heated in the oven of a forest fire. The American prairie is at its best, with the most species of grasses and the fewest shrubs and trees, if it catches fire about every eight years.

New life begins almost right away. The ground is bathed in sunlight where brush was burned away. All the foodstuffs stored in trunks and stalks that were burned are recycled as ash over the soil. Sprouting seeds are brightly lit and roots are super-nourished. The prairie grows lush, the forest floor becomes green with grass and tender seedlings. A generation of browsers and grazers has more to eat after a forest fire than before.

As foresters have come to understand the role of small, renewing fires—and the danger of large, destructive ones in places where fire has been prevented for too long—they have begun to set controlled fires in our national forests on a regular schedule. They are by no means the first people to torch the woods on purpose.

American Indians set their own forest fires to make the land easier to travel and game easier to see. Controlled burning of grasslands goes all the way back to *Homo erectus,* who set grass fires to herd game into a trap.

An Elephant Hunt

A site in Spain from 400,000 years ago shows that *Homo erectus* hunters waited in valleys for migrating herds to pass through on their way south for the winter. When a herd of big game was in the right spot, the hunters set grass fires to drive the animals toward swamps, where they became mired in muck and were most easily killed. Hunters even trapped elephants this way. The animal bones show that meat was cut from the carcass on the spot, and bones were cracked open for marrow. One elephant's fossil is only half an elephant. The other half was carried home.

The people of the cave in Beijing, China, enjoyed venison and hackberries. They left about 3,000 deer bones and innumerable hackberry seeds strewn about their cave, where both meat and berries were roasted.

Tools used for hunting and preparing meals improved as *Homo erectus* grew smarter. The oldest tools in the cave are the same sort of crude choppers *Homo habilis* could make by flaking a sharp edge from a water-rounded pebble. But then came the new inventions: spear points for attaching to a wooden handle, scrapers for cleaning hides. The earliest of these new shapes are large, clumsy things

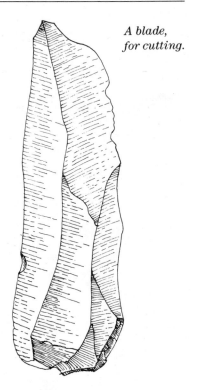

A blade, for cutting.

Complicated stone tools like these were made by pressing, not banging, to remove small flakes.

made from soft sandstone. By the end of their stay, these cavemen were making almost none of their tools out of easily worked stone. They flaked them from hard quartz and tough flint. And they didn't just bang away at the stone to form the edges. They applied steady pressure, removing tiny flakes to make tools that are small, keen edged, and precisely shaped for specific kinds of work.

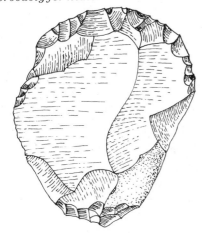

A scraper, probably for hides.

A borer, for making holes.

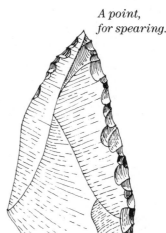

A point, for spearing.

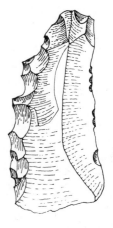

A serrated blade.

A QUESTION

Maybe they chatted as they worked. Judging by what such people must have had to communicate, they couldn't have done it in grunts. Where is the elephant herd now? Which way is the wind blowing? Who is setting the fire? Did anyone remember to bring the torch? The complicated techniques of tool-making couldn't be reinvented from scratch every generation. People must have told people what to do and how to do it, if not in words then at least in sounds and gestures more meaningful than those of apes.

All of the languages humans speak now have certain things in common. For instance, it's not proper in any language to say "I'm loving you." The same rule holds in sign languages invented by the deaf, which are not learned from any spoken language. There is the same rule in all of the creole languages—languages invented solely by the children of immigrants to places where many languages are used, and none is dominant. Creole speakers use the vocabulary of whatever languages are available, but they use the grammar of none. Curiously, creoles are the only languages in the world that allow a double negative as in "I don't want no spinach." More curious still, three-year-olds who have never heard any creole, invent that "error" in grammar in whatever happens to be their native tongue. In fact, there appears to be a Basic Child Grammar that accounts for many of the errors toddlers make as they attempt to learn language from adults, and it is the same grammar that rules all 27 creole languages, all of which were invented by children. The most basic patterns of early human languages may be written in our brains, traces of the actual evolution of language perhaps half a million years ago. Everyone in the whole world lifts their voice to ask a question.

CHINS BEGIN

Over the thousands of years of occupation, the Beijing cave gradually crumbled. Chunks of limestone

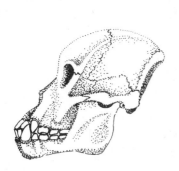

An early ape, perhaps similar to our ancestor.

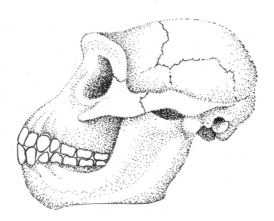

Australopithecus afarensis, *an early australopithecine.*

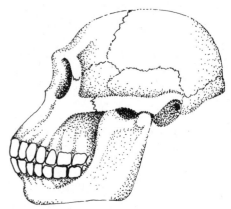

Australopithecus africanus, *a later australopithecine.*

ceiling fell, whole sections collapsed. By about a quarter of a million years ago, there was no longer enough living space, and the final group abandoned the cave. Human remains elsewhere by that time can no longer be called merely upright (*erectus*), but wise (*sapiens*).

Our present human species, *Homo sapiens,* has a different face from that of the cave dwellers of Beijing. *Homo erectus* had large teeth, and his jaw therefore jutted out like a short muzzle, with no chin. Our teeth are smaller and require less jawbone to hold them. As the tooth-holding portion of the jaw grew smaller, the bottom arch stayed about as it had been, leaving the bulge of our chin.

Homo erectus had bony ridges over his eye sockets. The whole skull was rather long from front to rear and rather flat on top. There wasn't much of a forehead. Modern human skulls are round, and there are usually no brow ridges (the Ainu people of Japan and the aborigines of Australia do have brow ridges). All modern humans have foreheads.

Skulls found in Europe that date back to about the time the Beijing cave was abandoned are somewhere between these two extremes. The eyebrows are heavy, but the teeth are small and the face begins with a low forehead and ends in a small chin. Dressed in modern clothes these people might pass unnoticed in a crowd. Intellectually, they had earned the name *sapiens*. Their brain was double the volume of *Homo habilis*'s brain, and fell well within the modern range of 1,000 to 2,000 cubic centimeters (61 to 122 cubic inches). They were beginning to think about themselves in new ways. For the first time, their bones are found in cemeteries. They buried their dead with flowers.

These people are named *Homo sapiens* with the added subspecies name *neanderthalensis* (after the Neander valley in Germany, where their remains were first found) to

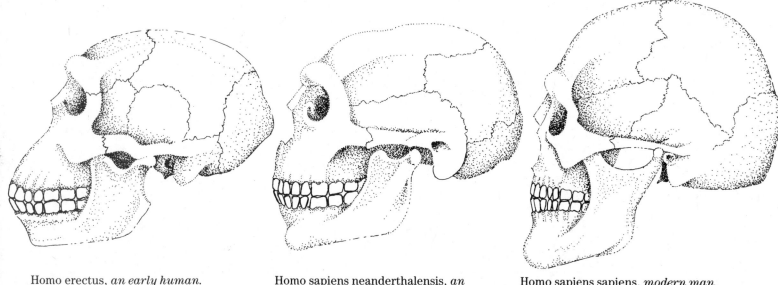

Homo erectus, *an early human.*

Homo sapiens neanderthalensis, *an advanced human.*

Homo sapiens sapiens, *modern man.*

indicate that they were different from the present species. Neanderthal man's homes, workplaces, and burial grounds have since been found all over Europe, in the Middle East, and beyond the Caspian Sea in Asia. The oldest fossils are perhaps from 300,000 years ago, making them contemporaries of *Homo erectus,* from one group of which they had descended.

Homo erectus became extinct about 200,000 years ago. Neanderthal lived for a quarter of a million years, replaced in turn by *Homo sapiens sapiens,* the subspecies that includes every human in the world today. *Homo sapiens sapiens* appears in the fossil record 50,000 years ago, in the Middle East and in Europe. Neanderthal man lingered on in some places as next-door neighbor to modern man for another 10,000 years, or until 40,000 years ago, when the heavy-browed subspecies either became extinct or was absorbed into the newer population by intermarriage. The head of even the earliest *Homo sapiens sapiens* is exactly like ours: high forehead, domed skull, flat face, small teeth, and full chin. There is no difference in brain size between these "cave men" and us.

WEATHER REPORT

During all this time, from when chinless people moved into the Beijing cave to when modern man thrust his jaw into human affairs, the weather remained cold. The dates of the earliest glacial comings and goings aren't known exactly, but the worst part of the Great Ice Age, including three huge ice advances, began 70,000 years ago and lasted until about 10,000 years ago. Neanderthal man lived through the first of these advances, all 30,000 years of it. Our present subspecies lived through the very worst of the Ice Age in Europe about 25,000 years ago, and entered the North American continent when it, too, was locked in glaciers about 20,000 years ago.

At the height of the Ice Age in

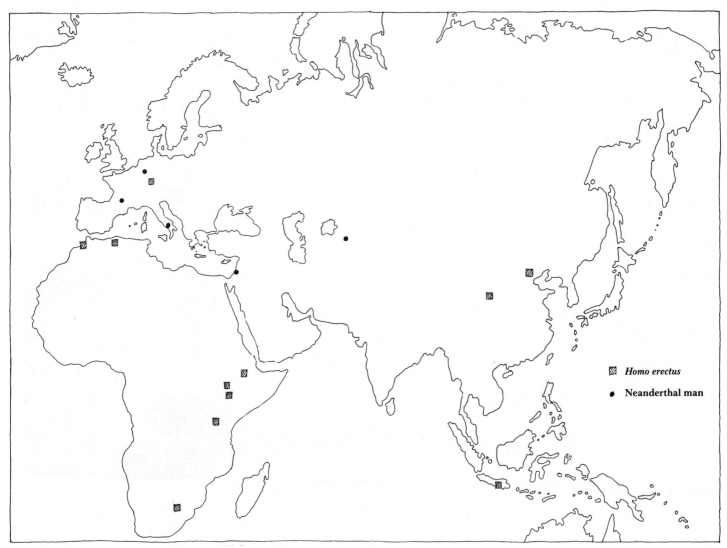

Places where the fossils of early man have been found

North America, glaciers had crept beyond the Canadian border in the West, covered New England and the Atlantic Coast to just below New York City in the East, and reached as far south as Kansas in the middle.

In Europe, most of England and Ireland and all of Scandinavia and the European portion of Russia were buried in ice. Cold air flowing off glaciers caused heavy precipitation—blizzards in winter, rainstorms in summer—wherever it hit humid southern air. The presently

THEN WHY DO WE LOOK DIFFERENT?

Woolly hair insulates the brain from overheating in hot climates. Dark skin protects against damage from the sun's ultraviolet rays. Light skin absorbs more light needed to produce vitamin D where sunlight is scarce. A stocky build and a layer of fat insulate against heat loss in cold climates. Tallness and skinniness aid the shedding of heat in hot climates. Narrowed lids shade the eyes from glare in snow and desert. Different nose and nostril shapes are good for different things: warming cold air, keeping out dust. All these shapes, sizes, colors, and textures evolved as workable answers to local conditions. That's why we are the only large mammal that has been able to live everywhere.

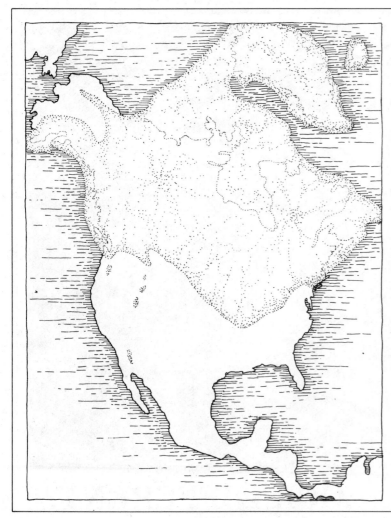

The greatest extent
of the ice in
North America.

The greatest extent of the ice in Europe.

dry Mediterranean shores were then leafy woodlands, and just to the north grew evergreens. Eastward across Asia, where the climate was drier, stretched vast grassy plains called steppes. Forests grew in the Sahara Desert.

Everywhere else, from the middle of Spain all the way to the northern ice caps, there was nothing but tundra: treeless, covered in lichen, moss, and stunted shrubs, permanently frozen only a few feet below the surface even in summer. There

is no tundra south of the Arctic today.

HUNTING SEASON

The land bridge between Alaska and Siberia had been flooded over for several million years. Then, by

COME DASHER! COME PRANCER!

Reindeer—caribou to us—migrate across the tundra far in the north, where the climate is similar to much of Ice Age Europe. A herd may number 200,000 animals. To picture steppe and tundra in the Ice Age, imagine similar herds of mammoths, bison, aurochs (wild cattle), and horses, all moving across the land in vast groups following routes that were the same from year to year. Stone Age peoples may have hunted them as Eskimos hunt caribou now, by intercepting the herd in the same place, at the same time, each year. Or, like Siberian tribal peoples, they may have followed a herd throughout its annual circuit. So picture people, too, on the move. Travel is not the invention of modern technology; it dates back to the Stone Age.

SKINNING AND DRYING AN ANIMAL SKIN

Drying is one way to preserve animal skins. These instructions are for preserving the body hide only, as freeing the whole skin is difficult. After drying, the hide will be stiff not soft like leather, but the fur will feel natural. (Before beginning, read again the warning about handling dead animals on page 270.) This is not an easy project and adult supervision should be requested if you've never worked with animals before.

You need:
Sharp, pointed scissors
An animal that has recently died (for example, a raccoon or opossum)
Sharp-bladed knife, such as a hobbyist's knife or scalpel
Heavy shears
Pocket knife
Large wooden spoon
1 gallon water
1 pound coarse (kosher) salt
Bucket
Plastic food-storage bag
Newspapers
Paper towels
Work gloves

1. With the sharp, pointed scissors, make a slit in the belly skin of the animal from tail to chin. Don't cut deeper than the skin. (The contents of the belly might smell very bad.) Pull the skin away to either side of the slit with your hands. Use the sharp-bladed knife to lightly cut through the web of connective tissue where it holds the skin to the muscle beneath. Aim the knife at the muscle so that you don't knick the skin by mistake. Continue pulling and cutting until the skin is completely free from the body all the way around. The hide is now connected only at the head, the tail, and all four legs. Cut free the body skin with the shears.

2. Clean the inside of the skin as best you can by scraping away fat and shreds of muscle and connective tissue with the pocket knife. Pull the shreds free with your fingers.

3. Use a large wooden spoon to mix the one gallon of water with the coarse salt in the bucket. Soak the skin for six hours. Wring the skin out and sprinkle it heavily with more salt. Fold it in from the edges so that all the salt is inside. Roll the skin up, fur side out, put it in the plastic bag, and leave the bundle overnight.

4. The next day, scrape the skin again with a pocket knife. Put out newspapers to work on, and keep paper towels handy. Wear gloves to avoid blisters. Lay the hide on the newspapers skin side up and sideways to you. Hold tight to the far side with one hand; with the other hand, scrape in short, hard strokes toward you. As you scrape, greasy crud will accumulate on your knife blade. Wipe that off with a paper towel. The skin where you are scraping will begin to turn white under your blade. When no more crud comes up and the skin is quite white, move on to the next spot. It may take an hour to scrape the skin of an animal the size of a raccoon.

5. The skin is now ready for drying. Stretch the skin flat in the shade to dry it. It will dry flattest if it is stretched and tacked at the edges to a wall or board. Beware of dogs: They will steal the skin and chew it up.

A raccoon skin, stretched and tacked down to dry.

about 20,000 years ago, as more and more water from the ocean froze into glaciers, sea level fell revealing the bridge. The Bering bridge between Alaska and Siberia reopened, allowing mammals to move back and forth again between the continents until 13,000 years ago, when meltwaters refilled the ocean basins and covered the connecting link with a 90-kilometer (59-mile) stretch of sea. Northern Alaska and Siberia were themselves never covered with ice.

As barren as tundra looks, it supports large herds of animals. In herds that may number 200,000 individuals, caribous (called reindeer in Europe) browse on lichen, moss, grass, berries, mushrooms, and just about anything else they can find. Their total number before the twentieth century was close to four million animals, all living far in the north in what is still an Ice Age climate. Dry steppes are full of life, too. Endless grass supports mammals such as horses, bison, muskoxen, cattle, and camels. Moist Mediterranean woodlands were home to deer, bears, and pigs, and so were the strips of evergreen forest that verged on the tundra and served as a winter home for tundra herds.

All of this was when glaciers were at their peak. During retreats, grass raced over the tundra way in advance of trees, covering the land in pasture. The only place in the world today that has as much meat on the hoof as there was in those days is the African plains.

The Great Ice Age was therefore the best of times as well as the worst of times. Or, to put it another way, it was the best of times for change because it was the worst of times for staying the same.

SOCIAL LIFE IN THE STONE AGE

Cave dwellings have become famous because human remains are well preserved there, but there are villages preserved in bogs or covered by dust during windstorms that tell more about how social life was changing in the Ice Age.

In the Ukraine groups of houses were built of mammoth bones by people who lived there between 18,000 and 14,000 years ago, when winter temperatures dipped to 5°C (41°F). Each house was beautifully designed with arching tusks, jawbones stacked in a herringbone pattern, and an entrance lined with leg bones or guarded by a pair of skulls. Some of the houses would have taken 10 men nearly a week to build. Some of the bones are decorated with carved or painted pictures. These people traded with other groups as far away as 800

TANNING AN ANIMAL SKIN

Tanning is a chemical process that shrinks an animal skin, which makes it thicker and tougher. Opossums and raccoons have thick hides that are easy to work with. Rabbits are nearly impossible for a beginner because their thin skins tear easily even when tanned. If you haven't worked with animal skins, ask assistance from an adult who has.

You need:
Large wooden spoon
Bucket
1 gallon water
½ pound coarse (kosher) salt
2½ ounces alum (potassium aluminum sulfate) or 4 ounces of tannic acid (both available from your druggist)
1 scraped animal hide (see page 346)
Strong detergent or ammonia
Broomstick or broom
Hand-held single-bladed food chopper
Vise
Coarse sandpaper
Neats-foot oil
Cornmeal

1. Prepare the tanning solution. Use a large wooden spoon to mix in a bucket the one gallon of water with the coarse salt and either the alum or the tannic acid. Tannin darkens the leather; alum leaves it white. Submerge the scraped hide in the solution for two days, stirring it a couple of times a day.

After 48 hours, lift the hide out of the solution with the wooden spoon and rinse it well in the bathtub until there is no salt left. Wash the skin several times in strong detergent or ammonia to remove oil and dirt. Rinse well.

2. Dry the skin slowly in the shade by hanging it, fur side out, over the top of a propped-up broomstick for two days, then turn it skin side out for two days more.

The dried, tanned skin will be stiff and hard. To give it the softness of leather requires more scraping and stretching. Dampen the skin slightly by sprinkling it with water, and roll it up like a piece of clothing that is to be ironed. Leave it rolled up for an hour so the moisture spreads evenly. The moisture will soften the skin enough that you can work with it, but it has to dry while you're stretching it. If it is too moist, you'll wear out before it dries.

3. Clamp the food chopper into the vise, blade up. Hold the damp skin taut between your hands, and carefully scrape it back and forth over the edge of the blade. As you scrape, the hide will stretch, soften, turn lighter in color, and develop a shredded look on its surface. Keep stretching and scraping the skin over the blade until the whole hide is dry and supple. When you are finished, the hide will be leather.

4. For a nice finish, sand the skin with coarse sandpaper. A skin that feels too dry and hard may need additional oil. Rub it well with an oil intended for leather, such as neats-foot oil, then trample it underfoot to work the oil in. Remove any excess oil by working cornmeal into both sides of the skin, leaving it for a day, then brushing it out.

A tanned skin in the final stages of drying.

kilometers (496 miles) to get shells and amber for necklaces. They sewed clothes with needles that had eyes. While some built, carved, painted, sewed, and traded, others hunted. There were as many as 50 people to support in such communities.

About 13,000 years ago in Chile a community of at least 60 people built a neat town of wooden row-houses lining both shores of a stream. Each home, built of poles hammered into the ground and covered with hide, had its own small hearth, and had food-processing equipment such as mortars and grindstones. Meals were cooked communally at two large outdoor hearths, and were reheated in each family's home. Toilet pits were dug for the whole community's use—two for the village, not one per household. A large workshop was set apart from the residential area. There tools were manufactured, mastodons and other large animals were butchered, and, judging from the remains of medicinal herbs, medicine was practiced. Some of the tools required so practiced a hand that only expert craftsmen could have made them.

Until recently, no one guessed that people so long ago lived in such large groups and in so complicated a way, in homes and workshops, with domestic chores and industrial ones, with individual jobs and communal ones, with ordinary skills, and with special talents. But when you stop to think how you might cope with an outdoor winter in the Ukraine, or a many-generations-long journey over the Bering land bridge and all the way down to Chile, surely you'd be dumb to do it alone.

SELVES AND OTHERS

One result of having an intelligence shaped by complicated social lives is our ability to see ourselves as others see us. The trick is something like climbing out of your own skin and looking at yourself from the outside. That's what a child becomes able to do when he or she begins to understand that *you* are *me* to yourself, and *me* is *you* to others. Seeing one's self as though from outside the self means seeing a lot of different selves. A person can look at himself through one person's eyes and see a charmer, and through another's and see a brat. It all depends on one's perspective.

Also, we can step outside ourselves and look at ourselves as though we were an object. In fact, we spend lots of thought on self-examination. As far as we know, no other animal has this "movable mind" of ours, and therefore no other animal can examine itself.

GOLDENROD DYE

Coloring yarn with natural dyes is like magic: You brew green bayberry leaves, the yarn dyes bright yellow; you cook up brown lichen, the yarn turns rosy. These mysterious results are due to the fact that each of these plants contains quite a few pigments whose colors aren't visible until one wonderful one is captured by a chemical in which the yarn has been soaked.

The chemical is called a mordant. Depending on which one is used, the same dye may color something green or gray or brown. Without a mordant, pigment molecules don't "stick," and the yarn isn't dyed at all.

In these general instructions an easy mordant—alum—is used. Goldenrod is only an example of the plants you can try. Experiment with lichens, alder and privet twigs, birch bark, bracken ferns, onion skins, bloodroot roots, sumac berries, and marigold, dahlia, coreopsis, queen-of-the-meadow, and bedstraw blossoms. An adult should supervise the heating of yarn in mordant or dye.

Mordant the Yarn

You need:
1 pound natural, undyed wool yarn
Cotton string
Soap flakes
Old bath or kitchen towels
Long wooden spoon
3 ounces alum (potassium aluminum sulfate, available from your druggist)
1 ounce cream of tartar
Kitchen scale
4 gallons water
5-gallon stainless steel or enamel pot
Wire hanger

1. Open out the skein of yarn and tie it with cotton string (as shown) in three places to prevent tangling.

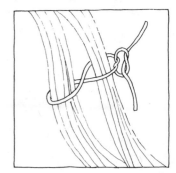

2. Fill the kitchen sink with cool, soapy water made from soap flakes, not detergent. Natural yarns are naturally oily. Wash the oil from the yarn by squeezing the soapy water gently

through it, then rinse it well and pat the water out between towels.

3. Measure out the alum and cream of tartar on a kitchen scale. Use the wooden spoon to stir the alum and cream of tartar in four gallons of water in the pot. Heat over a low flame until the mordanting bath is just warm and the chemicals are dissolved. Put the damp wool in the pot, stirring gently to spread it. Let the pot continue to heat slowly over low heat for the next hour, or until it is close to boiling. Then turn the heat down even more so the water doesn't boil, and simmer the yarn for another hour. Carefully carry the pot to the sink. Cool the wool slowly by running cool water into the pot (you might think heating wool to nearly boiling would shrink it, but the yarn will be fine so long as all temperature changes are gradual).

4. Lift the yarn from the cooled water and pat the extra moisture from it again. Hang it up to dry on the wire hanger over the kitchen sink or in the shower.

Making the Dye

You need:
2 quarts goldenrod blossoms
5-gallon stainless steel or enamel pot
1 gallon water
Colander
Large mixing bowl
4-ounces mordanted natural wool yarn

Kitchen scale
Long wooden spoon
Large kettle
Wire hanger

1. Place the goldenrod blossoms in the pot, add the gallon of water, and bring to a boil over medium heat. Turn the heat down and simmer for half an hour.

2. In the kitchen sink, put the colander in the mixing bowl. Carefully pour the contents of the pot through it to strain out the plant material. Discard the simmered plants, rinse the pot, and pour the dye from the bowl back into the pot. Let the dye cool to lukewarm.

3. Measure out four ounces of wool on the kitchen scale. Moisten the wool if it has dried completely, and then submerge it in the dye. Dye the wool in the same way you mordanted it, heating it gradually to nearly boiling, then simmering it for half an hour as you occasionally stir it back and forth with the wooden spoon. Meanwhile, boil more water in a kettle.

4. Pour off the dye water and rinse the wool in the boiled water. Then pour that off and rinse the wool again in hot tap water. Rinse several more times, each time with cooler water, until the yarn is cool. Lift it out of the rinse water and hang it up to drip-dry from a wire hanger over the kitchen sink or in the shower.

Evolution is a lens through which to see ourselves in revealing ways. We have been hunter-gatherers for 99 percent of human history. Our biological evolution is rooted in that niche. What we are like now was shaped by what things were like when our species got together to hunt elephants and gather hazelnuts in the face of the Great Ice Age.

THE ARITHMETIC OF GENEROSITY

Our most precious heritage is unselfishness—putting the good of others ahead of our own good. Generosity that costs more than its reproductive reward, however, can't evolve. Look at the arithmetic. An individual who sacrifices himself for the good of others doesn't live to pass that trait along. If there were genes for self-sacrifice they would die with the martyr. Nevertheless, self-sacrifice for the sake of others is the foundation of human morality.

The fact is that generosity costs less than its reproductive reward in the hunting society in which humans evolved. Stone Age bands evolved as family units. The more closely related two individuals are to one another, the more genes they have in common, and the more likely they are to resemble one an-

KINSHIP SNAPSHOTS

If you've ever been to a family reunion, you know that a lot of relatives spend a lot of time trying to figure out in what way they're related. The exercise jogs memories, and kinship is sorted out. Yet by the next family get-together, everything has become muddled again.

You could do your family a big favor by starting a kinship album. This photographic who's who can begin at home—the first page would be for you. Then you might put in a page for your brothers and sisters. The third page is for your parents. The fourth is devoted to the brothers and sisters of one parent, and the next to the broth-ers and sisters of the other parent. Your parent's brothers and sisters are, of course, your aunts and uncles. The photos could be of them as children, or they could be more recent ones. That doesn't matter, so long as each is identified.

Now complete these two genera-tions, your own and your parents'. Send an album page to each of those aunts and uncles. Ask them to paste in wedding pictures to record marriages—their spouses are another set of aunts and uncles, but not blood relatives—and snapshots of their chil-dren, your cousins. It would be nice if they could write in their own hand-writing the dates of marriage, birth, and death, and where these events happened.

By now your album may be many pages thick, yet your grandparents aren't in it yet. Each pair of grandpar-ents should have a page. Grandmoth-ers' names should include their maiden names, which would help you to add your great-grandparents, too.

That's a real challenge. You have eight great-grandparents. Some grandparents may no longer be alive to recall for you who your great-grandparents were, or to locate pho-tographs of them. Even if all four grandparents are alive, not all may recall their mother's maiden name, or the whens and wheres of birth, mar-riage, or death. Do the best you can.

Now think, if you could interest cousins in doing the same, what the albums would show all together. No two would be the same. Cousins share with you only half their grandparents and great-grandparents, for the other half are related to the person your aunt or uncle married. Some of their aunts and uncles are no kin of yours, and some of their cousins are not your cousins. Further, every album is a stingy one, for it doesn't include parents' aunts, uncles, and cousins. The total number of people in four generations of a family may be stag-gering. No wonder, when your life depended on your kin, knowing who was who not only jogged the memory, but sharpened the mind.

other in looks and personality. A mother shares half her genes with her child; so does the child's father. Brothers and sisters are somewhat less closely related to one another, since each receives a different mix of genes from each parent. But even cousins have an eighth of their genes in common, and although each more-distant relative shares fewer genes, they still share them. Therefore, whatever combination of traits may lead to self-sacrifice, that combination is more apt to outlive the martyr if his martyrdom benefits his close kin. On the other hand, risking life and limb for strangers is taking a genetic chance.

Humans are more likely to put themselves out for family than for anyone else, are less likely to help strangers, and are least likely to help those who look the most alien—the least related—to themselves. Yet generosity between strangers can evolve if both believe that one good turn deserves another. If an individual risks his own fitness to help out a nonrelative, but the favor is returned, the generous traits of both those individuals might find their way into more offspring than would the selfish traits of people who refuse to help one another. But there are several catches.

First, you must be able to recognize the person who owes you a favor in order to call on him in time of need. Second, the person must be available when, in the future, you need the favor returned. And third, you must believe that the person really will return the favor: You must trust him or her.

SMALL-TOWN VIRTUES

Humans originally lived in smallish groups. Certainly they could recognize one another: Humans are notable among mammals for their distinctively individual faces, and we also have the ability to never forget a face. Members of a small group were certainly likely to be available in the future, as they are in a rural village now. People in a small town, where everyone recognizes everyone else, and where those who grew up together remain friends for life, are much more likely to obey the golden rule than are people who live in big cities, where few people are familiar and friends come and go.

The biggest catch is trust. How do you know that a person you help will help you? We have evolved ways to test, and ways to demonstrate reliability. A steady gaze means honesty; shifty eyes make us suspicious. We judge people by the firmness of their handshake, the readiness of their smile, the sincerity of their voices and faces. Acquaintances become friends only after an exchange of not-very-important favors and confidences. We don't trust liars.

ENTER THE CHEATER

Societies that live by trust are vulnerable to cheaters. Someone who can pretend to be sincere, cadge favors, and then refuse to return them benefits himself and his selfish offspring for free.

But cheaters can never get the upper hand. As their numbers increase, too many of those they try to cheat are cheaters themselves. Having to get along with some cheaters in a society also favors those individuals who are good at recognizing them and who therefore avoid getting cheated. Of course, that in turn favors cheaters who are particularly clever at disguising themselves, like charming con artists.

Moral standards help us to penetrate those disguises. They are our standardized tests, and they are easier to score than smiles and handshakes. Moral standards in the form of laws, customs, and beliefs are the core of every human culture. Although each society has a somewhat different version of how a person should behave, all cultures are in keeping with our evolution.

There's been an argument around for a long time over whether we should blame what we are on our nature or on our cul-

Baby faces ask for cuddling, whether they belong to dolls or pigs.

ture. The answer is that our culture is how we express our nature. If biology whispers what we are, culture shouts it out. Every culture, for instance, elevates the old mating bond to the ceremony of marriage, not only honors leaders, but spells out how they are to be chosen, and doesn't just vaguely acknowledge that people should be generous to one another, but regulates rights and responsibilities.

But can culture get rid of cheaters? Probably not. Morals are gotten around by hypocrites, who say good things but do bad ones, and criminals, who do as they please. There are always bad guys, but most people are good.

THE CABBAGE PATCH CRAZE

People are downright foolish toward babies. That, too, goes back a ways. The rigors of the Great Ice Age favored more intelligent individuals, so babies began to be born with bigger and bigger heads. Up to a point, women's hip bones could evolve to allow the baby to be born. Modern human females have much broader hips than *Homo habilis* had. But broad hips interfere with a woman's ability to walk and run. Too great a width would have been crippling and couldn't evolve. Therefore, evolution was left to babies. Those infants who were born immature, before their heads had grown very large, were favored.

A newborn baby's head is only half the size it will be by the end of childhood. Its brain is so immature that it is smooth, not crinkled as it will become. Many of the brain's nerve cells aren't even connected yet at birth. Not only the brain but

A Brain Game

It's interesting to catch your brain acting on its hard-wired information. There is probably no one who has not filled in the letter O with two eyes and a mouth. An oval shape says "face" to the brain, and we can't help completing it. But why no nose? Babies will offer their first smiles to an oval piece of cardboard with two dots for eyes, a line for the mouth. They are born with that noseless scheme of the human face; they don't smile at other patterns. No one knows why.

Young children often draw "face-houses" with two windows for the eyes above a door for the mouth. Cartoonists draw cars with headlight eyes and radiator mouth. Try drawing a dog's face from the front, then a cat's, an owl's, a monkey's. An animal whose eyes are placed to the sides, like those of a dog, is very hard to draw from the front. We naturally draw it in profile. But, the opposite is true of animals whose eyes are placed to the front of its face, as ours are. Who would think of drawing an owl from the side or an eagle from the front? Our brains so clearly instruct us to gaze into the face of anything that looks human that we hardly know what an owl looks like in profile.

Mental patterns that you are born with determine emotional responses even to inanimate objects. You might, for example, notice a house that strikes you as charming. Probably it is small, chunky, and its windows oversized in comparison to its bulk. It is, your brain insists, a baby house, and therefore automatically charming. Why are the Volkswagen "bug" and the Model T Ford cute cars? Look at their proportions; they are babies, too. Sports cars, on the other hand, are built along the lines of swooping or pouncing predators, and that's the way we see them. Just try to see a Jaguar as cute!

the baby's whole body is immature. "Behind" at birth, our infants are remarkably slow to develop, even slower than would be expected if it were only a question of catching up on the extra weeks a smaller-skulled baby might have been able to stay in the womb. A baby isn't able to walk for a year, which is months later than an ape. A chimp can, if it must, take care of itself from the age of six years. Children can barely get themselves ready for school in the morning at that age.

Because our babies are so helpless for so long, parents who had the most powerful urge to care for them were also favored. The result is that our brains are prewired to want to cuddle and care for anything that looks babyish. What looks babyish to us is a chubby, short-legged creature with an oversize head, round face, and large eyes set wide apart. That describes baby dolls and newborn pigs and pups. They are cute and adorable, and we are crazy about them. Babyishness is probably what made humans take wolf babies into the family 20,000 years ago and turn them into pet dogs.

Big Babies

The story of how the wolf became a domesticated dog ought to be noble, a tale of hunting companions and guardians of the home. But that may not be the way the story goes. The bones of the earliest domesticated dogs resemble those of the present-day wild dog, or dingo, which lives only in Australia. Dingoes, like the first dogs, represent a stage at which domestication had begun, but had not been finished. Dingoes live in and around human settlements, where families often

LOVE A HOG

Frank Perdue claims chickens need tender loving care. He is quite right. Chickens grow to roasting weight faster and have better resistance to disease if people talk to them and handle them. Pigs are the same. Not only do pigs who get tender attention from people grow faster, but beloved sows produce more babies. The lesson of domestication is painful but true: Want a drumstick, love a hen; want a pork chop, love a hog.

raise them as pups. But no one feeds them once they have grown up (except for whatever they can scavenge from refuse heaps), and although they hunt by themselves, no one uses them for hunting. The only useful purpose dingoes serve is to cuddle up with their family to warm them through chilly nights. They are teddy bears, and pets.

Although dingoes have longer muzzles and more wolfish teeth than, say, a labrador retriever, they look more babyish than wolves. Their legs are shorter, their snouts are blunter, their heads are rounder, and their fur is fuzzier. They come in colors: tawny, rust, brown, black, and white. Often they have white paws and a white-tipped tail.

These traits are always signs of domestication, for they are rare in the wild. One has to assume that Stone Age man chose as pets those animals that looked different from the wild type, that had unusual colors or markings, or droopy ears, a curly tail, and softer fur. It would be natural to encourage the dogs they liked the best to stay around, and to chase away or kill the dogs they liked the least. Tossing bones at those they liked and throwing stones at those they didn't, these first domesticators selected for certain traits more efficiently than selection happens in the wild. Wolves were turned into domesticated dogs in no more than a few thousand years.

WELCOME TO THE FAMILY

The domesticated sheep, cattle, pigs, and horses that followed dogs into the human family went through the same transformation. They grew fuzzier. Wild sheep have long, coarse hair, not fleece. The wild horse has a bristling mane, but the mane of the domesticated horse falls softly over neck and shoulders and grows in a fetching tuft over the forehead. Everything that sticks out from an animal grew blunter, or curled. Snouts shortened, legs got stumpier, ears rounded or flopped. Wild goats have long horns shaped like scimitars; domestic goats have spiralled horns or short ones or none at all. Barnyard pigs have no tusks. People favored unwild colors and markings: black and white Jersey cows, gray and white dappled ponies, spotted pigs, black goats, white stallions.

Every domestic animal is plumper than its forebears. Wild animals lay on stores of fat in and around internal organs, such as the kidneys or liver. Domestic animals are plump on the outside. Prime steak is marbled with fat all through the muscle. Pigs are bacon beneath the skin. They are all big babies.

END OF THE ICE AGE

It was only between 15,000 and 8,000 years ago when glaciers began retreating toward the high latitudes and high altitudes where they are

DON'T RUN TOO SOON

If you saw a lion strolling along and it was a football field away from you, you'd probably keep your eye on it, but you probably wouldn't turn and run. On the other hand, if you saw a lion strolling through your backyard, you'd get out of there fast. Other animals are just as smart. They run from predators when they have to, but don't run until they have to. The distance between predator and prey at which the prey makes its getaway is called the prey's flight distance.

Now here's the wonderful point: For most of human history, we hunted with short-range weapons like spears, bolos (a thong with a rock tied to it), and bows and arrows. Flight distances must have been quite short—short enough for us almost to wander among the herds we hunted. Think of deer continuing to graze as you walk through the meadow, of bison barely skirting your camp, of caribou merely sniffing and gazing in your direction, and then going about their business. Primitive peoples must have known their prey as intimately as you know your dog. Then came guns.

Today, the flight distances of prey animals are so long that we barely get a glimpse before they're gone. That's sad, but not permanent. Where shooting isn't allowed, deer are positively bold. Their flight distance is no more than the few feet between the front hedge and the front door, and the only way to be rid of them is to plant shrubs they hate to eat.

Dingo

today. The weather warmed, reached its warmest between 7,000 and 5,000 years ago, then teetered back and forth for the next few thousand years. Climate cooled steadily again from A.D. 1500 to 1880, then warmed up until 1950. Now glaciers are advancing in many mountain areas. Will they creep on? Are we still in the Great Ice Age?

The difference in average temperature between Earth's usual

balmy climate and its rare Ice Age climate is only 10°C (18°F). Our present interglacial climate is smack in the middle, five degrees colder than what dinosaurs were used to and five degrees warmer than what cavemen endured.

Temperature is controlled by how much of the sun's heat is held onto and how much escapes back into space. Forests absorb as much as 95 percent of the heat that arrives here in sunlight, and water holds onto even more. Grasslands and deserts are more "shiny"; they reflect back into space, and therefore lose, as much as a third of the heat that hits them. Snow, ice, and clouds fail to capture from one-half to more than three-quarters of the sun's Earth-bound warmth.

One possible trigger for the beginning of the Great Ice Age was the raising up and drying out of continents, which created more "shiny" land than "dull" forests and seas. The world's newest mountain ranges—the Rockies, Andes, Alps, and Himalayas—had formed not long before. Continents embroiled in mountain making were lifted higher as the crust below them heated and expanded. Volcanoes formed along hot seams, where crust was rifting apart or knitting together.

THE SNOW LINE

The climate at a certain latitude is something like the climate at a certain altitude. In ordinary times, snow accumulates over America down to a certain latitude, just as it accumulates over mountain ranges down to a certain altitude, even if the mountains are in warm places like Arizona.

Come summer, only snow high up near the Poles or high up on mountains remains frozen. The place where a climber would first encounter snow in summer is the snow line.

As an ice age begins, the snow line lowers. A climber would then come upon snow in the higher valleys that had once been upland meadows in the summer. A northward-bound traveler would come upon ice fields that had once been tundra in the summer.

Finally, as glaciers become miles thick, they flow over lower latitudes and lower altitudes, where there may have been no snow in winter. The snow line is by then beside the point. The ice was made far away, not on the spot, and flows below the snow line on its own steam, regardless of the steamy climate.

There were stupendous eruptions, more violent than any known in historic times except, perhaps, the explosion of Krakatoa in Indonesia in 1883. That blast was heard 3,000 miles away.

It was just before the Ice Age, in the period between five and two million years ago, that a chain of volcanoes along the edge of the Pacific Plate spewed up the land of Central America. Most of Yellowstone Park is rimmed with the remains of a volcano that exploded 600,000 years ago. It threw up 600 cubic miles of dust and ash that drifted to Earth as far east as the Mississippi Valley, and south to the Gulf of Mexico. The plug blew out of another volcano along the border between California and Nevada 700,000 years ago. Searing clouds of gas traveling at 161 kilometers per hour (100 miles) an hour burnt the land to a crisp, and buried an enormous area under ash. Dust spread north over Wyoming, east through Kansas, and clear across Missouri. A blast as recent as 4,600 years ago belched out 10 cubic miles of the Cascade Mountains, leaving the gaping hole called Crater Lake and burying Indian sandals in its ashes.

The dust from such outbursts made the climate even colder. When Krakatoa exploded, its dust in the atmosphere reflected away as much as 10 percent of the sun's light as far away as Europe, and for three years.

WHY ICE OOZES

During Earth's long balmy periods there is no permanent ice anywhere, not even at the poles. Under its ice, Antarctica is a continent once covered with meadows and forests. Snow falls over mountaintops and near the poles where the air is cold in winter, but most of whatever accumulates melts away during the summer. Some snow does survive from one year to the next, so that each winter more snow falls than melts the following spring. Snow accumulates into a glacier, and gets deeper and deeper each year.

The fresh snow on top of a glacier is the usual stuff snowmen are made of. Underneath, the weight of the pile compresses snow to ice, as happens when you squeeze a snowball hard enough. Deeper still, molecules are squeezed together so hard that they form a kind of ice that oozes slowly, like Silly Putty. Under the weight of a miles-thick heap, the bottom ice flows outward in all directions like a thick liquid, carrying the rest of the glacier on top of it.

A growing, flowing glacier itself cools the climate. It reflects sunlight and cools the winds that blow across its icy surface. Warm climate at its edge doesn't stop the flow. During the Great Ice Age, glaciers flowed down from East African mountains right over jungles that lay on the equator. And in North America, the alligators and tortoises living in Nebraska survived the early days of the Ice Age nearly at the foot of glaciers.

WARMING WITH THE WOBBLES

The more ice there is that covers the land, the colder the temperature grows. The colder it grows, the more it snows. The more it snows, the more ice accumulates. What keeps the situation from getting worse and worse is that the Earth wobbles.

All is not smooth sailing in our planet's ages-old voyage around the sun. Earth tips and wobbles on its axis, and steers a slightly erratic course through the solar system. These eccentric motions give us sometimes more of the sun's heat and sometimes less in super seasons that last about 100,000 years.

Super cool seasons aren't cold enough to start an ice age without a trigger, such as a change in the globe's reflectiveness, but a super warm season is enough to halt an ice age. Each retreat of the glaciers during the Great Ice Age has been at a time when our uneven space trip has given us the maximum amount of sunlight. The last warming was 10,000 years ago; the next cold snap will be in 90,000 years.

Meanwhile, people are doing things that might invite the ice back sooner or melt it away for good. We are burning up the carbon trapped from ancient forests as coal and oil. There are two results. One is that the carbon released into the atmosphere combines with oxygen to form carbon dioxide, transparent to incoming sunlight, opaque to outgoing heat. As heat is trapped in this world-enclosing greenhouse, the temperature will rise and the Great Ice Age will be over. Unless we are making too much dust.

The same fossil fuels we burn form a layer of reflective dust in the atmosphere. More heat is bounced back into space, causing the temperature to drop. At this moment, there are measurable increases in both the carbon dioxide that would warm us, and the dust that would cool us. No one knows which way the temperature will go.

Either way, we're not going to like it. If all the ice melts, every coastal city in the world will be drowned in the rising oceans. If glaciers advance again, the whole population of the world will have to crowd toward the equator.

MELTING BACK

Forests that had retreated far to the south of the glaciers' leading edges crept northward as the glaciers melted. Grasses led the march but were overtaken by trees, and the tundra shrank back toward the Arctic. To the south, where ice-cooled clouds had once dumped their moisture, the woodlands dried and died. The Mediterranean coastlands became baked dry. The Sahara Desert spread in North Africa and deserts grew in the North American Southwest; these deserts are still growing now.

Horses, which had originated in North America, became extinct there. They survived only in the Eastern Hemisphere, which was cut off from the West as the Bering bridge flooded over, and they were not to return until the Spanish ex-

Rhinoceroses were woolly during glacial periods...

plorers brought them back only a few centuries ago. Camels, too, became extinct on this continent; American herds of all kinds became few and smaller. Many of the extraordinary mammals that had ushered in the Great Ice Age perished everywhere. The last of the cave bears died, as did the last of the stabbing cats, woolly rhinos, and Irish elk. There were no more giant bison, beaver, or glyptodonts. The giant ground sloth whose red hair was found in the cave in South America may have been one of the last to survive. Mammoths drowned in bogs and killed in blizzards a mere 8,000 years ago have been found so well preserved in perma-

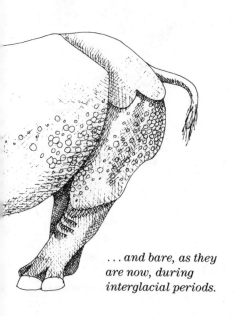

... and bare, as they are now, during interglacial periods.

ONE AFTER ANOTHER AFTER ANOTHER

When plants repopulate a bare patch of soil, whether it was bared by a glacier or by a plow, they march in in a certain order. You can watch this parade yourself.

In early spring, lay bare a patch of soil a couple of yards square. Over the summer, watch what comes up. Among the pioneers will be crabgrass, dandelions, and ragweed—weeds that survive well even in poor soil in exposed, dry places. Quickly, before other plants put down their roots, pioneers grow up and make huge batches of seed. Then they die. While their seed awaits the next opening, longer lived, less prolific grasses move in. Next summer, the bare patch will contain mostly grasses. But not for long.

Say you have a whole disused field to observe (or even a railway or a road). Say that three years have passed. Already, now that the grasses are shading the soil somewhat, wild roses, alder, sumac, juniper, and birch are sprouting up. They tolerate dryness well, and they don't demand much in the way of soil. In 10 more years, the junipers will have grown 10 feet, and hardy oaks will have begun to march in among them.

Check in again in another 30 years, if you can find the meadow for the trees. You are now in an oak woodland. You may find some of the original junipers, but most of them are dead, shaded out by the taller trees to whose seedlings they had given shade. The birches are old. Few new ones are sprouting. Plants that could never have coped with the dry, sterile meadow are thriving in the damp, acidic, oak-leaf mulch of the woodland floor—laurel perhaps, and ferns. Here and there is a sapling-size beech tree, a knee-high hemlock. Wait a century.

On your Rip van Winkle return, the field—road, railroad track—will be a deep forest of beech and hemlock, so dark hardly anything else can grow there. This is called a climax forest. The succession of plants that gradually nurtured the bare patch to maturity, and the climax forest itself, differ from place to place. This example might be in Connecticut, or in New York. Your climax forest might stop at oak and go no further, or end in towering firs. Find such a forest— there are remnants of America's originals in many parks and reservations—and gaze at it. Your backyard, if you never cut the grass again, could look like that in 150 years.

nently frozen ground that humans can read the genes in their cells, and dogs could eat their meat.

The extinction of mammals continues. Warm brown furry things have been declining for a million years. A few more species are lost each century.

A MULTIPLICATION MYSTERY

As other mammals declined, people multiplied. Populations practically never do that. However organisms manage to replace themselves in the population, whether by a million larvae of which only two will grow to adulthood, or by two babies, both of whom will grow up, the number of individuals in a species is regulated by the way the species earns its living in the kind of workplace in which it evolved. The number varies from time to

HOW DOES YOUR GARDEN GROW?

How tall your corn is, how large your melons are, depend on how much your cornstalks and melon vines get to eat. They get a lot to eat in floodplains: Each year a flooding river delivers minerals freshly ground from rock upstream, conveniently packaged as fine silt, and laid down for roots to suck on. Agriculture started along the floodplains of such rivers as the Nile, the Tigris, and the Euphrates in the Middle East, and along large rivers in China, too. The fact that farming ever got a foothold away from riverbanks before the days of fertilizer factories is probably due to the Ice Age.

Except along rivers that flood each spring, soil south of where the glaciers reached is very old. Minerals have been dissolved and washed away. After a few decades of farming, little nourishment is left, and farmers must feed their plants or move on.

Wherever the glaciers reached, soil is brand new. It is chock full of min-

eral grit scraped off the craton in Canada and bulldozed south. Without the wealth glaciers brought to our finest farmland, we would have to feed our dirt much more in order to feed ourselves.

time, but if, for example, the species nests only in tree cavities or eats only nuts, the population cannot multiply beyond its environment's capacity to supply nuts or provide holes. That number is called the carrying capacity of that environment for that species. To multiply beyond the carrying capacity of its environment, a species has to find a new way to earn a living in the old workplace, or a new way to earn a living in a new workplace. To do either, however, it usually has to undergo so many changes that it has evolved into a new species.

People multiplied without becoming a new species. In a way, they also didn't change jobs or workplaces. They still gathered crops and killed herd animals in the places where they had lived before. But instead of taking their food where they found it, people learned to put food where they wanted it. They planted crops. They herded animals. And, eating well on less land, they multiplied.

Both farming and herding began about 10,000 years ago in the eastern Mediterranean, which was then becoming a hard place to be a hunter-gatherer. As the climate warmed and dried, food grew scarce and patchy—more was found along rivers, less in between. New technology wasn't needed. Pet

POPULATION EXPLOSION

The population of the world was perhaps 250 million in the year A.D. 1. By 1830 it had reached the billion mark. It had doubled to 2 billion by 1930, only a century later. In another 30 years, 1960, there were 3 billion people in the world, and in only 15 more years, 1975, there were 4 billion. In 1980, there were 4½ billion humans on our planet, one for each of the 4½ billion years of its existence.

animals became farm animals. Digging sticks became planting sticks. Everyone knew what seeds were for. But planting crops and caring for herds is more work than gathering nuts and going fishing. People "discovered" agriculture only when they had to.

A LATE STONE AGE SUPPER

Drop in for supper at a late–Stone Age farm. The menu has been reconstructed by sifting through refuse dumps left 7,000 years ago by people who lived on the Polish plains. Like hunter-gatherers, they took food where they found it; like farmers, they put food where they wanted it. They slashed and burned clearings, grew grain, milked cows, fattened pigs, and all the while filled their bellies with whatever was there for the plucking.

There were 450 species of wild plants in their neighborhood to gather for meals, including fruits and berries, mushrooms, leafy greens, succulent roots, and nuts. Perhaps wild greens were served with the perch and bream these people fished out of a nearby lake, and the turtles they caught and may have simmered in a soup. Mussels were a favorite. There were duck and goose eggs, perhaps to hard-boil for lunch, rabbits for stew, and songbirds to skewer and roast over the fire like shish kebab. These might have been seasoned with aromatic herbs or flavored with wild onions and garlic.

Cows gave milk to drink, cream to pour over berries, and butter to melt over greens. Soured milk was made into pot cheese, and maybe other cheeses that required drying and aging. These farmers probably enjoyed yogurt, too.

They grew wheat and barley in clearings, and fattened pigs in the forest. Grains might have been

A WILD MEAL

Wild foods served up 10,000 years ago are still available now, if you look for them. Nearly every place but the desert has fish for the fishing (so, too, do cities, but the fish may be contaminated by polluted water). If you want to be authentic, roast a fish over an open fire with a stick stuck through its gills.

There are hundreds of wild vegetables to go with the fish. These few grow almost everywhere; look for more local ones in books about edible wild foods in your library. Anything you plan to eat should first be checked in a field guide or, safer still, with an experienced gatherer before trying it. Some wild plants and funguses are poisonous.

Fried Puffballs

Only those puffballs that are pure white inside are safe to eat. Among the best, commonest, and easiest to recognize is the gem-studded puffball. It is roundish, with a tapered bottom and a rough, granular surface that rubs off under your fingers. It grows along roadsides and in open woods even in cities. Check the identity carefully in a field guide, or with someone used to picking mushrooms for food. When sliced in half lengthwise, the puffball should be completely solid inside, with firm flesh

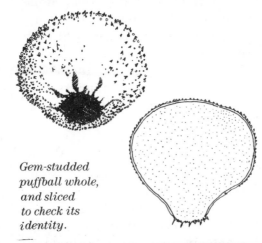

Gem-studded puffball whole, and sliced to check its identity.

snow white through and through. If the cut shows it to be mushroom-shaped inside, or discolored, throw it away.

To cook a puffball, cut off and discard the tough bottom, slice the rest, and fry on both sides in a little salted butter or margarine until the slices are golden brown.

Steamed Daylily Buds

Daylilies produce large green buds that are delicious. Lay a single layer in a pan, and add a very small amount of water. Bring the water to a

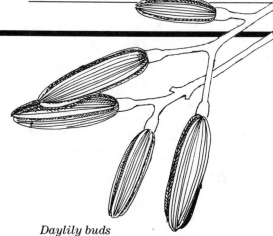

Daylily buds

boil with the pan covered, then turn the heat off and leave the buds for a few minutes without uncovering the pan. Then uncover the pan, pour off the water, and season the buds with salt, pepper, and butter or margarine.

Roast Jerusalem Artichokes

Jerusalem artichoke is a fancy name for a common sunflower that has spread nearly everywhere across the country. The edible portion is a roundish tuber—a food-storage root—that must be dug for. The plant is easiest to identify in the fall, when it is in flower, but once you locate a stand of Jerusalem artichokes, you can harvest their tubers anytime. Peel them, roll them in a little vegetable oil, and roast them on a glass pie plate in a 350°F oven for about 45 minutes, or until they feel soft when pierced with a fork.

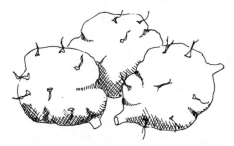

Jerusalem artichoke tubers

Acorns

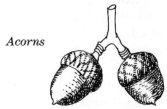

Boiled and Dried Acorns

Most everybody has tried to eat an acorn, and most everybody has spit it out. The nut is made bitter by tannin, that old tonic against worms. Tannin, however, is soluble in water. Once tannin is dissolved away, the nut is nutty, though some species of oaks have sweeter nuts than others. Shell the nuts with a pocket knife, first cutting off the tops where they fitted into their caps, then peeling down the sides. Put them in a large pot of water, and boil them until the water turns the color of tea. Throw that water out, and boil them again in fresh water. Repeat until the water no longer gets discolored and the nuts no longer taste bitter. Spread the nuts on a cookie sheet, and dry them for 45 minutes in a 300°F oven.

eaten as wheat pancakes, hot cereal, or thick barley soup. Perhaps pork was smoked and served as ham, but preserving meat to get through the winter wasn't really necessary because there were autumn duck and goose hunts as waterfowl flocked for migration and, later, deer hunts as deer herded for the winter.

Modern as this balanced diet sounds, these people hunted deer with stone weapons that *Homo erectus* had used a million years before, and roasted hearty meals of venison over open hearths similar to those in which wildfires had first been tamed. In fact, what cavemen ate, what Stone Age farmers ate, and what we eat now is dictated by our evolution.

NO BRAKES BUT THE BELLY

These days, researchers figure out what's healthy, educators spread the news, dieticians translate the information into menus, industries cook up the dishes, and you get the result: school lunches. You'd think that since the hundred thousand or so generations of *Homo* that preceded ours didn't know what we know now, they couldn't have escaped dying of malnutrition. But fossil bones show that primitive people were well nourished, even if they knew nothing about food groups and calories.

WHEAT AND TARES

"Wheat and tares together sown, unto joy or sorrow grown" go the words of Harvest Home, our Thanksgiving anthem. But what is a tare, and if it is a crop that brings sorrow, why plant it along with the wheat? The tare in the song is a bitter-tasting weed whose intimacy with wheat is an unfortunate accident of domestication. As wheat was being domesticated, tares took advantage of the situation by evolving a seed that resembled a wheat grain. When the grain was harvested, tare seeds were harvested, too. And when the grain was sown the next spring, the farmer willy-nilly planted tares, watered tares, fertilized tares, and harvested tares. To his sorrow, for such a crop makes bitter bread.

We now have to be told what to eat because biology is a tortoise and culture is a hare. All of the developments you can read about in history books—farming and herding, writing and calculating, urbanization, industrialization, and the space age—happened only in the last 10,000 years of our cultural evolution. That is too short a time for biological evolution to have caught up. We're stuck in bodies tailored for a life we no longer live.

Every creature has an automatic pilot system that guides it to dinner. We have a tongue to identify salt and sugar; a nose to identify ripe fruits, starchy vegetables, and roast meats; and an appetite that says anything sweet, starchy, salty, or fatty is "good food." The problem is that this nutritional guidance system works only when our choices of food are limited, as they were when our guidance system evolved. When people lived in the wild—hunting their meat and gathering everything else—eating everything their automatic pilot indicated was "good," until their full stomach switched off their appetite, gave them just enough sugar, salt, starch, and fat, packaged in meats and vegetables with just enough proteins, vitamins, and minerals—and no more. We, however, can douse our dinner with salt and pig out on chocolate cake. By the time our full stomach says we have eaten enough, we have actually eaten too much salt and too much sugar. Such excess wasn't possible in the Stone Age.

Deer and wild pigs are lean animals; they don't have so much cholesterol as beef and pork today. Wild fruits and berries aren't very sweet; they don't compare to candy bars. The wild tubers you could dig with an antler, or the hazelnuts you could gather in a skin, wouldn't give you the overdose of oil that you can get in a pizza. No wild foods are as salty as a sausage. The automatic pilot is still switched on, guiding us to eat what's sweet, fatty, and salty, but the only brake it ever had is the one it still has—is a full stomach.

WHY SUGAR IS SWEET

So old friends have become new enemies. Sugar, for instance. You like sugar because it's sweet, but why is it sweet? Sugar molecules are only atoms of carbon and hydrogen that came together in the ancient seas. Atoms and molecules have size and shape, but they have no flavor.

But if a creature is to eat what's good for it, it had better be able to recognize it. Our sugar identifiers are taste buds shaped to cling to molecules that are "sticky" in certain places. When a molecule that has the right specifications—whether it is sugar or Nutrasweet—lands on a taste bud, a nerve connected to the receptor fires a message to the brain. The message is only that the nerve has been fired. No nerve says anything more than that; a nerve fired by a sugar molecule carries the same electrical message as a nerve fired by a hair stuck on your tongue. The meaning of the impulse is added at its destination in the brain, so that if the impulse arrives in one place, it is a

HOMEMADE CHEESE

Cheese is fermented by various microorganisms—bacteria, funguses—that give it a distinctive flavor. Some cheeses can be made only in certain caves where their specific fermenters thrive. Cream cheese is fermented by such common bacteria that anyone can make it at home. This recipe makes 1½ cups.

You need:
1 quart whole milk
1 cup heavy cream (not ultrapasteurized)
¼ cup very fresh buttermilk
2-quart stainless steel, enamel, or glass saucepan, with lid
Kitchen spoon
1 rennet tablet (dessert type, available at health-food stores)
1 tablespoon water
Cheesecloth
Large sieve
Large mixing bowl
¼ teaspoon salt

1. Put the milk, cream, and buttermilk into the saucepan. Heat over low heat, stirring, until the mixture feels the same temperature as your skin. Take it off the stove and set it aside.

2. Dissolve the rennet tablet in the tablespoon of water and add it to the milk mixture. Stir for a minute or so, then cover the pot and leave it alone (that means no touching) at room temperature until it forms a curd, the solid white mass, and whey, the yellowish liquid that Miss Muffet ate. That may take anywhere from 16 to 24 hours.

3. Now you will find our how cheesecloth got its name: It is used to strain the whey from the curd. You will need a piece two layers thick and large enough so it can be folded completely over the whey later. For now, dampen the cheesecloth with water, line the sieve with both layers, and set the sieve over the bowl. Spoon into the sieve as much whey as you can, then gently lift the curd into the sieve, too. Let the curd drain until only an occasional drop of whey still drips.

4. The curd is already cream cheese, but it is too soft to use. To get more liquid out of it, fold the cheesecloth over the cheese, put a saucer or small plate on top, and weight the bundle with anything that weighs about a pound (two cups of raw rice or raw split peas in a plastic bag is about right). Refrigerate the whole contraption, sieve, bowl, and all. Double the weight after a couple of hours, and leave the cheese to drain overnight, or until it is as firm as you like it.

5. The only other thing that has to be done to make this the most delicious cream cheese you've ever had is to add a little salt. Discard the liquid from the bowl and dump in the cheese. Using your clean hands or a spoon, blend in the salt.

taste, and if at another, it is a touch, a sight, or a sound.

At the destination of a nerve impulse from a sugar receptor, nerve cells in the brain fire off signals that together create the sensation you feel as sweetness. Cats, who get all the sugar they need from meat, have no sugar receptors; the carbon and hydrogen atoms that seem sweet to you are so much grit to them. Primates early on switched from a diet of mostly leaves to a diet of mostly fruit, thereby taking advantage of the great store of energy fruits contain. Much of a fruit's calories are stored as sugar, and the amount of sugar also indicates how ripe—how energy filled—the fruit is. Sugar receptors were necessary; they are rough calorie counters.

At the same time that the brain creates the sensation of sweetness, it creates a sense of pleasure by releasing soothing molecules called endorphins. Pleasure pushes you toward those things that give you good feelings, like a ripe plum. Displeasure steers you away from things that give you bad feelings— bitter substances, for instance, many of which are poisons, or sourness, which warns of an unripe fruit not yet rich in calories.

What's so terrific about humans is that with our wonderful brains we can examine ourselves to understand why we eat too much sugar, and then we can do something about it. If culture creates problems, culture can also remedy them. Researchers, educators, dieticians, industries, and school lunches support our biological evolution: We can't change the amount of sugar that's good for us, and we can't

A GOOD REASON TO HATE MILK

If livestock have evolved because of their association with us, have we evolved because of our association with them? We sure have. Mammal infants produce an enzyme, lactase, that snips apart milk sugar—lactose—so that it can be digested. In most mammals, lactase production falls off after weaning age, and adults produce little or none at all. The same is true of most humans. But not all.

People who are descended from northern European ancestors can digest all the milk they can drink all through adulthood because they continue to make large amounts of lactase. People who are descended from ancestors who lived in the Mediterranean area do okay with milk, but they don't produce enough lactase to drink a lot of it. People whose ancestors came from Asian and African lands don't produce enough lactase to digest the milk sugar.

A person's ability to digest milk in adulthood depends on what his ancestors had to eat. In northern Europe, cow's milk has been an important source of nutrition. Those individuals who could tolerate milk in adulthood had a special ability to survive hard times, so those who produced larger than normal amounts of lactase were favored. The weather around the Mediterranean is too warm to keep milk from spoiling without refrigeration, so the people fermented milk to produce yogurt and cheeses. Fermenting microorganisms use up a good deal of the milk sugar themselves, so people who depended on yogurt and cheese would not have had to evolve the ability to produce lots of lactase in adulthood. Oriental and African peoples rarely depended on milk in any form, and so they are like normal mammals, intolerant of milk sugar.

Undigested milk causes bellyaches. Unconsciously, those who don't digest milk completely connect the discomfort with the food, and come to the conclusion that they hate milk. They are quite right to insist on that dislike.

quickly evolve a new physiological control system, so we replace the biological pilot with a cultural guidance system.

THE THIRD EYE

Most of your brain is given over to automatic pilot systems of one sort or another. Only 1 percent of what goes on in your head is conscious, that is, thoughts you are aware of. Scanning techniques that show brain activity indicate that microseconds before you are aware of a thought, it has been formulated in a part of the brain that is beyond your awareness. Your brain decides what to think before you think it. But that's not so bad. Unconscious thinking carries the wisdom of the ages.

There is a strange organ inside your head that was invented by armored fish in murky water hundreds of millions of years ago, and that all vertebrates still have. It was originally a sort of eye, called the pineal eye, that was smack on top of the skull.

The pineal eye was a light-sensitive switch that controlled the production of melatonin, a skin-darkening hormone. Darkness turned the switch on, deepening the animal's color. Daylight turned it off, lightening the animal's color. Maybe the fish used the switch to camouflage themselves—dark in

LEARNING TO WRITE

Evolution is as much a fact of culture as it is of nature. Take writing. The first "writing" about 6,000 years ago was small clay tokens of various shapes by which temple accountants in Sumer, in what is now Iraq, kept track of such things as how many animals or bushels of wheat had been received in offerings. The first clay tokens were probably very like the objects they stood for: tiny baskets, little jars. Later they were simplified: a small cylinder instead of a basket, for instance. But tokens can get lost, or can get mixed into another heap, and then the accounts are messed up.

The next step was to keep accounts straight by storing tokens in clay envelopes. So that the envelopes would not have to be broken to check their contents, each was stamped with the type of token that was inside; the number of impressions gave the number of tokens. Eventually, temple workers were able to give up the comforting ability to count actual tokens and rely instead on flat tablets stamped in the same way as the envelopes had been. Finally, the stamps were replaced by symbols that stood for tokens and that were pressed into the wet clay tablets with a stylus, a small stick with a wedge-shaped point.

"Barrels"

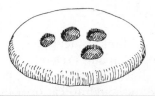

Barrel counters wrapped in clay and used as printers to mark the contents of the envelope.

A clay tablet, on which the number of barrels is written.

the darkness, light in the daylight. It might also have been used a second way by terrestrial vertebrates: a dark animal on a cool night absorbs more heat; a light animal on a hot day reflects heat away.

Your pineal "eye" is a gland inside your brain that also produces melatonin. No light can reach it, but it is hooked up to the part of the brain that receives light messages from the eyes. As day dawns, the flow of melatonin is switched off. As night falls, melatonin is re-

WHY PINEAPPLE SLICES HAVE HOLES

You may think pineapple canning companies remove the cores of pineapple slices because they are too tough to eat or because they contain seeds. Not so. The core of a pineapple is cut out because it contains an enzyme that digests protein. If you eat it, as it is possible to do with a fresh pineapple, your tongue will sting and your gums will bleed. The enzyme is digesting you.

leased. You don't change color. Melatonin is one of several hormones that make you sleepy.

Children make more melatonin during the night than adults do, and the amount of melatonin falls off the older a person gets. Children, who make the most, sleep the most. Old people, who make the least, sleep the least.

The same hormone, controlled by the same light switch, seems to make people feel depressed as well as sleepy. Long winter nights, which increase the amount of melatonin, are depressing. Maybe that emotional hookup is reptilian. Lizards brighten when they win a contest, darken when they lose. Maybe we didn't quite invent "bright" and "dark" to describe our moods. Maybe greeting the day and dreading the night is ancient wisdom.

LOOKING CLOSER

Going toward what's good for you and turning away from what's bad for you are as old as life itself. Even bacteria know the sweet from the bitter. That's why they're living in your mouth and not in your Listerine.

Each of us carries life like an Olympic torch that has been handed down from the first blob of life through all the kinds of animals that have preceded us. Our family tree includes bacteria, fish, amphib-

ians, pelycosaurs, therapsids, tree shrews, and apes. In fact, we're related in some way to every form of life, even toadstools and snakes. The evidence is in us, in how our bodies work and our minds think.

You think with chemicals called neurotransmitters, which were first produced by bacteria and have since been passed along to every sort of animal. Your brain cells are sending and receiving such molecules right this very second, as you read these words. Octopuses think by using the same chemicals. The mitochondria that run the energy department in your cells energize clams and caterpillars, too.

Your cells communicate with one another long-distance by using hormones—insulin, which carries messages about sugar; adrenaline, which you understand as feelings of excitement or fear; and estrogen, which in females plays a part in the sexual changes of adolescence. Some funguses send and receive estrogen messages among themselves, perhaps to say that they have found food or that they are ready to reproduce. Some bacteria communicate in insulin.

Your body cells inherit their shapes and skills from cells that originally needed no body to live in. White blood cells creep amebalike on jelly arms and still hunt their prey—dead cells and

AN ODD NUMBER

Although people object to the idea that there are differences between girls and boys because the differences seem unfair, they can't deny there are some, and that they're not taught. Grown-ups don't care if kids pal around in threes or sixes. But as early as nursery school, girls group themselves in pairs and threesomes, while boys begin to gang in larger groups. The difference doesn't go away. In any neighborhood you can see small clusters of girls, whole bunches of boys.

The odd numbers may be our history showing. None of the jobs most females did through most of human evolution needed more than a few of them. Most of the jobs most males did needed lots of them. That leads to other differences. Boys, girls notice, make up rules, cook up plans, and follow the leader. Girls, boys notice, care more about being close to one another than they care about technicalities, strategies, or who is boss. Evolution doesn't fit a species for its future. We are what we were, and when we are young, we prepare for what we used to do when we grew older.

A STRANGE COMMAND

Newborn babies obey a built-in command that makes no sense. When they feel a sudden loss of support, they circle their arms and legs forward, close their hands, and flex their toes.

You can safely observe this ancient self-help reflex in babies no more than a few weeks old this way: Lay the baby on his back, with his feet toward you, on a bed. Lean over the baby and put your hands on the mattress to either side. Push hard into the mattress so that the baby for a moment feels no support under him.

The Moro reflex, as the automatic movement is called, does nothing to help support him. But if a monkey in its mother's arms were to make the same gesture, its arms and legs would hug it closer to its mother's body, its hands and feet would grasp her fur, and it would save itself from falling.

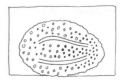

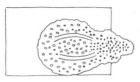

White blood cells move by circulating their insides onward through the center like a fountain.

bacteria—by engulfing them. Ciliated cells that used to wave themselves through water now wave dust from your nose. You, as a fertilized egg, were once waved into your mother's uterus by ciliated cells. Half your genes were delivered by a flagellated cell, a sperm, that looks like some flagellated, one-celled creature you might see through a microscope in a drop of pond water. While you were a fertilized egg, you lived for a while free floating, like any microorganism, absorbing nourishment in a watery world.

THE SEA IN YOU, YOU IN THE SEA

Seventy percent of your body is water, most of it salty and laced with sugar molecules so that it is very like the seawater all life began in. When you were a free-floating fertilized egg, you divided into the hollow-ball plan of a *Volvox* and then punched in into the two-layer umbrella plan of a jellyfish. The tissues an embryo makes to attach to its mother and tap into her blood supply are the same kind of tissues a turtle makes inside its egg.

The ways you sense the outside world are ancient. Pigment molecules in the retinas of your eyes are changing shape now as the light from this page hits them. They did the same stunt in the eyes of giant squids that lived in the seas 450 million years ago. Hairs in your ears are bending to sound waves as the hairs on lobster legs do. While your

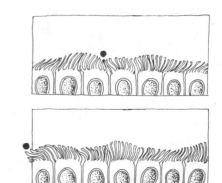

Ciliated cells, like those in a nose, perform a power stroke to move debris away, and a return stroke to prepare for the next push.

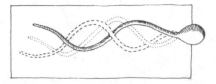

Flagellated cells, like sperm, whip along by twirling their tail.

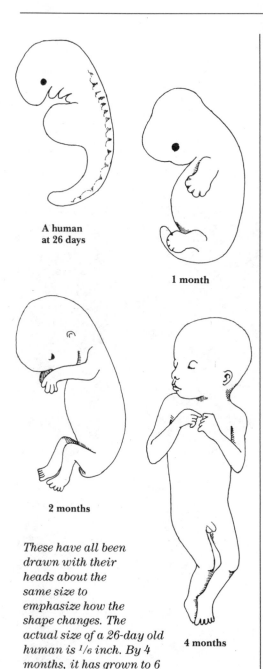

A human
at 26 days

1 month

2 months

4 months

These have all been drawn with their heads about the same size to emphasize how the shape changes. The actual size of a 26-day old human is 1/6 inch. By 4 months, it has grown to 6 inches, or 36 times bigger.

hand supports the weight of this book, tips of nerve cells are being squeezed, triggering a wave of electrical signals to your brain. You know the book is heavy the same way a trilobite knew if it was getting squashed.

You sense all these things in your mind because you are inside out—or rather, outside in. As you developed from your jellyfish stage, the outside, sensory surface turned inward to form your brain and spinal cord; that means that light, sounds, touches, tastes, and smells from the outside world have pathways to the interior. Your eyes are part of your brain; so is the smelling surface in your nose.

You're a tube like a worm, hollow from mouth to anus. And your rows of ribs, string of vertebrae, pairs of muscles, nerves, blood vessels, and limbs originated in the segmented plan of worms.

The ultimate evidence for the unity of life is in your genes. Every organism there has ever been—ameba or dinosaur, alga or oak, worm or man—has been instructed on what to be and how to live by the same genetic code. All life on Earth is directed in the genetic language that evolved, perhaps, in clay organisms before there was life at all. The words that tell a mushroom how to be are the same as the words that tell you how to be. Only the sentences are different.

You are very old in very many ways. Four thousand million years have passed since the molecules you are first came together. Yet each self is a brand new self that the world has never seen. And tomorrow is a day that has never been before.

COMING HOME

Now the sun is setting on this journey through time. Other suns, the ones we call stars, are appearing in the night sky. Maybe other lives on other planets are turning toward light and sweetness, spurning dark and bitterness. On our small planet, across our own continent, people are listening to their pineal glands whispering of sleep, and are thinking about tomorrow. It's another day added to the 1,460,000,000,000 behind you.

Watch the sunset somewhere over the middle of the continent. It is ending a day that is now rather longer than days were when the Earth was young and spun faster. When nothing taller than moss greened the craton, there were 400 sunsets every year.

Corn covers the craton now. The level where seas once washed its shores can be reached by an elevator that descends below the very bottom of the Great Lakes into a salt mine owned by Morton, Inc., from which workers are now ascending to go home to dinner. Over the last 24 hours, McDonald's has sold about 12 million more hamburgers, which are made of steer that now roam the prairies in place of herds of three-toed horses, and the herds of dinosaurs that came before them. Before night falls, cows with milk invented by therapsids will be milked by machines powered by electricity that was made by steam turbines that were heated with coal that was mined from tree-fern and horsetail forests that were buried in swamps 300 million years before the present.

In the West, Californians are being carried along a little farther toward Alaska as their fragment grates along the San Andreas fault. People in Utah are being budged apart somewhat as the latest rift spreads there. In the East, the rock rises under New Englanders, and Bostonians head homeward on the subway through what once was part of Africa. Floridians, pleased to have just brushed their teeth with diatoms, shake sand from their feet as they climb into bed, unconcerned that their land isn't part of the continent at all.

The sun is getting lower, and it's getting too dark now to play golf among the kames and kettle holes that mark the Great Ice Age glacier's former place. People driving across the continent on Route 80 are turning their headlights on, lighting up the roadbed cut in places through the roots of mountains no human ever saw, and through layers of coal, redstones, basalts, granites, and sparkling limestone right down to the old seafloor, almost to where life began. Everybody is breathing oxygen, the toxic waste that once killed off almost all the life there was.

As you lay your head on your pillow, life all over the globe is still evolving. There are about as many tomorrows as there have been yesterdays, about as many new kinds of life to come as there have been old kinds of life in the past. So far, you are the only kind of life on this Earth that can think about that, know the yesterdays, and wonder about the tomorrows.

You are the only kind of creature that can try to understand itself.

INDEX

PHOTOGRAPHY CREDITS

We would like to thank the following children who made such patient and wonderful models:

Julia Beame, Richard Beame, Andrew Beame, Sydney Beame, Peter Blair, Paul Blair, Cory Breen, John Breen, Rob Breen, Marco Caffuzzi, Gian Feleppa, Jason Fisher, Danny Guest, Drew Haller, Paul Haller, Carolynn Hayde, Lisa Iodice, Elizabeth Kang, Esther Kang, Jason Kuntz, Elizabeth Lee, Jenni Margolies, Ryan Meyers, Chris Millen, Jacob Miller, Polly Miller, Jenny Anne Nickles, Lara Orian, Kalim Pearson, Danny Perez, Hector Ramirez, Hillary Reddi, Owen Rice, Ariel Schiff, Alex Schiff, Josh Stine, Alexis Stoll, Meredith Stoll, Geoff Suval, Amanda Taylor, Steven Taveniere, Zoe Van Baron.

Also, we are grateful for the gracious cooperation of Tom Wood and Ken Soltesz of Teatown Lake Reservation, Inc., Ed Kanze of Ward Pound Ridge Reservation, Bedford Hills Pet Plaza, Muscoot Farm, Karl Ehmers Green Chimney Farm, Joanne Wolgast, Corrie Lapin, and the whole Blair family.